Introducing Mudbox™

Introducing Mudbox™

ARA KERMANIKIAN

Wiley Publishing, Inc.

Acquisitions Editor: Mariann Barsolo
Development Editor: Lisa Bishop
Technical Editor: Keith Reicher
Production Editor: Elizabeth Ginns Britten
Copy Editor: Sharon Wilkey
Editorial Manager: Pete Gaughan
Production Manager: Tim Tate
Vice President and Executive Group Publisher: Richard Swadley
Vice President and Publisher: Neil Edde
Media Associate Project Manager: Jenny Swisher
Media Associate Producer: Doug Kuhn
Media Quality Assurance: Shawn Patrick
Book Designer: Caryl Gorska
Compositor: Kate Kaminski, Happenstance Type-O-Rama
Proofreader: Nancy Bell
Indexer: Ted Laux
Project Coordinator, Cover: Lynsey Stanford
Cover Designer: Ryan Sneed
Cover Images: Ara Kermanikian and Ashley Wood

Dear Reader,

Thank you for choosing *Introducing Mudbox*. This book is part of a family of premium-quality Sybex books, all of which are written by outstanding authors who combine practical experience with a gift for teaching.

Sybex was founded in 1976. More than 30 years later, we're still committed to producing consistently exceptional books. With each of our titles, we're working hard to set a new standard for the industry. From the paper we print on, to the authors we work with, our goal is to bring you the best books available.

I hope you see all that reflected in these pages. I'd be very interested to hear your comments and get your feedback on how we're doing. Feel free to let me know what you think about this or any other Sybex book by sending me an email at nedde@wiley.com. If you think you've found a technical error in this book, please visit http://sybex.custhelp.com. Customer feedback is critical to our efforts at Sybex.

Best regards,

Neil Edde
Vice President and Publisher
Sybex, an Imprint of Wiley

To Erin, William, Jacob, and my parents—love always and forever

Acknowledgments

This book is a result of many deliberate and accidental events, and there are many people to thank and acknowledge for their involvement in making these events happen. If it weren't for them, you wouldn't be reading this book. ■ A very special and heartfelt thanks to my parents for their love, dedication, faith, and support over the years. Thanks to my dear soul mate, Erin, for her encouragement, understanding, and devotion while I worked on the book. Thank you to my dearest sons, William and Jacob, for letting me see life as I had never seen it before; I hope this book is the start of my being able to do the same for you. ■ Another person pivotal to making this book possible is a dear friend and fellow trench mate, Eric Keller. As a classmate, he asked to include an image of one of my ZBrush digital sculptures in his book *Introducing ZBrush* (Sybex, 2009), and it started a friendship that continues to grow. ■ This book would not have been possible without Mariann Barsolo, who asked me to take the leap and write it, and then rode shotgun throughout the process. I would also like to thank Mariann for putting together an excellent team to work with me. Thanks to Keith Reicher for serving as technical editor and providing information about the Mac-specific features of Mudbox, and to Lisa Bishop for being an excellent development editor. Thanks to Liz Britten for her magic touch as production editor, and for letting me see the content in book form rather than a Microsoft Word file and a bunch of images. Thanks to Ryan Sneed for his cover design. Thanks to Sharon Wilkey, copy editor, and all of the wonderful people at Sybex/Wiley who were involved in the production of this book. Finally, a special thanks to Neil Edde, publisher, and Pete Gaughan, editorial manager, for their involvement in the synchronicity of this book coinciding with the release of the 2011 version of Mudbox. ■ I was elated and surprised when one of my favorite artists, and constant source of inspiration, Ashley Wood, responded to an email I sent asking to use his robot creation Bertie as the subject of the exercises in Chapters 1, 3, and 4. I would like to extend my extreme gratitude to him for allowing us to use it. To model Bertie in 3D was a very cool experience, and it is my hope that your work with Chapters 3 and 4 will create interesting variations as well. Please note, however, that Bertie is copyrighted, and the likeness and files on the DVD can be used only as the subject for the exercises and for personal education, noncommercial projects. ■ Thanks to the artists Maik Donath, Marcia K. Moore, Kenichi Nishida, Andreja Vuckovic, Rudy Wijaya, and Pete Zoppi for contributing work to the Gallery. It is good to know that there are such amazing artists creating incredible art with Mudbox. Their work continues to inspire me. ■ Thanks to the original creators of Mudbox, Andrew Camenisch, Dave Cardwell, and Tibor Madjar, and the Autodesk team that continues to develop and enhance the program. A huge thanks to Dave and Andrew for answering my questions. Also, thanks to Brittany Bonhomme, Jodi Anderson, and Elizabeth Garreau from Autodesk for their help and support. ■ Very special thanks to Domi Pitturo and Mimi Tran at Icon Imaging for providing me with the 3D scan data and helping me with the content in Chapter 7. It is truly a pleasure and privilege to work with artists so integral to the development and implementation of 3D scanning technology. Please note that the scan data for the Chapter 7 is copyrighted, and the likeness and files on the DVD can be used only as the subject for the exercises and for personal education, noncommercial projects. ■ Big thanks also to Dan Gustafson from NextEngine for his help with the NextEngine desktop scanner information and images in Chapter 7. ■ Thanks to Phil Dench at Headus for making UVLayout, one of the most brilliant software applications I have ever used. ■ Thanks to Thomas Teger at Luxion for assisting me with KeyShot in Chapter 9. ■ Thanks to Ofer Alon for creating ZBrush and launching the world of digital sculpture. ■ A huge debt of gratitude to Scott Spencer for being an incredible anatomy and advanced ZBrush teacher at the Gnomon School of Visual Effects, and writing two indispensable books on digital character design and sculpting human anatomy. I feel extremely fortunate to have taken your class, and appreciate your feedback on the anatomy of the model in Chapters 7 and 8. ■ I also want to acknowledge Kevin Hudson at the Gnomon School of Visual Effects, and Rudy Wijaya, lead modeler at shadedbox, for teaching me everything I know about polygon modeling. ■ I want to take this opportunity to thank all my instructors at the Gnomon School of Visual Effects: Jeremy Engleman, Ryan Kingslien, Loren Klein, and Ergin Kuke, for the excellent education I received in their areas of expertise, and want to extend that gratitude to Alex Alvarez for being the beacon of education in this field. ■ A special thanks to Joey Jones from shadedbox for his excellent Maya animation class at the Art Center College of Design. ■ Thanks to my friend Brian, who cured my cabin fever by dragging me out to see a movie or have a coffee break in between writing sessions.

About the Author

Ara Kermanikian is a freelance character, vehicle, and set designer in the entertainment industry. He has been working in the field since 2007, after a 22-year career in the software industry, 18 of which were at Microsoft as a systems engineer, engineering manager, and technology director.

He holds a bachelor of science degree in computer science from California State University, Northridge, and has studied numerous courses with leaders in the field such as Scott Spencer, Kevin Hudson, Jeremy Engleman, and Joey Jones at the Gnomon School of Visual Effects and Art Center College of Design.

Ara has been passionate about building models from his childhood years. His exposure to VU-3D on the Sinclair Spectrum fueled his passion for computer graphics, which continues to the current day. Ara loves modeling and digital sculpting because he can bring characters and images that fuel his imagination onto a digital canvas and visualize them in three dimensions.

He has written reviews and master classes for publications such as *3D Artist* magazine, and has had his work showcased in galleries of several Sybex books.

CONTENTS AT A GLANCE

Contents

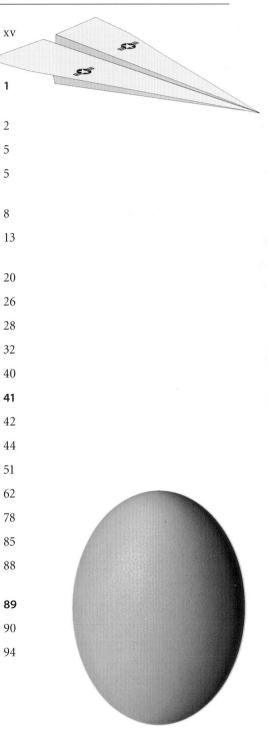

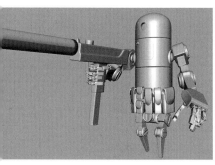

Introduction

Digital sculpting gives you the ability to create anything you can imagine. You can model, paint, and present characters, props, sets and environments in ways never before possible. After learning ZBrush, the leading digital sculpting software in the industry, I was curious to see what Mudbox had to offer. Upon using the software, I discovered that it provided greater accessibility to artists who were too intimidated by ZBrush's interface, or who wanted to transfer their skills and familiarity with leading 3D software packages, such as Maya, to this medium. However, I found limited resources in my search to learn about the software, and even though I find the help in Mudbox to be top-notch, discovered that there were no books on the topic. I decided to write this book to fill the gap.

The aim of this book is to be a companion that teaches you the concepts of digital sculpting and 3D painting via Mudbox, to produce results that can stand on their own or that are part of a workflow. The book is organized to teach you the concepts in waves. Chapter 1 takes you through the pipeline and gives you an idea of the workflow, and subsequent chapters give you more detail on specific stages of that workflow and expand on the requirements, concepts and capabilities of Mudbox.

I recommend going through Chapter 1 and using what you learn there to experiment further. When you run into situations where you need to ratchet up the complexity of what you are working on, jump to the specific chapter on that topic to get more information and exercises. You can also go through the book sequentially to learn the topics, because the chapters build on each other. Chapter 2 provides an in-depth tour of the software to help you understand the details of the user interface.

This is a pivotal and exciting time in the entertainment industry, as software such as Mudbox and ZBrush can contribute exponential advances to the production pipeline of special effects. Revolutionary capabilities continue to be added with every release, and the possibilities of what can be visualized with this art form are soon becoming limitless.

I hope this book will fuel your interest in learning about digital sculpting and 3D painting with Mudbox and will help you learn the intricacies of how to use it to achieve your potential in creating your own visions.

Who Should Read This Book

This book is for digital artists who want to use Mudbox to sculpt and paint high-definition digital models, such as characters, vehicles, props, or sets for film, television, advertising, video games, and both 2D and 3D print. Chapter 1 uses a simple exercise to run through the Mudbox production pipeline. The subsequent chapters delve deeper into these stages and produce results that would be required at different stages of the pipeline.

This book is intended for readers with a background in art, and an understanding of the basics of 3D space and the basic workings of 3D software. It assumes you to be a sophisticated beginner or intermediate user of Mudbox. The book is mostly focused on Mudbox, but also covers other tools such as Maya, Photoshop, UVLayout, and KeyShot. Although a basic knowledge of the workings of those tools is assumed, I have also included the results from those programs for the various exercise steps if you do not have them available to you.

Mudbox is an artist's tool, and I cover the topics from an artistic as well as a technical perspective. My hope is that upon reading this book, you will have all the answers to your questions about the technology and workings of Mudbox to maximize your workflow and to focus on creating your art.

What You Will Learn from This Book

This book introduces you to the tools and capabilities of Autodesk Mudbox 2011. You will learn the different stages of a production pipeline in which Mudbox is applicable, and the workflow of those stages.

You will learn how to start your model from a basic primitive shape, develop it into a sophisticated, realistic-looking digital sculpture, and render it using Mudbox, mental ray in Maya, and Luxion KeyShot.

You will learn how to import models into Mudbox and to sculpt high-frequency detail to give the surface a weathered and realistic look.

You will also learn how to tune surface materials and paint your model in 3D as well as how to use paint layers to create composite surface results to further your model's realistic representation.

You will learn about planning your sculpture and taking it through the various stages such as posing, laying out UVs, and sculpting on various subdivision levels while customizing the Mudbox sculpting tools to get the results you want. I also cover the basics of 3D meshes and UVs and how to troubleshoot and optimize their use in your Mudbox workflow. You will learn how to import 3D scan data and how to use Mudbox to extract the details of the scan and place them on geometry you can sculpt and paint.

All the content on the DVD was specifically created for the purpose of demonstrating the concepts in the chapters. I greatly enjoyed creating this content and hope you get the same enjoyment in sculpting and painting your own creations.

Hardware and Software Requirements

To complete the exercises in this book, you will need Mudbox 2011 and a computer that meets the systems requirements listed for Mudbox on the Autodesk website.

I highly recommend that you pay close attention to the requirements for the video card, making sure you that you are using a certified video card for Mudbox. Mudbox uses OpenGL as its rendering engine, and you need a video card that will accelerate OpenGL. Certified Nvidia Quadro or AMD FireGL cards are your best bet.

The next most important hardware requirement is memory. As you subdivide your models, the memory requirement to store and process them also grows. Even though the system requirements mention 2GB, I highly recommend you have at least 4GB, if not 8GB or 16GB of RAM if you can accommodate for it.

The next important requirement is the operating systems, which are linked to the preceding memory requirement. You can use Mudbox in Windows XP, Vista, or 7, or on Mac OS X 10.6.2. The Mudbox interface is mostly identical in all of these; however, you probably want to use Mudbox on the 64-bit version of these operating systems because 32-bit operating systems can only access 4GB of RAM. With the 2011 version, Mudbox exclusively works in 64 bits on the Mac, so if you are on version 10.6.2 and above, you probably have the required Core 2 Duo or newer processor to support Mudbox. In Windows, you need the 64-bit version of Windows XP, Vista, or 7 and an Intel EM64T processor or an AMD Athlon 64 or AMD Opteron processor.

Make sure you also have plenty of hard disk space because, in addition to taking up a lot of memory, Mudbox models, which could easily be made up of multimillion polygons, also take up hard disk space when you save them.

Finally, you need a digital tablet, such as a Wacom Intuos or Cintiq, based on your preference of having the tablet functionality detached or superimposed on the screen you are working on. Although you can follow the exercises in this book by using a three-button mouse, I have yet to see someone who is a proficient digital sculptor and 3D painter use just a mouse to achieve good results.

How to Use This Book

The chapters in the book are organized in a sequential manner; the content of latter chapters builds on the concepts introduced in earlier ones to help you delve deeper into the topic. The chapters are also broken up by topic, so you may jump to any chapter that pertains to the topic with which you need immediate help. Much thought was given to which chapter exercises would be best accompanied with videos to help you watch the sequence of the exercise steps as a movie clip.

All of the topics are augmented and supported with artistic concepts such as form, gesture, proportion, rhythm, balance, and composition.

The book also has a full chapter dedicated to lighting and rendering your model in Mudbox, as well as in mental ray in Maya and in a top-notch rendering software called KeyShot.

Chapter 1, "Getting Your Feet in the Mud: The Basics of the Mudbox Production Pipeline," runs you through the pipeline by creating a model of an egg and giving it the surface texture of an eggshell. Then you will paint it to have the material and texture of an egg. Finally, you will view your output in Mudbox, or export your work to Maya and render it in mental ray.

Chapter 2, "The Mudbox User Interface," gives you an in-depth tour of the interface of Mudbox with explanations of regions, panels, icons, tools, dialog boxes, and options.

Chapter 3, "Detail-Sculpting an Imported Model," goes through an example of importing an intricate model and using Mudbox to sculpt real-world wear and tear in fine detail on the surface of the model.

Chapter 4, "Painting and Texturing an Imported Model," takes the work you did in Chapter 3 and allows you to apply paint to the surface features to push the realism of the model further.

Chapter 5, "Digital Sculpting, Part I," goes deeper into digital sculpting concepts, such as the foundation of 3D models, and the stages they would need to go through in Mudbox. The chapter also covers advanced sculpting techniques and delves deeper into the sculpting tools and their properties.

Chapter 6, "Digital Sculpting, Part II," builds on the previous chapter with the inception of a base mesh model in Maya, for which you will then create UVs in UVLayout, and pose it and sculpt it in Mudbox.

Chapter 7, "Working with 3D Scan Data," is the final sculpting chapter. Here you will learn how to import a 3D scan of a human head into the software and run through the workflow of further sculpting it.

Chapter 8, "3D Painting," focuses on the second core capability of Mudbox: painting. You will learn more about the paint tools in Mudbox while painting the model you created in Chapter 6.

Chapter 9, "Lighting and Rendering," provides you with in-depth information on how to use the lights in Mudbox in addition to the viewport filters, which enhance the presentation of the model you are working on. The chapter also covers how to export images of your work and composite them in Photoshop, and how to export your model and textures to render it with mental ray in Maya and in KeyShot.

The Companion DVD

The companion DVD includes all the files in the lessons saved at several stages along the process. It is organized by folders for the nine chapters, in addition to a Stamps folder, a Stencils folder, and a 3D Primitives folder that contain 2D images and objects you can use for the lessons or future projects. Some chapters include a Videos folder that has movies of some of the lessons and some bonus movies related to the topic of the chapter. All the video files were recorded using TechSmith Camtasia using the H.264 codec. Because Mudbox scene files tend to get big when you subdivide a model into multimillion polygons, we have compressed the chapters as zip files. You can use tools such as WinZip or 7-Zip to uncompress these files. Please copy and uncompress the contents of the chapter you are working on from the DVD onto your hard drive before proceeding with the exercises. The head scan model on the DVD is provided by Icon Imaging. The Bertie robot model on the DVD is based on paintings and comic books by Ashley Wood. Both models are to be used for education purposes only. Commercial use is not allowed.

Essential Mudbox and Digital Sculpting Resources

The most essential resource of all is the community website built right into the software under the Mudbox Community tab. There you will find tutorial videos to take you beyond the offerings of this book, and demonstrate the work styles and tips and tricks of talented artists.

Another useful resource is the Autodesk AREA website (`http://area.autodesk.com`), which is a superset of what is included within the Community tab in Mudbox covering some of the other Autodesk products such as Maya, 3ds Max, and Softimage.

It is impossible to talk about Mudbox without mentioning Wayne Robson and his community website, Mudbox Hub (`mudboxhub.com`). Here you can find additional tutorials, a forum dedicated to Mudbox, and some useful plug-ins.

It is also impossible to talk about Mudbox without mentioning PixelCG and Ashraf Aiad's blog (`www.pixelcg.com/blog`). Here you can find some indispensible tutorials on Mudbox, as well as the extremely useful process of adding the environment variable to disable LZW compression on `.tif` files saved out of Mudbox to be used in mental ray.

Another thriving and excellent community for digital sculptors is ZBrush Central (www.zbrushentral.com). Although it is mainly aimed at ZBrush users, you can find some excellent techniques and inspiration from expert and seasoned digital sculptors.

As for resources on art and sculpting, there are too many to mention in this section, but I will list a few that I have within arm's reach at all times for reference and inspiration.

Anatomy Essentials

- *Modeling and Sculpting the Human Figure* by Edouard Lanteri (Dover Publications, 1985)
- Female and male anatomy reference figures from www.AnatomyTools.com

Lighting and Rendering

- *Digital Lighting & Rendering, Second Edition* by Jeremy Birn (New Riders, 2006)
- *Lighting & Rendering in Maya: Lights and Shadows* DVD by Jeremy Birn

Online Learning and DVDs

- Gnomon Workshop online and DVD training at www.thegnomonworkshop.com

How to Contact the Author

I would love feedback from you regarding the content in this book, or future titles and topics you would like to see. Please feel free to contact me at kermaco@live.com. For more information about me or my work, visit www.kermaco.com.

Sybex strives to keep you supplied with the latest tools and information you need for your work. Please check their website at www.sybex.com or the website for this book at www.sybex.com/go/intromudbox, where we'll post additional content and updates that supplement this book should the need arise.

Thank you for your support in purchasing this book. It has been a great adventure writing it and figuring out relevant exercises for you to understand the foundation concepts and the workings of Mudbox 2011. When I set out to learn Mudbox, there were no books on it. I hope that I have bridged that gap for you in a way that is helpful, and that the content builds a good foundation for you to create your artwork by using the amazing capabilities that the developers of Mudbox have put in our hands.

CHAPTER 1

Getting Your Feet in the Mud: The Basics of the Mudbox Production Pipeline

Digital sculpting and 3D painting software is a relatively recent and significant milestone in computer graphics imagery (CGI). Audiences expect more and more from special effects that suspend their disbelief when the most extreme visions of an author's imagination are brought to visual reality. As movie directors and game designers push the envelope to meet the demands of the market, tools such as Mudbox are becoming a requirement in every visual effects production pipeline.

Mudbox is a sophisticated digital sculpting and painting software package that lets artists sculpt and paint digital models using software as their modeling clay or paintbrush. Mudbox enables you to create the realistic and detailed characters, props, vehicles, and sets that satisfy the audience's expectations. The artists' imagination and creativity are fast becoming the only limits to what they can show their audience.

This is the most important chapter in the book because it introduces all the concepts and stages models go through in the production pipeline. After learning this pipeline and the concepts, you will be ready to delve into the rest of the book, so make sure you are comfortable with this chapter's contents, even if you have to go back through the steps before moving on.

This chapter includes the following topics:

- **Understanding the Mudbox workflow stages**
- **Loading a base mesh**
- **Using the camera to navigate your scene**
- **Blocking in the general shape and adding image planes**
- **Sculpting your model**
- **Adding paint layers and painting your model**
- **Rendering your image in Mudbox**
- **Exporting the results from Mudbox**
- **Rendering your image in Maya**

Understanding the Mudbox Workflow Stages

Mudbox is used throughout the multiple stages of a production pipeline (Figure 1.1). It is used for speed-sculpting concept designs, digital sculpting art assets such as characters, sets and props, painting models, sculpting blend shapes for animation, and projection painting environments. Although these seem like completely different stages, the Mudbox work is fairly similar, so as you get a good grasp of what the software can do, you can apply it to any of the stages in the pipeline, or come up with completely new areas where Mudbox could help your project.

Figure 1.1

Typical workflow stages of a visual effects (VFX) production pipeline ; the darker sections indicate where Mudbox could be used

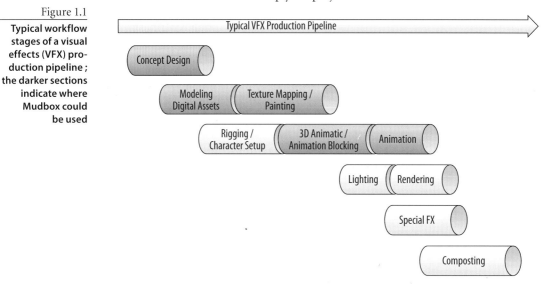

Mudbox can be used as a stand-alone application, enabling a user to start with one of the provided primitives and end up with a final render of a sculpture. However, most artists use it in a production pipeline in which inputs flow into the program, and outputs flow out to 3D and 2D applications. The data flowchart (Figure 1.2) demonstrates this sequence.

The starting point of Mudbox is a model. This model can be one of the provided Mudbox starter meshes, or a primitive or base mesh model you generate in a 3D program such as Maya, or a scan from 3D digital scanner. You can also import 2D images to use as textures, stamps, or stencils.

In Mudbox, you pose, sculpt, and detail the geometry of the model, and then use the 3D painting capabilities to texture and paint it. Mudbox includes some rendering capabilities—such as lighting based on high dynamic range imaging (HDRI) and ambient occlusion (AO)—which give you a good idea of what your model will look like when output to an external renderer.

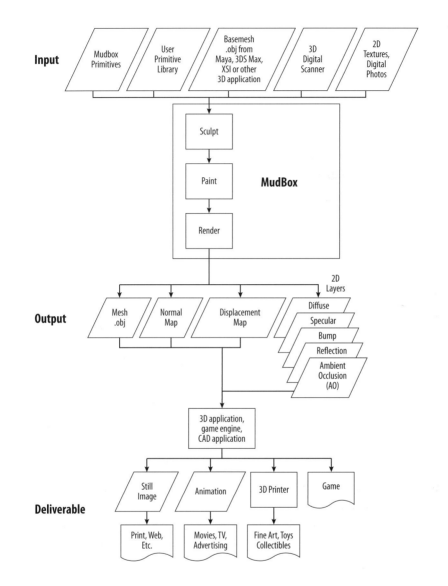

Figure 1.2

Mudbox data flow

After you are finished with your model in Mudbox, you will output the following files:

- A lower-subdivision-level version of your sculpted model, which has polygon counts that the intended 3D application or game engine can support. These models have the overall shape of your final sculpture but lack the detail. These are exported as .obj or .fbx files.

- Two-dimensional images, called *normal* and *displacement maps*, to wrap around the lower-resolution version of your model that you exported as an .obj or .fbx file. These 2D images give the illusion of the detail you had on the high-subdivision-level, high-polygon-count sculpture but require significantly less computing resources to render and animate.

- Two-dimensional images of all the paint layers that you painted your sculpture with, to composite onto your final deliverable.

Before moving to the next stages, I recommend you take some time to go through the five one-minute movies that come with Mudbox. You can find them on the Welcome screen that comes up when you launch Mudbox. If you closed this screen, you can also access the movies through Help → Learning Movies, which brings up a Welcome screen for you to click on the movies. These movies will get you started with Mudbox by showing you how to navigate with a mouse or a tablet, and how to paint and pose.

I can't stress how important and indispensible a tablet is for digital sculpting and 3D painting in Mudbox. Even though it is possible to do the lessons with a mouse, it will be extremely tedious if not impossible to get good results. Tablets come with varying capabilities and sizes. Some come with a display that you can directly draw and sculpt on, others are wireless, and some have more sensitivity levels. I use the medium-size Intuos4 tablet from Wacom.

I will go through how to set up and optimize settings for the tablet in Mudbox, but for now, just make sure your tablet stylus buttons are set to Middle Click for the front button and Right Click for the back button. To do this for Wacom tablets, make sure Mudbox is running, open the Wacom control panel (Figure 1.3), and follow these steps:

1. Near the top of the dialog box, click the plus sign to the right of Application.

2. Click Mudbox and then click OK. Notice that Mudbox is added to your application list and has a highlight around it, indicating that it is selected.

Figure 1.3
Tablet control panel

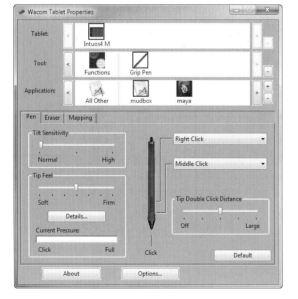

3. Make sure you are on the Pen tab. Click the drop-down menu that is mapped to the back button and choose Clicks → Right Click.

4. Click the drop-down menu for the front button on the stylus and choose Clicks → Middle Click.

5. Close the Wacom control panel.

If you are using a tablet, henceforth in this book, substitute a tap of the stylus for clicking the left button of the mouse, a tap of the forward button on the stylus for clicking the middle button of the mouse, and a tap of the back button on the stylus for clicking the right button on the mouse. Tap the stylus and drag on the surface of the tablet to substitute left-clicking and dragging the mouse.

In the rest of this chapter, you will go through the Mudbox pipeline to produce a realistic-looking egg.

Loading a Base Mesh

A *base mesh*, or *cage* as it is sometimes referred to, is a 3D polygonal object that has been modeled in a 3D application and saved or exported as an .obj file.

To paint this model, we need to unwrap it into 2D before we bring it into Mudbox. If an object has been unwrapped and has UV coordinates associated with it, the UV information will be included in the .obj or .fbx file. Chapters 3, 4, 5, and 6 explain in depth what UVs are and how to generate them. For the examples in this chapter, where needed, the UVs are done and provided for you.

To load your base mesh into Mudbox, follow these steps:

1. Load Mudbox.

2. Close the Welcome screen by clicking the Close button.

3. Choose File → Import.

4. Open the bertie_low.obj file in the Chapter 1\Bertie folder on your DVD.

THE ART OF ASHLEY WOOD

Bertie is a robot that can be found in Ashley Wood's paintings and graphic novels. I have been inspired by Ashley's work over the years and thought Bertie would be a perfect subject for sculpting details and 3D painting because of the bold shapes and amazing aesthetic of the robot. You will be working more with Bertie in Chapter 3, "Detail-Sculpting an Imported Model," and Chapter 4, "Painting and Texturing an Imported Model." To see more of Ashley's work, go to his website at www.ashleywoodartist.com. (Please note that the Bertie images, and Bertie Maya and Mudbox models on the DVD are provided for your personal education only, and not for use in any commercial projects.)

Using the Camera to Navigate Your Scene

Now that the base mesh is in Mudbox, you can look at it from any angle and zoom in and out to enlarge areas you will be working on in depth. When you are performing the following actions, you are not moving the object but rather the camera through which you are looking at the object. This is similar to framing, let's say, a statue in a museum, in the viewport of a point-and-shoot digital camera. You point your camera at the statue, and walk around it while using the zoom features to perfectly frame the feature you wish to capture in the camera's display viewport before taking the snapshot. Becoming comfortable with navigating the camera is critical to your workflow. Practice as long as you need to, until you are comfortable getting to the area you need to manipulate with minimal steps.

To work with the camera, follow these steps:

1. Press and hold down Alt and tap and drag your stylus tip on the tablet to tumble or spin the model; with a mouse, hold Alt while left-clicking and dragging.

2. To pan, press and hold down the Alt key and the forward button on your stylus, and hover the stylus over the tablet without touching it. The equivalent movement with a mouse is holding Alt while middle-clicking and dragging.

3. To zoom in and out of your model, press and hold down the Alt key and the back button on the stylus, and hover the stylus over the tablet without touching it. The equivalent movement with a mouse is holding Alt while right-clicking and dragging.

4. Press W to show or hide the wireframe on the model.

5. To focus on a specific area, point to it with the cursor and press the F key on your keyboard. Now tumble around as you did in step 1, as you can see the center of your rotation is now your focus point. This is a handy way to set the focus on your work area.

6. To see all of your model, press the A key.

7. From the Window menu, choose Object List (see Figure 1.4). The Object List shows you all the cameras, lights, objects, and materials in your scene.

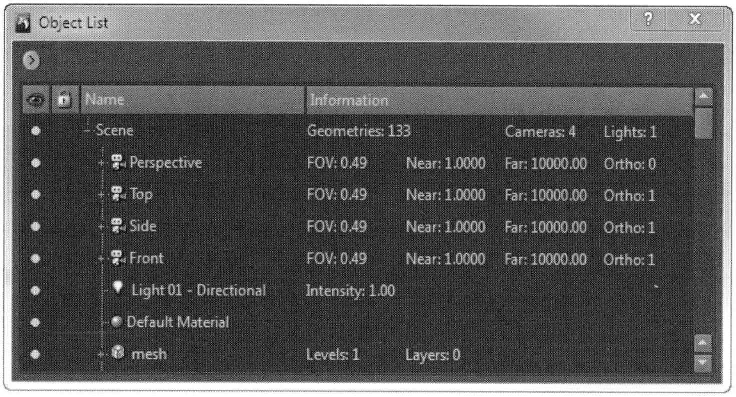

Figure 1.4

Object List

8. Notice that you have four default cameras already available to you. If you use other 3D applications, you are usually looking at your object in four views (Figure 1.5). In Mudbox, you work in only one viewport. You can switch from one camera to another by right-clicking the appropriate camera with your mouse, or by pressing the back button on your stylus, and selecting Look Through from the drop-down menu. Look through all four cameras.

9. Notice that as you select a camera, the properties of that camera are displayed below the Object List in the Properties tray (Figure 1.6).

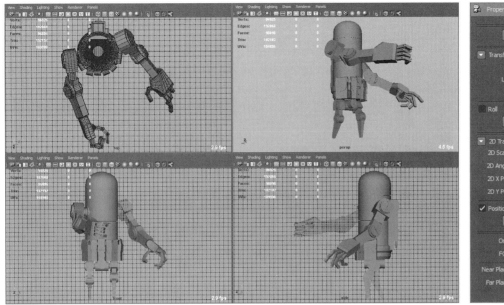

Figure 1.5
Four viewports as seen in Maya

Figure 1.6
Camera properties

10. Look through the Front camera. Use the navigation methods I explained earlier to move around your model. Now look through the Top camera. Look through the Front camera again. You will notice that you are not looking at the model in the front view, but the view you actually left your model in. To get the camera to snap back to the front view, in the Transform properties of the camera, select the Roll, Rotate, Track, and Dolly check boxes and click the Reset button (Figure 1.7). This reverts your model to the original front view.

11. Note that there are three lock options in the Transform properties of your camera: Lock Pan, Lock Rotate, and Lock Zoom. When you want to restrict any of the three transform capabilities of the camera either for convenience or because you have attained a desirable camera view state, you can lock the change in the camera position, orientation, and magnification by choosing one, two, or three of these options. Note that the Front, Side, and Top cameras have the Orthographic option selected by default, which means they do not show your objects with any perspective depth. Experiment by navigating around your model with these options to get an idea of how they work.

Figure 1.7
Resetting the camera view

WORKPLACE HINT

When I sculpt, I usually bring up a second Object List window (by choosing Window → Object List) that I can move anywhere on the screen. I usually have this second Object List either on my second monitor or somewhere on my first monitor but out of the way of my sculpting. I then make sure the Lock Rotate option on all three of the Front, Side, and Top cameras is selected, which it should be by default, unless they were changed in a prior session. This helps me not to confuse the camera I am looking through, and even if I pan and zoom the camera, I am still looking at the model in the view that corresponds to the name of the camera.

You have now navigated the 3D view with your tablet or mouse and the Alt key. The introductory movies in the Welcome screen give an excellent demonstration on how to do this. Table 1.1 is a cheat sheet to get you started, but this will become second nature for you after your first few sessions.

Table 1.1

Navigating with the Mouse and Tablet

ACTION	TABLET	MOUSE
Tumble or spin	Alt + click down and drag stylus	Alt + left-click and drag mouse
Pan or track	Alt + forward button and drag stylus	Alt + middle-click and drag mouse
Dolly or zoom	Alt + back button and drag stylus	Alt + right-click and drag mouse

- To focus on an area on your model, move your cursor to it and press the F key.
- To see all of your model, press the A key. This repositions the camera so all the visible geometry is in the 3D view.

Blocking in the General Shape and Adding Image Planes

Now that you know how to navigate the camera around your model, you will go through the entire Mudbox pipeline with a simple example of an egg. You will start with a primitive sphere and then shape it into an egg. You'll then sculpt the eggshell and paint it. Finally, you'll output displacement, normal, and texture maps to Maya and use mental ray to do a final render of the model.

You can follow these instructions step by step, or watch the movies of this project in the `Chapter 1\videos` folder of the DVD. These videos are divided as follows, based on the four stages in the chapter:

1. `Blocking in shape: Chapter1-part1.mov`

2. `Subdivide and sculpt: Chapter1-part2.mov`

3. `Paint and render: Chapter1-part3.mov`

4. `Export and render in Maya: Chapter1-part4.mov`

To block in the egg shape, follow these steps:

1. Start Mudbox and click the Close button in the bottom-right corner of the Welcome screen.

2. Choose Create → Mesh → Sphere.

3. Press W to show the wireframe, if it's not showing. Tumble around the sphere and observe the polygons that compose the sphere. Notice that there are at most four edges coming out of each vertex, except for eight vertices that have only three edges. Also, notice that all of the polygons composing the sphere are four-sided quadrilaterals (or quads). Chapter 3 covers why this type of geometry layout is ideal.

4. Click the UV View tab on the top left of your screen to see the UVs of the sphere. Notice that the sphere is unwrapped perfectly into quads with no overlapping lines. Also note that the UVs fit perfectly into the first quadrant square (Figure 1.8). When you are finished looking at the UV view, click the 3D View tab.

5. The two sections on the right and bottom of the screen that contain tools and trays are referred to as the *East and South Frame trays*, respectively, even though they are not labeled as such. Click the Object List tab at the top of the East Frame tray. Notice that there are four cameras created for you already: Perspective, Top, Side, and Front. You also have a default Directional Light, a default Material, and the Sphere mesh geometry. Right-click the Sphere object in the list, choose Rename Object, and type egg.

6. Click the plus sign next to the mesh you just renamed to see the first-level mesh. Move your mouse between the Name and Information columns in the Object List, and resize the Name column by dragging the divider bar to the left so you see more information on the mesh. Notice that the Sphere primitive has two subdivision levels labeled level 0 and level 1. Notice that the first subdivision level, level 0, has 384 polygons, and level 1 has 1,536. As you add layers, they will be listed under the mesh name. The Information column beside the Name column also gives you more details on the different objects in the scene.

Figure 1.8

The Sphere primitive's UV view

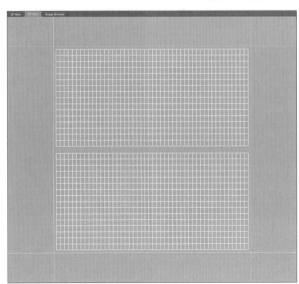

7. Right-click the Front camera and select Look Through. Notice that the Properties tray under the Object List has the properties of the camera. Make sure the Lock Rotate check box is selected. This prevents you from accidentally rotating the camera. If you accidentally change the camera view, select the Roll, Rotate, Track, and Dolly check boxes and click the Reset button to reset the camera to its original view.

8. Click the plus sign next to the Front camera and click ImagePlane. Notice that the ImagePlane properties replace the camera properties in the Properties tray underneath the Object List. Click the drop-down arrows next to Advanced and Transformation properties to open them. Click Import and navigate to the `Chapter 1\egg\ reference and image plane files` folder and load the `egg_side.jpg` image. It will load in front of your ball and might take up most of the 3D view.

9. In the Advanced section of the ImagePlane Properties tray, change the Depth to 100. Now you will see the sphere in front of the egg.

10. If you do not see the top and bottom of the egg in the 3D viewport, click in the Scale text box in the Transformation section of the ImagePlane Properties tray, and type **1** or **0.8** or **0.6** (80 percent or 60 percent resizing of the image) until you can see both the top and bottom of the egg in the 3D viewport. Notice that you can also rotate and translate the image plane, but for our example, this is good enough.

11. Now use Alt + middle mouse button, or Alt + forward button on the stylus, to position your egg so the leftmost and rightmost edges of the sphere line up with the leftmost and rightmost edges of the egg in the picture (Figure 1.9). Also line up the center as best as you can.

12. In the Object List, right-click the Side camera and select Look Through. You will no longer see the image plane, just the sphere. This is because you are now viewing the sphere through the Side camera that does not have an image plane yet.

13. Click the Image Browser tab at the top left of your Mudbox window.

Figure 1.9

Sphere and egg lined up

14. Click the Open Directory button.

15. Navigate to the `Chapter 1\egg\reference and image plane files` folder on the DVD.

16. Click the `egg - high frequency detail.jpg` thumbnail in the left Image Thumbnail tray and press Alt while clicking and dragging on the image to see the finer detail of the egg's surface. As you can see, it is not smooth. Note the roughness that shows up, especially in the white, shiny specular region. Also note the variation of oranges in the diffuse color and the reddish blemishes on the surface. Observing reference material is critical to the creation of art. Whether you are imitating, exaggerating, or distorting what you see, you really need to look at it and understand its nuances first. Click the `egg_top.jpg` thumbnail and notice that from the top, an egg looks circular. Finally, click the `egg_side.jpg` thumbnail.

17. On the toolbar, click the Set Image Plane button.

18. Click the 3D View tab in the top-left corner. Notice that the egg is set as the image plane and is in front of your sphere. Click the plus sign next to the Side camera and click ImagePlane. In the ImagePlane properties, click the drop-down arrows next to Advanced and Transformation properties to open them. Change the Depth to 100. Now you will see the sphere in front of the egg.

19. Click Scale and choose the same scale that you used for the front image plane, either 1, or 0.8, or 0.6.

20. Switch back to the Front camera by right-clicking it in the Object List and choosing Look Through, and select Lock Zoom in the camera's properties.

21. Click the Select/Move Tools tab at the bottom of the screen that contains the Mudbox tools. This area is referred to as the South Frame. Click the Objects icon and click on the sphere. Notice that it now appears a yellower shade of brown, which means it is selected. You can also select the egg by clicking on the egg mesh in the Object List.

22. Click the Scale button.

23. Click and drag the red square (x-axis) on the horizontal scale manipulator to widen the sphere so the edges line up with those of the egg. Align the sphere by pressing Alt + middle mouse button, or Alt + forward button on the stylus, to pan the camera and position your egg so the leftmost and rightmost edges of the sphere line up with the leftmost and rightmost edges of the egg in the picture (Figure 1.10).

24. Now click and drag the green square (y-axis) on the vertical scale manipulator to change the height of the sphere so the top and bottom edges of the sphere line up with those of the egg in the image plane. If needed, align the sphere by pressing Alt + middle mouse button, or Alt + forward button on the stylus, to position your egg so the top and bottom edges of the sphere line up with the top and bottom edges of the egg in the picture (Figure 1.11).

Figure 1.10

Scale horizontally

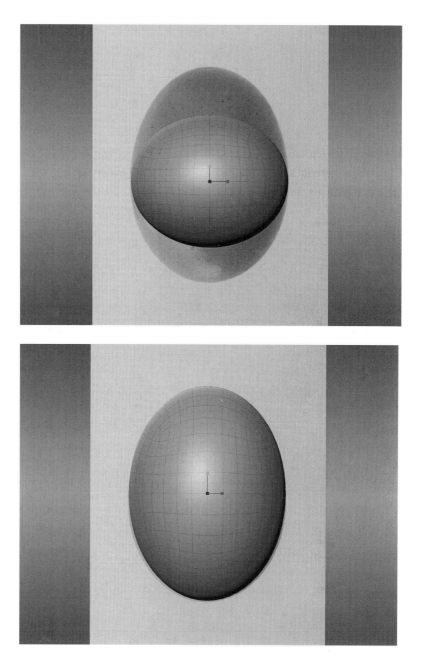

Figure 1.11

Scale vertically

25. Switch to the Side camera by right-clicking it in the Object List and selecting Look Through.

26. Align the top and bottom of the sphere with the image plane by pressing Alt + middle mouse button, or Alt + forward button on the stylus. Click and drag the blue square (z-axis) on the horizontal scale manipulator to widen the sphere so the edges line up with those of the egg. Align the sphere by pressing Alt + middle mouse button,

or Alt + forward button on the stylus, to position your egg so the leftmost and right-most edges of the sphere line up with the leftmost and rightmost edges of the egg in the picture.

27. Right-click the Perspective camera in the Object List and select Look Through. Tumble the camera around your egg and examine your work. Next press the L key and click and drag your mouse, or tap and drag your stylus, to change the direction of your light.

28. Click the Material Presets tab in the South Frame tray and select the material (Gesso). You can identify a material's name by hovering your mouse over it; Gesso is one of the white materials. This changes your egg color to white. To see the name of a material, hover your cursor on top of it in the Material Presets tray and wait for a pop-up that gives you a larger thumbnail and the name of the material.

29. Save your work by choosing File → Save Scene As **egg_step_01.mud**. You can see me going through the stages in this section in the `Chapter1-part1.mov` video in the `\Chapter 1\Videos` folder.

Sculpting Your Model

Suppose that this egg will be used in a commercial or movie clip, where it is impossible to use a real organic prop because eggs are brittle and delicate. In the storyboard, we see that we'll have a close-up shot requiring the details on the surface of the egg to be visible.

Now that you have the egg shape, you need to add the rough texture that you saw in the reference image. You can either continue from the previous lesson or load the scene file egg_step_01.mud from the `Chapter 1\egg\egg_project\Mudbox` folder on the DVD.

Press Pg Dn to go to subdivision level 0 on the egg. In the Object List, you can see that your egg has only 384 faces at level 0. Even though the egg looks smooth in the middle, you can see some faceting when you look at the edges of the egg. *Faceting* means you see big squares or polygons making up the surface instead of a smooth, polished surface. When we sculpt on a model, we are moving the vertices that make up the polygons. If we have only these few faces and we move the vertices at level 0, we will not be able to get the level of detail we want.

IMAGE PLANE ERROR

If you do load the egg_step_01.mud file from the DVD, upon loading the file, you will see a dialog box indicating that Mudbox is unable to find the egg-side.jpg image plane file. This is because Mudbox saves a hard-coded image plane path name. Because it is extremely unlikely that you have egg-side.jpg in the exact same path on the hard drive of the computer you are working on as I do on mine, you will get this error dialog box. Click OK to dismiss the dialog box. Because we have two image planes in our scene, the dialog box will come up again. Just click OK a second time to dismiss the second dialog box. You can reload the front and side image planes into your scene again from the DVD, or from a location on your hard drive to which you copied the DVD files.

The lower levels of a mesh are great for blocking in the shape, but not for adding detail. If, for example, you want to make a character's chin longer or work on the overall shape of your model, use the lower subdivision levels. This is where you will get the best result for the least amount of manipulation.

One of the skills that you will need to develop to be an effective digital sculptor is knowing which subdivision level best suits the task at hand. Another skill is knowing the optimal amount of geometry needed to display the required detail. It is a constant struggle between what the software and hardware can handle versus the detail level your project demands. As I noted before, our egg has too few polygons for us to to get the result we want, so we need to subdivide it to get more subdivision levels.

Adding Subdivision Levels to Your Model

Follow these steps to add subdivision levels to your model:

1. Press Pg Up to go back to subdivision level 1 at 1,536 polygons. Choose Mesh → Add New Subdivision Level. Notice that as you do this, status information about the new subdivision level appears at the top-right corner of the 3D view. It stays on for only a few seconds. If you missed it, don't worry, the same information is available to you if you click the plus sign next to the Egg mesh object in the Object List, and in the status line at the bottom-right of the Mudbox window. You can see that now you are at 6,144 polygons, which is four times the number of polygons you had. Every time you subdivide your model, you will end up with four times the number of polygons you had. At the lower levels, the number of polygons is not significantly greater than those of the previous level; however, as you get to higher subdivision levels, the numbers start going up significantly. For our simple egg, notice that as you get into level 6, you are already at 1.5 million polygons (Figure 1.12).

Figure 1.12

The growth in polygon count at every subdivision level of a model

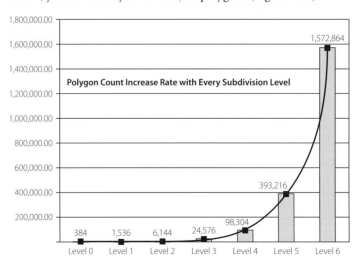

2. Press Shift+D to subdivide your model one more time. If you don't have the wireframe display on, press the W key to see the wireframe on the egg, and notice the new polygons that the new subdivision level has added. You are now at level 3, with 24,576 polygons. Also notice that a new line has been added to each of the levels under the Egg mesh object in the Object List.

3. To move up or down in levels, hover your cursor on the egg model, and press Pg Up or Pg Dn, respectively. To find what level you are on at any time, look at the status bar at the bottom right of your Mudbox window. The current level is listed as the Active level. You can also press Pg Up or Pg Dn and look at the information that pops up in the top-right corner of the 3D view. Subdivide your model up to level 6. If you have the wireframe on, you will notice that the lines show up as very dense on the surface, so turn off the wireframe by pressing the W key.

As the mesh is subdivided, notice that Mudbox creates a smooth-surfaced result. In our egg model, we do want that smooth subdivision result. However, if you are working on a model requiring creased, hard-surface edges (for example, the edges of a box), you need to subdivide your model with the Smooth Positions option off in the Mesh → Add New Subdivision Level Options dialog box (Figure 1.13).

To access the subdivision options, you need to click the options box next to the Add New Subdivision Level menu item (Figure 1.14). On the Mac, you need to select the Subdivision Level Options menu item.

Figure 1.13

Subdivision Options dialog box

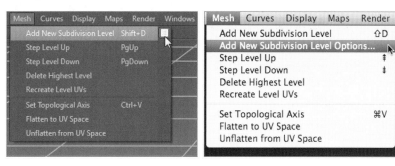

Figure 1.14

Subdivision options menu

Adding Sculpting Layers

Now that you have your egg of 1.5 million polygons, you will start adding the surface detail. But before you do that, you will add two sculpting layers. One layer is for the uniformly rough, high-frequency detail on the surface of the egg, as you saw in the reference picture egg - high frequency detail.jpg on the DVD. The other layer is for the nonuniform spots and bumps on the surface. The reason we do this in layers is so we can dial the detail of the sculpting layer up and down as needed. This will become clearer in the following steps. Sculpting in layers is a powerful capability you will learn to love because it will save you a lot of time during your work, specifically for exploring *what if* scenarios, undoing a whole bunch of sculpting in one swift step, and layering effects of surface detail. Follow these steps to add the two layers:

1. Click the Layers tab in the East Frame tray. Click the Sculpt button (Figure 1.15).

2. Click Pg Up until you are at subdivision level 6. Click the arrow under the Layers tab to open the Layers window menu and choose New Layer (Figure 1.16). Do this again to add another layer. Notice that you now have two sculpt layers in the Layers list.

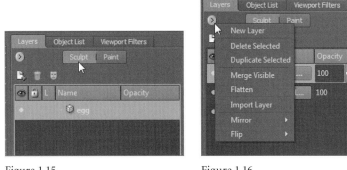

Figure 1.15
Sculpt and Paint layer buttons

Figure 1.16
Layers window menu → New Layer

3. Double-click sculpt layer 1, rename it **eggshell**, and press Enter. Do the same to sculpt layer 2 and call it **spots**. You now have your two sculpting layers.

Notice the five columns in the Layers tray. The first column indicates visibility of the model and can be toggled on and off by clicking the small circle next to the name of the layer. A full circle indicates that the layer is visible, and an empty circle indicates that the layer is hidden. The second column is Lock, which allows you to lock that layer from being edited. The third column shows the subdivision level assigned to this particular layer; this column is just informational and cannot be manipulated. The fourth column is the name of the layer with an icon in front of it, and it can be changed. The fifth column is the opacity of the layer (Figure 1.17). Note that Figure 1.17 is just for reference of the user interface and does not indicate what your Layers tray should look like for this project.

The five columns in the Layer tray are as follows:

Visibility You can turn on the visibility of a layer by clicking the small circle in the Visibility column. If you use Photoshop, you are familiar with this because Photoshop uses the same method of showing and hiding layers.

Lock To lock a layer and disable editing on it, click on it in the Lock column. You will see an image of a closed padlock when a layer in the column is locked.

Level This column indicates the subdivision level assigned to this layer.

Figure 1.17

The Layers tray

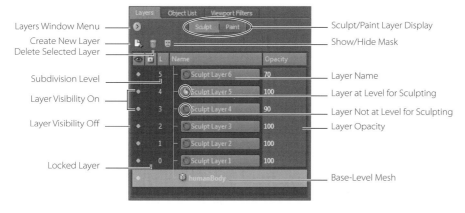

Name You have already seen how to rename a layer. The icon in front of the layer name denotes whether you can sculpt on that layer. Even if there is no lock on the layer, you might not be able to sculpt on it because you may not be at the subdivision level the layer was created in. A sculpt layer can be assigned to only one single subdivision level. You can have multiple layers that have the same subdivision level, but each layer is assigned one and only one subdivision level. For example, sculpt layers 4, 6, and 7 can all be of subdivision level 5. However, you can work only on subdivision level 5 in sculpt layers 4, 6, and 7. The way you assign a level to a layer is to be at the desired level before you make your first sculpting stroke on it. This could cause some frustration because you could be on a layer and not be able to sculpt on your model. If this happens, look at the layer to see whether there is a red circle with a line through it next to the layer name. If there is, you are at a different level than what this layer was set to. That's why you are not able to sculpt on it. To fix this, create a new layer for the level you are on, click on the base-level mesh in the Sculpt Layers tray, or press Pg Up or Pg Dn to get to the subdivision level to the left of the layer name.

Opacity You can either enter a numerical value or use the slider to show the opacity of your sculpt layer. This is useful for dialing up or dialing down the detail on a layer.

Sculpting the High-Frequency Detail

You are now going to sculpt the detail on the surface of the egg. This is a really simple example of sculpting, or rather surface detailing; you will do some more shape sculpting in Chapters 3, 5, and 6. Here are the steps:

1. Click on the eggshell layer in the Layers tray to select it.

2. Click on the Sculpt Tools tray in the South Frame tray panel and choose the Spray tool. Notice that the Spray tool properties come up in the Properties window.

3. As you move your cursor onto the egg, you will notice a circle with a dot in the middle of it moving on the egg. This is your brush. The circle is the area you are affecting with your brush.

4. In the Falloff tray, choose Falloff 4 (the fifth one, because they start at 0). You will see the Falloff name pop up when you hover your cursor over it.

5. From the Stamp tray, look for and choose the bw_dots stamp (the 11th one). You will see the stamp name pop up when you hover your cursor on top of it. Notice as you choose the stamp that the Use Stamp Image check box gets selected in the Spray Tool properties.

6. In the Spray Tool properties, click the arrow to open the advanced options (Figure 1.18) and select the Remember Size and Orient to Surface check boxes. The Remember Size check box sets your brush size to the size it was when you used the tool last. Orient to Surface makes your brush wrap around the model.

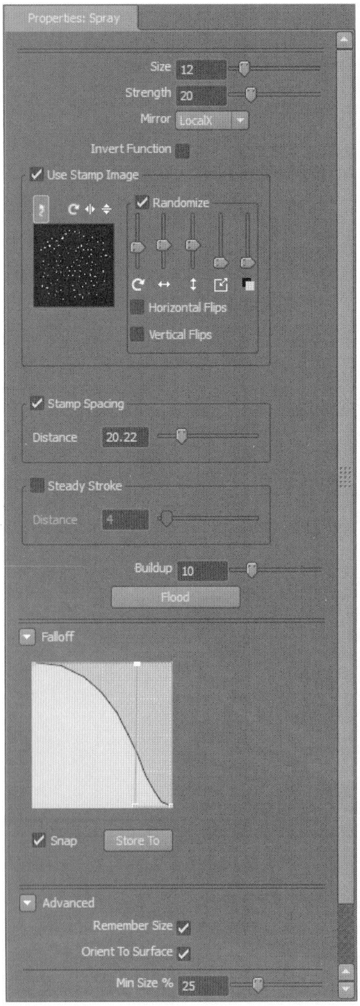

Figure 1.18

Stamp tool properties

7. While your cursor is on your model, press and hold the B key on your keyboard and drag. This changes the size of the circle and your brush. You will do this a lot to adjust the size of your brush.

8. While your cursor is on your model, press and hold the M key on your keyboard and drag. This shows you a line going up from the center of the circle. This is your brush strength, which determines how much the sculpt tool affects the surface. The longer the line from the center of the circle, the deeper an imprint your brush will make on the surface of your model. I recommend you start with a lower strength and dial it up as needed. Notice that you can enter numerical values for both Size and Strength of your tool in the Spray Tool properties (Figure 1.18).

9. For this lesson, let's type in the strength and size of your brush. Set Size to 14 and Strength to 2.

10. Click the Mirror drop-down and select Local X. Also select the Randomize, Horizontal Flips, and Vertical Flips check boxes.

11. While holding down the Ctrl key, place your cursor on the top of the egg and then click and drag your mouse to start creating the eggshell pattern on the egg's surface. Zoom in to see the detail (Figure 1.19). You are holding down the Ctrl key so you sculpt inward, into the egg, instead of creating a relief off the surface. You can also sculpt without holding down the Ctrl key to add some relief and create even more variation to the surface. Cover the entire surface of the egg with this pattern, alternating between pressing down and not pressing down Ctrl. Rotate your egg to make sure you cover all of it.

12. To check that you have covered the entire surface of the egg with this pattern, hold down the l (light) key and click and drag the cursor on the surface. This moves the light and shows you more of the detail on the surface by changing the lights and shadows. You might see

some anomalies as you are doing this, but don't worry, that's Mudbox rendering the details, and it will eventually catch up to display the correct detail. Notice that this detail is a little exaggerated, but that's by design, because you are going to dial it down by using the Opacity of the layer after you are finished sculpting.

13. A 6 appears next to the `eggshell` layer in the Layers tray, indicating that this layer is on subdivision layer 6 of the egg; the layer is at opacity level 100. Either type **0** or drag the opacity slider to 0 to hide the `eggshell` layer. You are back to your smooth egg.

14. Click the `spots` layer to select it.

15. In the Spray tool properties, select Off from the Mirror drop-down list. Also deselect the Randomize, Horizontal Flips, and Vertical Flips check boxes.

16. Change the Brush size to 50 and Strength to 2.5. Make short strokes on the surface by using the Ctrl key on and off to get some spots that poke out, and some that poke in. You want to have a very few of these, so go easy on the strokes. If you end up making a bad stroke, you can always use Ctrl+Z to undo your strokes. You should end up with an egg with some protruding and some indented spots (Figure 1.20).

17. Use the opacity sliders on your two layers to get the perfect look for your egg's surface. An opacity of 46 on the `spots` layer and 59 on the `eggshell` layer looked appropriate for me. If yours doesn't look right, load the scene file `egg_step_02.mud` from the `Chapter 1\egg\egg_project\Mudbox` folder on the DVD to see an example of the results you are going for and try again (remember to dismiss the two dialog boxes that come up by pressing the OK button). When you are happy with your results, save your file as **egg_step_02.mud**. You can see me going through the stages in this section in the `Chapter1-part2.mov` video in the `\Chapter 1\Videos` folder.

Figure 1.19
Eggshell layer detail

Figure 1.20

Spots layer detail

The detail you have just sculpted onto the surface of the egg is called *high-frequency detail*. You will be using this to add fine detail such as wrinkles, cloth patterns, scratches, and dents to your sculptures. If you feel adventurous at this juncture, reload the egg_step_01.mud file and use some of the different sculpting tools to add other details to the surface. I will cover all of the tools in later chapters, but for now, just remember that if you press Ctrl, you depress the surface, and if you use a tool without pressing Ctrl, you add to the surface. Also try different stamps to get a feel for what they do.

Adding Paint Layers and Painting Your Model

If you have used Adobe Photoshop, Corel Painter, or any image-processing or compositing application that has paint layers, you understand the benefits of overlaying layers, placing them in a certain order, and fine-tuning their opacity to get amazingly realistic results. In most 3D productions, texture artists usually paint textures in layers and then composite them onto the model at render time so adjustments can be made to them on an individual level.

In this section, you will paint a base layer of paint on your egg, accent it with a second layer of paint, and then add red spots. Then you will use a variant of the side image plane file (where I have removed some of the specular highlights in Photoshop) as a stencil to project paint the exact color of the egg in the picture onto yours. You will then add some specular and gloss highlights to your image. Let's get started:

1. Either continue from the previous lesson or load the egg_step_02.mud file from the Chapter 1\egg\egg_project\Mudbox folder from the DVD.

2. In the Layers tray, click the Paint button to activate the Paint Layers tray (Figure 1.21). Please note that Figure 1.21 is a reference to explain paint layers and is not what you will see in the current project.

3. Click the Layers window drop-down menu and choose New Layer (Figure 1.22).

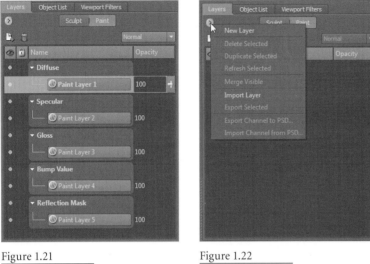

Figure 1.21
Paint Layers tray

Figure 1.22
Layers window menu → New Layer

4. This brings up the Create New Paint Layer dialog box (Figure 1.23). Type **base coat** as the name for your layer, choose 2048 as the size, and TIFF [8 Bit, RGBA] as the image format. The 8 bits give us 16.8 million colors, which will work for this scenario. This will be one of three diffuse layers. Diffuse is the base color we see, without highlights or shininess, just the base paint color.

5. Add a total of three diffuse layers: **base coat** (which you already created in the previous step), **red spots**, and **projection**.

6. Add another layer, call it **highlights**, and choose Specular from the Channel drop-down menu. In this color image, the lighter colors will show up with specular highlights, and the darker areas will not shine at all. A specular map is a way to indicate the areas on your model you want to highlight because they are part of surfaces that have a more shiny, reflective property (for example, oily areas of the forehead).

7. Finally, add a layer, call it **glossiness**, and pick Gloss from the Channel menu. Like the specular image, this one's lighter colors represent areas that will appear glossy, and the darker areas will not. Areas that have high gloss values look wet, while areas with high specular values look shiny.

Figure 1.23
Create New Paint Layer dialog box

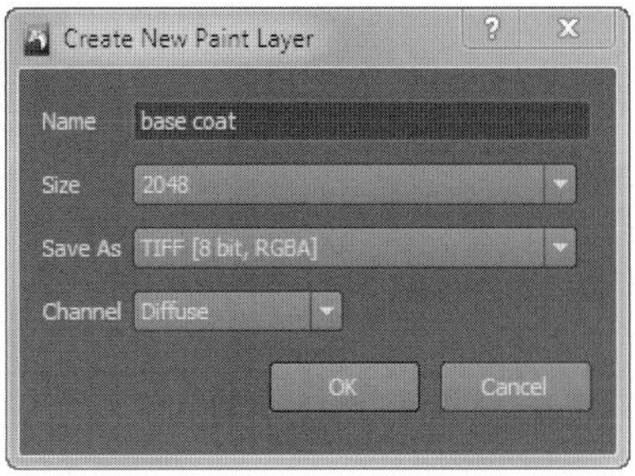

8. Bring up the Object List and look through the Side camera. The image plane of the egg should still be in the background. Move the egg to the side by clicking the Translate tool in the Select/Move Tools tray, and clicking and dragging the red or green arrow on the move manipulator that appears in the 3D View. From the paint tools in the South Frame, click the Eyedropper tool and move the eyedropper icon onto the image of the egg to choose the base color of the egg. Do your best to pick the general color that does not have any highlights or shadows or pigmentation, somewhere in the middle of the egg.

9. Click the Airbrush tool and notice that in its properties, the color is the orange of your egg. In the Object List, look through the Perspective camera. Click the Airbrush tool again, and in its properties, turn Mirror on to Local X, and choose a brush Size of 60 and a Strength of 30. Click the Layers tab and make sure the base coat layer is selected.

Figure 1.24

Color Chooser

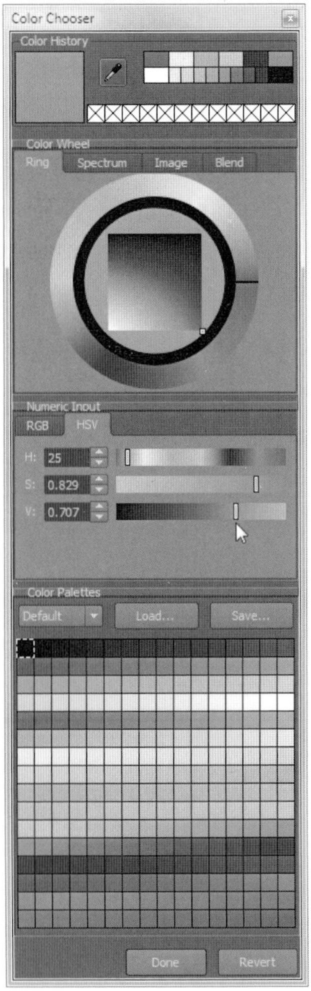

10. Paint your egg with the base orange color; make sure you color the entire egg evenly. You can check this by pressing Pg Dn to get to the lowest subdivision level of your model and looking at the UV view to see whether you missed any spots. If you see missing color in any areas of the unwrapped UV shell, you have missed those areas. Remember to press Pg Up to get back to the highest subdivision level before you continue.

11. Click on the color in the Airbrush tool properties tray to open the Color Chooser. Choose a color that is a slightly lighter version of your current color by either using the color wheel, or expanding the Numeric Input section and choosing a color with slightly less Value by dragging the slider to the right (Figure 1.24).

12. In the Paint Layers tray, make sure the base coat layer is still selected. Choose the bw_dots stamp from the Stamps tray if it's not the selected stamp for the Airbrush tool. Make sure Use Stamp Image and Randomize are selected. Also make sure that Horizontal Flips and Vertical Flips are selected. Move the five Randomize sliders to about the middle. This will ensure that you paint a very random pattern. To find out what each of these sliders does, check Chapter 2, "The Mudbox User Interface." Click Off from the Mirror drop-down list.

13. Paint on the surface of the egg so you have an even pattern of dots all around, and you have some room to see the color you painted before, underneath or between the dots of your current paint work. Painting a surface with various subtle variations of the base color makes it look more realistic.

14. Click and select the `red spots` layer in the Paint Layers tray. Click the Airbrush tool again and click on its color property. Choose a dark reddish-brown. Of course, you can sample the exact color of spots off the egg image by using the Color Chooser technique you used previously.

15. Type **150** in the Size text box of the Airbrush properties. Notice that if you drag the slider to the end, it caps out at 100, but you can type greater values in the text box.

Figure 1.25

`red spots` **layer**

Paint random large red spots on the surface of the egg. Turn off the `base coat` layer to see your work. If you notice that you have too many red spots, use the Paint Erase tool in the Paint Tools tray to erase them. When you are satisfied with your random smattering of red dots, turn on the `base coat` layer and examine your work (Figure 1.25).

Depending on the color distribution and your painting ability, you have probably ended up with a good rendition of the egg's surface color. To add an extra level of realism, you will use the actual egg image to project paint on the surface of the egg. To do this, I have taken the image of the egg shot from the side into Adobe Photoshop and used the Patch tool to remove some of the specular highlights in the photo.

16. Click the Image Browser tab and navigate to the `Chapter 1\egg\reference and image plane files` folder on the DVD and look at the `egg_no_specular.jpg` image. Ideally, you would not want to use `.jpg` images in production to save textures or to paint textures from because `.jpg` is a lossy format. *Lossy* file formats use algorithms to average the color of pixels in order to compress an image so it's smaller in size when you save and load it. These images are called lossy because they lose some of the original color information in favor of reducing file size. Although lossy images might look OK at first glance, they often produce anomalies that create undesirable, blocky results in the picture when you zoom in or process them. In our example, it will not be an issue, but be aware of lossy compression for your projects and if at all possible use nonlossy, uncompressed image formats for textures. Click the Set Stencil button.

17. Click on the `projection` paint layer to select it. Hide all the other layers by clicking on the small circles under the eye column so they are hollow.

18. Click the 3D View tab and choose the Projection tool from the Paint Tools tray. Notice that there is a transparent image of your stencil overlaying your egg model

(Figure 1.26). Also notice that there is some help in the bottom-left corner of the 3D view for manipulating the stencil. During this session, randomly press the S key and click and drag your stylus to rotate your stencil, and occasionally press the Q key to show and hide your stencil. You will not need to scale or move the stencil in this case, but note that you can scale and move the stencil with the S key and right and middle buttons of the mouse (or back and front buttons of your stylus).

Figure 1.26

A stencil overlay on the model for projection painting

Move Stencil: 'S' + Middle button
Rotate Stencil: 'S' + Left button
Scale Stencil: 'S' + Right button

Hide Stencil: 'Q'

19. Use your camera to roughly align the egg to the stencil image.

20. Tap and drag the cursor on the surface of the egg. You will project the image of the stencil onto the surface of the egg. You might want to choose Orient to Surface from the Advanced drop-down list in the Projection tool's properties.

21. Rotate the egg and project-paint the egg's surface. Notice that though this image looks pretty even in color, some areas are lighter than others because of the light illuminating the surface. Rotate your egg so you paint uniform color while also generating a random pattern of the surface. You can press the Q key to toggle the stencil image on and off to look at your work and erase areas that do not work for you. Remember that the stylus has sensitivity levels, so if you gently stroke on the tablet, the color variations will be more subtle on the surface.

22. Click on the Stencils tray in the South Frame and click Off to turn off the stencil.

When you are finished, examine your work. Look for color variations that are too strong, any edges of the projected egg's image that bleed onto your egg model, and

repeating patterns that distort the believability of the texture. Watch the video
`Chapter1-part3.mov` of this lesson in the `Chapter 1\videos` folder of the DVD to
see how I paint my model. When you are finished, compare your newly projection-
painted layer with the previous three to see how quick and effective projecting from
a picture is versus painting the image yourself. The good news here is that you can
composite the two layers that you painted with the base coat and the red spots with the
one that you projection-painted from the real picture of an egg—and play around
with the opacity of the three paint layers you created—to get an even more perfect
texture. To do this in the Layers tray, click on the opacity number and move the sliders
up and down to see the results in real time in the 3D viewport. In my example, an
opacity of 70, 40, and 60 worked best for the three diffuse paint layers of `projection`,
`red spots`, and `base coat` (Figure 1.27).

23. Click the `highlights` layer in the Layers tray to select your specular layer. Choose
    the Airbrush tool, make sure that the `bw_dots` is selected, and that Use Stamp Image,
    Randomize, Horizontal Flips, and Vertical Flips are also selected. Choose white or
    a light gray for your color. Turn off all other layers and paint a nice random pattern
    on the surface of your egg with a brush size that's about a quarter the size of the
    egg. Start with a weaker strength and dial it up until you get a nice specular pattern
    similar to that in the close-up reference picture `egg-high frequency detail.jpg` in
    the `Chapter 1\egg\reference and image plane files` folder of the DVD. These are the
    areas you want to show up when a light is shining on the surface.

    Specular layers enable you to specify parts of your texture that are shinier than oth-
    ers and reflect more light, creating specular highlights. If you have some matte paint
    chipped off a metal surface, for example, you might want to paint the metal surfaces
    with a specular map so that when light shines on that surface, the metal parts show
    up shiny while the matte paint does not.

24. Choose the Paint Brush tool from the Paint Tools tray, and click on
    the `glossiness` layer in your Paint Layers tray. Make sure all your paint
    layers are visible by clicking the circles so they are filled in the Visibil-
    ity column. Paint on your egg to make some areas look a bit glossier.
    On these areas, the egg might have a little bit of "sweat" from being
    taken out of a cold refrigerator, or have some egg white dripped on it
    from a hand that has cracked another egg. Again you can dial in the
    glossiness with the opacity slider of the `glossiness` paint layer.

    You are now done with your egg model (Figure 1.28). You have the
    eggshell texture sculpted onto the surface of the model, and have
    painted on a texture that looks like the reference image.

Figure 1.27

Adjusting the opacity layer of the paint layers to get the perfect compos-ited look

Figure 1.28

**Finished egg model
(see color insert)**

25. Turn on the visibility of all the sculpt and paint layers, and work with their opacity to get as close to the look of the egg in the picture as possible.

26. Save your work as **egg_step_03.mud**. When you save your work, Mudbox automatically creates a folder and saves all of your paint layers as individual files in that folder. You can see me going through the stages in this section in the Chapter1-part3.mov video in the \Chapter 1\Videos folder.

27. In the Image Browser, navigate to the folder where you saved your file and click the egg_step_03-files folder. You will see all of your paint layers. These are separate images that can be manipulated individually or composited in Adobe Photoshop or your favorite image-editing application.

Next you will create a mock-up of what your final render will look like.

Rendering Your Image in Mudbox

In most 3D applications, you set up your scene, and your materials, textures, and lights, and then that information is taken into a renderer that outputs the results in the desired photorealistic or stylistic image. This can take a while, depending on complexity; every time a change is made, you need to re-render and wait.

The really good news is that all rendering happens in real time in Mudbox. Whenever you make any changes, whether they are sculpting, material assignment, texturing, or lighting, all the results are displayed as you are making the changes.

You also have some viewport filters that add additional effects to the 3D view, such as Ambient Occlusion and Depth of Field. I will go into detail about what these various viewport filters do, but for now, you will just use the Depth of Field for your egg. Depth of Field simulates a camera effect; some parts of the picture appear blurry or out of focus, while other parts appear sharp and in focus. This is a good method to draw the viewers' attention to the important parts of the image and use the blurry areas to create interesting gradations in the foreground or background. To add a Viewport Filter follow these steps:

1. Click the Viewport Filters tab in the East Frame (Figure 1.29). Turn on the visibility of the Depth of Field layer, and click on the layer name so the Depth of Field properties come up.

2. Make sure the grid is on by clicking the Display menu item and selecting the Grid check box. Move the Blur Amount slider until you get a slight blur around the edge of the egg. If you get too intense of a blur, move the slider slightly and then double-click the slider handle; this limits the range of the slider. A value of about 0.001 should be good. Move the Focus Distance slider and notice how the focus shifts on the egg and the grid. Move the slider until the front or top-front part of the egg is in focus.

Figure 1.29
Viewport Filters tab

Now move the Depth of Field slider to get a nice soft edge on the egg. You can find detailed descriptions of these three sliders and what they do in the UI tour in Chapter 2. You might want to experiment with some of the other viewport filters to get an idea of what they do. Don't worry if you mess things up; you can always turn off the filters by clicking the eye icon to the left of the filter. By using a combination of viewport filters, I got the results shown in Figure 1.30.

3. In earlier versions of Mudbox, you would have had to take a snapshot of the screen to export your image by using Print Screen or a third-party utility such as TechSmith Snagit, but since Mudbox 2010, this deficiency is not only addressed but addressed with an extremely powerful feature. Not only can you now save the screen by choosing Render → Save Screen Image, but you can also save it in whatever image size you like. This is really useful if you want to save your image in sizes for posters or billboards. Save your image using your screen size by clicking the Use Screen Size button, or type in any size you would like in either the Width or Height text boxes. When you are finished, turn off the Depth of Field by clicking the eye icon next to it in the Viewport Filters tray. I have saved a copy of the screen for you in .psd format called Mudbox Render.psd in the Chapter 1\egg folder of the DVD. When you are finished, turn off all the viewport filters.

Figure 1.30
Mudbox render of egg

Exporting Results from Mudbox

You now have everything you need from your Mudbox session. It's time to export all the assets to be used in external applications.

Exporting the Geometry

Let's start by exporting the geometry. This is the wireframe mesh of the egg at the various subdivision levels (0 to 6). Although you can export all these levels individually, you will extract only levels 0 and 6.

Low-resolution geometry is used in scenarios where the geometry must conform to computational compromises—for example, in animation in a busy scene or as an asset in a fast-moving game. The less geometry, the faster the model can be manipulated in an animation or real-time game engine. There are great advancements in technology to fake the display of the high-resolution work on the low-resolution geometry in animation and game pipelines. These are done through normal and displacement maps. These are computationally less-demanding methods of displaying detailed light interaction and surface detail using low-resolution geometry.

Higher-level geometry is in most cases unusable for animation and games. Even with processing power doubling every year and a half with multiple cores, parallel processing grids, and graphics processing unit (GPU) advances, churning 1.5 million polygons for a simple egg is an impossible luxury. Instead, this level of geometry would be useful in these situations:

- A high-resolution render of a still image in which the detail is critical—for example, if our egg was the subject of a billboard advertisement or a product shot for a glossy brochure. This high-resolution mesh can be imported into renderers that can handle this level of geometric complexity, such as Keyshot by Luxion.

- Geometry that needs to be imported into other digital sculpting applications, such as ZBrush by Pixologic, for further manipulation in a production pipeline. Most production pipelines use multiple applications that complement each other, or sometimes even do the same thing because of various in-house artists' expertise. But in most cases, the final output from whatever application your high-resolution model is exported to will still eventually be a normal or displacement map.

To export the two levels of geometry:

1. Load the `egg_step_03.mud` file from the `Chapter 1\egg\egg_project\Mudbox` folder on the DVD, or continue working from your previous session.

2. In the 3D view, hover your cursor on the egg model, and press Pg Dn until you are at level 0 of detail. Tumble around the egg. Notice that even though you are at the lowest level of geometry, your surface detail on the texture still shows up. The only features of the egg that might not look right are the edges that look like straight lines. Press the W key to see the wireframe.

3. Click the Objects icon in the Select/Move Tools tray in the South Frame.

4. Click on the egg to select it. You will notice that it has a yellowish hue when selected.

5. Choose File → Export Selection. Save your file in a work folder you create for your project as **egg_model_Level_0.obj** in the .obj file format.

   The .obj file format is a simple data-format that represents 3D data most commonly used for importing and exporting geometry. It contains the position of each vertex in a very specific order, the UV texture coordinate associated with a vertex, the normal at each vertex, and the faces that make up the polygons. It was developed by Wavefront Technologies and has been adopted by most 3D graphics application vendors as an import/export format because of its open architecture. As mentioned, .obj files contain not only the geometry information but the UV data as well.

6. Press W to turn off the grid, and press Pg Up until you get to subdivision level 6.

7. Click the Objects icon in the Select/Move Tools tray in the South Frame and click the egg to select it.

8. Choose File → Export Selection and save the model as **egg_model_level_6.obj** into the work folder for your project.

Note the difference in the file sizes of 182MB for the high-resolution .obj file versus 36KB for the low-resolution .obj file. We see a difference in scale of 3,000 from the smaller sized file to the bigger.

Exporting the Texture Maps

Exporting the texture maps is already done for us in Mudbox. Whenever you save a Mudbox file that you have created paint layers for, Mudbox automatically creates a folder with the filename and places each layer in it as an individual file in the format and size you specified when you created the paint layer. You can also save or export individual layers while you are working, before you save the Mudbox file, by clicking the Layers window drop-down menu in the Layers tray and then choosing Export Selected (Figure 1.31). You need to do this for each layer you want to export.

Figure 1.31
Exporting the paint layer

For our example, the texture maps are in the egg_step_03-files folder. They are all .tif files because that's what we chose as our export format when we created our layer. Most image formats have either three or four channels: red, green, blue, and alpha. The alpha channel is used as an opacity channel. If a pixel has a value of 0 percent (or black) in its alpha channel, it is fully transparent, and if it has a value of 100 percent in the alpha channel, it is fully opaque.

Mudbox has support for multiple image formats such as Targa (.tga), TIFF (.tif), Portable Network Graphics (.png), and OpenEXR. Chapter 2 covers these formats in depth.

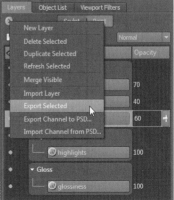

Exporting the Normal and Displacement Maps

To export the normal map, make sure you are at subdivision level 6 of your model and then follow these steps:

1. Choose Maps → Extract Texture Maps → New Operation.

2. In the Extract Texture Maps dialog box (Figure 1.32), select Normal Map. Make sure your settings match those in Figure 1.32. I will discuss these settings in more depth in later chapters.

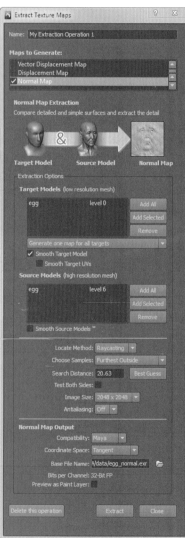

Figure 1.32

Normal map extraction dialog box

3. If it's not already populated for you, in the Extraction Options section, make sure the egg at level 0 is selected in the Target Models (Low Resolution Mesh) text box by clicking the Add All button. This is the low-resolution mesh onto which you will project the normal map.

4. In the Source Models section, also make sure egg is selected again, but at level 6. This will take into consideration the highest subdivision level from which to generate the normal map. Again this should be populated for you; if not, click the Add All button to the left of the Source Models section.

5. For the Locate Method, choose Raycasting, and for the Choose Samples option, select Closest to Target Model. For the Search Distance option, type **20.63** or use the result from clicking the adjacent Best Guess button. Choose an Image Size of 2048 × 2048 to match our texture maps. The bigger the size you choose for these maps, the finer the projected detail will be in your final destination application.

6. Click the Maya option in the Compatibility drop-down list.

7. Click the folder icon next to Base File Name and type **egg_ normal** as the filename. Select OpenEXR [32 Bit Floating Point, RGBA] as the file format and click Save. Note that this does not generate the normal map; it just sets the name.

8. Click the Extract button to extract the normal map. The Map Extraction Results dialog box appears, your normal map is generated, and a new dialog box comes up letting you know whether your normal map extracts without errors. You are finished extracting the normal map.

To export the displacement map, make sure you are at subdivision level 6 of your model and then follow these steps:

1. Choose Maps → Extract Texture Maps → My Extraction Operation 1.

2. In the Extract Texture Maps dialog box (Figure 1.33), select Displacement Map. Note that the Normal Map check box is also selected; leave it selected because it has all the settings from our prior normal map generation steps. The map generation settings are saved with the scene, and you can have multiple sessions with different settings saved under one scene. Make sure your settings match those in Figure 1.33. I will discuss these settings in depth in later chapters.

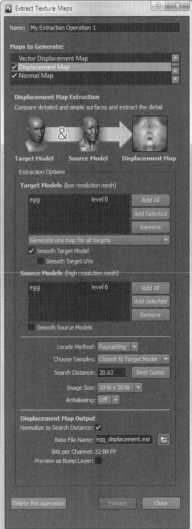

Figure 1.33

Displacement map extraction dialog box

3. In the Extraction Options, make sure egg is selected. This is the low-resolution mesh onto which the normal map is projected.

4. In the Source Models section, make sure egg is selected. This takes into consideration the highest-subdivision level from which to generate the normal map.

5. For Choose Samples, select Closest to Target Model. The Search Distance of 20.63 is fine. To find out what Choose Samples does, hover your mouse on Closest to Target Model, and pop-up help will detail the difference in diagrams. I will go in depth into the different options in later chapters, but for now use the default of Closest to Target Model. Choose an Image Size of 2048 × 2048 to match our texture maps.

6. Click the folder icon next to Base File Name and type **egg_displacement** as the filename. Select OpenEXR [32 Bit Floating Point, RGBA] as the file format and click Save. Make sure you choose RGBA and not the Black & White OpenEXR file format. Note that this does not generate the displacement map; it just sets the name.

7. Make sure the Preview as Bump Layer check box is not selected.

8. Click the Extract button to extract the displacement map. The Map Extraction Results dialog box appears, your displacement map generates, and a dialog box appears to let you know whether your displacement map extracts without errors. You are finished extracting the displacement map.

Note that you can extract both the normal and displacement maps in one step by selecting both of the check boxes in the Extract Texture Maps dialog box.

Rendering Your Image in Maya

You are at the final stage of our pipeline in this chapter. After you have your model and your texture, normal, and displacement maps, you have everything you need to render your model for its destination. You can input these components into animation, rendering 3D printing, or game engine applications to use your model for its final purpose.

In this section, you will transfer your files into Maya 2011 and render an image. I will cover other applications in later chapters. The steps might be different, but the concepts and workflow are the same. If you have access to Maya 2011, follow the steps, or look at the rendered images in the Chapter 1\egg\egg_project\images folder from the DVD, or watch the step-by-step movie on the DVD.

1. Copy Chapter1\egg\egg_project and all of its subfolders to your hard disk and remember the location.

2. Start Maya 2011 and choose File → Project → Set.

3. Navigate to the egg_project file on your hard disk and click OK.

    A Maya project is a folder structure that Maya creates to organize all of your files for the project you are working on. Our exported .obj files are in the egg_project\data folder. Our texture, normal, and displacement maps are in the egg_project\source-images folder. The Maya.ma scenes of what we are working on are in the egg_project\scenes folder. We also have a Mudbox folder that I manually created to store all of our Mudbox files.

4. Choose File → Import.

5. If you are not automatically in the egg_project\data folder, navigate to it and click egg_model_level_0.obj. Then click the Import button to load it.

6. Make sure you are in the perspective view by choosing Panels → Perspective → Persp in the Panel menu (Figure 1.34). Make sure this panel is the only one open by pressing the spacebar.

7. Select the egg model by clicking it. Press 6 to activate hardware rendering, and then press 3 to activate Maya's Smooth Mesh Preview mode. Notice that the jagged edges of our model are now nice and smooth. Even at 384 faces, we have a nice-looking model. This model will render smooth in mental ray without our having to subdivide it, or use the smooth operator on it to generate a smoother version of the model.

8. Choose Window → Settings/Preferences → Plug-in Manager.

9. Make sure that the Loaded and Auto Load check boxes are selected next to Mayatomr and OpenEXRLoader.mll.

10. Click the Render Settings button on the toolbar.

11. In the Render Using drop-down list, select mental ray.

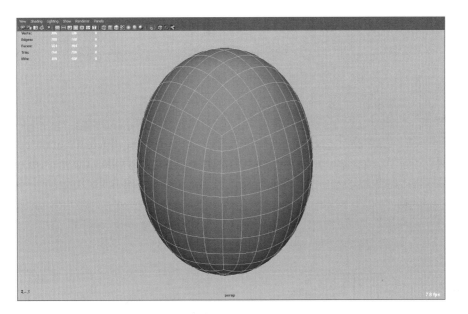

Figure 1.34

Imported egg_
model_level_
0.obj **file**

12. Click the Quality tab. In the Quality Presets drop-down list, click Production: Fine Trace. This automatically sets the output quality to the best setting while compromising render time. Because we are rendering only one image, a longer render time is tolerable. Close the Render Settings dialog box by clicking the Close button at the bottom.

13. Choose Window → Rendering Editors → Hypershade.

14. Click Blinn to create a new Blinn shader.

15. Make sure that the egg is selected by clicking it. Right-click the Blinn node and, from the marking menu that comes up, select Assign Material to Selection.

16. Double-click the Blinn shader to open its attributes in the Attribute Editor (Figure 1.5).

17. Click the checkered box next to the Color attribute.

18. Click File to connect the Color of our shader to the file node.

19. This opens the file node attributes.

20. Click the folder icon next to Image Name and click the egg_texture_comp_8_2K.tif file. This is a composite of the three texture files we created in Mudbox (Figure 1.36).

    I have loaded the three individual paint layers in Photoshop, composited them into a flattened image, and saved it as an 8-bit .tif file. To see what this looks like, open the file Chapter 1\egg\egg_project\sourceimages\egg_texture_comp_8_2K.psd in Photoshop. And look at the layers and their opacity.

    You should now see our texture applied to the egg (Figure 1.37).

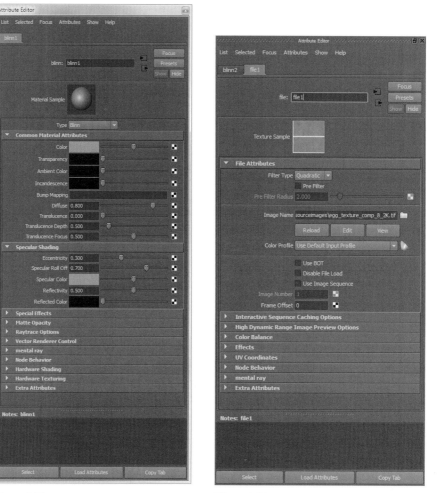

Figure 1.35

Blinn shader attributes

Figure 1.36

File node attributes

MENTAL RAY WILL NOT RENDER LZW-COMPRESSED *.TIF* FILES

Note that in Maya 2011 and prior versions, mental ray will not render images that have shaders linked to `.tif` files with Lempel-Ziv-Welch (LZW) compression. Unfortunately, Mudbox saves all `.tif` files with LZW compression, and that is also the default setting for Photoshop. If you want to use `.tif` files in Maya and mental ray, you must first load them into Photoshop and save them as `.tif` files, making sure that you save them as uncompressed files that do not use LZW compression. There also is a way to set an environment variable on both Windows and Mac so that Mudbox does not save the files with LZW compression. You can look up how to do this at `www.cgpixel.com`. Note that disabling LZW compression as a default makes the texture files take more storage space on your hard disk.

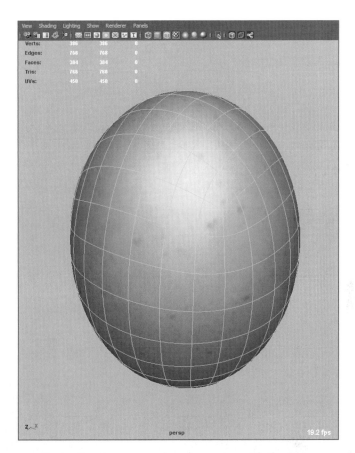

Figure 1.37

Texture preview using the hardware shader capabilities of Maya

21. Click the Render button on the toolbar to see a render of your egg with the texture applied to it. We are using the default light in Maya, but you can set up a more elaborate lighting setup with three-point lighting, image-based lighting (IBL), or one of many lighting methods. You can also adjust the Eccentricity and Specular Roll from the Blinn shader to make the surface of the egg take on the characteristic of a real eggshell surface.

22. I have set up a scene with three-point lighting that you can load and render. Choose File → Open Scene and click the egg_texture.ma file in the Chapter 1\egg\egg_project\ scenes folder on the DVD and click the Render button. Some things I have done in this setup besides adding and positioning three spotlights and a camera are adjusting the specular highlight of the Blinn shader, and modifying the Background color of the camera to a dark gray. Experiment by looking at the egg from different angles with different specular settings.

23. Select the egg and choose Window → UV Texture Editor. Notice that the texture is applied to the UVs of the egg just as it was in Mudbox.

24. Close the UV Texture Editor and choose Window → Rendering Editors → Hypershade.

Figure 1.38

Shader network

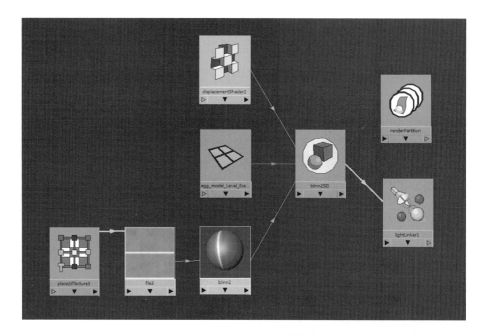

25. In Hypershade, right-click the Blinn shader you created and choose Graph Network from the marking menu. You will now add the displacement map.

26. In Hypershade, middle-click and drag a displacement node onto the Blinn shader you just created. From the menu that pops up after you let go of the middle mouse button, click Displacement Map.

27. Click the Blinn shader, and then click the Input and Output Connections button on the toolbar to see the entire shader network (Figure 1.37).

28. Double-click the displacement shader to open its attributes in the Maya window.

29. Click the checkered box next to the Displacement attribute.

30. Click File to connect the color of our shader to a file node.

    This opens up the file node attributes (Figure 1.39).

Figure 1.39

File node attributes

31. Click the folder icon next to Image Name and click the `egg_displacement_32_2K.exr` file that we created in Mudbox. Your shader network should look like Figure 1.40.

32. Render your image and notice that the displacement map applied to your image is the high-frequency detail sculpting we did in Mudbox. See Figure 1.41.

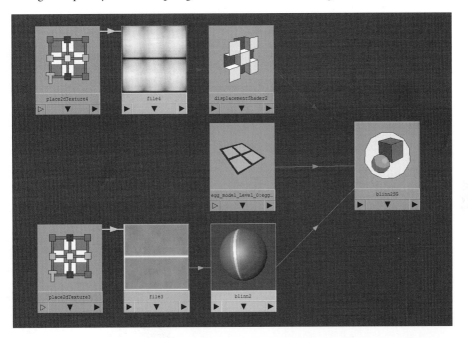

Figure 1.40

Shader network

Figure 1.41

Egg render with displacement map

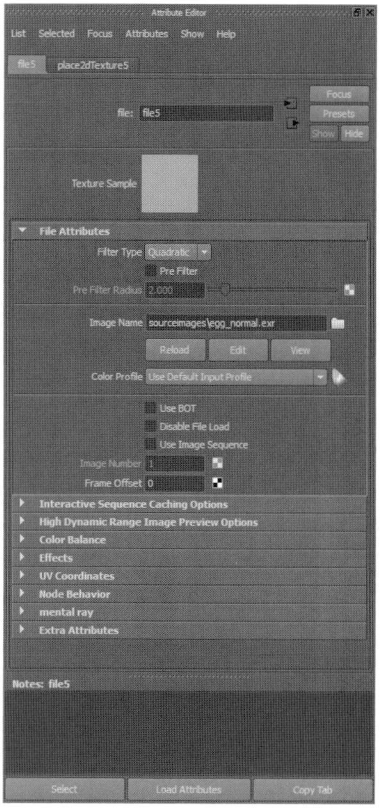

33. Next, you will create a shader for the normal map. In Hypershade, create a new Blinn node.

34. Make sure that the egg is selected by clicking it in the Maya Perspective viewport, and right-click on the Blinn node. From the marking menu that comes up, select Assign Material to Selection. That should make the egg look gray.

35. In Hypershade, click the Bump2d node and middle-click and drag from the Bump2d node onto the Blinn shader. From the menu that pops up after you let go of the middle mouse button, click Bump Map.

36. Double-click on the Bump2d shader to open its attributes in the Maya window.

37. Click the checkered box next to the Bump Value attribute.

38. Click File to connect the color of our shader to the file node.

    This opens the file node attributes.

39. Click the folder icon next to Image Name and click `egg_normal_32_2K.exr` file (Figure 1.42). This is the normal map we created in Mudbox.

    Your shader network should look like Figure 1.43.

40. Render your image and notice that the relief of your high-frequency detail on the surface of the egg is greatly exaggerated (Figure 1.44). That's because you need to change one more setting to let Maya know that this is in fact a normal map and not a bump map.

Figure 1.42
File node attributes

Figure 1.43
Normal map shading network

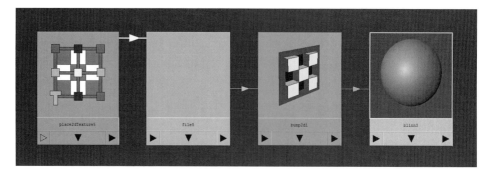

Figure 1.44

Exaggerated relief due to using a normal map as a bump map

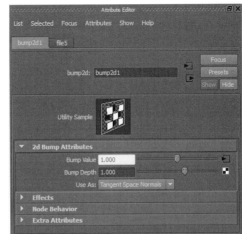

Figure 1.45

Bump2d attributes used as tangent space normals

41. In Hypershade, double-click the Bump2d node. This brings up the attributes for the node. In the Use As drop-down, select Tangent Space Normals and render your image (Figure 1.45).

42. Render your image and notice that you have the normal map applied to your model.

    The true value of normal maps and their importance to the production pipelines can be demonstrated when we use Maya's ability to render normal maps to give you a real-time preview of the high-frequency detail that you sculpted in Mudbox that resulted in over 1.5 million polygons to display in real time on our 384-polygon model in Maya.

43. In the Perspective panel, choose Shading → Wireframe on Shaded and note that we still have our simple 384-poly egg model. Choose Shading → Hardware Texturing. This will not do anything to the display until the next step.

44. Choose Renderer → High Quality Rendering. You will now see the high-frequency detail appear on the surface of the egg. You can tumble around the egg to see all the details in real time. There is an anomaly that appears at the edges of the UVs on the egg that you can easily fix in the next step (Figure 1.46).

45. In Hypershade, double-click the file node. This brings up the attributes for the file node.

46. In the file node attributes, expand the High Dynamic Range Image Preview Options section. In the Float to Fixed Point attribute, click Clamp. This fixes the UV edge issue, and now you are previewing the relief on the surface of your egg in real time using the normal map (Figure 1.47). You can see me going through the stages in this section in the `Chapter1-part4.mov` video in the `\Chapter 1\Videos` folder.

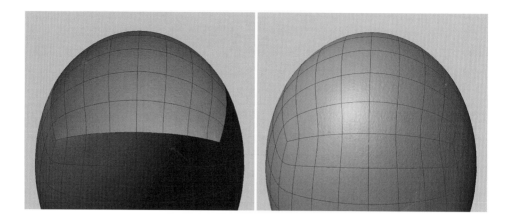

I have included a finished version of the normal mapping section on the DVD called `egg_normal.ma` in the `Chapter 1\egg\egg_project\scenes` folder. Try adding the texture map to the Blinn node to see a fully textured normal mapped version of your egg, or open the `egg_normal_texture.ma` file from the `Chapter 1\egg\egg_project\scenes` folder to see your egg texture and high-frequency detail in real time. You can see the real power and benefit of normal maps here, where you have a very low-polygon egg that can easily be manipulated in games and movies, and yet be able to display high-frequency detail on its surface that reacts to light with minimal cost in processing power.

Figure 1.47

Set the Float to Fixed Point attribute to Clamp

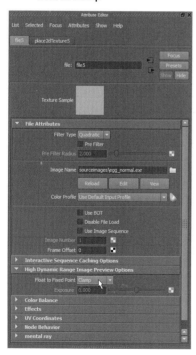

Summary

As I mentioned at the beginning of the chapter, this is the most important chapter in the book. Everything you will do from this point forward is expanding on the concepts you worked on here. Go through the steps, watch the videos, or load the finished files from the DVD to make sure you have a good comprehension of all the stages in this chapter.

You started out with a Mudbox primitive sphere. You learned how to move around your model by manipulating the camera view in Mudbox. Then you proceeded to block in the shape of the egg, subdivide it, and sculpt layers of high-frequency detail. You painted the model with our best approximation of what an egg surface would look like, in addition to projection-painting it with the surface of an actual egg in a digital photo. You used Mudbox's real-time preview to see what your model looked like and proceeded to export all the components out of Mudbox. You imported the geometry, texture, normal map, and displacement map files into Maya to output the final results of your work.

Hopefully, this chapter has set a good stage of the Mudbox production pipeline for you to build on in the chapters that follow.

CHAPTER 2

The Mudbox User Interface

This chapter provides a reference or orientation of the Mudbox user interface (UI). I will cover the Mudbox interface, identify the different sections you see on the screen workspace, and outline the functions of the tools.

When you work with any program, you will initially focus on areas that are particular to the project at hand, as you did in Chapter 1, "Getting Your Feet in the Mud: The Basics of the Mudbox Production Pipeline." In most cases, users develop a comfort zone of features in the application they are working with and then go on to explore the interface to find other software features that can streamline their workflow or enable them to explore new areas of creativity in their work. This chapter lists the components of the Mudbox interface and what they do from a definition level. You will learn more about the usability of the key features in other chapters of the book.

If you are working in Mudbox and see something interesting yet unfamiliar to you, this chapter is the place to look it up. I recommend that you initially read through this chapter to get your bearings, and then refer back to it when you need to know where things are or for information about a specific tool or a section of the screen.

This chapter includes the following topics:

- Starting out with the Welcome screen
- Navigating the main viewport
- Exploring the East Frame window
- Working with the South Frame tray
- Performing map extraction

Starting Out with the Welcome Screen

When Mudbox first launches, you are greeted with the Welcome screen (Figure 2.1). The Welcome screen also comes up when you choose the New Scene option from the File menu.

Figure 2.1

Welcome screen

The main function of the Welcome screen is to jump-start your work session. If you are a beginner and need help with the basics, the first column of the Welcome screen displays five, one-minute tutorial movies to familiarize you with the essentials. These are as follows:

- Navigate the View Using a Mouse
- Navigate the View Using a Tablet
- Start Painting
- Start Sculpting
- Start Posing

If you have not yet done so, I recommend that you run through all the tutorial movies at least once to familiarize yourself with the most basic and critical actions you will be performing throughout your sculpting session. If you have used Maya or other 3D applications, some of these functions will be familiar to you. After you run through the five basic tutorials, you can click the QuickStart Tutorial button to launch Mudbox's help, which covers 11 topics to get you further along (Figure 2.2). These topics are as follows:

- Configure your Wacom tablet or mouse
- Launch Mudbox

- Navigate the 3D view

- Load a model

- Increase the resolution of a model

- Sculpt a model

- Sculpt using layers

- Sculpt using stencils

- Paint a model

- Paint using stencils

- Save your work

Again, for a beginner, I recommend that you go through these sections at least once. You can access many more tutorials in the Mudbox Community by clicking the More in the Mudbox Community tab.

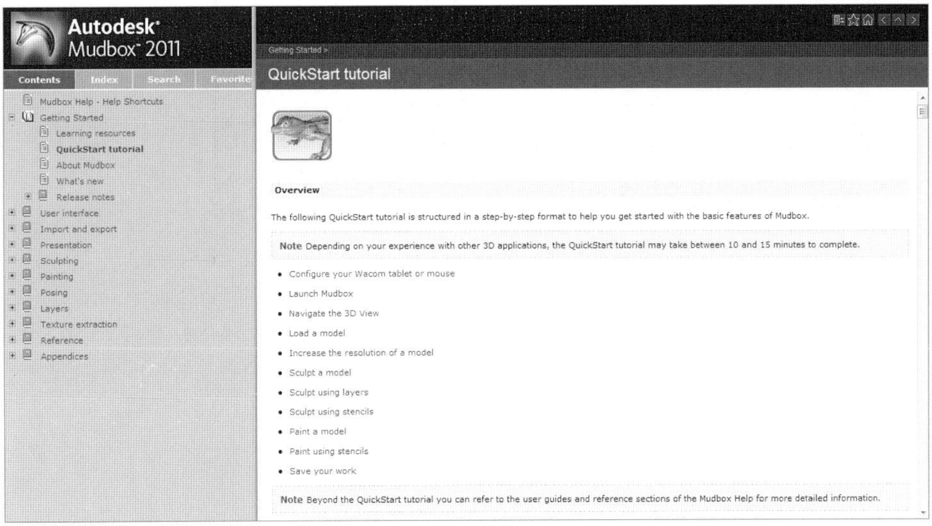

Figure 2.2

QuickStart tutorial help screen

After you feel comfortable with the topics covered in the one-minute movies and the QuickStart tutorials, you can streamline your Welcome screen by clicking the Do Not Show Learning Movies Again check box at the bottom of the Welcome screen. You will learn how to revert back to showing the learning movies at the end of this section.

The next column of the Welcome screen give you the option to pick one of Mudbox's starting-point primitives, such as the Basic Head, Cube, or Sphere, to start your sculpting session. These primitives are provided for you to start from a basic generic shape and develop it into your personal creation. Although these shapes are good for practicing and doing some concept sculpts, you will soon discover their limitations and eventually develop your own library of primitives, or import models called *base meshes* from Maya or your favorite 3D modeling application. We will go into depth about the reasons that you might want to do this in Chapter 3, "Detail-Sculpting an Imported Model," Chapter 5, "Digital Sculpting Part I," and Chapter 6, "Digital Sculpting Part II." Clicking on one of the basic shapes closes the Welcome screen and launches you into Mudbox's user interface with your selected shape loaded.

Figure 2.3

Preferences menu options

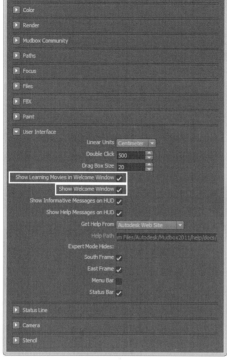

The last column has an Open button to open a Mudbox scene from your hard drive. It also has a list of recent files, to save you time navigating the folders on your hard drive to find them. Note that when Mudbox saves a scene or exports models, it will save a thumbnail image with the file and display that thumbnail in the Recent Files section of the Welcome screen.

Some folks find Welcome screens cumbersome and like to launch right into a new scene when they launch the application. If you are one of them, you can click the Do Not Show This Welcome Window Again check box, and the Welcome screen will no longer greet you when you first launch into Mudbox.

If you accidentally click the Do Not Show Learning Movies Again or Do Not Show This Welcome Window Again check box, and want to bring them back, you can do so in either of two ways:

- Choosing the Learning Movies menu item under the Help menu
- Selecting the Show Learning Movies in Welcome Window and Show Welcome Window check boxes in the Windows → Preferences menu item (Figure 2.3)

Navigating the Main Viewport

After you either pick a primitive or open a file from the Welcome screen, you are in the main viewport, where you will be doing all your work in Mudbox. The main viewport is divided into three main frames (Figure 2.4): the Heads-Up Display (HUD), the East Frame window, and the South Frame tray.

There is also a menu bar at the top of the screen and a status bar at the bottom of the screen that give you information about your scene, errors, and information relative to your actions.

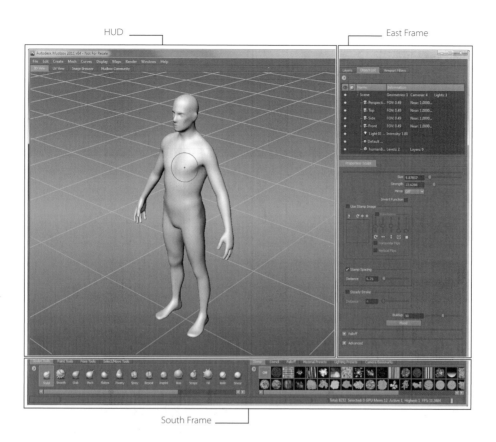

HUD

East Frame

South Frame

Figure 2.4

Three frames of the Mudbox interface

Heads-Up Display

The Heads-Up Display (HUD) has four tabs:

- 3D View, where you will sculpt and 3D-paint your creation. This is where you will spend the bulk of your time in Mudbox.

- UV View, where you will see the way your textures and paint are applied to the UVs of your image. If you are unfamiliar with UVs or what they do, don't worry, because they are covered in depth in Chapters 3, 4, 5, and 6.

- Image Browser, where you will browse your texture and image libraries to pick the textures and image-based lighting (IBL) images to apply to your creation.

- Mudbox Community, where you can find and share resources such as stamps, stencils, base mesh models, tutorials, and samples of your work. You can also vote on community members' work and get feedback on yours. You have to be online and connected to the Internet to access the Mudbox Community.

3D View

The 3D view is where all the creative magic happens. When you first see the 3D view, it consists of a gradient background and a grid. Imagine the rectangle where the 3D view is located as a viewfinder of a camera that you are looking through. There are many other standard and customizable viewports, but the one you start with is called the Perspective camera.

You will go through changing the camera to standard orthogonal or custom cameras in later chapters, but whatever your camera choice, you are able to see only one camera's contents in the 3D view. This is different from other 3D applications, because most of them usually have three or four camera views when you first start up.

There are some other things that pop up in the 3D view as you start working on your model. After you start dividing your model or stepping through its subdivision levels, you will see the subdivision level as well as the number of polygons in your model in a window at the top-right corner of the 3D view (Figure 2.5).

Figure 2.5

3D view

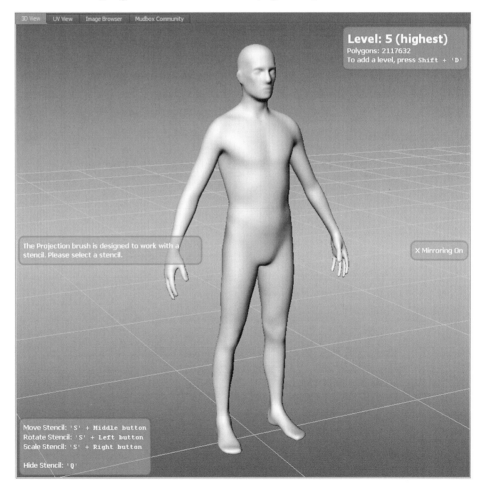

You will also get a status indicator at the center right of the 3D view, telling you which mirroring method is activated Figure 2.5). You will learn more about how to use mirroring to sculpt and paint symmetrically in Chapters 5 and 7.

You will also occasionally get tool help that shows up in the left part of the 3D view. You can turn off the informative messages if you wish; you can do so in the User Interface Section of the Windows → Preferences (Mudbox → Preferences on the Mac) dialog box.

You can turn off the gradient background by deselecting the Gradient Background option in the Display menu.

You also have context-sensitive menus that you can activate in the 3D view by right-clicking on either the canvas or an object in the canvas. When you right-click on the canvas, you get a subset of the Display menu. When you right-click on an object, you get a menu that enables you to assign a new or existing material to the object, edit the material that is assigned to it, and rename or delete it or find out about its properties.

UV View

The UV view is where you see your active model's UV texture coordinates in addition to the active paint layer (Figure 2.6).

Figure 2.6

The UV view

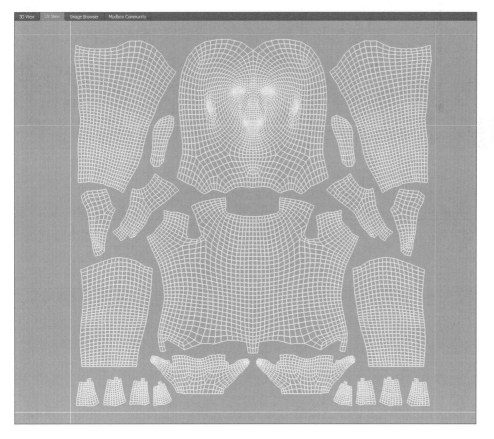

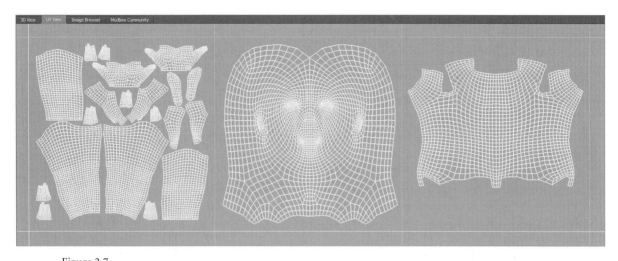

Figure 2.7

UV view with multiple quadrants

This view enables to you to see UVs in the first quadrant (or tile region) in addition to ones that are laid out in multiple tiles (Figure 2.7). Here you will also see your different maps and layers applied to your UVs.

Note that all of your UVs should be laid out before your model gets into Mudbox. This view is just for viewing the UVs and textures applied to them and not for creating, interacting with, or changing the UVs.

Image Browser

The Image Browser is a viewer that helps you view your 2D image library. You can visually select images to be stamps, stencils, image planes, or high dynamic range (HDR) image-based lighting (IBL). Think of it as a sophisticated version of a File Open dialog box for 2D images.

The Image Browser is divided into three parts: the toolbar, or ribbon, on top; the thumbnails on the left; and the 2D view in the center (Figure 2.8).

The ribbon, or toolbar, is where you sort through your images, get information about them, and assign them to the various roles such as image plane backdrops, a stamp to sculpt with, or a stencil to paint on your model (Figure 2.9).

To point the Image Browser at an image folder, do one of the following:

- Type the image path in the File Path text box.

- Click the Open Folder button and navigate to the image folder with a familiar File Open dialog box.

- Click the Open Parent Folder button to move up a level in the folder hierarchy.

- Use the Browse Back or Forward buttons to cycle through the folder you worked with in the session. This is similar to the Back and Forward buttons in your favorite browser.

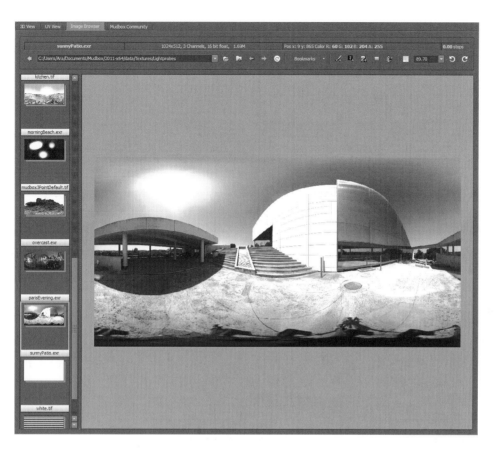

Figure 2.8

Image Browser

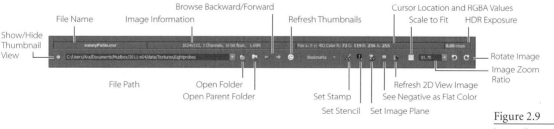

Figure 2.9

Image Browser toolbar

Pick a folder from the list in the Bookmarks drop-down list. Within this drop-down list is also where you set your favorite image folders as bookmarks to save time navigating to them in future working sessions, or to quickly jump from one bookmark to another without having to navigate your hard drive to get to them. Setting bookmarks for your texture, stamp, stencil, and current working directories will save you a lot of time during a working session. After you select a folder or directory, the images in that directory will show up in the thumbnails strip to the left of the Image Browser. You can enlarge this strip to see more thumbnails by dragging the separator between the thumbnail strip and the 2D view.

In addition to thumbnails, you will see folders in the left pane of the Image Browser view with the name of the folder on the bottom of the picture of a folder. Make sure you click on the picture of the folder above the name and not the folder picture below the name. Because the image of the folder appears closer to the name of the folder above it, it is a common practice and source of frustration to mistakenly click the folder under the name.

You can show and hide the thumbnails by clicking the Show/Hide Thumbnail View arrow icon to the left of the file name text box. You can cycle through the images sequentially by pressing the spacebar.

After you have selected an image, the information section of the toolbar Figure 2.9) displays the image's name, dimensions in pixels, number of color channels, bit depth (8, 16, 32), and file size. Next to the image information you will see an information area that changes values as you move the mouse over your image. This section shows information about the image under the pointer, such as the X and Y position, the Red, Green, Blue, and Alpha (RGBA) values, and whether you have a high dynamic range (HDR) image, and its exposure value.

When you are viewing an HDR image, you can use the + and – keys to go up or down, respectively, in exposure value. These values are also called *stops*, based on the photography term *f-stop*, used to measure exposure. I cover HDR imagery and the significance of HDR photography in Chapter 9, "Lighting and Rendering." Press the 0 key to reset the stop, or exposure value, to zero. Note that after you go up or down in exposure value to a setting for a particular image, that exposure setting does not change as you subsequently click on different images, whether they are HDR images or not.

It is a good practice to press **0** right after you navigate to a new image, especially if it is looking too dark or blown out to return the exposure level to the default value so you can see subsequent images you click on at a neutral exposure level.

The buttons on the right side of the toolbar enable you to set the image you are looking at in the 2D view as a stamp, a stencil, or an image plane (see Figure 2.9 earlier). These are covered further in future chapters, but for now, just know the location of the buttons, and that this is where you can make the assignments. If you are looking at a 32-bit floating-point HDR or a grayscale extracted displacement map image and wish to differentiate the pixels that contain negative floating-point values, click the See Negative as Flat Color button (see Figure 2.9 earlier). Negative displacement is displayed as positive values by default, and using this option helps you troubleshoot problems in an extracted normal map by seeing the negative values in green.

If you are working on your image in another application such as Adobe Photoshop, or loading an update image from a digital camera to replace the one you are looking at, click the Refresh Thumbnails button (Figure 2.9) to see the latest saved version of the image.

To have your image zoom up, down, or fit the size of the 2D view of the Image Browser, click the Scale to Fit button. You can zoom in or out of the image by using the Ctrl and + or – keys, respectively. Hold down the Alt key and click and drag your mouse or tablet on the image in the 2D view to pan around an image that is zoomed bigger than what fits in the 2D view. You can also zoom up your image at a preset value of 1×, 2×, 3×, 4×, 5×, or zoom down your image to ⅔×, ½×, ⅓×, ¼×, ⅙×, ⅛×, or ¹⁄₁₂× by clicking the down arrow of the Zoom Ratio combo to the right of the Scale to Fit button (Figure 2.9). You can also type an arbitrary number in the combo box to zoom your image to that size.

To rotate the image in 90-degree increments, click either of the Rotate Image buttons to rotate clockwise or counterclockwise. Note that this does not rotate the image permanently; it just does so in the image viewer. Also note that if you do rotate an image and grab it as a stamp, stencil, or image plane, the rotated image will be grabbed even though the original remains in its original orientation.

Mudbox Community

When you click the Mudbox Community tab, your main viewport essentially becomes a browser window connecting you to the `http://area.autodesk.com/mudcom` website, where you can download and upload resources, view community posted tutorials, browse and rate the work of Mudbox community members all over the world, or submit some of your own work to get rated by others. Community users need to use their Autodesk AREA user credentials to log in to the site.

Exploring the East Frame Window

The East Frame is grouped into two sections. The top section is composed of three tabs:

- Layers, where you create and manage sculpt and paint layers
- Object List, where you select and manage all the objects in your scene, such as your model, lights, cameras, and materials
- Viewport Filters, which controls the rendered look of the 3D view

The bottom section of the East Frame contains the Properties window, which changes to display the properties of the currently selected object or tool, such as the sculpt tool, paint brush, camera, material, or light.

Depending on your preference, you can dynamically (as you are working) increase or decrease the room each section takes by moving the separator between the top and bottom section. You can also add more horizontal room to both sections by moving the separator on the edge left and right (Figure 2.10).

Figure 2.10

**Resizing the
East Frame**

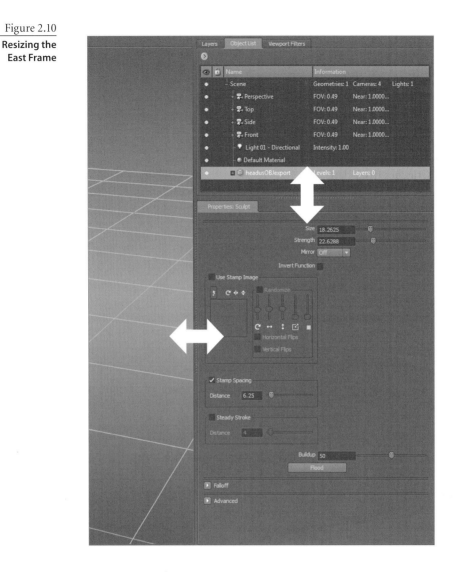

Layers Window

In the Layers window, you manage one of the most powerful capabilities of Mudbox: the ability to sculpt and paint on layers. If you have experience using Photoshop, Corel Painter, or any image-editing or compositing program that uses layers, you are familiar with how powerful and useful they can be.

The reason the skin on a Rembrandt portrait looks so vibrant and realistic is that Rembrandt used layers of oil paint with various opacities to represent the intricacies of how faces are composed of dermal and subdermal layers with various heat points and oily film. Lights in the environment reflect, refract, and react to these layers to give the subtleties of appearance that we are subconsciously conditioned to see. In Mudbox, you can do the same by painting or sculpting each layer individually, and then compositing them with different levels of opacity to achieve realistic or stylistically beautiful results.

Mudbox has both sculpt and paint layers. Sculpt layers are really useful when you are working on a model and you want to dial up or down sculpted features in a nondestructive manner. For example, if you are sculpting damage on armor for a game character and presenting it to your art director for approval, you can sculpt damage from ballistic weapons on one layer, scratches from claws or swords on another layer, and deformation from blunt-force weapons such as hammers or spikes on yet another layer. You can show and hide each one of these layers, and also dial up or dial down the opacity of the layer to choose the appropriate level of damage and fine-tune it until it looks perfect. You can also use these layers to generate blend shapes, such as expressions on a face. This is a huge time-saver and will prevent you from having to resculpt to accommodate for revisions.

You can switch between sculpt and paint layers by clicking the Sculpt or Paint layers buttons (Figure 2.11).

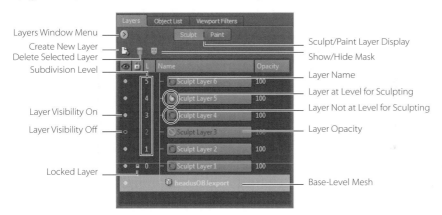

Figure 2.11

Layers window

The Layers window enables you to do the following:

- Create, name, duplicate, mirror, flip, and delete layers.
- Merge or flatten layers.
- Navigate layers.
- Show and hide layers.
- Lock layers.
- Show and hide masks on a layer.
- Control the opacity of a layer.

Sculpt Layers

It is very important to understand the relationship between sculpt layers and subdivision levels. *Sculpt layers* are layers that contain differences in the surface of the model that have been sculpted specifically in that layer. *Subdivision levels* denote how many times the mesh has been subdivided to get more polygons, and, in turn, display more-granular detail. This relationship can be a source of frustration if you don't understand it well. I will go over it in a couple of places in this book. Read this section and go through the example in Chapter 3 until you are completely comfortable with the relationship between sculpt layers and subdivision levels.

Your model can be subdivided many times to add more polygons so you can sculpt finer details. You start with your model at level 0. As you subdivide, your model will progress to subdivision level 1, 2, 3, and 4, and so forth based on how much detail you need and of course what your hardware is capable of crunching. Each subdivision level you go up increases the number of vertices you have, by multiplying it by 4. So if you have 24 vertices in the model you start with at level 0, subdivision level 1 will result in 96 vertices, which is 24 vertices times 4. Level 2 will have 384 vertices, the 96 vertices from level 1 multiplied by 4.

You add a new subdivision level by clicking Mesh → Add New Subdivision Level in the menu or using the keyboard shortcut Shift+D. Doing so adds a subdivision level to your model and places your model at the newly created subdivision. You have to be at the highest existing subdivision level to be able to add a new level; otherwise, when you click Mesh → Add New Subdivision Level or press Shift+D, you will go up to only the next level that's already there. For example, if your model has four subdivision levels, and you are sculpting on level 3, if you press Shift+D, you will go to level 4 rather than add level 5. But if you are sculpting on level 4 and press Shift+D, you will add level 5. So if you are not at the highest existing subdivision level, Shift+D does not add a level, but has the same effect as Mesh → Step Level Up, or pressing Pg Up on the keyboard.

A sculpt layer is assigned one and only one subdivision level. However, multiple sculpt layers can have the same subdivision level. For example, three sculpt layers named scars, pores, and wrinkles can all be assigned subdivision level 5. This means you will sculpt these three skin details on individual sculpt layers, and these details will be sculpted on your model at the geometry detail provided at a subdivision level of 5 in their individual layers. However, you can work on these three sculpt layers only in subdivision level 5.

You can't go down a subdivision level while you are in a sculpt layer, because it is locked at the subdivision level it was created in. For example, if you are on the wrinkles layer at subdivision level 5 and you press Pg Dn to go down a subdivision level, you will get a No icon in front of the wrinkles layer in the Layers window, and you won't be able to sculpt your model until you either go back to subdivision level 5 or move off the layer by selecting another layer that is assigned the subdivision level 4. If you attempt to sculpt on a layer at a different subdivision level, you will get a dialog box explaining that the layer is locked at a specific subdivision level, and the options you have are either to be able to sculpt on this layer by going the subdivision level assigned to it, or creating or going to an existing layer that has the current subdivision level assigned to it.

You assign a level to a sculpt layer by selecting the sculpt layer in the Object List and by being at the desired subdivision level before making your first sculpting stroke on it. After you make that first stroke and the subdivision level is assigned to your sculpt layer, it is not possible to change the subdivision level assigned to that sculpt layer.

This can be frustrating because you can be on a layer but not be able to sculpt on your model. Before you start digging around in properties or thinking there is a problem with the software, look at the sculpt layer to see whether a red circle with a line through it appears next to the layer name. This symbol indicates that you are at a different level than the one to which the sculpt layer was assigned. That's why you are not able to sculpt on it. To fix this, either create a new layer for the level you are on, or click on the base-level mesh in the Sculpt Layers window.

DEMYSTIFYING SUBDIVISION LEVELS AND SCULPT LAYERS

Subdivision levels and sculpt layers can be really frustrating when you first start out, so refer to the following tips as many times as needed to get comfortable with how they work.

You have to be at the highest subdivision level to add a new level. Otherwise, clicking Mesh → Add New Subdivision Level or pressing Shift+D will only go up to a next level that's already there.

A sculpt layer can be assigned to only one single subdivision level. You can assign multiple layers to a subdivision level, but each layer is assigned one and only one subdivision level.

To assign a subdivision level to a new sculpt layer, first determine the level that should be assigned. If that level exists, go to it by pressing the Pg Up or Pg Dn keys, create the layer, and as soon as you make your first sculpting stroke, the subdivision level you are currently on will be assigned the sculpting layer. You will see this assignment in the L column of the Sculpt Layers window.

As you are working on your sculpture, if you are unable to sculpt on the layer you are on, look at the L column in the Sculpt Layers window to see what subdivision level is assigned to that layer and then notice the red circle with a line through it next to your layer name. Either go to that level by using the Pg Up or Pg Dn keys, or create a new layer for the level you are on.

To create a sculpt layer, do one of the following:

- Click the Create New Layer icon (refer back to Figure 2.11).
- Click the Layers window drop-down menu icon and choose New Layer.
- Right-click anywhere inside the layer list area and choose New Layer.

To delete a sculpt layer, do one of the following:

- Click on the layer to be deleted, and then click the trashcan icon (Delete Selected Layer) in the Layers window (Figure 2.11).
- Click the Layers window drop-down menu icon and choose Delete Selected.
- Right-click anywhere inside the layer list area and choose Delete Selected.

To duplicate a sculpt layer, do one of the following:

- Click the Layers window drop-down menu icon and choose Duplicate Selected.
- Right-click anywhere inside the layer list area and choose Duplicate Selected.

To select a sculpt layer, click on it. You will not be able to select multiple layers, but you can merge multiple layers by making sure they are visible and that other layers are not, and then choose Merge Visible from the Layers window menu. To show or hide a sculpt layer, click the little Layer Visibility dot or circle under the eye icon (Figure 2.11). To flatten or merge all sculpt layers into one, choose Flatten from the Layers window menu.

You can save a version of your sculpture, make changes to it, load the original back in as a layer, and use the opacity slider to blend the two sculpts. To do this, choose Import Layer from the Layers window menu, navigate to the .mud or .obj file, and then use the opacity slider to blend them.

You can also flip and mirror the layer along the x-, y-, or z-axis or the tangent by choosing the appropriate option from the list in the Flip and Mirror submenus from the Layers window drop-down menu icon. Chapter 5 covers mirroring.

Paint Layers

The steps for operations on sculpt layers (such as selecting, deleting, duplicating, and showing and hiding) that you learned in the previous section all apply to paint layers as well, with one exception. When you create a new paint layer by selecting New Layer, you get the dialog box in Figure 2.12.

Figure 2.12

Create New Paint Layer dialog box

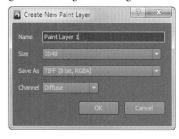

Here is where you choose the size of your images, which are referred to as maps, for the paint layers 256, 512, 1024, 2048, and 4096. These numerals refer to the number of pixels, and of course, a map is square so 2048 is actually 2048 × 2048 and is also referred to as a 2K map. You will mostly use 1K, 2K, or 4K maps depending on how much detail will be visible in your resulting output. In film or TV, close-ups require more detail; in games where textures have to be loaded and rendered in real time in the midst of action, you want to optimize memory usage by having smaller textures.

Figure 2.13

File formats

The Save As drop-down menu is where you choose the file format for your maps (Figure 2.13). The options are as follows:

- PNG [8 bit, RGBA]
- TIFF [8 bit, RGBA]
- TIFF [16 bit Integer, RGBA]
- TIFF [32 bit Floating Point, RGBA]
- Photoshop [8 bit, RGBA]
- Targa [8 bit, RGBA]
- OpenEXR [16 bit Floating Point, RGBA]
- OpenEXR [32 bit Floating Point, RGBA]

You can save your images in four lossless file formats in 8-, 16-, or 32-bit depth, and all the images formats save four channels: Red, Green, Blue, and Alpha (RGBA). The four lossless file formats are as follows:

PNG Portable Network Graphics, a popular graphics format.

TIFF Tagged Image File Format developed by Aldus, now Adobe, is popular with the print and document imaging world.

TGA Truevision Graphics Adapter, or Truevision Advanced Raster Graphics Adapter (TARGA) is a ubiquitous file format for storing textures because of its ease of implementation.

OpenEXR OpenEXR is a high dynamic range (HDR) file format released as an open standard by Industrial Light & Magic (ILM).

As for which format is the best to use, it depends on the project or the company's production pipeline. Many game studios use TGA for textures, but OpenEXR is a growing open standard that has support for 32-bit depth and HDR. In this book, we will mostly be using TIFF, TGA, and OpenEXR.

You choose a channel type when you create a new paint layer. These are Diffuse, Specular, Gloss, Incandescence, Bump Map, and Reflection Mask (Figure 2.14). You can have multiples of these layers, and they are grouped in the Paint Layers window by channel (Figure 2.15).

Diffuse Specifies the base color of your sculpture. Think of it as the pure color in an environment that has no external influencing factors.

Specular Specifies the color of the specular highlight on the material. This is best described as the property that gives objects their shine. This is a grayscale image that specifies which parts of your model are allowed to show specular highlights (white and lighter grays) and which parts are not (usually black or darker grays).

Figure 2.14

**Paint Layers
window**

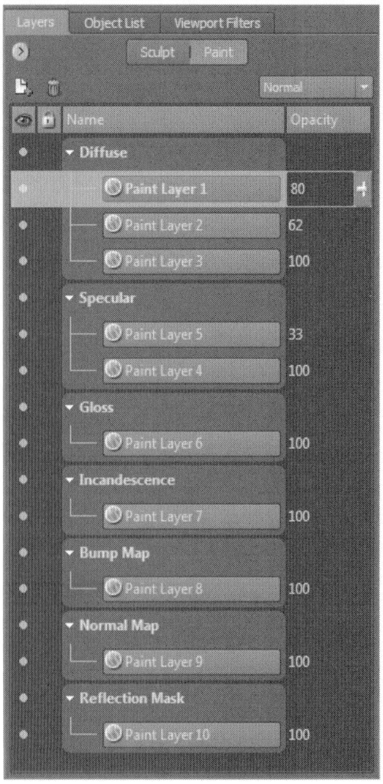

Figure 2.15

Paint Layer channels

Gloss Specifies the size of the specular reflection. It is also a grayscale image for which the darker the value, the smaller the size of the specular highlight.

Incandescence Incandescence simulates the emission of light by the material, independent of the lights in the scene. This paint layer indicates the brightness of the color on a material but does not affect or illuminate other models or parts on the scene.

Bump Map Bump maps give a fake sense of depth. Darker values appear to be inset, and lighter values appear to bulge out. You will not see the effects of a bump map on the edge of the geometry of a model because there is no displacement or chiseling in, it's just an optical illusion. The bump map is a grayscale image in which areas that are at 50 percent gray are flush with the surface of the model. Areas with darker colors are indented, and lighter ones appear to bulge out. The Bump Map is also the channel in which you can visualize an extracted displacement map on your model.

Normal Map The Normal Map channel, based on RGB colors, is the channel at which you can visualize an extracted normal map on your model.

Reflection Mask This is a grayscale image that specifies what part of your model reflects the environment.

Note that the Mudbox Material used in the 2009 and 2010 versions of Mudbox had some additional channels such as Specular 2 and Gloss 2, and did not have others such as Incandescence and Normal Map. It also had some naming differences such as Bump Value instead of Bump Map. The channels in the older Mudbox Material are still supported with later versions of Mudbox to maintain compatibility; however, they are not available to you when you are creating materials:

Specular 2 A second specular that affects the fringes of the specular highlight. This setting is useful in low and oblique lighting situations.

Gloss 2 A second gloss component that affects the size of the outer regions of specular highlights. This setting is useful in low and oblique lighting situations.

Of all these channels, Diffuse and Normal are the only two in which color is relevant. Even though the others can be in color too, only their saturation is relevant, unless you want the specular highlight to have a particular hue. Note that you can have multiple diffuse maps layered on top of each other to represent the layers found in nature. For example, a face has subdermal and epidermal layers that you can paint; using the powerful layers capability of Mudbox, you can dial up or down the opacity of each layer to get your perfect desired blend of the two.

To merge or flatten paint layers into one layer, click Layers window drop-down menu →
Merge Visible. This is a good practice if you are finished with the layers and don't need
to make further adjustments and edits to them or their opacity, because this reduces the
number of texture files and saves texture memory.

Some things to note when merging layers:

- All visible layers are merged for the selected paint layer channel. You can temporarily
  turn off any layers you don't want merged by using the Layer Visibility setting (click
  the little dot or circle under the eye icon in the Paint Layers window and make sure the
  circle is not filled). You will then select one of the existing layers to be the resulting
  layer.

- When layers are merged, the existing layer opacity values are frozen. Even though
  you can still adjust the opacity of the resulting layer, you can no longer adjust the
  opacity of the original individual layers.

- When layers of different resolutions are merged, the layer with the highest resolution
  determines the resulting layer's resolution. If you merge an image with a resolution
  of 1K with two images that are 2K, the resulting layer adopts the highest resolution, in this case 2K. Similarly, when layers with different bit depths are merged, the
  resulting layer has the same bit depth as the image with the highest bit depth.

> Before you merge layers, it is a good practice to first save or export your initial layers, and
> take notes on their opacity, in case you do have to go back and correct something. In that
> case, you just import the images, make the adjustments, and merge the layers again.

If you want to export paint layers, select them and choose Layers window drop-down
menu icon → Export Selected. You can also import images as layers by choosing Layers
window drop-down menu icon → Import Layer.

When you save your model (for example, torso.mud), Mudbox stores all your layers as
image files in a folder (for example, called torso-files).

You can rearrange the top-to-bottom order of paint layers within their channels by
dragging and dropping them in the Paint Layers window.

Paint layers can also be composited by using one of five blend modes that work similar
to blend modes in Adobe Photoshop layers. Every layer starts out with the default Normal
blend mode that you can change by using the blend mode drop-down menu. To determine the blend mode of a paint layer, click on it, and its blend mode will be indicated in
the blend mode menu. The five blend modes available in Mudbox are as follows:

Normal The default blend mode for a paint layer. With this blend mode, the composite of all the layers will result only in the top paint layer in the layer stack unless
you change the opacity setting to a number less than 100, or it has some transparent

regions due to the image having an alpha channel that indicates what parts of it are transparent.

Multiply The value of each pixel in the layer is darkened by a value greater than or equal to the value of pixels occupying the same location on layers on top of it in the layer stack. It is useful for darkening an image, especially with an ambient occlusion map. Multiplying with white does nothing, while screening with black produces black.

Add The value of each pixel in the layer is brightened by a value less than or equal to the value of pixels occupying the same location on layers on top of it in the layer stack. Although Screen seems to do the same thing as the Add blend mode, the lightening effect produces no change in contrast because of the mode being applied in a linear fashion, producing a more extreme lightening result than Screen.

Screen The value of each pixel in the layer is brightened by a value less than or equal to the value of pixels occupying the same location on layers on top of it in the layer stack. The resulting effect is the opposite of the Multiply blend mode. Screening with black does nothing, while screening with white produces white.

Overlay Is a combination of Multiply and Screen. The Multiply blend mode is applied to a pixel if it is at the bottom 50 percent of the overall brightness of the image , and the Screen blend mode is applied to the pixel if it is at the top 50 percent. The base color on the layer is not replaced but is mixed with the blend color to reflect the lightness or darkness of the original color. This blend mode is useful for replacing patterns and colors while preserving the highlights and shadows of the base color.

Now that you have read a description of the Layers window, we will cover the Object List and Viewport Filters windows in the East Frame.

Object List

The Object List lists everything in your scene. This includes all cameras with their image planes and stencils, lights, materials, selection sets (or groups), and polygonal meshes with their layers (Figure 2.16).

This window is similar to the Outliner in Maya. You can use the Object List window drop-down menu to filter what you see in the Object List window. You can view/hide and lock/unlock the components of this list by clicking the eye icon next to the item.

You can open another or multiple Object List windows by clicking Windows → Object List (or Window → Object List on the Mac) from the menu bar. This is a good practice because you will always want to have the Object List visible and accessible while you are working. You can open an Object List window and move it off to the side or to your second monitor if you have one. You can also open multiple windows of the Object List window and filter each one differently.

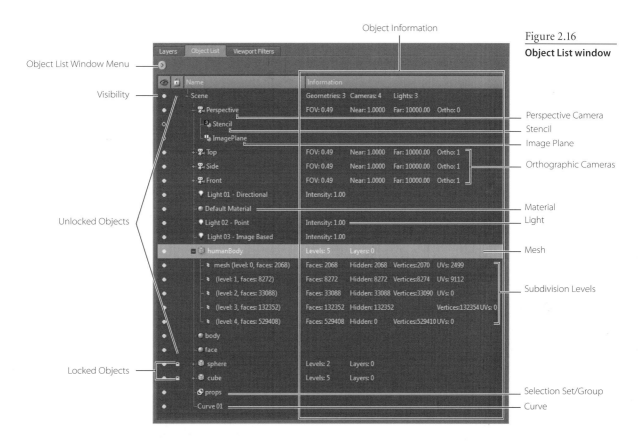

Object Information

Figure 2.16
Object List window

Object List Window Menu

Visibility

Perspective Camera
Stencil
Image Plane

Orthographic Cameras

Material
Light

Mesh

Unlocked Objects

Subdivision Levels

Locked Objects

Selection Set/Group
Curve

Viewport Filters Window

If the final result of your work in Mudbox is not destined to be rendered in another 3D application, renderer, or game engine, the rendering in Mudbox can be enhanced to produce some great effects. Mudbox gives you the capability to apply some post-processing visual effects to your scene in 3D view by using viewport filters (Figure 2.17).

The primary purpose of these filters is to re-create as closely as possible the environment of the application in which your sculpture will be rendered. You can, however, use the results of the render and variations of it created with the various viewport filters to composite it into proof-of-concept images. Another advantage of the Mudbox rendering engine and viewport filters is that they operate in real time, so you could actually work on your sculpture in real time with filters turned on.

The standard viewport filters included in Mudbox are:

- The Tonemapper filter enables you to change the color tone and gamma of your 3D view.

- The Depth of Field filter enables you to specify a range outside of which the image is blurry and out of focus, as you would with a camera lens.

Figure 2.17
Viewport filters

- The Ambient Occlusion filter gives your sculpture an occlusion effect that makes cracks, crannies, and corners appear darker. This effect makes your sculpture look more realistic, especially if you have a lot of high-frequency details such as wrinkles and scratches.

- The Screen Distance filter displays a depth map of the objects in the 3D view. Based on your settings, you see a gradation between black and white depending on the distance of the object from the camera's viewpoint. It's useful for creating a depth map to composite into your final image, or for quickly creating stencils, stamps, or displacement maps from sculpted objects.

- The Non-Photorealistic Effect filter makes the objects in your scene look hand-drawn on textured paper.

- The Normal Map shader shows objects by using color values based on the orientation of their surface normals. This filter is useful for previewing normal maps without having to use the extract texture maps feature.

Figure 2.18

Properties window for the Sculpt tool

To turn these filters on, click the circle icon next to them. To change the properties of a filter, click on the filter itself in the Viewport Filters window, and its properties will appear in the bottom section of the East Frame. Chapter 9 details the properties of these viewport filters, in addition to two others, the Nvidia Ambient Occlusion, and the CG filters, that are not displayed by default, in more depth.

Properties Window

The bottom section of the East Frame is the Properties window (Figure 2.18). It does not have tabs, and its contents change depending on what you choose in other windows. For example, if you choose a sculpting tool, the properties of that tool will appear in the Properties window. You can also open additional Properties windows if you need to work on more than one simultaneously, by clicking Window → Properties and choosing a property. This additional Properties window will appear in a floating window that you can move to another monitor or position.

Working with the South Frame Tray

The South Frame (Figure 2.19) contains your tools, stamps, stencils, presets, and bookmarks. Mudbox comes with some default options for these, but you can customize this list with your own additions, omissions, and order.

> The items on a tray can be reordered by dragging them while pressing the middle button of your mouse or the back button on the stylus.

The South Frame is grouped into two sections. To the left are your tools, and to the right are stamp and stencil libraries, material and lighting presets, and camera bookmarks. Depending on your preference, you can dynamically (as you are working) increase or decrease the room each section takes by moving the separator between the left and right section. You can also add more vertical room to both tray sections by moving the separator up and down (Figure 2.20).

Figure 2.19

The South Frame

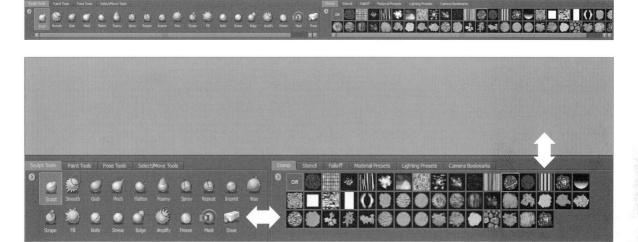

Figure 2.20

Resizing tray space

Sculpt Tools Tray

The Sculpt Tools tray (Figure 2.21) is where you will pick the tools that manipulate the geometry, or shape, of your model. There are 19 standard tools you can choose from, and all of these tools have properties that can be customized for your work session. These customized versions can be added to the Sculpt Tools tray if you need to use them on a future project.

Figure 2.21

The Sculpt Tools tray

Table 2.1 lists the sculpt tools and what they do in general. We will go into more depth about their properties and customization in examples of their use in other chapters.

Table 2.1

Sculpt Tools

ICON	NAME	FUNCTION
	Sculpt	The Sculpt tool (or a variation) is the tool you will use to do most of your sculpting in Mudbox. It is used to build up or take away surface depth on your model.
	Smooth	The Smooth tool gets rid of hard or pixilated edges to produce a smoother gradation in depth on your model. You will use this tool in conjunction with the Sculpt tool for the bulk of your work in Mudbox.
	Grab	The Grab tool enables you to move vertices and geometry on the surface of the model. This tool enables you to make adjustments to the form of the model.
	Pinch	The Pinch Tool pulls vertices together to create a pinched look. You will be tempted to use this to create hard edges and creases, but I strongly recommend against it because it creates problematic geometry. You will see why and learn other ways to get the same effect in chapter 5, "Digital Sculpting, Part I".
	Flatten	The Flatten tool is indispensible for creating planes in your geometry. Artists use planes to block out 3D shapes, and the Flatten tool enables you to make those planes.
	Foamy	The Foamy tool is a softer version of the Sculpt tool.
	Spray	The Spray tool uses a stamp from the Stamp tray and randomly places or sprays relief on the surface of your object. Very useful for adding pores or random scratches on a surface, among many other things.
	Repeat	The Repeat tool is perfect for creating repeating linear patterns such as for stitching, screws, bolts, or rivets. The repeating shape is determined by the stamp.
	Imprint	The Imprint tool is used to either depress or pop out an instance of the stamp on the surface of your model.
	Wax	The Wax tool builds up or removes material from the surface of your model as if you were adding material to it. This is a useful tool for sculpting because it simulates adding material to the surface, like adding clay in traditional sculpture.
	Scrape	The Scrape tool is used to remove or scrape off shapes that protrude. It establishes a plane at the first vertex you click on the surface and flattens everything above that plane.
	Fill	The Fill tool fills holes and cavities on your model. Upon clicking the surface, it establishes a plane at the average of vertices within the area of the circle around your cursor and fills holes up to that plane.
	Knife	The Knife tool is used to cut strokes into the model by using a stamp.
	Smear	The Smear tool moves the vertices under the area within the circle around your cursor in the direction you move the cursor. Like the Pinch tool, it could create problematic geometry and should be avoided if possible. It is useful for moving a group of polygons along the plane of the camera, Turn the wireframe on to see the effects of the Smear tool.
	Bulge	The Bulge tool bulges out geometry along the vertices' normals, which bulges out the geometry beneath the area within the circle around your cursor on all sides versus just upward, creating an inflated look.
	Amplify	The Amplify tool establishes a plane upon clicking a surface and moves vertices that are under it lower, and ones that are above it, higher. It is good for bringing out features that might appear too subtle, such as wrinkles or muted sculptural details.
	Freeze	The Freeze tool locks, or freezes, vertices on the surface of your model so they can't be moved with any of the sculpting tools. The frozen area will be a solid blue. Based on your falloff, the solid blues are not movable, and as the opacity tapers, the vertices will be more movable. The Freeze tool freezes vertices on all levels.
	Mask	The Mask tool lets you hide or show the sculpting done on a layer from the one beneath it. This is nondestructive, so you can dial in and out to determine how much of your sculpting on the level shows through. Think of it as having an opacity slider that works on parts of the model that you paint a mask on. This is a very powerful tool we will cover in depth in chapter 5, "Digital Sculpting, Part I".
	Erase	The Erase tool erases the sculpting you have done on a layer.

As you click these sculpt tools, their properties appear in the Properties tray (Figure 2.22 and Table 2.2). Note that all the sculpt tools have most of these properties, but some of the properties are available for only certain tools.

Table 2.2

Sculpt Tool Properties

PROPERTY	DESCRIPTION
Size	Radius of the tool. It is measured in world space units. A Size of 100 corresponds to a radius of 100 centimeters.
Strength	The strength with which the sculpt tool affects the surface. Depending on the tool, this property is either a percentage of the maximum Strength or a height expressed in world space units.
Mirror	Mirrors stroke from one side of a model to the other along the specified axis: Off: Stroke not reflected. X: Stroke reflected across world space x-axis. Y: Stroke reflected across world space y-axis. Z: Stroke reflected across world space z-axis. Local X: Stroke reflected across the local space x-axis. Local Y: Stroke reflected across the local space y-axis. Local Z: Stroke reflected across the local space z-axis. Tangent: Stroke reflected across the center line of a topologically symmetrical model. You must first identify the model's topological center by selecting two faces that are on opposite sides of the center line and then clicking Edit → Set Topological Center.
Invert Function	Inverts the function of the tool. If the tool function is to raise up the surface, inverting it will push down the surface. You can also press Ctrl to invert the function.
Use Stamp Image	Enables you to sculpt with the selected stamp. The tool will affect the surface of the model based on the grayscale values in the stamp image. The darker the values, the lower the strength of the tool.
Orient to Stroke icon	Orients the stamp so that as you draw, you stroke the top of the stamp points along the direction of your stroke.
Rotate, Horizontal, and Vertical Flip icons	Rotates and flips the stamp.
Randomize	Turns on the randomize sliders for the tool stamp. Hover your mouse on the various levers and options to see help images that show you what the various levers do.
Stamp Spacing	Controls the gap between the impressions your tool makes when you draw a stroke on the surface. The higher the setting, the greater the visible gaps on the stroke. The default setting is 6.25; the range is between 0 and 100. This is a relative value depending on the Size and Falloff of your tool.
Steady Stroke and Steady Stroke Distance	When Steady Stroke is turned on, as you draw a stroke on the surface of your model, you start out drawing a vector with the length specified by the Steady Stroke Distance. When the end of that distance is reached, your selected tool will do its work along that vector. This is ideal for drawing smoother, less jittery strokes.
Buildup	Represents the rate at which the tool response on the surface grows to reach the specified Strength value.
Flood	Floods the tool's function uniformly across the entire surface of your model.
Falloff	Specifies the depth of the stroke from the tool's center point to its outer edge. It is represented as a curve that can be edited.
Remember Size	Preserves the size of the tool between uses. If you turn it off, the tool will inherit the size of the tool used before it.

Figure 2.22

Sculpt tool properties

PROPERTY	DESCRIPTION
Orient to Surface	Orients the tool ring along the normal of the surface. This does not change what the tool does, just how the cursor is displayed.
Affect All Layers	This property is available for only the Smooth tool. When on, it causes the plane under the stroke of the tool to be recalculated at each stamp placement of the stroke. When turned off, the underlying tool plane is determined by the initial stamp and remains fixed for the duration of the stroke.
Update Plane	This property is available for only the Flatten, Wax, Scrape, Fill, and Contrast tools. When turned on, it causes the plane that the tool is affecting to be recalculated at each placement of a stamp during the current stroke. When off, the plane is determined by the initial stamp and remains fixed for the duration of the stroke.
Whole Stroke	This property is available for only the Flatten, Wax, Scrape, Fill, and Contrast tools, and works only when Update Plane is turned on. When on, it causes the plane that the tool is affecting to be recalculated from all the vertices affected during the current stroke.
Smooth Values	This property is available for only the Freeze, Mask, and Erase sculpt tools and works only if the Smooth and Paint Values setting is turned off. When on, it blurs areas on the model where the Freeze or Mask tool had been applied. You can press the Shift key to cause this effect while using the Mask or Freeze tools.
Smooth and Paint Values	This property is available for only the Freeze, Mask, and Erase sculpt tools. When on, it blurs the edges of the tool being applied.
Pen Pressure	This section controls the settings for customizing the tablet.
	Min Size: Controls the tool size when the lightest pressure is applied with the pen. It is expressed as a percentage of the tool's Size property. For example, if you set the Min Size to 100, there will be no size variance regardless of the applied pressure.
	Min Strength: Controls the Strength when the lightest pressure is applied with the pen. It is expressed as a percentage of the tool's Strength. For example, if you set the Min Strength to 100, there is no strength variance regardless of the applied pressure.
	Direction: Specifies the direction vertices are moved when the tool is applied:
	Center Normal: Moves vertices in the direction of the normal of the face directly under the center of the tool.
	Averaged Normal: Moves vertices in the direction of the average of the normals of all affected faces. This is the default setting.
	Vertex Normal: Moves each vertex in the direction of its own normal.
	Forward: Moves vertices in the direction of the stroke.
	Right: Moves vertices perpendicular to the direction of the stroke.
	X: Moves vertices along the world space x-axis.
	Y: Moves vertices along the world space y-axis.
	Z: Moves vertices along the world space z-axis.
	Camera: Moves vertices toward the camera.

Paint Tools Tray

The Paint Tools tray (Figure 2.23) is where you pick the tools that enable you to paint on the surface of your model. There are 16 standard tools you can choose from, and all of these tools have properties that can be customized for your work session. These customized versions can be added to the Paint Tools tray if you need to use them on a future project.

Figure 2.23

Paint Tools tray

Table 2.3 lists the paint tools and what they do in general. Chapter 8, "3D Painting," provides more depth about their properties and customization in examples of their use.

Table 2.3

Paint Tools

ICON	NAME	FUNCTION
	Paint Brush	Paints on the surface of the model and layer.
	Projection	Applies the color from images and textures by using a stencil image you select from the Stencil tray.
	Eyedropper	Picks up a color from your model, under the cursor, and assigns it as the current paint color.
	Airbrush	Applies paint on the surface like a real-world airbrush but with less opacity and feathered edges than the Paint Brush.
	Pencil	Draws a thin stroke with sharp edges.
	Paint Erase	Erases paint from the active paint layer.
	Clone	Samples paint applied on one area of a model and applies it onto another area of the same model. Ctrl+click to set a source point from which you will sample, and then paint in another location to clone the paint from the source point.
	Dry Brush	Applies paint based on the depth of the surface of your model. It will allow you to paint only raised areas or only recessed areas by inverting the brush's function.
	Blur	Blurs the painted area to which the brush ring is applied.
	Dodge	Enables you to lighten the painted area to which the brush ring is applied.
	Burn	Enables you to darken the painted area to which the brush ring is applied.
	Contrast	Increases or decreases the difference between light and dark pixels on the active paint layer to which it is applied.
	Sponge	Makes subtle adjustments to the color saturation of pixels on a texture on the active paint layer to which it is applied.
	Hue	Enables you to replace the hue of pixels on a texture on the active paint layer to which it is applied with a user-specified color hue.
	Hue Shift	Shifts the hue by the amount specified in degrees around the color wheel relative from its current value in a counterclockwise direction.
	Invert	Inverts the color hue under the region of the brush ring in the current layer.

As you click on these paint tools, their properties appear in the Properties tray (Figure 2.24 and Table 2.4).

	PROPERTY	DESCRIPTION
Table 2.4 **Paint Tools Properties**	Color	Indicates the color of the Paint Brush. Clicking the box displays a dialog box enabling you to select a color.
	Affect	A property of the Dodge and Burn tools that lets you bias the lightening of the Dodge tool, or the darkening of the Burn tool's influence within the tonal range of the areas you apply to the tool. You can set the affected tonal range to be All or just Highlights, Midtones, or Shadows.
	Blur Strength	A property specific to the Blur tool. Determines the radius of the area in pixels that is sampled for determining the amount of blur. Larger values produce greater blur.
	Exposure	A property specific to the Dodge and Burn tools that determines the amount of lightening or darkening for each stroke of the brush depending on the Affect property setting (Midtones, Highlights, Shadows, or All).
	Contrast	A property specific to the Contrast brush. Ranges from –10 to 10; positive numbers increase contrast, and negative values reduce it.
	Amount	A property specific to the Sponge brush. Ranges from –1 to 1; positive values decrease color saturation, and negative values increase it.
	Hue Shift	A property specific to the Hue Shift brush. The value of the texture areas painted with this tool are shifted by the Hue Shift amount entered as an angle in degrees around the color ring of the Color Chooser relative to their current value. The Hue Shift value can range from –1 to –180 for counterclockwise, and 1 to 180 for a clockwise shift on the Color Chooser ring.
	Size	Radius of the tool. It is measured in world space units. A Size of 100 corresponds to a radius of 100 centimeters.
	Strength	Determines the opacity of the paint tool. Depending on the tool, this property is either a percentage of the maximum Strength or a height expressed in world space units.
	Mirror	Mirrors the stroke from one side of a model to the other along the specified axis: Off: Stroke not reflected. X: Stroke reflected across world space x-axis. Y: Stroke reflected across world space y-axis. Z: Stroke reflected across world space z-axis. Local X: Stroke reflected across the local space x-axis. Local Y: Stroke reflected across the local space y-axis. Local Z: Stroke reflected across the local space z-axis. Tangent: Stroke reflected across the center line of a topologically symmetrical model. You must first identify the model's topological center by selecting two faces that are on opposite sides of the center line and then clicking Edit → Set Topological Center.
	Use Stamp Image	Enables you to paint with the selected stamp.
	Orient to Stroke icon	Orients the stamp so that as you draw your stroke, the top of the stamp points along the direction of your stroke.
	Rotate, Horizontal and Vertical Flip icons	Rotates and flips the stamp.
	Randomize	Turns on the randomize sliders for the tool stamp. Hover your mouse on the various levers and options to see help images that show you what the various levers do.
	Stamp Spacing	Controls the gap between the impressions your tool makes when you draw a stroke on the surface. The higher the setting, the greater the visible gaps on the stroke. The default setting is 6.25; the range is between 0 and 100. This is a relative value depending on your Size and the Falloff of your tool.

PROPERTY	DESCRIPTION
Steady Stroke and Steady Stroke Distance	When Steady Stroke is turned on, as you draw a stroke on the surface of your model, you start out drawing a vector with the length specified by the Steady Stroke Distance. When the end of that distance is reached, your selected tool will do its work along that vector. This is ideal for drawing smoother, less jittery strokes.
Buildup	Represents the rate at which the brush response on the surface grows to reach the specified Strength value.
Falloff	Specifies the depth of the stroke from the tool's center point to its outer edge. It is represented as a curve that can be edited.
Remember Size	Preserves the size of the tool between uses. If you turn it off, the tool will inherit the size of the tool used before it.
Orient to Surface	Orients the tool ring along the normal of the surface. This does not change what the brush does, just how the cursor is displayed.
Pen Pressure	This section controls the settings for customizing the tablet:

Min Size: Controls the tool size when the lightest pressure is applied with the pen. It is expressed as a percentage of the tool's Size property. For example, if you set the Min Size to 100, there will be no size variance regardless of the applied pressure.

Min Strength: Controls the strength when the lightest pressure is applied with the pen. It is expressed as a percentage of the tool's Strength. For example, if you set the Min Strength to 100, there is no strength variance regardless of the applied pressure.

Direction: Specifies the direction vertices are moved when the tool is applied:

Center Normal: Moves vertices in the direction of the normal of the face directly under the center of the tool.

Averaged Normal: Moves vertices in the direction of the average of the normals of all affected faces. This is the default setting.

Vertex Normal: Moves each vertex in the direction of its own normal.

Forward: Moves vertices in the direction of the stroke.

Right: Moves vertices perpendicular to the direction of the stroke.

X: Moves vertices along the world space x-axis.

Y: Moves vertices along the world space y-axis.

Z: Moves vertices along the world space z-axis.

Camera: Moves vertices toward the camera.

Table 2.4

(continued)

Figure 2.24

Paint tools properties

Pose Tools Tray

The Pose Tools tray (Figure 2.25) is where you will select one of four tools to pose your model

Table 2.5 lists the pose tools and what they do in general. Chapter 6 goes into more depth about their properties and customization in examples of their use

The pose tools have very limited properties. The Create Joint tool has only a falloff property. The Pose tool has an invert operation that also can be invoked by pressing down the Ctrl key. The Weights tool has properties similar to that of the Paint Brush tool, and the Move Pivot tool has no properties.

Figure 2.25

Pose Tools tray

	ICON	NAME	FUNCTION
		Create Joint	Enables you to create a joint, specify its area of influence falloff by a boundary axis, and the area affected by the joint.
		Pose	Enables you to rotate, translate, or scale the weighted region associated with a joint.
		Weights	Enables you to add to or erase from the weighted region that is associated with a joint by painting on or removing color from areas you want affected, the same way you would use a paint tool.
		Move Pivot	Enables you to move the position of the pivot point and shift the origin of the rotation, translation, or scaling posing operation.

Table 2.5

Pose Tools

Select/Move Tools Tray

The Select/Move Tools (Figure 2.26 and Table 2.6) tray has tools that enable you to select, reposition, rotate, or scale the models in your scene, or select faces on your model.

Figure 2.26

Select/Move Tools tray

You select faces on your model to specify an axis of symmetry. You can also select faces or objects to hide them in the 3D view when working on complex models.

You need to have an object selected to export or isolate it to a separate file. Selected faces on objects can be saved and restored by grouping them into selection sets. You create a selection set by selecting faces and objects you wish to group and clicking Create → Selection Set.

ICON	NAME	FUNCTION
	Faces	Selects faces along your stroke. Clicking off the model deselects the current selection. Press Shift+A to select all the faces.
	Objects	Selects the object you click. Clicking off the model deselects the current selection. A better way to select an object is to select it in the Object List by its name.
	Translate	Brings up the transform manipulator to move the object in the 3D view. Click the arrows to move the object in the direction of the axis.
	Rotate	Brings up the rotate manipulator to rotate the object in the 3D view. Drag the circular rings to rotate the object.
	Scale	Brings up the scale manipulator to scale the object in the 3D view. Drag on the center box to scale uniformly across all axes, or on the boxes at the edges of the axes to scale along one specific axis.

Table 2.6

Select/Move Tools

The properties for the Faces and Objects tools are the same as those for the Sculpt and Paint Brush tools.

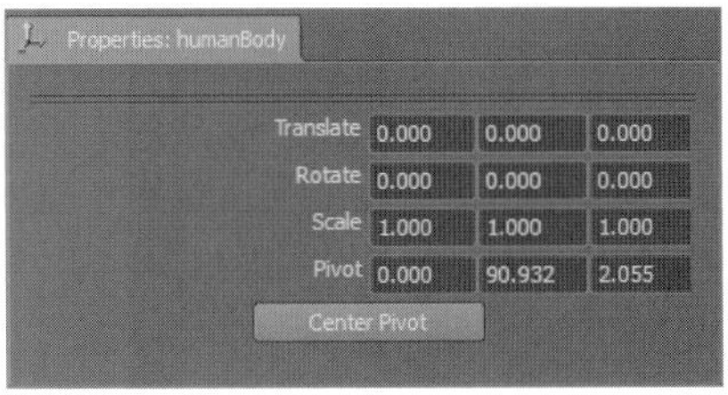

Figure 2.27

The Translate, Rotate, and Scale Properties window

The Properties for Translate, Rotate, and Scale consist of four rows of X, Y, and Z coordinates and a Center Pivot button (Figure 2.27).

This Properties window serves both as a place to input coordinates as well as a place to see what the coordinates of an object's pivot point are. Each object has a *pivot*, which is a point in space that you can think of as its handle. You move the object by its pivot. Rotate the object around its pivot or scale it up or down around its pivot. The pivot location is assigned to the object before it is brought into Mudbox, but you can change it in Mudbox if you so choose by typing the coordinates in the Pivot row of the Properties window. I highly recommend that you do all your translation, rotation, and scaling outside of Mudbox, because 3D applications such as Maya have much better and more-comprehensive translation, rotation, scaling, and pivot manipulation tools.

Stamp Tray

The Stamp tray (Figure 2.28) is where you will pick a stamp to use for sculpting and painting from thumbnails of your stamp library. Your selected stamp shows up with a highlight around it in the tray, and also in the Properties tray of your tool. If you do not want to use a stamp, click the Off thumbnail.

Figure 2.28

Stamp tray

If you are sculpting with a stamp, you are using it for its value, meaning the lighter areas are used to impress or indent the stamp on a surface, and the darker areas do not make as much of an indentation. Mudbox comes with a variety of stamps, and you can add your own. If you are painting with a stamp, you are using it as a brush to apply its color value to the surface of your model.

The Properties settings of your tool determine the frequency, spacing, and orientation of how the stamps are generated.

The Stamp tray menu enables you to add, delete, or rename a stamp. The best place to add stamps is in the Image Browser. Your stamp library is located in your user directory under the Documents\Mudbox\2011\data\stamps folder. I recommend you open a few stamps in Photoshop to see what they look like so you know what characteristics to apply when creating your own.

Stencil Tray

The Stencil tray (Figure 2.29) is where you will pick your stencil from thumbnails in your stencil library to apply on top of your 3D view in order to paint or sculpt the pattern of the stencil onto your image.

Figure 2.29

Stencil tray

Whereas a stamp is applied to the tip of your tool, the stencil is applied to the viewing plane of your 3D view, and you will sculpt or paint through it. If you are sculpting through a stencil, you are using it for its value, meaning the lighter areas are used to impress or indent the stencil on a surface, and the darker areas do not make as much of an indentation. Mudbox comes with a variety of stencils, and you can add your own. If you are painting with a stencil, you are painting its color value onto the surface of your model.

The Stencil tray menu enables you to add, delete, or rename a stencil. The best place to add stencils is in the Image Browser. Your stencil library is located in your user directory under the `Documents\Mudbox\2011\data\stencils` folder. I recommend opening up a few stencils in Photoshop and seeing what they look like so you know what characteristics to apply when creating your own.

Falloff Tray

The Falloff tray (Figure 2.30) lists some default Falloff presets and enables you to add your own.

Figure 2.30

Falloff tray

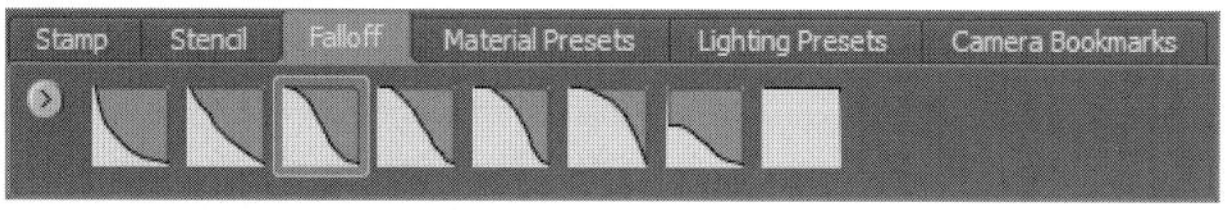

| Stamp | Stencil | Falloff | Material Presets | Lighting Presets | Camera Bookmarks |

You edit falloff curves in the Falloff section of your tool's Properties tray (Figure 2.31). After you determine that a falloff is the one you wish to use in the future, click the Store To button under the falloff curve to save it to your Falloff tray.

Figure 2.31

Editing a falloff in the Properties tray

When looking at a falloff, consider that the left is the center of your brush, and the right is the edge, and the higher the curve, the deeper the imprint.

In the Properties tray of your tool, you can modify the falloff curve by moving the points on the curve to adjust it:

- You can add points to the falloff curve by right-clicking (back button on the stylus) and selecting Add Point.
- Snap enables you to snap the curve points to the axes.
- To delete a point, right-click on it and select Delete Point from the menu.

Material Presets Tray

The Material Presets tray (Figure 2.32) is where you choose a premade material for your model. Again Lights, Materials, and Rendering settings in Mudbox are mostly to re-create as close as possible the environment your model will end up in. You will most likely not do too many adjustments to these settings.

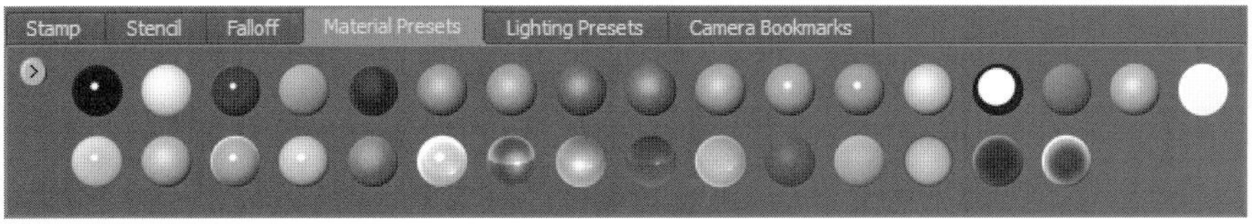

Figure 2.32
Material Presets tray

You assign a material to the model either by choosing from the thumbnails in the Material Presets tray or by right-clicking on it (back button on the stylus) and selecting Assign New Material from the menu. This opens the Material Properties tray (Figure 2.33), in which you can customize the material and add it to the Material Presets tray.

To edit an assigned material, right-click (back button on the stylus) on your model and select Edit Material.

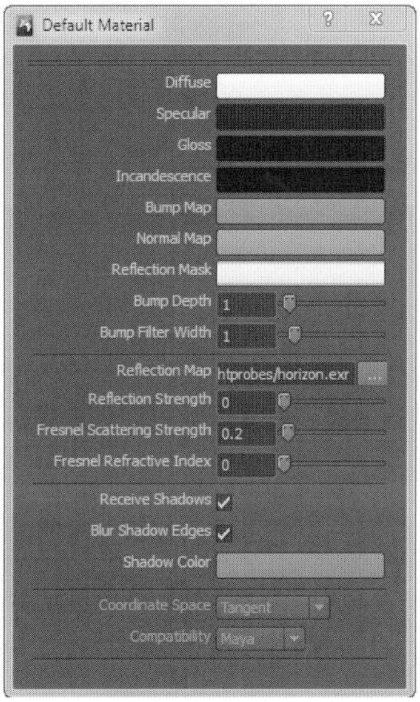

Mudbox uses four types of materials that produce different looks for your model:

Mudbox Material: Default and recommended base material

Simple Blinn Material: Simplified Blinn for unsupported graphics cards

Lit Sphere Material: A material defined by the light sphere around it

CgFX Material: Portable shader standard developed by Nvidia

We will go into working with materials in Chapter 4, "Painting and Texturing an Imported Model," and Chapter 8.

Each of these materials have properties specific to them, as seen in Tables 2.7, 2.8, and 2.9.

Figure 2.33
Material Properties tray

PROPERTY	DESCRIPTION	
Diffuse	Specifies the base color of the material. Click the color box to change the Diffuse color and edit it by using the Select Color window.	Table 2.7
Specular	Specifies the color of the highlight on the material. Click the color box to change the Specular color and edit it by using the Select Color window.	**Mudbox Material Properties**
Gloss	Specifies the size of the specular reflection. The lower or darker the value, the smaller the size of the specular highlight. Click the color box to change the Gloss color and edit it by using the Select Color window.	
Incandescence	Specifies the self-illuminating brightness of the color on a material independent of the scene lighting. This property is used to simulate the emission of color from an object independently of the lighting setup in the scene.	
Bump Map	Specifies the file path of the bump map image.	
Normal Map	Specifies the file path for the image to be used for a normal map.	
Reflection Mask	Specifies the file path for the image to be used for the reflection mask.	

	PROPERTY	DESCRIPTION
Table 2.7 *(continued)*	Bump Depth	Controls how high or low the appearance of bumps display on the surface when a bump map is applied. Increase the value to make the surface bumpier. Decrease the value to make the surface smoother.
	Bump Filter Width	Specifies the level of filtering performed on a texture used as a bump map. Values greater than 1.0 produce more filtering, making the bumps smoother. Values less than 1.0 produce less filtering, making the bumps appear sharper.
	Reflection Map	Specifies the file path for the image used as a reflection map. An environment is simulated around the model that appears in the material's reflection component depending on the value of the Reflection Strength property.
		Note that whenever an image-based light is specified in the scene, the reflection map image is replaced with the image specified by the image-based light source.
	Reflection Strength	Controls the visibility of the reflection map. A value of 1.0 causes the image to be fully visible and overrides any of the diffuse color on the model. A value of 0 causes the reflection map to be invisible.
	Fresnel Scattering Strength	Specifies the intensity of the Fresnel glow effect. The Fresnel effect is the variance of reflectivity of a surface based on the viewing angle of observation.
	Fresnel Refractive Index	Specifies the surface area of the model that is affected by the Fresnel glow effect. A low number specifies that only the edges get illuminated. A higher number indicates that more of the model is illuminated by the glow effect.
	Receive Shadows	Turns on shadows for the material. At least one scene light must also have its Cast Shadows property turned on for shadows to appear on a model.
	Blur Shadow Edges	Specifies the softness of shadow edges. The softness of shadow edges is also influenced by the Depth Map Resolution property for the shadow casting light. Keep these two properties in mind if shadow edge artifacts appear.
	Shadow Color	Controls the shadow color. Colored shadows help to simulate reflected light when self-shadowing of colored surfaces occurs or in simulating the shadow produced by transparent, colored surfaces (for example, colored glass). The default setting is black.
	Coordinate Space	Specifies the normal map's coordinate space based on how it was originally extracted. This setting must match the setting used when the map was originally extracted for the normal map to display properly on the model. (If you are unsure, try each option in turn and view the results in the 3D view.) Options include the following: Tangent : The coordinate space on a face defined by the normal, tangent, and the binormal. Object : Local coordinate space for the model. World: Coordinate space for the 3D scene.
	Compatibility	When the Normal Map option is turned on, set this property to match how the Compatibility setting was set during the original map extraction so the normal map previews correctly. Options are Maya or 3ds Max.

	PROPERTY	DESCRIPTION
Table 2.8 **Simple Blinn Properties**	Diffuse	Specifies the base color of the material. Click the color box to change the Diffuse color and edit it by using the Select Color window.
	Specular	Specifies the color of the highlight on the material. Click the color box to change the Specular color and edit it by using the Select Color window.
	Ambient	Specifies the minimum darkness of the material.
	Shininess	Indicates the size of the specular reflection. The lower values result in wider highlights.

PROPERTY	DESCRIPTION
Lit Sphere Image	Specifies the image to be used for the lighting environment. This image is used to calculate the light source and works with the scene lights in your environment.
Bump Value	Specifies the file path of the bump map image.
Bump Depth	Specifies how high or low bumps display on the surface. Higher values make the surface look bumpier.
Bump Filter Width	Specifies filtering on the texture used as a bump map. Values greater than 1.0 make bumps smoother, and values less than 1.0 make bumps appear sharper.
Reflection Map	Specifies the image to be used as a reflection map. This creates a simulated environment around the model. If an image-based light (IBL) is applied to the scene, the reflection map image is replaced with the IBL image.
Reflection Strength	Controls the visibility of the reflection map. A value of 1 causes the image to be 100 percent visible, and a value of 0 makes the material show no reflections.
Reflection Mask	Specifies the file path for the reflection mask image.
Fresnel Scattering Strength	Specifies the intensity of the Fresnel glow effect on the model.
Fresnel Refractive Index	Specifies the surface area of the model that is affected by the Fresnel glow effect. A low number specifies that only the edges get illuminated. A higher number indicates that more of the model is illuminated by the Fresnel glow effect.

Table 2.9

Lit Sphere Material

CgFX-Based Materials CgFX shaders plug into applications that use the Cg programming language for programming graphics hardware. Cg was developed by Nvidia with close collaboration of Microsoft Corporation to help generate real-time cinematic-quality experiences on multiple platforms such as OpenGL, DirectX, Windows, Linux, Macintosh OS X, and console platforms such as the Xbox.

There is a README.cgfx-support.txt file in the \effects folder of your Mudbox installation folder for more information on the CgFX annotations and semantics supported by Mudbox. Further information on Cg is available at the following site:

http://http.developer.nvidia.com/CgTutorial/cg_tutorial_chapter01.html

Lighting Presets Tray

The Lighting Presets tray (Figure 2.34) has thumbnails of lighting setups and enables you to add your own. When you set up lights and create the lighting environment you want to see your model in, you can save it as a preset and apply it to other models by clicking its icon in the Lighting Presets tray.

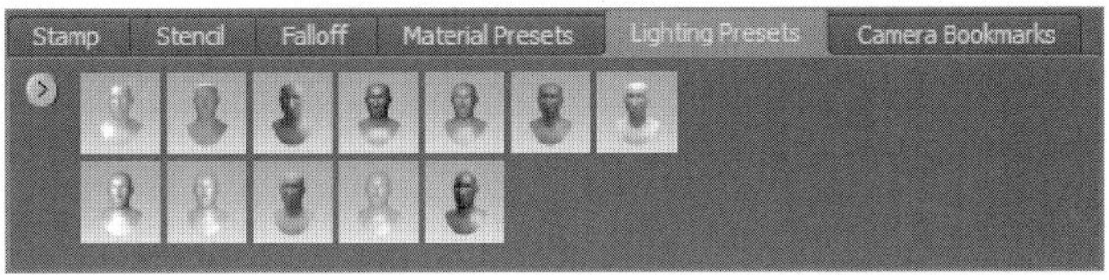

Figure 2.34

Lighting Presets tray

Mudbox supports three types of lights:

Point lights Point lights emit light evenly in all directions from a point in your 3D space. A point light is used to simulate an incandescent light source such as candles or lightbulbs.

Directional lights Directional lights simulate light emanating from a distant light source so that its light rays are parallel to each other when they reach the object they affect. Directional lights are used to simulate sunshine or distant light sources.

Image-based lights (IBL) Image-based lights simulate lighting in the scene based on an image wrapped around the environment. Image-based lighting uses HDR images for generating very realistic lighting and reflection effects.

You can add many point and directional lights to your scene, but only one IBL. When you add an IBL to your image, it replaces the reflection map assigned to the materials in the scene.

All three lights have properties indicated by Tables 2.10, 2.11, and 2.12 for point, directional, and image based lights, respectively.

Table 2.10 Point Light Properties	PROPERTY	DESCRIPTION
	Diffuse	Specifies the color of the light.
	Intensity	Specifies the brightness of the light.
	Light Decay	Specifies how the light's intensity decreases with distance.
	Scale	Enables you to change the scale of the displayed light source sphere. This does not affect the amount of light produced, but just makes it easier to see where the light source is.
	Show Manipulator	Displays the light's transform manipulator, letting you reposition the location of the point light in X, Y, and Z space.
	Show Light	Displays a sphere to show the light's location.

Table 2.11 Directional Light Properties	PROPERTY	DESCRIPTION
	Diffuse	Specifies the color of the light.
	Intensity	Specifies the brightness of the light.
	Scale	Enables you to change the scale of the displayed light source direction arrows. This does not affect the amount of light produced, but just makes it easier to see where the light source is.
	Locked to Camera	Locks the position of the light source to the camera. When the camera is tumbled, the light also gets rotated with the camera.
	Show Manipulator	Displays the light's rotate manipulator, letting you rotate the orientation of the light source.
	Show Light	Displays four arrows to show the light's direction.
	Cast Shadows	Indicates whether this specific directional light casts shadows.
	Depth Map Bias	Indicates the offset of the depth map toward or away from the light.
	Depth Map Resolution	Indicates the light's shadow depth map resolution. The higher the resolution, the smoother the shadow.

Table 2.12 Image-Based Lighting Properties	PROPERTY	DESCRIPTION
	Intensity	Specifies the brightness of the light.
	Locked to Camera	Locks the position of the light source to the camera. When the camera is tumbled, the light also gets rotated with the camera.

PROPERTY	DESCRIPTION
Show Manipulator	Displays the light's rotate manipulator, letting you rotate the orientation of the light source.
Image Based Light File	Specifies the file path for the IBL image. Upon adding an IBL, this file replaces the reflection map file assigned to the materials in the scene.

Table 2.12

(continued)

Camera Bookmarks Tray

The Camera Bookmarks tray (Figure 2.35) is a container for storing camera settings. When you set up a camera or change the settings of an existing camera, you can save it as a bookmark and apply it to other scenes by clicking its icon in the Camera Bookmarks tray.

Figure 2.35

Camera Bookmarks tray

You can look at, customize, or modify cameras by clicking the camera in the Object List. Table 2.13 lists the camera properties.

PROPERTY	DESCRIPTION
Transform	Lock Pan, Rotate, Zoom: Locks or unlocks your ability to pan, rotate, or zoom the camera. Reset: Resets the camera's Roll, Rotate, Track, and Dolly transforms. Select the check boxes you want to reset and click the Reset button.
2D Transform	Transforms the scene based on the plane of the camera. Select the check boxes and click Reset to reset 2D transforms.
Orthographic	Turns off the perspective.
FOV	Specifies the camera's field of view.
Near Plane	Specifies the distance of the near clipping plane from the camera. Clipping planes define the range the camera sees.
Far Plane	Specifies the distance of the far clipping plane from the camera. Clipping planes define the range the camera sees.

Table 2.13

Camera Properties

You can specify a stencil and an image plane for each camera. The stencil enables you to sculpt or paint through the image of the stencil. The image plane is an image you can load behind your model for reference.

You can associate a single image to a camera as an image plane. Table 2.14 lists the properties of an image plane. Table 2.15 lists the stencil properties.

PROPERTY	DESCRIPTION
File	Indicates the file path for the image plane.
Import	Imports an image plane.
Export	Exports an image plane.
Visibility	Specifies the transparency of the image plane.

Table 2.14

Image Plane Properties

PROPERTY	DESCRIPTION
Depth	Specifies how far the image plane is from the camera in relation to the model in the 3D view.
Transformation	Moves the image plane in 3D space by specifying coordinates, and rotates and scales in 2D by specifying rotation angle and scale percentage.

Table 2.14
(continued)

PROPERTY	DESCRIPTION
On	Toggles the stencil on and off.
File	Indicates the file path for the image plane.
Import	Imports an image plane.
Export	Exports an image plane.
Transformation	Moves the stencil in 3D space by specifying coordinates, and rotates and scales in 2D by specifying the rotation angle and scale percentage.
Invert Values	Inverts the values of the stencil.
Hide When Sculpt	Hides the stencil when you are sculpting but not when you are painting.
Flip Vertical, Flip Horizontal	Flips the stencil.
Use Tiles	Use tiles, and repeats the stencil in a tile pattern in the 3D view.
Show Tiles	Shows the tiles if the preceding option is selected.
Visibility	Specifies the transparency of the stencil.
Multiplier	Specifies the strength of the stencil.
Offset	Specifies the stencil deformation relative to the surface of the model. The higher the number, the more vertices are raised and pulled out. The lower the number, the more they are pushed in. Using a middle value of 50, brushing over black pixels of the stencil image pushes vertices down, and brushing over white pixels pull vertices out.

Table 2.15
Stencil Properties

Performing Map Extraction

Map extraction is not a permanent fixture in the Mudbox interface, but a dialog box that comes up when you click Maps → Extract Texture Maps → New Operation. I included it in this chapter because map extraction is a critical operation in Mudbox to export your sculpting detail work to other applications, and the Extract Texture Maps dialog box, or variation of four dialog boxes, has many components that should be available for reference in a UI tour.

In Chapter 1, we generated a displacement and normal map for the egg we created in Mudbox and transferred the surface detail to lower versions of the egg in Maya for rendering or real-time viewing. In this section, we will go through the settings in the map extraction dialog boxes in detail.

When you click Maps → Extract Texture Maps → New Operation, one dialog box comes up, but the contents of that dialog box expand out and change slightly when you click any one of the four options in the Maps to Generate section: Ambient Occlusion Map, Vector Displacement Map, Displacement Map, and Normal Map (Figure 2.36). Note that you can change the options for the listed map types only when that option is highlighted in the dialog box. This can be confusing because the options also have check boxes next to them. If you select the check boxes, you are opting to generate that specific map when you click the Extract button. If all four are selected as they are in Figure 2.36, all four maps will be generated when you click the Extract button.

Figure 2.36

The four options of Maps to Generate

To change the dialog box to the particular map, you need to click that map option to highlight it. Notice the similarities and variations in the four renditions of the map extraction dialog box as you click Ambient Occlusion Map, Vector Displacement Map, Displacement Map, and Normal Map (Figure 2.37).

After you go through this operation, the settings will be saved for reuse in the future. The settings subsequently appear in the Maps → Extract Texture Maps menu , after allowing you to have multiple map extraction settings for different parts of a model.

You can individually or as an aggregate generate four types of texture maps: ambient occlusion (AO) maps, vector displacement maps (VDMs), displacement maps, and normal maps. There is a graphic and text description of each map at the top of the dialog box that describes what the maps are, what the extracted maps look like, and what they do.

Figure 2.37

Variations of the Extract Texture Maps dialog box

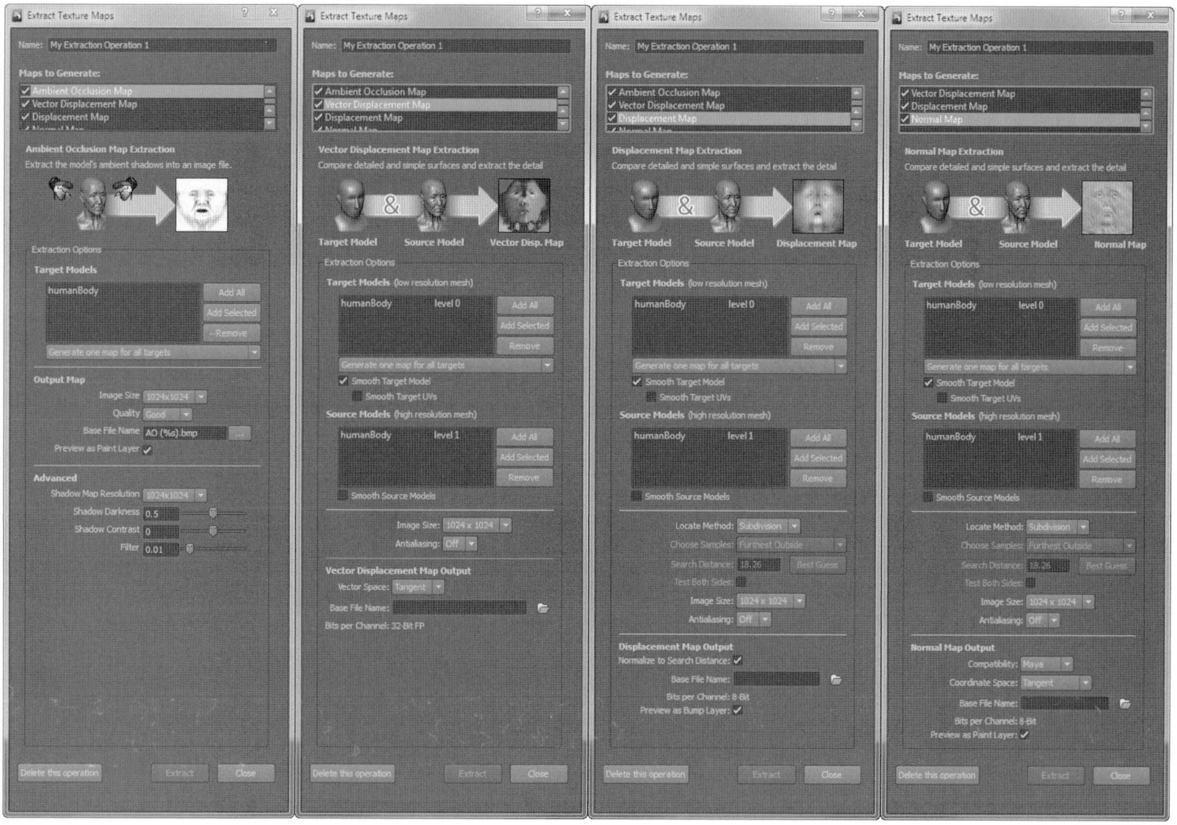

Target Models

All four variations of the dialog box contain the target models, which indicate the name of the model to receive the extracted ambient occlusion, normal, or displacement map. This is the low-resolution version of the model that will be exported, and of course, it should have UV coordinates so that the map generated will correspond to it. You will see more on UV coordinates in subsequent chapters.

The target model is generally either the lowest or one or two levels above the lowest subdivision level of a model. For normal and displacement maps, you can change this subdivision level after the fact, by using the subdivision level drop-down list to the right of the target model name. The normal or displacement map produced represents the difference between the target model or models and the source model or models.

For ambient occlusion maps, the currently active subdivision is used for the map extraction. If you want to extract the map for a different subdivision level, you need to be at that subdivision level before you extract the AO map. Also, by default, ambient occlusion map extraction generates a map for all the visible objects in the scene. If you don't want parts of your model to be in the AO map, turn off their visibility in the Object List.

Add All, Add Selected, and Remove Buttons

Add All and Add Selected enable you to add all the models or just the model selected in the Object List or 3D view. The Remove option removes the selected model in the Object List or 3D view from the target model name list.

Generate One Map for All Targets and Generate a Map for Each Target

If all the objects in the Target Models list share one UV tile, then when extracting maps for multiple targets, use the Generate One Map for All Targets option to generate one map for all of them.

If the target models use different materials or UV texture coordinates occupy the same UV tile location, use the Generate a Map for Each Target option.

Smooth Target Model and Smooth Target UVs

When the Smooth Target Model option is selected, the map extraction operation calculations use a smoothed version of the target model. However, if you are extracting texture maps for games in which a faceted model is generally used, you can turn this option off.

When the Smooth Target Model option is selected, the Smooth Target UVs option smooths the interior UVs of the target model as well during the texture extraction. This feature is also useful for rendering software such as Pixar RenderMan, as this capability carries over to smooth the UV texture coordinates on a mesh during rendering to get better results.

Source Models

The source model contains the sculpted details of the higher or highest subdivision level of your model. You can change which subdivision level you want to extract the map for by choosing the level in the subdivision level drop-down list located to the right of the source object name.

Add All, Add Selected, and Remove Buttons

As in the target models extraction options, Add All and Add Selected enable you to add all the models or just the model selected in the Object List or 3D view. The Remove option removes the selected model in the Object List or 3D view from the target model name list.

Smooth Source Models

When Smooth Source Models is selected, a subdivided and smoothed version of the source model is used for map extraction calculations. This prevents jagged and hard edges from being generated when you apply the extracted maps to models in other 3D applications.

Choose Samples, Search Distance, and Best Guess

If you envision both a low-resolution version of your model and a high-resolution version in the same place, you will have faces from the high-resolution model intersecting the surface of the low-resolution model in many places. The Choose Samples option enables you to specify which value to use for the extracted map if an extraction sample intersects the high-resolution version of your model more than once:

Furthest Outside samples farthest out from the source model, to the range specified by the Search Distance.

Furthest Inside samples from closest to the interior of the source model to either the target model, or the range specified by the Search Distance.

Closest to Target Model samples closest to the target model, ignoring the source model.

A tooltip image comes up when you hover your mouse over the Choose Samples property. The tooltip provides an excellent graphical depiction of the three options.

The Search Distance setting indicates the distance that samples can span to find the source model. This range samples on both sides of the target based on the Choose Samples option. The Best Guess button sets the Search Distance, taking into consideration the distances of the bounding boxes for the source and target model. If the two surfaces are not too far apart, this option generates a useful estimate.

Image Size

The Image Size indicates the height and width, in pixels, of the output maps. You can choose from the preset values of 256×256, 512×512, 1024×1024 (1K), 2048×2048 (2K), and 4096×4096 (4K).

Options Specific to Ambient Occlusion Maps

When extracting an ambient occlusion map, the Extract Texture Maps dialog box slightly changes to include the following properties.

Quality

Quality sets the granularity of the final ambient occlusion map. You can choose from the preset values of Fastest, Fast, Normal, Good, and Best. The higher the quality setting, the more number of shadow maps are produced and combined to generate a higher-quality map. However, this is at the cost of more time required to generate the ambient occlusion map.

Base File Name

The Base File Name field is where you indicate the name of the extracted map. AO(%s). bmp is used as a default if you do not specify a name, where %s is substituted by the name of the model. You can click the file button to the right of the Base File Name to bring up the Save As dialog box to set a directory and choose the file format (`.png`, `.bmp`, `.gif`, `.jpg`, `.tif`, or `.tga`).

 If your model contains UVs outside the 0 to 1 range in two or more UV tile spaces, this operation automatically creates separate ambient occlusion maps corresponding to each UV tile by adding a suffix of the coordinates of the tile—for example, `AOhead_u1_v1.tga` and `AOhead_u1_v2` for a model that has UVs in two adjacent tiles.

Preview as Paint Layer

If selected, Preview as Paint Layer adds the generated ambient occlusion map as a new Diffuse channel paint layer. This lets you preview the generated map on the model. You can also use it to view ambient occlusion on your model without using the Ambient Occlusion viewport filters.

Shadow Map Resolution

Shadow Map Resolution indicates the size of the shadow maps generated for the occlusion map calculations. You can choose from the preset values of 256×256, 512×512, 1024×1024, 2048×2048, and 4096×4096.

 The greater the Shadow Map Resolution, the more detailed the occlusion map and the more time it takes to generate. In general, the Shadow Map Resolution should be set to the lowest possible value that produces an occlusion map of acceptable quality.

Shadow Darkness

Shadow Darkness sets the brightness or darkness of the ambient occlusion map. Lowering the value from the default of 0.5 brightens the ambient occlusion map, and increasing the value darkens it.

Shadow Contrast

Shadow Contrast sets the contrast between shaded and nonshaded areas of the ambient occlusion map. This value ranges from –1 to 1, with a default value of 0. Lower values reduce contrast, producing gray values in the map, while higher values increase the contrast, producing more black and white values.

Filter

Lower Filter values improve the overall sharpness of the finer details in the generated ambient occlusion map, while higher values help reduce some visible artifacts that sometimes are generated by the shadow maps.

Options Specific to the Vector Displacement Maps

The options specific to vector displacement maps are limited to one, which is the Vector Space property.

Vector Space

Vector Space indicates the coordinate space for calculating vector displacement maps. The three options for vector space are as follows:

Tangent This default setting should be used if the model deforms during animation.

Object Use this option if the model is animated without deformation.

World Use this setting for environment maps.

Options Specific to Displacement Maps

When extracting a displacement map, the Extract Texture Maps dialog box slightly changes to include the following properties.

Normalize to Search Distance

When the Bits per Channel option is set to 8- or 16-bit, turning on the Normalize to Search Distance option maps the results of the extraction samples to the 0 to 1 color space for displacement maps instead of the –1 to 1 range used for normal maps. As a default, Normalize to Search Distance is selected.

Base File Name

As with ambient occlusion, the Base File Name field is where you indicate the name of the extracted map. You can click the folder icon to bring up the Save As dialog box to set a directory and choose the file format (.png, .jpg, .bmp, .tif, .psd, .tga, or .exr), some with 8-, 16-, or 32-bit depth.

Again, if your model contains UVs outside the 0 to 1 range in two or more UV tile spaces, this operation automatically creates separate displacement maps corresponding to each UV tile by adding a suffix of the coordinates of the tile—for example, disp_head_u1_v1.tga and disp_head_u1_v2 for a model that has UVs in two adjacent tiles.

Bits per Channel

Bits per Channel indicates the bit depth of the file type chosen in the Save As Type drop-down menu when you specify the name and location of the file to save.

Options Specific to Normal Maps

Normal mapping is a way to represent highly detailed surfaces on more-simplified low-polygon versions of the mesh. In addition to depicting the surface detail, normal maps contain information to make your surface detail react to environment lighting. Normal maps are needed where low-polygon meshes are a requirement, particularly in real-time hardware rendering applications such as games, previsualization, and 3D simulations. When extracting a normal map, the Extract Texture Maps dialog box slightly changes to include the following properties.

Coordinate Space

Coordinate Space indicates whether Tangent, Object, or World coordinate space will be used to calculate the normal maps. Just like XYZ and UVW coordinates, the Tangent coordinate space on a face is set by the normal, tangent, and the binormal. A *face normal* is a directional line perpendicular to a surface and represents the internal or external orientation of each polygon face on a mesh. The *tangent* is a vector that indicates the slope of the polygonal face at a given point, and the *binormal* is a vector orthogonal to both the normal and tangent.

Object is the local coordinate space for the model in which the lighting of the detail shown from the normal map is based on the object itself. World is the overall scene coordinate space, in which the lighting of the detail shown from the normal map is based on the environment. Tangent is the default and the one you should use unless you have a specific need for the lighting on the detail of your model to be affected by itself or its environment.

Compatibility

The Compatibility field sets compatibility of the calculated normal maps with other 3D applications. The tangent space vectors are calculated using one of two methods, either the left-handed or right-handed method of determining the normal orientation. These methods determine the sequence of axes in a Cartesian coordinate system. For example, with the right-handed method, the thumb, index finger, and middle finger of the right hand are held so that they form three right angles, and then the thumb indicates the normal, the index finger the tangent, and the middle finger the binormal. Maya defaults to the right-handed tangent space setting, while 3ds Max defaults to the left-handed tangent space setting. Look at the settings for any other 3D application you use to determine its tangent space setting, and use Maya or 3ds Max as the setting to indicate right or left tangent space setting, respectively. Obviously, this does not matter if you use World or Object coordinate space because both coordinate systems are absolute.

Base File Name

Just as for ambient occlusion and displacement maps, the Base File Name field is where you indicate the name of the extracted map. You can click the folder icon to bring up the Save As dialog box to set a directory and choose the file format (`.png`, `.jpg`, `.bmp`, `.tif`, `.psd`, `.tga`, or `.exr`), some with 8-, 16-, or 32-bit depth.

As with ambient occlusion and displacement maps, if your model contains UVs outside the 0 to 1 range in two or more UV tile spaces, this operation automatically creates separate displacement maps corresponding to each UV tile by adding a suffix of the coordinates of the tile—for example, `norm_head_u1_v1.tga` and `norm_head_u1_v2` for a model that has UVs in two adjacent tiles.

Bits per Channel

Bits per Channel indicates the bit depth of the file type chosen in the Save As Type dropdown menu when you specify the name and location of the file to save.

Setting Mudbox Preferences

The Mudbox preferences dialog box is another dialog box that is not part of what you see on the screen, but that has many components affecting how Mudbox looks and behaves. Rather than explain every option in the preferences dialog box, I will highlight some of the more commonly used ones.

It is important to know how to reset these settings to their defaults in case you set them to options that cause unwelcome results. The user settings files are saved in the following folders for various platforms:

Mac OS X:

```
/Users/<username>/Library/Preferences/Mudbox/<version>/settings
```

Windows XP:

```
<drive>:My Documents\Mudbox\<version>\settings
```

Vista:

```
<drive>:Users\<username>\Documents\Mudbox\<version>\settings
```

You can move or rename those files for Mudbox to re-create new ones with default settings.

Color

Color is where you specify the colors of the Mudbox user interface. The ones I find most useful are the first four: Viewport Top, Viewport Middle, Viewport Bottom, and Viewport Flat. The first three specify the top, middle, and bottom colors of the 3D view gradient. Viewport Flat will set the background color if the gradient option is turned off. The other color options are pretty self-explanatory.

Render

In the Render options, I use only the Limit Wireframe to Level option. This is extremely useful if you want to display a lower-level wireframe on a higher-subdivision-level model (Figure 2.38). Even though the grid is a good visual guide to tell you how high your subdivision level is, as you get into higher subdivision levels, the grid size gets really small and becomes more of a disruption. Figure 2.38 shows the difference between this setting at the default value, which is 10 on the image on the left, versus a value of 2 on image on the right. You can choose 0 to have the absolute lowest level.

Figure 2.38

Wireframe levels with a default value of 10 on the left and a value of 2 on the right

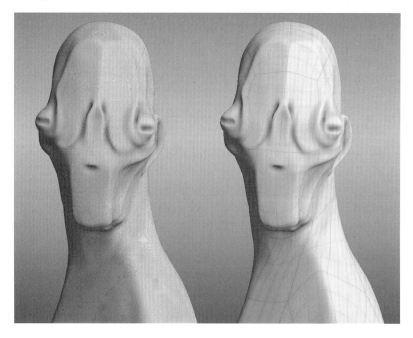

The other Render options will help speed up your display while working, but I recommend leaving them alone or recording their default values before tinkering with the settings.

FBX

FBX, which is short for *Filmbox*, is an interoperability file format owned and developed by Autodesk. The FBX section is where you specify the preferences with which you will use the FBX file format to import and export geometry, UVs, cameras, and materials in and out of Mudbox.

Export ASCII FBX

Export ASCII FBX is an option I usually select if I need to troubleshoot FBX export issues. I would leave this on as a default, but the ASCII version of FBX files take up a lot more hard drive space because the files are larger than their binary counterparts.

Export Layers as Blend Shapes

When turned on, the separate sculpt layers on the current subdivision level are exported as individual and separate blend shapes. When loaded into Maya or 3ds Max, separate blend shape targets can be modified with blend shape sliders very similar to the Layer Opacity sliders in Mudbox. The default setting for this is off, and the selected object is exported at its current subdivision when exporting it as .fbx.

Paint

The Paint section is where you specify the preferences of the paint tools and their effects in Mudbox.

Fast Dry Brush

When Fast Dry Brush is turned on, it accelerates the application of the Dry Brush tool. You should set this option to off only if the Dry Brush tool is not producing acceptable results because you will get better accuracy when the tool is slow to react to your stroke.

User Interface

There are many useful and self-explanatory options to turn on and off various user interface options in the User Interface section of the preferences dialog box. The one option I want to highlight is the Get Help From option. This is set to Autodesk Web Site by default, which is the setting you want if you are connected to the Internet.However, if you are at a location with slow or no Internet access or such as when you are mobile, or on a set, you can redirect this path to read the help from your hard drive. The challenge with setting the help to a local file is that Autodesk constantly updates and edits the help on the website, and accessing help locally from your hard drive will not have the latest

reversions. Note that you will have to initially download the Mudbox help files from www
.autodesk.com/mudbox-docs and unzip the help file in the location specified by the Help Path
text box. The default for Windows is `C:\Program Files\Autodesk\Mudbox2011\help\docs`
and for the Mac OS X is `/Library/Application Support/Autodesk/Mudbox 2011/help/docs`.

Status Line

This section of the preferences dialog box has various options of what to show and hide
in the status line. I always make sure that the Save Reminder option is on and set at an
interval of 20 or 30 minutes. Even though a blinking red Save in the bottom-right corner
of Mudbox can be really annoying, it reminds me to keep saving my model—and what
would be even more annoying would be to lose an hour or two of work because I forgot
to save.

Summary

The Mudbox user interface is organized intuitively, and as you continue to work with
it, you will discover many new features that will help you with your work. Chapter 2 is
a great place to come back to again and again if you want a description of a feature in a
Properties list, a dialog box, or anything else in the Mudbox interface. Please also note
that as you hover your mouse on a particular tool or area, sometimes, pop-up help will
give you more information about the particular tool or option.

Even though the Mudbox user interface is laid out intuitively, you will want to customize it to the way that you work. In the following chapters, we will go through some
customization options to give you the means to create your own perfect setup.

CHAPTER 3

Detail-Sculpting
an Imported Model

In the first chapter, you went through the Mudbox workflow with a relatively simple model of an egg, a model with one part. In this chapter, you will go through a much more sophisticated model with multiple parts.

You had a brief encounter with a low-resolution version of Ashley Wood's robot, Bertie, in the camera section of Chapter 1, "Getting Your Feet in the Mud: The Basics of the Mudbox Production Pipeline." In this chapter, you will work with a high-resolution version of Bertie and do some surface detail sculpting. But before you get started with Bertie, you need to understand some terminology and best practices of bringing models into Mudbox.

This chapter includes the following topics:

- **Modeling the base mesh**

- **Laying out UVs**

- **Using naming conventions and organizing the components of your model**

- **Setting the scale, pose, and location of the model**

- **Sculpting surface details**

- **Sculpting weathering and wear and tear**

Modeling the Base Mesh

All sculpting in Mudbox starts from a base mesh. A *base mesh* is a polygonal model made up of vertices that are connected to each other by edges to produce faces (Figure 3.1).

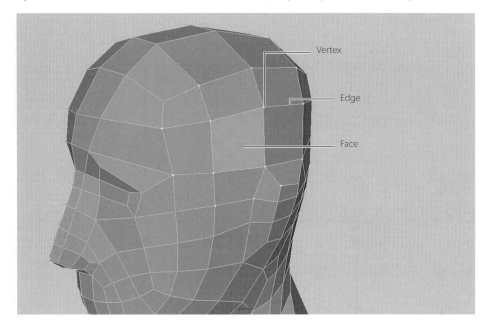

In the case of the egg created in Chapter 1, we used a Sphere primitive that we scaled to be our egg base mesh. Even though sculpting and painting your model is the core function and fun part of using Mudbox, having a problematic base mesh can bring that fun to an abrupt end and leave you extremely frustrated with an unusable sculpture you spent hours on. It is vital that you understand the requirements of a good base mesh and proper UV layout to get the results you want when you sculpt and paint your model.

Even if the original model did not start out as a polygonal model, its conversion to a polygonal model in either .obj or .fbx format is what you will start with in Mudbox. However detailed, this model and all its parts will be brought into Mudbox at subdivision level 0.

Triangles, Quads, N-gons, Poles, and Uniformly Spaced Geometry

As I mentioned, all models are made up of vertices, edges, and faces. The edges connect the vertices to form polygons. Even though Mudbox supports polygon faces with a maximum of 16 edges, your base mesh should ideally be composed entirely of four-edged polygons, which are also referred to as *quads*. The reason for this is that when you subdivide your model, polygons will be divided by 4, so if your model is a quad (that is, composed of four edges), then it will be divisible by 4 and will result in smaller quads inside each divided quad.

Figure 3.2 shows how Mudbox subdivides a tri (triangle), a quad, a pentagon, a hexagon, and an n-gon. All the resulting subdivision polygons produce quads on the inside. However, notice how uniform the subdivision is with the square quad shape and how the rest of the shapes produce a *hub*, or *pole*, in the middle. These poles produce a dense collection of polygons around the center of the pole, causing the surface to pinch and produce undesired visual artifacts when you sculpt, smooth, deform, and paint your model.

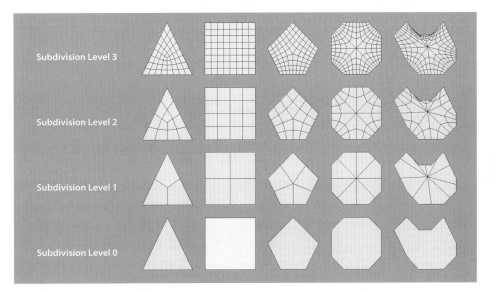

Figure 3.2

Subdivision of a triangle, a square quad, a pentagon, an octagon, and an n-gon

The number of edges coming out of a vertex is called the *valency*. If you generate poles that have a valency of more than 5, you should reposition those poles in inconspicuous locations where they will not be seen. This is even more critical when you are working on an organic model, such as a human being or creature, versus a hard-surface model, such as a car, robot, or spaceship, because hard-surface models usually are not intended to undergo deformation unless they are specifically intended to be deformable characters by design (for example, cartoony characters of cars, planes, or trains).

Another consideration is the size and distribution of your polygons. If you have long, thin polygons, they will get subdivided accordingly, creating artifacts when you sculpt. You want all your polygons evenly distributed in as close to a square shape as possible.

In Figure 3.3, planes A and B are both subdivided four times. Using the Sculpt tool on plane A produces jagged banding because each of the subdivisions is a smaller thin rectangle. In contrast, a subdivided plane B produces excellent results because you are subdividing squares with equal sides. The ratio of the width divided by the height of a rectangle is called the *aspect ratio*. A square has an aspect ratio of 1:1 because the height and width are the same, whereas the rectangles in plane A have an aspect ratio of 1:4. The only way we can get plane A to sculpt better is to subdivide it further, which wastes geometry and computing resources to get the same result we would have if we had used more uniformly spaced geometry.

Figure 3.3

Subdividing square quads versus rectangular quads

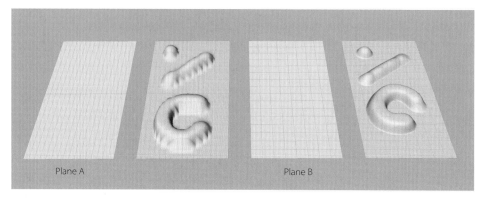

Plane A

Plane B

That said, it is impossible for all of your polygons to have an aspect ratio of 1:1. Getting some poles in your model is also unavoidable. Even if your model is entirely composed of quads, you will still have poles due to the topology of your edge loops. However, if you stick to the following three best practices, you will lessen your problems with subdividing, sculpting, and painting your model:

- Make sure your model is composed of quads. Occasional triangles or n-gons are acceptable only if you have a good place to hide them on the model, or if you have a hard-surface model that will not deform in the area where the triangles or n-gons are located.

- Make sure all the quads in your model have an aspect ratio as close to 1:1 as possible. If you find that you have skinny, long rectangles in your model, add some edge loops, to make the quad distribution more even. (Edge loops are explained in the following section.)

- Make sure the valency for all your poles is at 5 or less. If you absolutely need to have any poles that have a valency greater than 5, make sure they are tucked away somewhere not visible.

Topology and Edge Loops

Edge loops, or *edge rings*, are the flow of edges on your model where the last edge meets again with the first edge, forming a loop. They are critical for animation purposes because they determine how the model deforms to accommodate for the squashing, stretching, and bending of the geometry. The overall flow of edge loops on a model is referred to as the model's *topology*. Good modelers create edge loops that flow with muscle direction and follow wrinkle lines so that their models bend, stretch, and crease in a realistic way.

Perfectly edge-looped topology targeted for animation is not necessarily ideal topology for sculpting. It takes expert modeling to accommodate for both animation and sculpting topologies, if it is even possible. For sculpting purposes, you need geometry that is uniformly spaced and optimized for subdividing, is composed of quads, and has edge loops that flow in the direction that accommodates sculpting gestures and strokes. For animation, you need edge loops that accommodate for squashing, stretching, and deformation based on the motion of the limbs or movable parts of the model.

For Mudbox, it is better for your base mesh to have topology suitable for sculpting rather than animation. After the sculpting and painting is done, and the normal or displacement maps are extracted, the model can be re-topologized for animation. *Re-topologizing* is re-creating a mesh that represents the same model but with different edge loops and topology. This can be done in your 3D application or a variety of other applications such as TopoGun or the NEX tools plug-in for Maya. You will be visiting this topic in Chapter 7, "Working with 3D Scan Data," when you re-topologize 3D scan data into a topology fit for sculpting and digital painting.

Problematic and Nonmanifold Geometry

Mudbox supports two-manifold polygon topologies. Polygon meshes that have two-manifold topology can be split along various edges to unfold and form a flat surface with no overlapping sections. Mudbox does not support nonmanifold topology. All 3D modeling applications can produce nonmanifold polygons either by accident or by a modeling operation such as deleting faces, extruding, or Boolean operations. Some 3D modeling applications provide tools such as Maya's Mesh → Cleanup feature (Figure 3.4) for checking and fixing this problem.

Figure 3.4

Maya's Mesh Cleanup dialog box

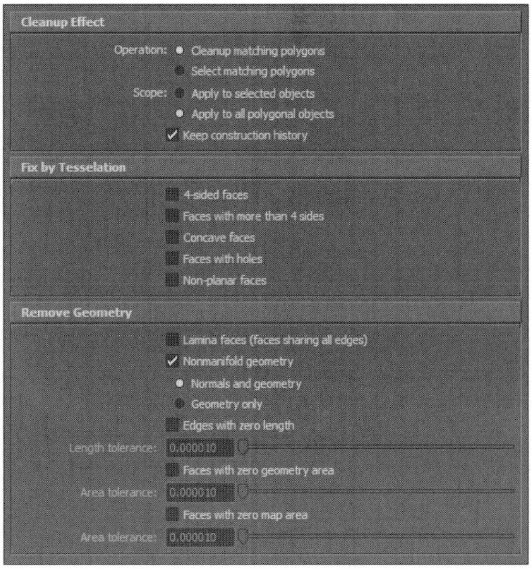

Every polygon has a *face normal* that determines which side of a polygon is the front and which side is the back. It is often represented by an imaginary line that is perpendicular to the surface of a polygon. Face normals are important because sometimes when you bring a model into Mudbox, certain parts of the model are not visible, and that is a good indication that the face normals are reversed. This situation can be detected and easily remedied in your 3D application just by reversing the face normals on the problematic faces.

Symptoms of problematic and nonmanifold geometry are as follows:

- Edges that do not connect to two faces, open seams, and overlapping edges in your model

- Polygons that are connected by only a vertex and no edges

- Vertices that are surrounded by more than one sequence of edges and faces
- Adjacent polygons with normals facing in opposite directions
- Floating or overlapping stray vertices in the model
- Lamina faces, which are faces that share all edges, mostly resulting from aborted extrude operations

If your base mesh is having problems loading or is displaying uncharacteristic anomalies when you load it, you likely have one of the preceding issues. To fix these problems, use cleanup features found in some 3D modeling applications, such as the Mesh → Cleanup feature in the Polygons menu set of Maya (Figure 3.4), read up on fixing these problems in polygonal modeling books, or seek the help of a polygonal modeling expert. Figure 3.5 shows some examples of nonmanifold geometry.

Figure 3.5

Three examples of nonmanifold geometry: T-shaped, bowtie, and flipped normal

Now that you have seen the importance of having a good base mesh to start with, you are ready to look at another important aspect of a base mesh, its UV layout.

Laying Out UVs

Just as X and Y are coordinates of a point in 2D space, U and V are coordinates of points on the surface of a model. It is easy to identify a point in flat 2D space by its coordinates, but to do the same with a complex polygon mesh, you first need to unfold it into a flat surface—making sure there are no overlapping sections, so that every coordinate corresponds to a unique point on the surface of the mesh. This unwrapped 2D surface called a *UV map* stores the correlation between the pixel locations in the image and the vertices on the model. A good example to better understand UVs is a paper airplane (Figure 3.6).

Figure 3.6

A paper airplane with a United States Air Force decal on its wings

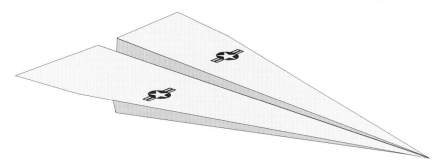

If we were to instruct a printer to print the United States Air Force insignia on a paper airplane, we would have to unfold the paper airplane (Figure 3.7) and indicate the coordinates of where the decals would go when the paper is completely flat (Figure 3.8).

UV coordinates are the positions of pixels on the surface of the 3D mesh. Those pixels can represent color, depth, and light orientation in the form of a texture, displacement, or normal map. The concept of unwrapping a 3D model is similar to the unwrapping of the paper airplane but is more involved because, unlike the paper airplane, complex 3D objects (such as a head, body, or spaceship) have many facets and we need to know where to cut seams to get the best flattened representation. You saw an example of an unwrapped UV map when you looked at the UV view of our egg in Chapter 1. All the mesh primitives in Mudbox, such as the Human Body (Figure 3.9), already have UV maps created for you. It would be a good idea to load all of them and take a look in the UV View at how the different models and shapes are unwrapped.

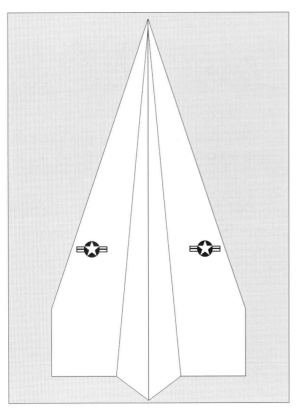

Figure 3.7
Unfolding the paper airplane

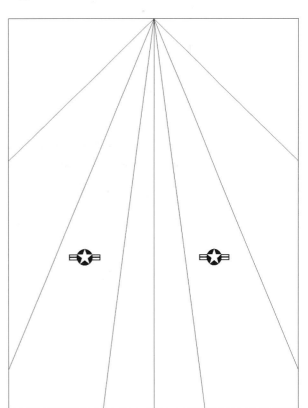

Figure 3.8
The unfolded paper airplane

Figure 3.9

**UV map for the
Human Body mesh
in Mudbox**

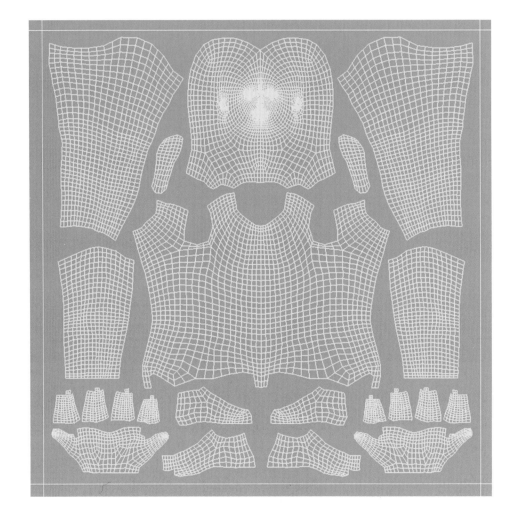

As mentioned, the two-manifold geometry that Mudbox supports, by definition, can be split along various edges to enable the shape to be laid out completely flat. There are different tools and methods available to you to create UV maps or UVs for your model. The process of creating UVs for a mesh is called *UV mapping*. Unfortunately, Mudbox does not contain any tools to create or modify UVs. Mudbox will, however, automatically subdivide the area within the UVs for you when you subdivide your model and choose to paint on it on a level greater than 0. Most major 3D applications, including Maya, have many UV mapping tools, such as automatic, planar, cylindrical, and spherical mapping.

There are applications that also create automatically generated UVs that are randomly arranged, and humanly unreadable, but these randomly laid out UVs do enable you to 3D paint without having to manually lay out UVs. Although this is a solution, it is not optimal because you will not be able to match any 2D patterns to the random layout of the flattened polygons. There are also tools and technologies being developed, such as

Ptex developed by Walt Disney Animation Studios, that might eliminate the need for manually laying out UVs in the future. This will be a welcome solution for our vocation because it automates a stage in the process. However, this technology is still in development and will hopefully find its way to the most commonly used 3D tools in the near future. In the meantime, we still have to unwrap UVs by using existing tools and applications. The tool I prefer to use to lay out UVs is a brilliant application called UVLayout by Headus (www.uvlayout.com), which makes the process extremely fast and easy.

A tool such as Maya or UVLayout enables a user to cut the seams on the model to break it into multiple pieces called *UV shells*. Then these UV shells are flattened individually to have no intersecting lines or overlapping pieces. As these UV shells are flattened, take care to evenly space the polygons so they don't compress or stretch too much. As you can see in Figure 3.10, the UVs provided for the Human Body mesh have areas that are subject to stretching and compressing. UVLayout color codes the areas that will stretch in variations of red, and the areas that will compress in variations of blue.

Figure 3.10

This UV map displays areas that are subject to stretching and compressing by coloring them in shades of red and blue, respectively (see color insert).

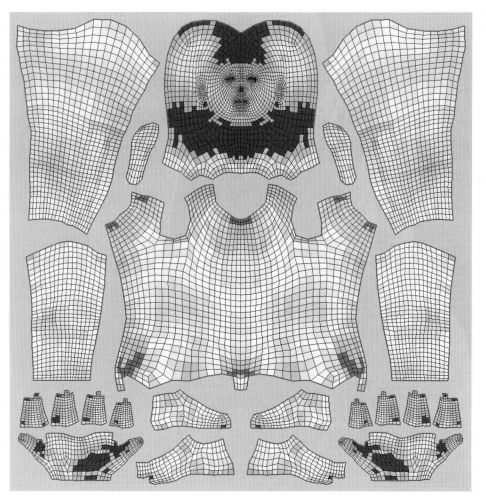

Stretching and compressing causes an even texture such as a checkerboard to appear nonuniform on the surface of a model. Figure 3.11 demonstrates a checkered pattern applied to the Human Body mesh, and as you can see, there is some stretching of this pattern on the chest, right below the clavicular notch, which is the indentation at the base of the neck. You can also see compression of the checkered pattern in the neck and forehead area. These can be easily remedied with a bit more work in UVLayout to produce Figure 3.12.

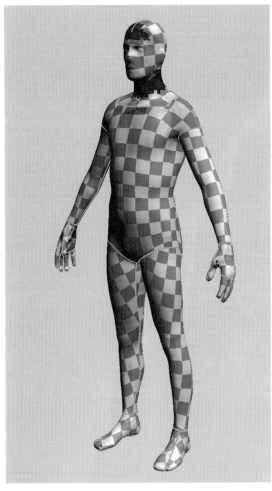

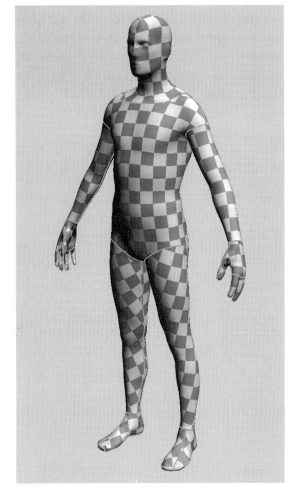

Figure 3.11

The Human Body mesh with the default UVs provided in Mudbox displaying stretching and compression (see color insert)

Figure 3.12

The Human Body mesh with modified UVs in UVLayout displaying a more uniform checkered pattern (see color insert)

The other feature you will notice in both Figures 3.11 and 3.12 is that the checkered pattern does not continue through the seams. Texture painters who used to have to paint on UVs as 2D images had to come up with creative ways to match the patterns so the seams would not appear. Of course, painting in Mudbox eliminates the need to do that because you can directly paint on the seams, and the continuity of your brush strokes will be preserved through the seams. This is one of the most powerful and useful capabilities of Mudbox, and many texture artists use Mudbox for this reason alone.

After the seams are cut and the pieces are unwrapped, they will have to be arranged or packed to fit in the first square tile of UV space, making sure that as little space as possible is wasted. As you look at the UVs for the meshes provided in Mudbox, you will notice that they all are contained within one square UV tile, or quadrant, within the UV texture space. This square UV tile matches up directly to a square image that is created when you paint on the model. You can specify as much or as little detail as you want by the size of the image that corresponds to the square UV tile. If the object is going to be looked at closely, you would need to specify a 2K or 4K map size; if it is going to be viewed from afar, you don't need as detailed a map size. You may recall that we chose a 2K map size for our texture, displacement, and normal maps for the egg in Chapter 1 because we were going to look at it up close.

You can distribute UVs outside the first tile, which is also referred to as the *0 to 1 UV range*, if the rendering application or game engine you will be outputting to supports this capability. This will enable you to place more-prominent or important parts of the model into their own UV tile region to paint greater detail on them. Then you will be able to paint multiple high-resolution maps and show much more texture detail on your models.

Another way you can save UV space is to fully overlap symmetrically opposite UV shells that will have symmetrical paint applied to them on top of each other, and use the space that is left for other parts of your model that require more detail.

The *winding order* of a UV is either the clockwise or counterclockwise direction in which the UV coordinates are stored for a face. If your texture maps appear flipped or display incorrectly, you probably have some UVs that have an opposite winding order from the rest. Errors in nonuniform winding order could be the result of flipped face normals, or errors during the modeling or UV mapping. The winding order can be easily detected in the UV Texture Editor in Maya by clicking the Shaded UV display button.

The polygons with a clockwise winding order are displayed in blue, and the ones with a counterclockwise winding order are displayed in red. To change the winding order of a UV shell, you can use the Polygons → Flip function in Maya's UV Texture Editor.

Finally, you may encounter situations where all the polygons in a UV are separated out even though they are still adjacent. This happens during importing and exporting of your model to other applications that have options selected to separate out all the polygons as individual UVs. A good way to check for this in the Maya UV Texture Editor is to click the Toggle the Display of Texture Borders for the Active Mesh button in the Maya UV Texture Editor.

This is better illustrated by looking at Figures 3.13 through 3.15.

Figure 3.13

UVs in default view

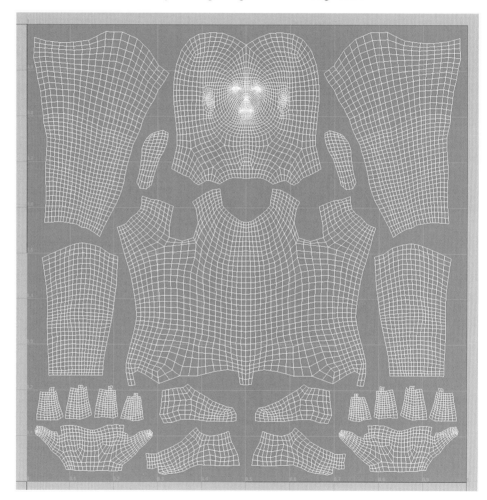

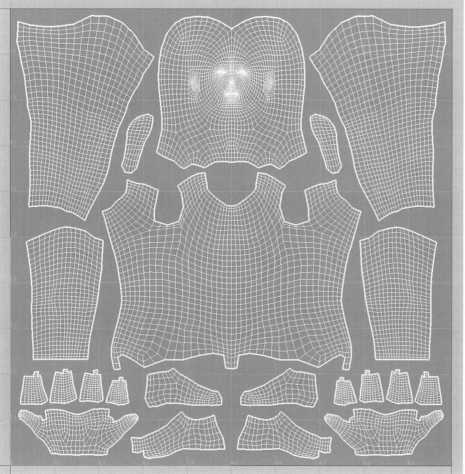

Figure 3.14

Good UVs with texture borders highlighted by clicking the Toggle the Display of Texture Borders for the Active Mesh button in the Maya UV Texture Editor

If you find that all your polygons in a UV are separated out even though they are still adjacent, you need to select all the polygons within the shell and sew them together by using the Sew the Selected Edges or UVs Together button.

Please note that other 3D applications besides Maya that have their own UV creation and manipulation capabilities may have similar features for you to detect and correct these UV issues.

Figure 3.15

Bad UVs with texture borders highlighted by clicking the Toggle the Display of Texture Borders for the Active Mesh button in the Maya UV Texture Editor

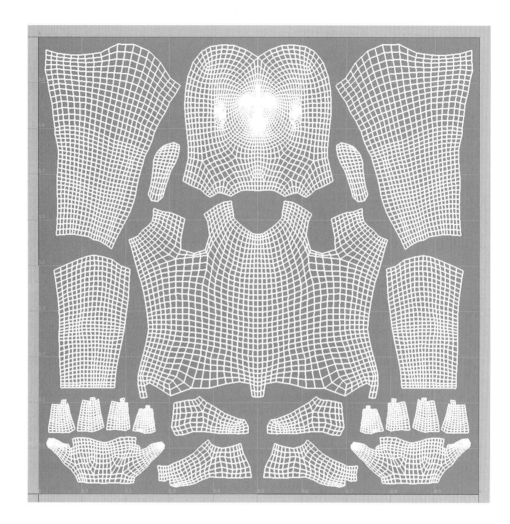

Proper UV layout of your model is critical for Mudbox because you can paint on your model or export texture, displacement, and normal maps from your model only if your model has UVs that follow these guidelines:

- No overlapping UV shells, or lines or pixels within your UV shells. This is especially the case for areas of dense pixel concentration.

- Spacing of at least 4 to 6 pixels between the UV shells and the borders of the 0 to 1 UV space.

- All UVs have the correct UV winding order.

- UV shells don't manifest extreme stretched or compressed areas.

Using Naming Conventions and Organizing the Components of Your Model

Whether you are the only one working on your model or you have a model in a pipeline, a well-documented model will save you a lot of time. Most production houses have their own naming conventions that you will have to adhere to, but you can also come up with your own. This is an indispensible practice because it will help you find parts easily in a list.

It's a good idea to name everything while you are creating the parts of your model, or at short intervals of creating your model. Because your model will be used on multiple platforms that treat capitalization and special characters differently, it is also a good idea to use only lowercase characters and to use an underscore to indicate a space. Always identify the work with your name and indicate whether the part is on the left (lf), right (rt), center (cn), upper (up), or lower (lw) section of the model. Be as specific as you can with your naming—for example, for humans, use anatomical terms, and for mechanical objects, get schematics to specify the correct names of parts.

Some good examples are as follows:

- `arak_bertie_arm_actuator_up_lf`
- `arak_bertie_thumb_rt`
- `arak_bertie_body_cn`

For the first example, I used an abbreviation of my name, `arak`; the name of the model, `bertie`; the part, `arm_actuator`; the distinction of the upper actuator denoted by the word `up`; and `lf` denoting that this is the left one.

In Mudbox, you can double-click on the name of an object in the Object List to name it. If you are bringing an `.obj` model into Mudbox from Maya, and you have named all of your objects in Maya, select the Groups On option in the File → Export Selection Options (Figure 3.16) in Maya, as this will bring the names from Maya into Mudbox.

Selection sets are a good way to group or organize components of your model. For example, you might want to group the entire arm with all of its pieces into a selection set so you can hide or freeze it. To do this in Mudbox, select all the individual pieces by using the Objects selection tool on the model. Alternatively, you can multiple-select them by holding down the Ctrl key in Windows or the Command key on the Mac in the Object List and then choosing Create → Selection Set and giving your sets a name. You can also create selection sets with faces by using the Select Faces tool to select faces on your models, and saving your selection by choosing Create → Selection Set.

Figure 3.16

Export selection options, with the Groups option set to On

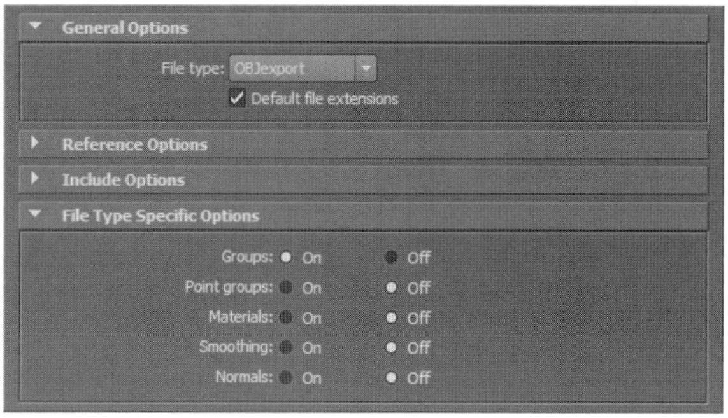

To create your selection sets in Maya, select all the geometry you are going to be working with and then choose Create → Sets → Quick Select Set. Make sure to export your `.obj` model from Maya with the Groups option set to On in the File → Export Selection Options (Figure 3.16) because that will transfer your quick select sets into Mudbox as selection sets.

Figure 3.17

Mudbox preferences Linear Units setting

Setting Scale, Location, and Pose of the Model

If no units or scale have been specified for your model, it is always safe to go with a true-to-life scale. In Mudbox, you can specify millimeter, centimeter, meter, or inch as the

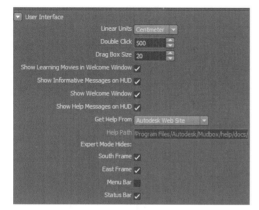

unit of measurement in the Linear Units drop-down menu in the preferences dialog box. To access the preferences dialog box, choose Windows → Preference in Windows, or Mudbox → Preferences on the Mac. Linear Units are in the User Interface section of the preferences dialog box (Figure 3.17). The default in Mudbox, as it is in Maya, is Centimeters.

In Maya, because I have the gridlines set to a foot, and the subdivision lines set to an inch, when we import the Human Body mesh exported as an `.obj` or `.fbx` file into Mudbox, we see that it is about 6 feet tall, which is the approximate height of a male human being (Figure 3.18).

However, as you can see when all of the meshes in Mudbox are brought into the same scene, their scales vary (Figure 3.19).

Before you import your model, position it in the center of the XYZ origin, so that you will be able to use the X, Y, or Z mirroring capabilities.

Whether the final presentation of your sculpture will be a 2D image, a 3D turntable, or an animation, you will be narrating something about your model, and unless your narration is about Leonardo da Vinci's Vitruvian Man or an action figure twist-tied in its packaging, the T-pose tends to be pretty boring to look at. Your model would be better presented telling a story, and that can be accomplished with a good pose along with its composition in a narrative environment.

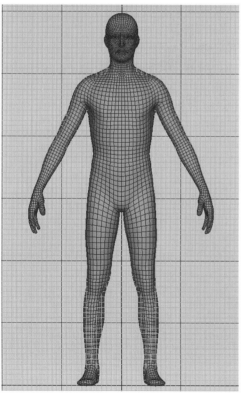

Figure 3.18

The Human Body mesh scale is approximately 6 feet tall.

If the model is to be animated, it will likely already have, or be destined to have, a rig in its development pipeline. A good rig, or skeleton with good controls and effective skinning, is the optimal way to pose a model. A *rig* is a skeletal system with joints that you rotate, and effectors that you move to pose your model. *Skinning*, or *enveloping* is determining the weight or influence the rig will have on the polygons of your model so that as you manipulate your skeleton, the intended parts of the model are translated or rotated.

It would be very easy to pose your model by using its rig and then output the resulting pose as an .obj or .fbx file and import it into Mudbox for sculpting. It is also very convenient because you can continually and easily modify or update your pose and export your model if needed.

If you are, however, not working in a pipeline where you will get an already rigged model, or have no rigging and skinning experience of your own, you will quickly discover that rigging and skinning is an in-depth expertise. If you don't have the help of a good rigger, and need to rig and skin a complex model, you will be out of your depth in a very short time.

Figure 3.19

The differences in scale among the default Mudbox meshes

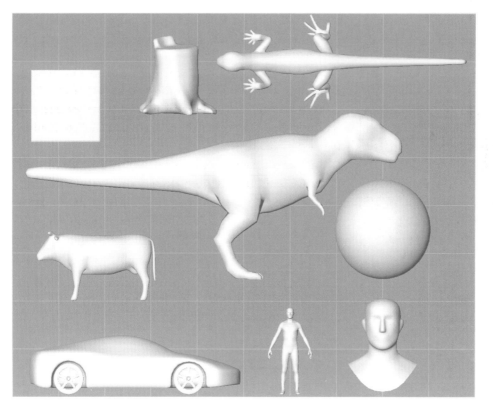

If the final output of your digital sculpture is a turntable animation, a 3D print, or a 2D image, you likely don't need to spend the time or go through the expense of rigging your base mesh. You can use the posing tools in Mudbox 2011 for almost all cases with a few exceptions.

Mudbox 2011 is the first version of Mudbox to introduce posing tools. Even though you could have used the Grab tool in earlier versions of Mudbox to push, pull, and reposition geometry, it was never intended to be a posing tool. If you are posing an organic biped or quadruped, the new pose tools in Mudbox 2011 are quite effective and powerful. You can also use the new pose tools to bend, deform, move, or twist and shape models that are nonorganic. We will go into these tools in depth and pose a character in Chapter 7.

There are, however, some instances where the pose tools in Mudbox 2011 are not effective, and you will unfortunately need to use alternate posing tools to get the results you need. A perfect example is the model we will be using in this chapter, which is a mechanical robot with many parts.

I modeled Bertie, the robot model we will be using in the rest of this chapter, in Maya in a neutral T-pose and rigged it by adding joints and a skeleton. I then posed the rig in a stance inspired by one of Ashley Wood's paintings.

Sculpting Surface Details

You will now load a mesh into Mudbox and sculpt some surface details. This mesh was modeled in Maya, rigged, posed, and then its UV maps were created in UVLayout. I have included the Maya project with the posed robot for you on the DVD in the `Chapter 3\` `bertie` folder.

Note that the very intricate UV map (Figure 3.20) has a lot of parts and would be a nightmare to paint in Photoshop, but this has no bearing on us because we are working in Mudbox. This is one of the biggest benefits of painting a model in Mudbox. In a production environment, we would overlap some of the repeated parts in the UV map and also pack the parts closer together, but for the example in this book, what we have will work just fine.

Note that even though we have a lot of parts, the pattern and surface distribution of the UVs are even with no stretching (Figure 3.21).

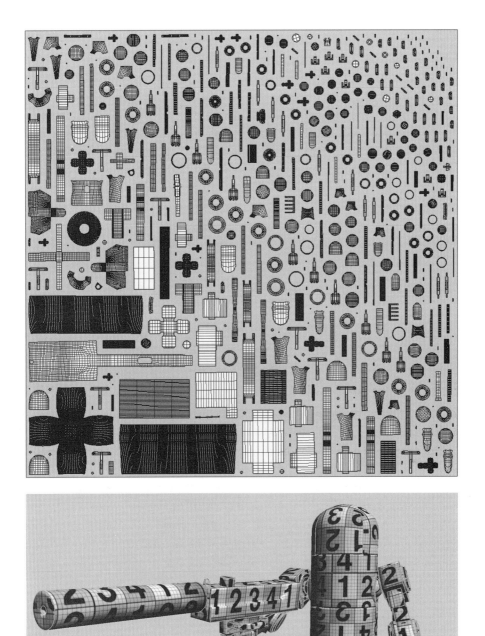

Figure 3.20

UV map for Bertie done in Headus UVLayout

Figure 3.21

Pattern applied to Bertie model in Headus UVLayout

Sculpting Paneling and Mechanical Details

You will not make any major structural changes to the model; you will just add some wear and tear, weathering, and surface details:

1. Start Mudbox and open the `Chapter 3\bertie\Mudbox\bertie_base.mud` file.

2. Press W and look at the wireframe of the model. You will notice that this mesh is pretty dense, and that is by design. I have modeled it in Maya so that the mesh will retain its shape when it is subdivided. You will look at a less dense base mesh in a future chapter, but in this one, because you are not going to be using Mudbox for sculpting the shape of the model, you will rely on the modeling that's done in Maya. Press the W key again to turn off the wireframe.

3. In the Object List tray, select Default Material. Click on the color swatch for Diffuse in the materials properties and change the Diffuse color to white.

4. In the Select/Move Tools tray, click the Objects icon and select the head of the robot; it will turn a yellowish hue to indicate that it is selected.

5. Click the Options box for Mesh → Add New Subdivision Level in Windows (Mesh → Add New Subdivision Level Options on the Mac). This opens the Subdivision Options dialog box (Figure 3.22). Make sure Smooth Positions is selected. This will smooth the model as you subdivide it. If you want your model to subdivide where it will have facets along the mesh edges, deselect the Smooth Positions check box. In our case, I have modeled Bertie so it will hold its shape when subdivided. You might want to experiment subdividing a Cube primitive with this check box on and then off.

6. Press Shift+D three times. Even though the status bar and the pop-up in the top-right corner of the windows mentions that you are at a 1.3 million polygon count, that represents your total polygon count and not just the head. To find out how many polygons you have subdivided your head into, choose Windows → Object List (or Window → Object List on the Mac) and move and scale the Object List window so it does not obstruct the model. I move the list to a second monitor and have it up while I work. Click the plus sign next to `bertie dome body` and notice that it has four levels of subdivision (0, 1, 2, and 3) and is at 1.17 million polygons at level 3 (Figure 3.23). Create a new sculpt layer and call it **head_detail**.

7. Click on the Sculpt Tools tray and select the Imprint tool. The Imprint tool imprints or embosses the stamp image into the model's surface. After you click on the model, you drag the stylus on the surface of the tablet or scale it, and when you let go, you will get an impression on the surface of your model based on the Strength value. Depending on the black-to-white values of your stamp, the Imprint tool will either press in or punch out the shape. If you get the opposite of your intended result, either use the Ctrl key or select the Invert Function check box in the tool's Properties tray to get the desired result.

Figure 3.22
Subdivision Options dialog box

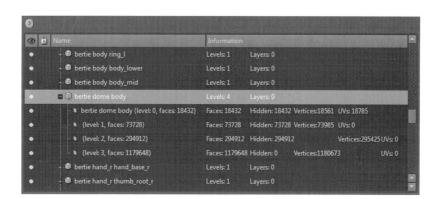

Figure 3.23

Using the Object List to find out the number of faces

8. From the Falloff tray, choose the last falloff on the list that has no slope to it. The falloff curve controls the difference in strength from the center of your brush to its edge. The left side of the curve is the center, and the right side is the edge. We'll talk more about falloffs in Chapter 5, "Digital Sculpting Part I."

9. Click on the Image Browser and choose the Stamps folder on the DVD. Select circle .tif in the Image Browser and click the Set Stamp button. Change the Strength to 200 and select the Invert Function check box. In the Advanced section of the tool properties, click Orient to Surface.

10. Using the Imprint tool, click and drag your mouse or stylus to paint the stamp on the surface (Figure 3.24).

Figure 3.24

Click and drag your mouse or stylus to draw where you want the eye to go.

11. Let go, and the eye becomes an indentation on the head of the robot (Figure 3.25).

Figure 3.25

The imprint of the eye on the robot

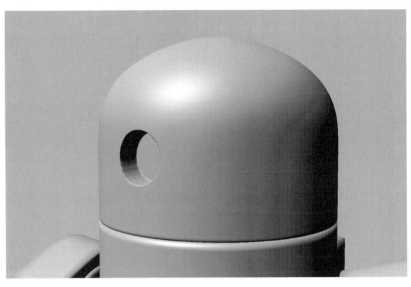

12. Change the Strength to 50 and make another smaller, shallower eye above and to the left of the original one (Figure 3.26).

Figure 3.26

The second smaller and shallower eye above and to the left

13. From the Select/Move Tools tray, click the Objects icon and select the middle body. Press Shift+D four times to divide it to 2,883,584 polygons. Check to make sure you have five subdivisions in the Object List. The part is called bertie body body_mid. Create a new sculpt layer and call it **midbody_detail**. Click the Imprint tool, deselect the Invert Function check box, and change the Strength to 80. Imprint a circle in the location shown in Figure 3.27. Click the Invert Function check box, or hold down the

Ctrl key and imprint another circle in the middle of the one you just made. Remember that Undo or Ctrl+Z is handy to undo the imprint if it's not in the right place.

Figure 3.27

Concentric circle protrusion and indent

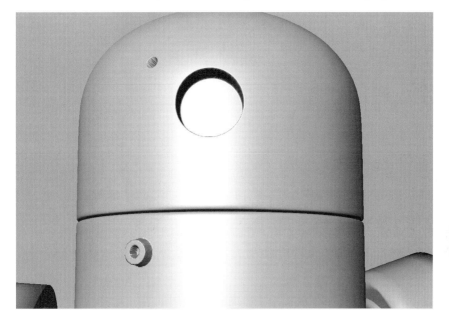

14. In the Image Browser, select the panel.tif stamp, click the Imprint tool in the Sculpt Tools tray, and click the Set Stamp button. In 3D view, deselect the Invert Function check box and set the Strength to 5. Click and drag from the bottom to the top to create an outdented panel in the center, between the shoulders of the robot (Figure 3.28). Note that this is not under the big eye because the head is swiveled off-center to look down the barrel of the gun.

15. Turn the robot around to see the engine on his back. Choose Mesh → Add New Subdivision Level Options and deselect the Smooth Positions check box. The reason for this is that unlike the rest of the model, the engine parts are not modeled, so they will hold their shape when subdivided. If you leave Smooth Positions selected, the shape will become more rounded, which is not what we want in this case. Select the Exhaust mesh and press Shift+D four times. Create a sculpt layer called **exhaust_ detail**. Using the circle.jpg stamp and a Strength of 50, make two holes next to each other (Figure 3.29).

16. Select the engine and subdivide it five times, still with the Smooth Positions option not selected. Create a sculpt layer called **engine_detail**. Using the Circle.tif stamp and a Strength of 50, make a large hole. Switch to the grill.tif stamp and place a grill inside the circle you just made (Figure 3.29).

17. Save your model as **bertie_stage_01.mud**.

Figure 3.28

Front middle panel

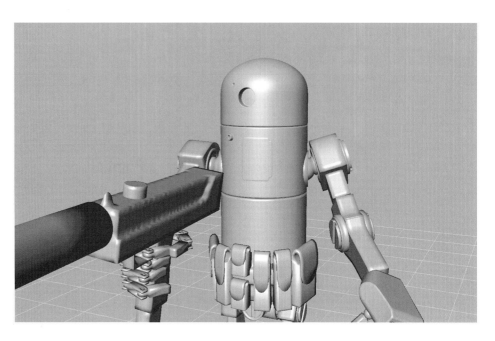

Figure 3.29

Engine detail

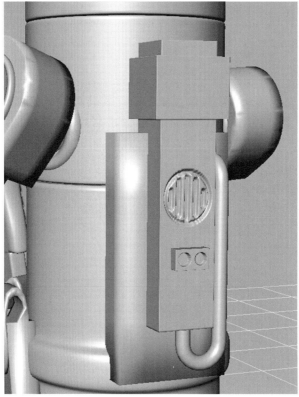

Sculpting Weathering and Wear and Tear

You will now add weathering and wear and tear to the model. Before you do this, you should envision the wear and tear a robot like Bertie would go through. Gather reference images online to use as examples for your work. You can search terms such as *banged up cars from the seventies*, *junkyard metal*, *Soviet WWII-era tanks*, and *old water heaters* in your favorite search engine or photo reference site to get images for examples.

Subdividing the Parts of the Model and Creating Sculpt Layers

Before adding the detailing, you need to further subdivide the pieces of geometry you will be working on so that you provide adequate geometry for the sculpting:

1. Load the `Chapter 3\bertie\Mudbox\bertie_stage_01.mud` file from the DVD or continue from your work in the previous section.

2. From the Select/Move Tools tray, click the Objects selection tool and Shift+select all the parts of the robot highlighted in Figure 3.30. With the Smooth Positions option selected, under Mesh → Add New Subdivision Level Options, subdivide by two levels each of the robot parts highlighted in Figure 3.30. You might need to reselect all the parts again after you press Shift+D the first time. Subdivide the gun one extra time to three subdivision levels. If you don't want to go through this tedious process, you can load the `bertie_stage_01a.mud` file from the `Chapter 3\bertie\Mudbox` folder on the DVD.

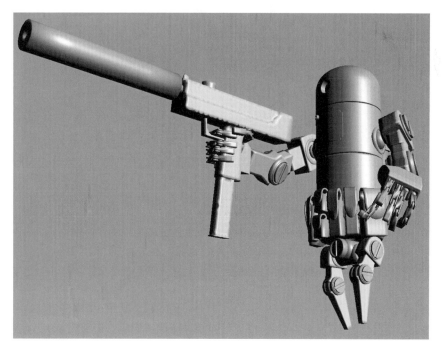

Figure 3.30

Subdivide highlighted parts by two subdivisions with the Smooth Positions option selected (see color insert).

3. From the Select/Move Tools tray, click Objects and Shift+select all the parts of the robot highlighted in Figure 3.31. With the Smooth Positions option not selected, subdivide by one level each of the robot parts highlighted in Figure 3.31. Subdivide just the silencer and the armpits two more times to three subdivision levels. Also subdivide the engine bottom two times because it is in the back of the robot and not visible in Figure 3.30. If you don't want to go through this tedious process, you can load the `bertie_stage_01b.mud` file from the `Chapter 3\bertie\Mudbox` folder on the DVD.

Figure 3.31

Subdivide highlighted parts by two subdivisions with the Smooth Positions option not selected (see color insert).

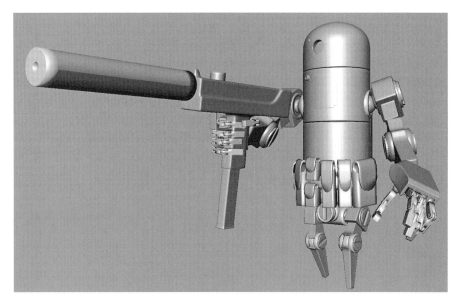

4. Select all the pouches and subdivide them to level 5, or load the `bertie_stage_01c.mud` file from the `Chapter 3\bertie\Mudbox` folder on the DVD.

Later in this chapter, you will create various layers of wear and tear on Bertie. The first layer is for dents, the next is for scratches, and finally a layer for rust. Note that every part has its own sculpt layers. You will not add layers for all the parts, but just the main ones—for example, the two parts of the body, the three parts of each arm, the two parts of each leg, the two hands (not the fingers), the two big engine pieces, and finally the gun. You can either add all the sculpt layers yourself or load the `bertie_stage_01d.mud` file from the `Chapter 3\bertie\Mudbox` folder on the DVD.

Understanding Sculpt Tool Basics

You will use the various sculpt tools with some custom settings to create the dents, scratches, and rust effects. When sculpting, you are constantly adding and subtracting from the surface of your model. At different stages of your sculpting session, you will add and subtract at different depths. Initially, as you are blocking in the general shape of your model, you will add, subtract, and move big chunks of surface on your sculpture, and as you get more to the detail and refinement portion of your work, you will work with smaller increments and decrements of surface detail. Whether blocking in the general shape or refining the sculpture, I find it best to do it in incremental stages, which will be easy to recover from in case of undesired strokes. While sculpting, you will need to balance between the size, the strength, the falloff of your tool, and the pressure you apply on the stylus.

Before getting started on Bertie, you need to understand some important tool properties and shortcut keys:

Size The size of the active tool is displayed as a circle with a center as you move your cursor onto your model. The inside of this circle is the area on the model that the tool will affect based on the tool's properties. You can change the size of the tool by holding down the B key and clicking and dragging your mouse or stylus on the surface of the model; you get visual feedback of the size, which corresponds to the size of the circle. Even though the B key also corresponds to the brush size in Maya, I assign the size to the Z key. This enables me to keep one hand at the bottom-left corner of the keyboard while sculpting, because Shift, Alt, and Ctrl are keys I constantly use and Z is closer to them. You will learn about keyboard customization later in this book.

Strength The strength of a tool corresponds to how deep an impression the tool makes on the surface of the model. Selecting the Invert Function check box or holding down the Ctrl key makes a stroke that pulls out the surface instead of pushing it in. You can adjust the strength by using the M key. However, I assign strength to the X key because, again, it is next to the Shift, Alt, and Ctrl keys that I constantly use while sculpting, enabling me to keep one hand at the bottom-left corner of the keyboard.

Stamp The Stamp image property of a tool uses a grayscale image ranging from black to white as the tip of your tool and modifies the surface based on the variation of color between black and white.

Falloff The falloff is a curve that displays the change in strength of your stroke from the center of the circle to the edge.

Stamp Spacing This is the frequency, or continuity, of the stamp on your stroke. The higher the setting within the range of 0 to 100, the more visible the gaps will be in your stroke.

Steady Stroke and Steady Stroke Distance Turning Steady Stroke on enables you to make a smoother, more continuous stroke. A vector displays on the tool cursor as you drag your mouse or stylus on the surface of your model, and the stroke is not drawn until the mouse or stylus has moved a distance specified in the Distance field.

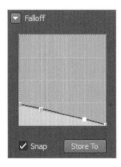

Figure 3.32

Smooth tool
falloff curve

Remember Size Selecting this option preserves the size of your tool if you move to another tool and return. If this is set to Off, the brush will inherit whatever the size of the tool used before it.

Smooth Tool The Smooth tool will smooth out the surface of your sculpture by averaging the vertices. This is one of the most useful tools in Mudbox. In fact, it is so useful that you can activate it by holding down the Shift key while you are using other sculpt tools. If the Smooth tool is not used properly, it may undo a lot of detail work, so it is important to make sure you have it set correctly before you start every sculpting session. First, make sure you choose a very weak strength for it, such as 10 or 20. Second, modify the falloff to match Figure 3.32.

Sculpting Dents

You will now add dents on the surface of Bertie so you don't have the fresh-out-of-the-factory look (Figure 3.33).

Figure 3.33

Dented body

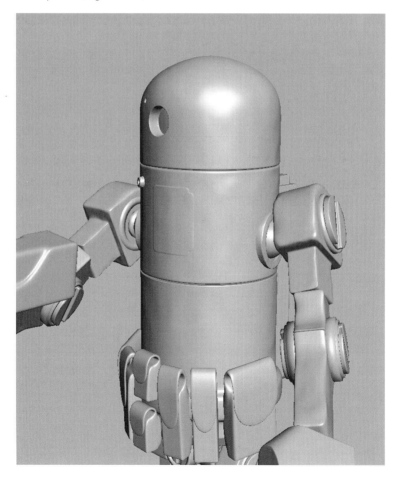

Continue from the prior section or load the `bertie_stage_01d.mud` file from the `Chapter 3\bertie\Mudbox` folder on the DVD. You will add some surface imperfections by using the Flatten tool:

1. Select the Flatten tool. Use the default falloff and a Strength of 4, and vary the Size between 10 and 30 as you sculpt. Use the Flatten tool preferences in Figure 3.34.

2. Sculpt the dents on the surface of your model by using small strokes. Press the L key and click and drag your stylus or mouse to move the light to see the variations on the surface and get a better view of your work.

3. Hold down the Shift key and click and drag your stylus or mouse to smooth out any areas that seem too severe.

4. Remember to sculpt the dents only on the `dents` sculpting layer by first clicking or tapping on the part and then selecting its dent layer in the Sculpt Layers tray. This is extremely useful because you might need to undo these dents as a whole, or dial up the opacity of your sculpt to go between a more dented or less dented version of your robot. Add dents to all three body parts, the arms, and the legs. Remember that only some of the parts have sculpt layers, and use more care when you are sculpting parts that don't have layers. If you change any parts that don't have sculpt layers, you will not be able to dial back their opacity.

5. Always look at your reference material for how the dents manifest themselves on the surface of metal vehicles or objects.

6. After you are finished sculpting, dial the opacity on the various layers of the parts to get to a weathered look you like.

7. Save your work as `bertie_stage_02.mud` after you are finished with each part. It is vital that you always save your work at intervals where you are happy with it. You can set an option to remind you to save at intervals you specify, by choosing Windows → Preferences in Windows (or Mudbox → Preferences on the Mac) and selecting the Save Reminder setting in the Status Line rollout (Figure 3.35). The reminder appears in the status line as a blinking red *Save Text*.

Sculpting Scratches

In this section, you will do the same thing you did when sculpting the dents, but now you will use different tools than the Flatten tool and will sculpt on a layer called `scratches` Figure 3.36). Continue from the prior

Figure 3.34

Flatten tool properties

Figure 3.35

Save reminder and interval setting in the preferences

section or load the `bertie_stage_02.mud` file from the `Chapter 3\bertie\Mudbox` folder on the DVD.

1. Click the Sculpt tool and use the properties in Figure 3.37. Create the falloff in the Falloff properties by clicking on the two middle curve points and dragging them to the bottom-left corner. This creates a very sharp point for your tool.

2. Using different tool Size and Strength settings, make some scratches on the surface of your model, making sure you are working on the model's `scratches` sculpt layer that we created. You can also enhance some of the surface details, such as the front panel, by adding more detail in the form of protrusions and indentations around the edge.

3. Select the Steady Stroke property to make linear scratches. Experiment with changing the Steady Stroke Distance.

4. Test out the Sculpt tool with different Strength and Size settings.

5. When you are finished, use the opacity dials to adjust the opacity of your `scratches` sculpt layers to a level that looks good to you.

6. Save your work as **bertie_stage_03.mud** after you are finished with each part.

Figure 3.36

Scratches

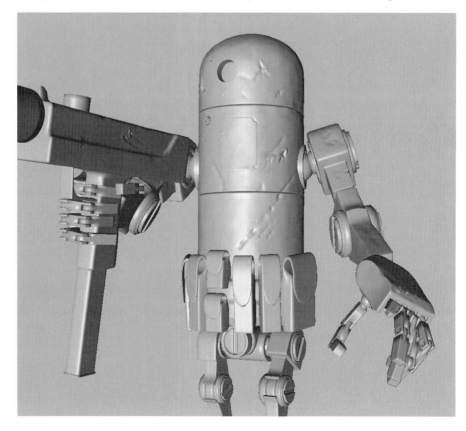

Sculpting Rust

Again, you will do the same things as in the two previous sections, but now you will sculpt some rust in areas where you feel Bertie would get corroded from water, engine liquid leaks, and general weather. You will mostly use the Spray tool with a stamp to achieve this look. The resulting sculpt will have some more weathering in the form of corroded edges and streaks (Figure 3.38). Continue from the prior section or load the `bertie_stage_03.mud` file from the `Chapter 3\bertie\Mudbox` folder on the DVD.

1. Turn on Ambient Occlusion by clicking the eye icon next to it in the Viewport Filters tray. Click on the Ambient Occlusion viewport filter so that the properties show up in the Properties tray and make sure they match Figure 3.39. This will darken corners and indentations on the model to make the sculpting detail stand out. In 3D applications, Ambient Occlusion is a render layer that is created after the model is finished. In Mudbox, you can turn it on and off and work in real time with it on. This again is a powerful capability because it gives you a good idea of how your final Ambient Occlusion layer will look, and also you can sculpt and see the depth and corners darkened to add more realism to your model.

2. Adding rust is very similar to what you did with the egg in Chapter 1. You will be using the Spray tool from the Sculpt Layers tray, with the preferences and stamp shown in Figure 3.40.

Figure 3.37

Sculpt tool preferences

Figure 3.38

Corrosion and rust

Figure 3.39

**Ambient Occlusion
preferences**

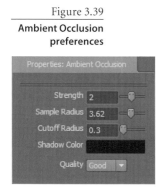

Figure 3.39

**Ambient Occlusion
preferences**

Figure 3.40

**Spray tool
properties**

3. Using different tool Size and Strength settings, sculpt some rust streaks and corrosion in areas of your model where water or a constant flow of corrosive fluids would create rusty texture. Remember to do your rust sculpting in the model's `rust` sculpt layer. Look at reference material on rusty metal to see the properties of a rusty surface, and replicate this on your model as best as you can. The Ambient Occlusion viewport filter gives you direct feedback on how the rusty areas will look.

4. When you are finished, use the opacity dials to adjust the opacity of your `rust` layer to a level that looks good to you.

5. Save your work as `bertie_stage_04.mud` after you are finished.

Sculpting Pouches

The last things to sculpt are the pouches. This is a departure from what you have been doing so far because you are not going to add detail to anything. Instead, you are going to sculpt an organic shape of ammo pouches from a blocky base mesh (Figure 3.41). To do this, you will hide the rest of the model and sculpt the pouches one by one.

The pouches have limited geometry, so you won't be able to add a lot of high-frequency detail. However, you will be able to provide a general shape of what a pouch looks like. When we are looking at the entire robot as a whole, the relative scale of the pouches is small, and any high-frequency detail would not be visible.

In this section, you will use the Grab, Bulge, Sculpt, Repeat, and Flatten sculpt tools. You can follow along with the `Chapter3-sculpting_pouch.mov` video in the `Chapter 3\videos` folder on the DVD. Here are the steps:

1. Using the Objects selection tool, select any pouch you want to start with.

2. Choose Display → Hide Unselected to hide all the parts except the pouch you selected.

The first tool you will use is the Grab tool, which moves the surface you click in the direction you drag the mouse or stylus. It is best to use it on lower subdivision levels to block the general shape of your sculpture. The Grab tool has a Direction property in the Advanced section of the properties that will constrain the movement of the tool to the direction of the Screen (which is the default), XY, YZ, or XZ planes, or Averaged Normal (the average of the normals of the surface). The Orient to Surface option in the Grab tool properties is extremely useful.

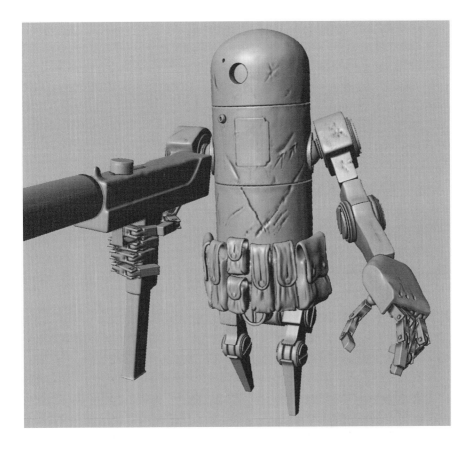

Figure 3.41
Sculpted pouches

3. Press Pg Dn until you are on subdivision level 3. Use the Grab tool to change the shape of the pouch to one that looks more realistic. Adjust the Size and Strength properties of the tool as needed by pressing the Shift+B and Shift+M keys; this may require a little bit of experimentation. Drag the edges of the top and bottom corners of the pouch to match Figure 3.42.

4. Press Pg Up to get back to level 5. Use the Bulge tool with a Size of 10 and a Strength of 2 to bulge out the bottom of the bag to accommodate for content that would be weighing it down and creating folds on the surface. Change the Size to 4, and press Ctrl to reverse the bulge to go inward in the top and bottom center of the pouch (Figure 3.43). Place the brush where the clasp or button would go, and click and drag your mouse or stylus in a small circular motion. If the bulge is too rounded, you can use the Flatten tool to flatten it out.

5. Use the Sculpt tool to create some indented seam folds at the bottom two corners of the pouch and a line for the buttonhole (Figure 3.44). Remember to use Shift to smooth out any severe strokes.

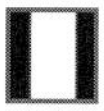

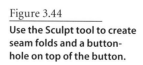

6. Click the Repeat tool and choose the rectangular-looking stamp. With a Size of 3, Strength of 2, and Stamp Spacing of 1, click and drag your mouse or stylus on the edge of the pouch flap (Figure 3.45). You may want to use Steady Stroke with a Distance of 3 to get a more stable stroke.

   Use the Bulge, Grab, Smooth, and Sculpt tools to further refine your pouch shape. Remember that you don't need to add too much detail, just enough to make the shape stand out when you are looking at the entire robot.

7. Repeat these operations on the rest of the pouches, because it will be good exercise for you with the various tools and their properties.

8. Save your work as **bertie_stage_05.mud** after you are finished.

There is a saved version of bertie_stage_05.mud on the DVD for you to load and examine.

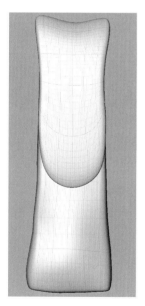

Figure 3.42

Blocking in the general shape

Figure 3.43

Use the Bulge tool to bulge out the pouch to accommodate for the weight of its contents.

Figure 3.44

Use the Sculpt tool to create seam folds and a buttonhole on top of the button.

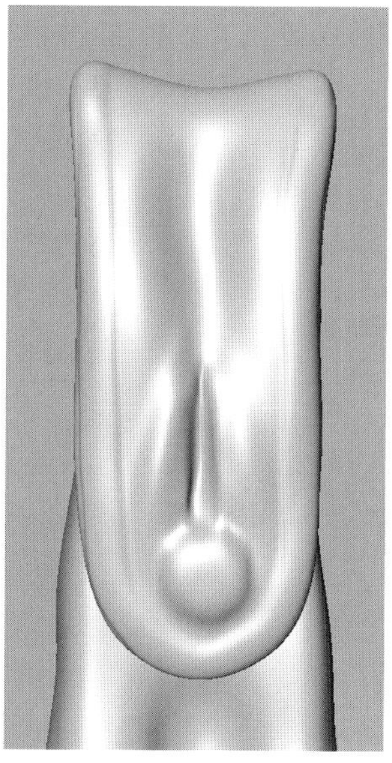

Figure 3.45

Use the Repeat tool on the pouch flap to create edging.

Summary

In this chapter, you have gone through the requirements of a good base mesh:

- Make sure your model is composed of quads. Occasional triangles or n-gons are acceptable only if you have a good place to hide them on the model or have a hard-surface model.

- Make sure that all the quads in your model have an aspect ratio as close to 1:1 as possible. If you find that you have skinny, long rectangles in your model, add some edge rings or edge loops to make the quad distribution more even.

- Make sure the valency for all your poles is at 5 or less. If you absolutely need to have any poles that are more than 5, make sure they are tucked away somewhere not visible.

- Make sure your topology is geared for sculpting.

- Make sure that your geometry is two-manifold geometry.

You learned about the definition of UVs and the importance of a good UV layout when you need to export maps from Mudbox:

- Make sure you have no overlapping UV shells, or lines or pixels within your UV shells. This is especially the case for areas of dense pixel concentration.

- Make sure you have a spacing of at least 4 to 6 pixels between the UV shells and the borders of the 0 to 1 UV space.

- Make sure all of your UVs have the correct UV winding order.

- Make sure that your UV shells don't manifest extreme stretched or compressed areas.

You went through the importance of a good naming convention and exporting your .obj files with the Groups option set to On. You learned the importance of posing and scaling your base mesh before you bring it in to Mudbox. Finally, you added sculpting details to the body of Bertie the robot and did your first sculpt in the form of a pouch.

You will be going through another more detailed sculpting session in Chapter 5, but hopefully by now you have a very good idea of how some of the main tools work and how their preferences can affect the surface of your model. Next you will paint Bertie.

CHAPTER 4

Painting and Texturing an Imported Model

In the preceding chapter you imported an `.obj` model from Maya and added some paneling detail, weathering, and wear and tear to the surface geometry. In this chapter, you will pick up from where you left off with Bertie, Ashley Wood's robot, to paint and texture it for its final output. However, before you do, you need to familiarize yourself with a few concepts.

This chapter includes the following topics:

- **Texture-painting models**

- **Laying out UV maps and arranging UV shells for texture painting**

- **Creating texture maps**

- **Using materials and textures**

- **Working with paint and texture layers**

- **Using specular, gloss, and bump maps**

- **Gathering reference images**

- **Painting Bertie**

Texture-Painting Models in 2D and 3D

The leading 2D texture-painting tool is Adobe Photoshop because of its wide range of paintbrushes, layering and masking features, and comprehensive set of image-processing capabilities.

In the not-too-distant past, 3D models were exclusively painted in Photoshop or other 2D image-processing and painting tools; texture artists had to paint all the textures in 2D on UV maps. One of the challenges with this process is interpreting how a 2D image will wrap around a 3D object without stretching or compressing textures. Another challenge is painting uniform patterns across seams that are cut when creating UV shells, because these UV shells are not connected on the flattened 2D UV layout. A third challenge is that, when you paint in 2D, you constantly have to go back and forth between Photoshop and your 3D application to see whether the results are acceptable.

With the introduction of 3D painting tools, this process has become easier; users can paint directly onto the 3D models in 3D. Mudbox, in addition to being a powerful and versatile digital sculpting application, provides some unique and extremely useful digital painting and texturing capabilities.

These 3D painting capabilities remove most of the barriers of 2D painting applications because you can paint directly on your model in 3D, across UV seams, and see the results of your brush strokes in real time. This does not remove the need for a 2D compositing or image-processing application such as Photoshop, but it is a huge time-saver and gives you greater creative control over the texture-painting process. The introduction of versions 2010 and 2011 now further integrates Mudbox with Photoshop by enabling you to save to Photoshop's native .psd file format, preserving the layers that can be brought directly into Photoshop.

Another big advantage of Mudbox is that you can paint on your 3D model in layers. This is useful because you can have layers that represent different details on the surface of the model. One layer could be a base material of the model; the second could be a paint layer; the third could be weathering such as dust or dirt or rust; the fourth could be decals, emblems, or posters; the fifth could be glossiness or shine; and the sixth could be bumpiness of the surface. Just as you can in sculpting layers, you can adjust the opacity and blend modes of these paint layers to show as much or as little of each layer to get the desired look.

The new Flatten to UV Space feature introduced in Mudbox 2011, which is accessible through Mesh → Flatten to UV Space, enables you to paint or edit textures on a flattened representation of the original. You can also use the Pinch or Grab tools to perform basic UV position adjustments on the model in this mode. This is extremely useful to get an idea of how your textures are distributed on the UV map and make adjustments to the textures and the UVs themselves to accommodate the results you want.

Laying Out UV Maps and Arranging UV Shells for Texture Painting

I mentioned UVs in the preceding chapter and indicated that they represent coordinates on the surface of the model. You will revisit them in this chapter as they pertain to texture painting. All UV editing on a model needs to be finalized before painting and texturing your 3D model in Mudbox to avoid misaligning UVs and your painted areas. (Chapter 6, "Digital Sculpting Part II," covers how to lay out UVs for a sculpture by using Headus UVLayout.)

For the most part, UV maps for a model take up one square UV tile, or quadrant. Some applications, such as Mudbox and Maya, support UV shells distributed to multiple-square UV tiles. The benefit of distributing the UV shells across multiple UV tiles is that you get more room per shell to add detail to your texture. However, for the most part, you will do all your UV work in the first quadrant, or 0 to 1 tile.

Whether UV shells are laid out in one quadrant or many quadrants, the UV shells should not overlap. Overlapping UV shells will cause unpredictable results in 3D applications and in your final result. The only time UV shells can overlap is when you intend to take advantage of symmetry in your model and save texture space by overlapping symmetrically identical UV shells precisely on top of each other to reuse a part of the image that is symmetrical or repeated on the model.

Make sure to leave 4 to 6 pixels of space between UV shells, and between UV shells and the four borders of the UV tile. If you fail to do so, the textures will bleed from one shell to the other, producing streaking lines on the paint you apply to your model.

The shells in your UV map can be off scale. For example, if you are texture-painting a human being and you need more space to paint the details of a face, you would want to scale up the UV shell that corresponds to the head. However, if you do that, you will have broken the proportionality of the shells. For example, if you have all the shells in the same proportion and you apply a checkered pattern to a human model, the checkered pattern will be uniform throughout the body (see Figure 4.1).

However, if you apply the same checkered pattern to the model on which you scaled up the head, you will notice smaller checkered squares on the head than on the body (Figure 4.2), because you have more UV space allocated to the head.

If you need more UV space for the entire body because, for example, you need to paint intricate tattoos on the body in addition to details on the face, you can scale up all the shells and distribute them across multiple UV tiles. Note that even though you can distribute UV shells across multiple UV tiles, they should be laid out so they are contained within the square UV tile and do not cross any UV tile borders.

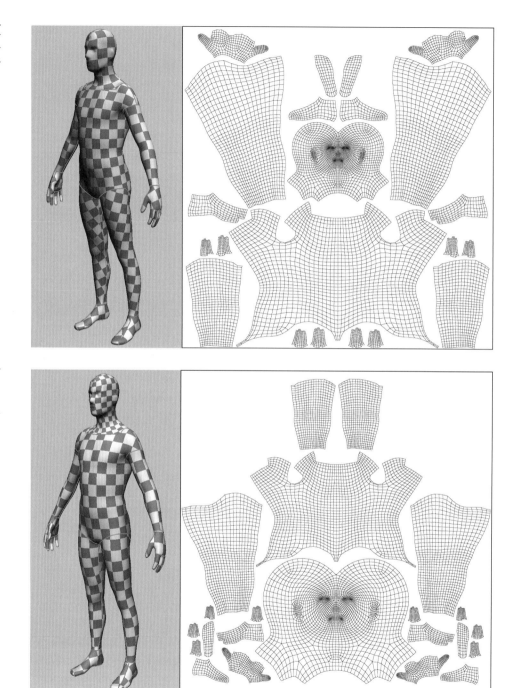

Figure 4.1

A uniform check-
ered pattern on pro-
portional UVs

Figure 4.2

The checkered
pattern appears
smaller on the head
because more UV
space is allocated
to it.

The way to determine the distribution of shells to UV tiles depends on the following factors:

Variation of detail on the model If you have a section with minimal variation in color and texture detail, and the UV shells corresponding to the section are receiving a uniform color, then you can give its UV shells less UV space. On the flip side, if you have sections that need more detail, such as a head with facial details or a mechanical part with intricate surface paneling and text, you want to give the shells corresponding to that section more UV space.

Game requirements For games, you will want to constrain all of your UV shells into one UV tile because games need to load textures really fast and game machines need to manipulate models in real time. Games might even cram UVs for multiple objects or characters on one UV tile.

Texture types UV shells might also be distributed among different tiles by type of texture—for example, all metal UVs on a metal texture UV tile, all leather UVs on a leather texture UV tile, skin textures on a skin tile, and so on.

UV space usage Rotate and move the UV shells to take up minimal room in the UV tile and maximize UV space usage. Try to have the least number of shells possible because this maximizes the amount of utilized UV space. This must be, of course, balanced by making sure you have the minimal stretching or compression of UVs, which is usually done by cutting more seams or dividing UVs into more shells.

Creating Texture Maps

Texture maps are 2D images that you generate either in 2D image-processing applications such as Photoshop, or in a 3D painting application such as Mudbox. These 2D images are then wrapped around your model much like wrapping paper around a present.

After you have laid out the UVs, you can output the UV map as a flat bitmap image. Most UV layout tools, such as Headus UVLayout or UV Texture Editor in Maya, allow you to output the UVs in any desired map size. Usually these are 1K (1024×1024), 2K (2048×2048), or 4K (4096×4096) bitmap images. This UV image will serve as a good base layer to use if you are going to do any 2D painting on your model or as a point of reference to see where the various paint regions align with the model.

All the texture painting you will be doing will be on the tiles on which you laid out your UVs. *Texture maps* are generally RGB or RGBA 2D images in one of the nonlossy, popular image formats such as TIF, TGA, or OpenEXR. You can create one or multiple texture maps to apply to your UV map. Multiple images are subsequently composited as layers and flattened to form the final texture map that will be mapped on your model for its final presentation.

Using Materials and Textures

We can generally tell what an object is made of by the way it looks. This is because our eyes and minds are trained to look for certain characteristics that distinguish one object from another. These characteristics help us discern glass from metal, wood from plastic, and rubber from rock. We are so good at this that we don't even think about it; we just know from years of experience.

When we are creating computer-generated imagery, we need to convince these well-trained eyes and minds, whose suspension of disbelief can be stretched only so far, that what they are seeing in the image looks like the object in the real world. To do this, we have to reverse-engineer what our eyes see to create believable or even stylistic objects that convey characteristics of the world around us. Even though software has the capability to generate these characteristics, we still need to know how to manipulate the features to get the desired appearance.

To do this, the first step is to start training our eyes to look at characteristics that differentiate the appearance of the objects around us. What is it about the characteristic appearance of an object that makes it metal, plastic, marble, or glass? How does it reflect, refract, or absorb light? What surface properties define rubber, velvet, brushed metal, rust, and water? Why can we still tell what something is made of even under varying lighting conditions such as candlelight, neon, or sunlight?

Two characteristics to take note of when looking at objects are their material and texture. People new to the field mistake one for the other or start out thinking they are one and the same, but material and texture are, in fact, two distinct characteristics of the way an object looks.

In 3D applications, both materials and textures can be represented with *shaders*, which are sets of instructions that tell the rendering software how to render a material with a set of properties that can be adjusted by the user to represent real-world objects.

Understanding Materials

A *material* is the base substance of an object—for example, metal, wood, glass, or rubber. Most everything around us is never in its pure material form, but many characteristics of the base material still come through in its final appearance. We can identify these characteristics by many surface properties such as color, surface finish, and the way light reflects the world around it on the surface of the object. For example, we may know that a table is made of painted wood because we can see the wood grain on the surface. We know whether a toy is plastic or metal, even if it is painted, by the reflective properties and graininess of its surface.

Materials are generated in 3D packages by sets of code that represent mathematical algorithms; as I mentioned earlier, these are called shaders. Some commonly used shaders in 3D packages are Lambert, Blinn, Phong, Lafortune, and others. Many of these shaders have properties, such as reflectivity, transparency, and translucency, that can be dialed in to produce characteristics of real-world materials.

Mudbox has four shaders you can use to assign materials to your model: Mudbox Material, Simple Blinn, Lit Sphere, and CgFX. Of the four, the one you will use the most is the Mudbox Material because it supports most material shading needs. This is because it can represent both Blinn and Lafortune shading models. By adjusting the properties of the Mudbox shaders (for example, color, glossiness, or specularity of materials), we can get them to simulate materials we see around us.

The properties of the Mudbox Material shader are more limited than some of the properties found in shaders in other 3D packages and renderers. However, the big advantage of the Mudbox Material shader is that it displays the results of changing the properties of your material in real time, while you are moving the camera around your model and sculpting on it or painting it.

By default, models in Mudbox are assigned the default Mudbox Material. You can edit the properties of this material or assign other premade materials from the Material Presets tray. This is also the material you should use if you intend to paint or assign textures to a model because it provides texture channels for Diffuse, Specular, Gloss, Incandescence, Bump Map, Normal Map and Reflection Mask.

The simple Blinn shader is provided in Mudbox for computers equipped with older, unsupported, or low-performance graphics cards to provide basic sculpting and limited color properties. It does not provide texture channels for painting on your 3D model, and it should be used only if you have unsupported or low-performance graphics cards and intend to use Mudbox for digital sculpting.

Creating, Assigning, and Deleting Materials

To create a material and assign it to any selected object, choose Create → Materials → Mudbox Material. Alternatively, you can right-click the model in the 3D view or its name in the Object List and choose Assign New Material → Mudbox Material.

To assign an existing material to a model, right-click the model either in the 3D view, or its name in the Object List, and click Assign Existing Material. Then select a material from the list of materials we have already created in the scene.

To edit a material, right-click the model and select Edit Material. Alternatively, you can select the material in the Object List and then edit its properties in the Properties window.

You can delete a material only if it is not assigned to an object. To delete a material, right-click it in the Object List and select Delete Material.

Using Textures and Patterns

Although a material defines the basic properties of a surface (for example, its overall color, glossiness, and reflectivity), *textures* or *patterns* define visual detail that give the surface a more realistic look. Consider the example of a brick wall. You may pick a non-reflective red color as the material, but the grout, the aging, and the weathering of the bricks would have to be done with a texture or pattern. Another example is a metal pipe that would be assigned a semiglossy material but would need texture to denote aging, peeling paint, rust, and wear and tear from its surroundings.

Maya and other 3D applications have computational shaders such as granite, leather, or rock that can be aggregated in a shader network to simulate textures. These can be very helpful in generating naturally occurring textures if they are competently layered to disguise their computational patterns that our extremely skilled eyes can easily detect. However, Mudbox does not contain any of these computational textures. If you want to use them in Mudbox, you will have to generate them in a 3D application that supports them, export the maps, and then import them as paint layers in Mudbox.

Mudbox does, however, let you paint directly on a model by using the paint tools to create texture maps. You can also project imported digital camera or texture library images and paint them on in layers to create a more realistic appearance of real-world surfaces.

The most significant skill you need to create realistic-looking images is your vision and the ability to interpret surfaces into their various layers of textures. It is important to discern the overall pattern that a surface manifests, and then block those patterns in as a material or overall base coat texture, and finally discern the different layers of more-specific textures and paint those on. Open the files `Rust Stages` and `Barrel patina` in the `Chapter4\reference` folder of your DVD. Look at the rusted pipe and take note of the different layers of rust, the color, luster, surface detail, and texture of the pipe. Now look at the barrel. It is a pretty simple image, but if you were to re-create it, you would have to represent a metal barrel that is painted, rusty in spots, and that has developed a patina and various layers of dirt patterns on it. Although it is not possible to represent every detail on a surface, we should train our eyes to see the characteristics that stand out and then be able to fool the viewer's suspension of disbelief into interpreting the characteristic details of the real world in our models.

Working with Paint and Texture Layers

Just as the grand masters put down layers of oil paint on canvas to paint realistic images, you need to layer textures on your image to achieve a believable look to your model.

These layers can be complementary to a specific pattern on the surface. In Chapter 1, "Getting Your Feet in the Mud: The Basics of the Mudbox Production Pipeline," for the egg we used a base coat layer that we painted on, added a projection-painted layer of the image of an egg on top of that layer, and then adjusted the opacity of the two to get a more realistic look. Layers can also represent different surface patterns such as drips, rust, patina, and decals.

Paint layers are different from sculpt layers because with sculpt layers, each object can have its own subdivision levels and one or multiple layers independent from the other objects in the scene. However, with paint layers, objects that are in the UV map together are all on the same paint layer. As you are painting on different parts of your model, you are changing only one paint layer.

Paint layers cannot be subdivided; to add finer detail to a paint layer, give the texture map associated with the layer higher pixel resolution. Even on a model with a few subdivisions, you can paint a very detailed and nonpixelated texture map if you chose a large texture map size such as 4K or 8K.

We control the results of layering texture maps in Mudbox by the order and opacity of the layers. The ordering is done top to bottom, with the topmost layer in front (as the outermost layer on the model), and the subsequent layers behind it in order (inside the model, like layers of an onion). The opacity is controlled by a slider that ranges from 0 to 100, where 100 is fully visible and 0 turns off the layer completely.

In 2D or compositing applications such as Adobe Photoshop or Corel Painter, you have long been able to add layering effects including multiplication, addition, hue, soft light, and so forth. Mudbox 2011 introduces the ability to apply some of those compositing effects to your Mudbox paint layers as layer blend modes. You are now able to use Multiply, Add, Screen, and Overlay paint layers to produce various blending or compositing functions.

Blending layers is extremely useful because certain effects need these blending layers to work effectively. For example, if we extract an ambient occlusion map, or generate one in another 3D application, the way to apply it to the model would be to Multiply the layer it is on to the overall paint layer stack. This will ensure that the occluded darker areas show up in the composite while the other areas do not. We will go into blend paint layers in depth, and see their effects in Chapter 8, "3D Painting."

It is important to know that the Mudbox Material shader has various channels that can have layers of their own. These channels are Diffuse, Specular, Gloss, Incandescence, Bump Map, Normal Map, and Reflection Mask for the Mudbox Material in Mudbox 2011, and Diffuse, Specular and Specular2, Gloss and Gloss2, Bump Value, and Reflection Mask for the 2009 and 2010 versions. The Mudbox Material used in versions 2009 and 2010 can still be used with later versions to maintain compatibility. As mentioned, all these channels can have multiple layers or maps of their own. The Diffuse channel contains the color maps. The Specular and Specular2 channels contain the highlight and fringe highlight maps. The Gloss and Gloss2 contain the size and fringe size maps for the specular reflection. The Bump Value channel contains the bump maps, and the Reflection Mask channel contains reflection maps that mask and restrict reflections.

One last important aspect to know about layers is transparency. For example, if you have a layer that has decals on it, you need the decals to show up on the surface of the model, but not the areas on the layer surrounding the decal.

The transparency is achieved with the image's alpha channel, which stores the transparency information for each pixel. Just as the RGB (red, green, and blue) channels store information about the amount of red, green, or blue each pixel has, the alpha channel stores information about how transparent each pixel is. If the alpha value is white, the pixel is opaque; if it is black, then it's fully transparent. The different levels of transparency are represented by 256 values of white to black.

By default, all the file formats for paint layers in Mudbox are created with an alpha channel. However, if you are importing images as texture maps into Mudbox, and you want details from inner paint layers to show through parts of your imported image, you need to make sure the image you are importing includes an alpha channel, that is, it is an RGBA image. Look at the file formats in Chapter 2, "The Mudbox User Interface," to determine which ones have an alpha channel.

Using Specular, Gloss, and Bump Maps

Like texture maps, specular, gloss, and bump maps are 2D images that denote where the surface of the model is shiny, glossy, or bumpy. This is usually done with value, meaning that areas on the specular or gloss map that are lighter or white are the shiniest or glossiest, while the darker colors are duller and less glossy.

The surfaces of objects do not reflect light evenly. For example, if you look at someone's face, even though it has the same skin throughout, there are spots such as the nose or the forehead that might be shinier than other areas because of some surface oil, so they have a different specularity than the rest of the face. A car's surface might have a different shine or specular value in areas that are more prone to friction than those that are not. Even a shiny surface such as the cover of this book might have different specular values from fingerprints or scratches.

The different values of gray on a bump map denote relief on the surface. Darker areas with less value are indented, whereas lighter values protrude from the surface of your model.

In general, these maps are grayscale, but they could be in color. Of course, if they are in color, only the value of the image will be used.

Gathering Reference Images

Whether we are creating something that does or does not exist in our world, we still need to base it on something that has visual familiarity. The best way to do this is to find objects that represent that familiarity either in the form of images or in the real world.

With the advent of digital photography, Internet image searches, and photo-sharing sites such as Flickr, Picasa, and Photobucket, you can find thousands upon thousands of images of what you are looking for. It is a good idea to devote a sufficient amount of time to reference gathering before you sculpt or paint your model. Digital images are plentiful and extremely useful, but it's also helpful to go out and physically look at your subject matter. Images can never substitute for walking around your subject, touching it, smelling it, squinting your eyes at it, or viewing it in different lighting conditions.

All sorts of reference images need to be compiled. As you progress in your career, you will start putting together a reference library that you tap into again and again for your sculpting and texture-painting needs. For bigger projects with big pipelines, reference images will be given to you by an art director or the art department, but it's always helpful to augment that with reference material of your own if possible.

Reference images can have many aspects, and you should gather your information to cater to most if not all of them. The types of reference materials include the following:

Environmental setting Gather reference images of location and setting indicating where your model will be in your final output, the environment around it, the weather conditions, the age of the environment, similar objects in that setting, and so forth.

Color Color is a powerful communication vehicle that sets the mood of a scene and needs to be balanced delicately to achieve the results you need. Gather references that show the values and saturation of the colors you want to convey. The color of an object can diametrically vary based on its environment and lighting; it's indispensible to have images of the colors you want to convey in their natural setting so you can simulate these aspects in the environment to achieve the look you are going for in your reference.

Composition Another critical aspect of your final output is the juxtaposition of your model with respect to other models in its environment and surroundings. This adds visual interest to your image and guides the viewers' eyes when they view the scene. It's best to have some images that give you visual cues of how to balance the composition of your scene to achieve the impact you want to achieve with your final output.

Lighting Just like color, lighting sets the mood of your output. You need to have reference images of the lighting settings you are looking to achieve. When you look at your lighting images, you need to ascertain where the different lights are emanating from that are showing on the surface of the subject. What is the light source? Is it the sun, the moon, a lightbulb, or a candle? What angle is the light coming from? How many light sources are there? Are they direct light sources, or are they bouncing or reflecting off surfaces around it? All these questions will need to be answered, and they will be easier to answer if you have reference images of the lighting you want to achieve.

Pose References of figures in the pose of your model will also be helpful, especially if the images are from multiple angles, so you can achieve the same pose on the model.

Materials and textures and stencils   Gather or take as many images as you can of materials that portray the same characteristics as what you want your model to look like. Get overall pictures as well as zoomed-in pictures that will give you more detail as to how the texture is formed. Not only are these references good to look at while you are working, but you can actually use them to either paint the texture on your model in a 2D image-processing application such as Photoshop or to projection-paint them as a stencil in Mudbox. You can also use desaturated and manipulated versions of these texture and material images as bump, specular, or gloss maps.

Stamps and Photoshop brushes   Reference images that represent various textures can also be used as tools to paint and sculpt with. When you see a pattern that you like, you can desaturate it and use the 256 levels of gray in it to sculpt relief on the surface of your model, or you can use it as a color image to add texture to your model.

Painting Bertie

As mentioned before, Bertie is a robot from Ashley Wood's various comic books and paintings. Even though I have all the books that his images are in, an Internet search also found collectible action figures of Bertie and various images of those action figures. I first created a reference folder of all the images I found. I also spent a good amount of time looking at the comic books, reading the stories, and thinking up scenarios that Bertie would be in.

Then, I thought of real-world materials and the wear and tear a robot like Bertie would manifest. I did a search for images of WWII tanks, metal barrels, and mechanical robots in extreme conditions and came up with some surfaces that I liked. I then determined the number and nature of paint layers I would need. I envisioned three distinct materials on my model of Bertie: the metal that makes up his body, the leather pouches, and the metal that makes up his gun.

I also determined that I would be working with four diffuse paint layers and one specular layer. The four paint layers would be as follows:

Base coat layer   This would be the metal base that Bertie is made from. Through my research, I found that big lumbering machines are made of galvanized metal sheets that are cut and bent into shape. Doing research on the Web and using Photoshop, I made a tileable galvanized metal texture (included as `galvanized_steel_tileable.tga` on the DVD in the `Stencils` folder). The Web has multiple tutorials on how to make tileable textures in Photoshop and other applications. As the paint would scratch off Bertie, this layer is what would show up underneath. This layer would mostly take care of the metal portions of Bertie, and I would paint the leather pouches a neutral leather color to set their base coat.

Paint layer   The paint layer would include the basic color of Bertie's different parts. His body would be a dark greenish-gray, the leather pouches would be black, and the gun would be dark gray steel.

Weathering layer This would be the grime, rust, and wear-and-tear layer.

Decal This layer would include all the spray-painted or glued-on insignia and stickers.

I also planned to include a specular layer that would distinguish between the various specularity areas of Bertie's body, gun, and leather pouches.

The Base Coat Layer

To start, you will make the base coat layer, which is the galvanized metal that will show up through scratches on the edges or when paint is scraped off.

You will be using two paint tools in this first section to create the base coat layer. They are the Paint Brush and the Projection tool:

Paint Brush This is the standard workhorse painting brush. It uses the chosen stamp and color to paint on the surface of your model. The Strength setting controls the opacity of your stroke. You can adjust the various properties to get the effects that you want with your stroke.

Projection tool This is one of the most useful and powerful tools in Mudbox. It allows you to paint portions of your stencil image onto the surface of your 3D model. It is useful for painting real-world textures from digital photos and images right onto the surface of your model. Make sure to retain the relationship of the stencil and the zoom level of your model. What you projection-paint is the exact representation of the stencil on the surface of the model at the zoom level at which you are on the model. For example, if you zoom out on the model so it is small on the screen and projection-paint on it, when you zoom back in, you will lose the detail of your stencil and get a distorted and blocky texture. This is because at that zoom level, you didn't paint enough texture information on the surface to account for the details of the stencil. Make sure you are projection-painting the stencil at the detail level that relates to the zoom level of your model, and refrain from zooming in and out to maintain the scale of your stencil on the surface.

To create the base coat layer, follow these steps:

1. Either load your last saved version of Bertie, or load the `bertie_stage_06.mud` file from the Chapter 4 folder from the DVD. This is my final project file for this chapter (Figure 4.3).

   Tumble the camera around and observe the various surface details on Bertie. Click the Viewport Filters tab and turn on Ambient Occlusion by clicking the circle to the left of it in the display column with an icon of an eye as the column heading. This darkens the various crevices to give the model surface a more realistic look. I will be going into depth as to what the settings are for the Ambient Occlusion viewport filter in Chapter 9, "Lighting and Rendering," but for now, choose a Strength setting of 4, a Sample Radius setting of 5, and a Cutoff Radius of 1.16. Leave Shadow Color blank, and choose a Quality setting of Best (see Figure 4.4) because it will render a better view of Bertie for you to look at. Note the various surface details.

Figure 4.3

Final painted version of Bertie

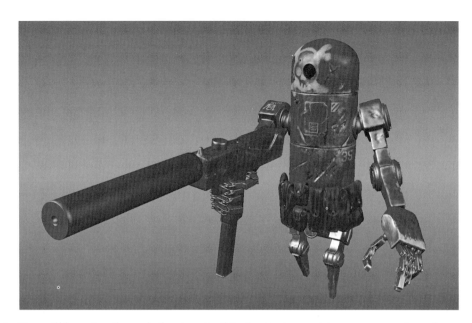

2. You will be going through the steps in this chapter to create your own version of a painted Bertie, but in the interest of saving space on the DVD to include more information for you, I unfortunately need to put you through a few extra steps of loading the final version and subtracting out layers and steps to get to the beginning of the stage. From the Select/Move Tools tray, click the Objects selection tool and click on any part of Bertie. After he is selected, click anywhere outside Bertie in the 3D view to remove the highlight. This will leave Bertie selected. In the Layers tray, click the Paint button and notice the five paint layers. Starting with the diffuse group, start from the top and click the little dot next to each one of the diffuse paint layers to hide them until you get to the base_coat layer (Figure 4.5). It is a pretty convincing paint-stripped metal robot. Now turn off the specular layer to see how much of the realism disappears.

3. In the Layers tray, right-click each of the paint layers and select Delete Selected from the menu. This might take a little bit of time while Mudbox processes each of the deletions, but it is unfortunately necessary to save room on the DVD for the material in the book. Then, turn off Ambient Occlusion in the viewport filter to get back to the original Bertie sculpt that you did in the preceding chapter (Figure 4.6). Save the scene just in case you need to start back from this stage and don't want to go through deleting all the layers. I have done a little bit more surface detailing using the process familiar to you from Chapter 3, "Detail-Sculpting an Imported Model," of using the Spray tool from the Sculpt Tools tray and a stamp. In this case, I used the bw_clifface.tif stamp to add more of a rough surface to Bertie after seeing pictures of tanks that had the same painted metal effect.

Figure 4.4

Ambient Occlusion settings

Properties: Ambient Occlusion		
Strength	4	
Sample Radius	5	
Cutoff Radius	1.16	
Shadow Color		
Quality	Best ▾	

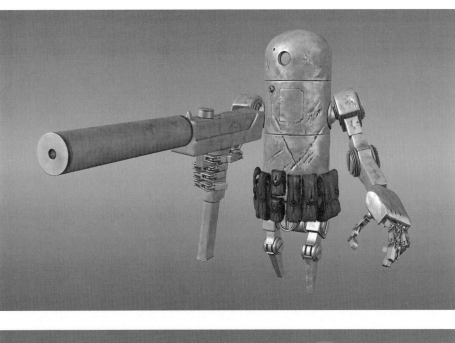

Figure 4.5

Base coat paint layer with specular map and Ambient Occlusion on

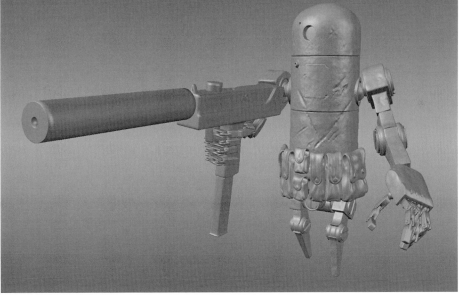

Figure 4.6

Original Bertie sculpt

4. For the material, leave everything as the default Mudbox material. You could change the color of your material to white, but it will not make any difference after adding the texture layers.

5. You are now at the starting point and need to add the base coat to Bertie. You could paint on the base coat, but it is easier to import a tileable texture of galvanized metal.

I created this one in Photoshop by using some references and various filters, and then using the Offset filter. You can find numerous free tutorials online explaining how to make a texture tileable in Photoshop. The result of my work is shown in Figure 4.7, which I have supplied for you on the DVD. To import a tileable texture, go to the Layers tray and click the Paint button. From the Layers tray's window menu, click Import Layer. From the DVD Stencils folder, select galvanized_steel_tileable.tga to load it as a paint layer. Double-click the name of the layer and type in the name **base_coat.**

For the most part, the tileable layer covers most of your model pretty well, except for some seams (Figure 4.8). To get rid of the seams, you will use the same texture as a stencil and paint over the seams.

6. Click the Image Browser tab and navigate to the Stencils folder on the DVD. Select it, choose galvanized_steel_tileable.tif in the Image Browser window, and click the Set Stencil button on the toolbar. Click back on the 3D View tab and you will see a dimmed version of the image on top of your model (Figure 4.9).

7. Next, you will scale the stencil to match what you have on the model. Notice the help messages on the bottom left of the screen. Click and hold down S on the keyboard and right-click and drag to scale up the image. Scale it up so it roughly matches the texture on the robot in Figure 4.9. Click the Projection tool in the Paint Tools tray and paint over the seam. Because this pattern is so random, this works really well to hide the seams. Press Q to hide your stencil and examine your work. Notice that

you have very easily gotten rid of the seam. Do the same for all the other seams that you feel stand out on the model. There are four on the head, one on the parts of the center body, and many on the edges of the arms. Do this for practicing projection painting, but don't worry about getting every seam because most of this layer will remain hidden. When you are finished, click on the Stencil tray and click Off to turn off your stencil.

Figure 4.7

Galvanized metal texture created in Photoshop

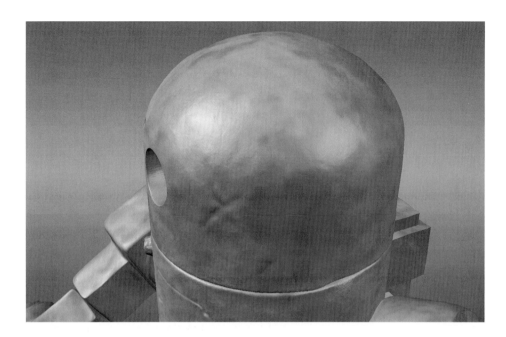

Figure 4.8

Seams when you import a layer

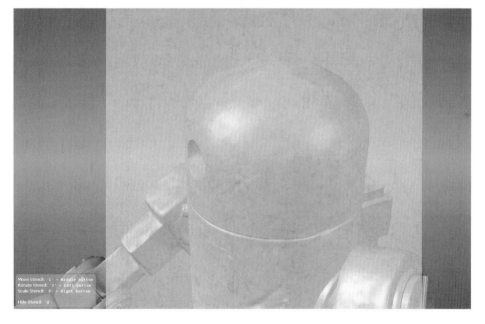

Figure 4.9

Galvanized metal stencil loaded

8. You now will put a different base coat on the ammo pouches because they are not made of metal. First, you will need to hide everything but the pouches to make it easier to work on them and not affect the rest of the model. In the Object List, select all the pouches either by clicking on the topmost pouch and then holding down the Shift key and clicking the bottommost pouch, or by holding down the Ctrl key and clicking each pouch in the Object List (Figure 4.10). As you select the pouches, they become highlighted with a yellowish sheen in the 3D View.

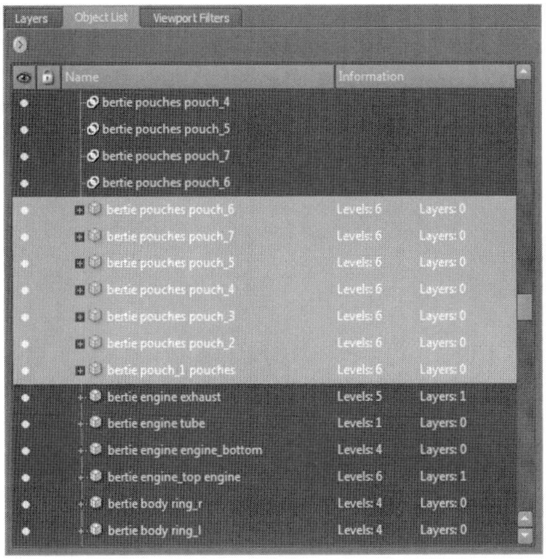

Figure 4.10

All the pouches selected in the Object List

Choose Display → Hide Unselected to hide the rest of Bertie and to display just the pouches (Figure 4.11). From the Select/Move Tools tray, click the Objects selection tool and click anywhere in the 3D view to deselect the pouches.

9. From the Paint Tools tray, select the Paint Brush tool. In the Properties tray for the Paint Brush tool, pick a dark gray or dark green color. With a large brush size and strength of 100, quickly apply uniform paint to the pouches.

10. Press U or choose Display → Show All to redisplay all of Bertie.

11. Save your work. Then right-click the base_coat paint layer in the list of Paint Layers and click Export Selected from the drop-down menu. Save the file as **base_coat.tga**.

Figure 4.11

Show pouches only

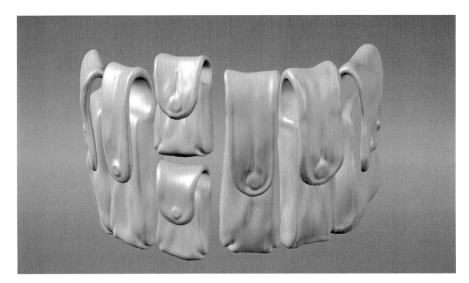

The Paint Layer

The next layer to be painted on is the paint layer. This will include the paint that is applied to Bertie, his gun, and his leather pouches. You will also strip away some of the paint in areas that could be scratched to reveal the galvanized metal beneath it. You will again block in the major swaths of paint and then texture the gun and pouches afterward.

Figure 4.12

Create New Paint Layer dialog box settings

1. Click the Layers window drop down menu and select New Layer from the drop-down menu. Create a new diffuse paint layer with a size of 2048 × 2048 (2K) and use the Save As Targa [8 bit, RGBA] format (.tga). Call it **paint** (Figure 4.12).

2. Right-click the layer you just created and click Export Selected. Export it as **paint.tga**. Now right-click it again and click Delete Selected. You could have skipped this step and just created your image in Photoshop, but this process automatically creates an alpha channel for you.

3. Load the paint.tga file into Photoshop or your favorite 2D painting application and fill it with a uniform military dark gray-green or any other color of your choice and save it back out as a 24-bit .tga file. You can alternately use the camo.tif camouflage pattern I have supplied in the Stencils folder on the DVD. However, you will have to use the same technique we used with the galvanized metal texture to projection-paint the camo pattern on the seams.

4. Click the Layers window drop down menu, click Import Layer, and re-import the paint.tga file. Make sure it imports on top of the base_coat layer.

5. Select the Paint Brush tool and then a black color. Color the two holes on Bertie's head black.

6. Select the Paint Erase tool from the Paint Tools tray, and reduce the size to a small size such as 2 or 4, and select a strength of around 10. Choose the bw_bristol2.tif stamp, and start erasing areas that you feel might have paint chipped or scratched off, such as the borders of the hatch, the insides of the scratched and gouged areas on the model's surface, the edges where Bertie's head and torso would turn, and the sharp edges of the arms, legs, and fingers (Figure 4.13).

   Look at references of paint chipping off tanks, tractors, and construction vehicles to get some ideas of how paint would chip or scratch off a painted surface. If you make mistakes, you can use Undo to go back a few steps, or you can delete the paint layer and re-import a pristine version of it. You may also want to save different versions of your paint layer by exporting texture map versions such as paint_slight.tga or paint_extreme.tga.

7. When you are happy with your results, it is time to move on to the gun. Select all the gun parts in the Object List (Figure 4.14) and click Display → Hide Unselected. From

the Select/Move Tools tray, click the Objects icon and click anywhere except on the gun in the 3D view to deselect the gun.

8. In the Image Browser, if you are not already there, navigate to the Stencils folder on the DVD, and select the metal_strip.jpg file. Set this as the stencil by clicking the Set Stencil icon on the toolbar.

9. From the Paint Tools tray, select the Projection tool and start painting on the gun. Notice that as you paint on a surface that faces you, and your brush goes over the edges, you get streaks when you rotate the model (Figure 4.15).

Figure 4.13

Paint chips and scratches

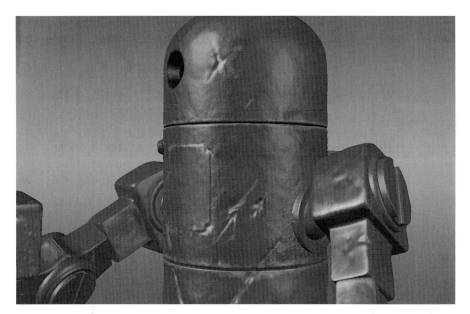

Figure 4.14

Select gun parts.

Figure 4.15

Streaks on the edge of a model while projection painting

This is overcome with two easy steps. First, make sure your brush fits on the surface you are painting and does not go over the edge. Then rotate the gun so that the top edge of the gun is facing you at an angle, as in Figure 4.15, and projection-paint on the angle. This is a good exercise for you to practice projection painting and not have any streaks because you will be working on flat, angular shapes as well as the cylindrical shape of the silencer.

10. Remember that you can move, rotate, and scale the stencil by holding down the S key and clicking and dragging with the middle, left, and right buttons of the mouse. You can also press the Q key to hide the stencil and view your model; another press of the Q key toggles the stencil back into view.

11. After you are finished applying the stencil as evenly as you can, it is time to paint over it with a dark gunmetal gray while letting some of the underlying details show. Pick the Paint Brush tool and a very dark gray color. Set your strength to about 2. Gently paint on top of the stencil pattern, letting bits and pieces of it show through to get a realistic metal finish (Figure 4.16).

12. Use the same process to color the leather pouches. Find a leather reference or shoot your own. Isolate the pouches by selecting them and hiding the rest of the model. Use your images as stencils and projection-paint the pouches.

13. Save your scene, and then right-click the paint layer in the list of Paint Layers and click Export Selected from the drop-down menu. Save it as `paint.tga`.

In addition to using the Paint Brush and Projection tools, you also used the Paint Erase tool in this section.

Paint Erase is used to remove paint from the currently active paint layer. If a model has multiple paint layers, erasing paint on one layer reveals the visible layers below it.

Figure 4.16

Gunmetal finish

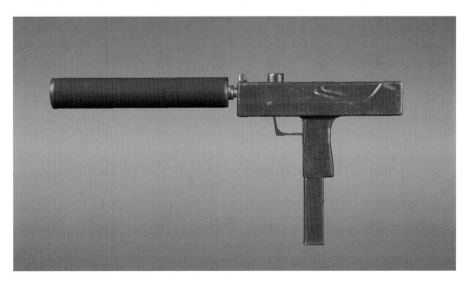

The Weathering Layer

For the weathering layer, you will add some more scratches, rust, dirt, and various other elements that would be the effects of a battle environment on Bertie. In this section, you will use two more painting tools, the Dry Brush tool and the Pencil tool. The only painting tool you will not use in this chapter is the Clone tool.

The Dry Brush tool is used to paint in areas that are either raised or recessed. By default, the Dry Brush tool paints protruded areas on your model; pressing Ctrl will paint recesses. The distance in from the top of a protruded area or the distance out from the bottom of a recessed area is controlled by the tool strength.

The Pencil tool is used to draw thin, sharp lines.

The Clone tool is similar to the Clone tool in Photoshop, which is used to sample paint on one area of a model and to apply it onto another area of the same model. To use the Clone tool, Ctrl+click the region you want the paint to be copied from. This sets the location of the starting point from which the Clone tool copies the paint. Then position the Clone tool where you want the cloned paint to appear and begin painting.

To create the weathering layer, follow these steps:

1. Click the Layers window drop down menu and select New Layer. Create a new diffuse paint layer with a size of 2048 × 2048 (2KB) and the Save As Targa [8 bit, RGBA] format (`.tga`), and call it **weathering**.

2. Use the Paint Brush tool to paint some dirt and scratches on Bertie.

3. Use the Projection tool and some of the rust textures in the `Stencils` folder on the DVD to paint some rusty areas on Bertie (Figure 4.17). Use some of the references you gathered as a guide to paint some rust streaks and spots.

Figure 4.17

Using the Projection tool to paint on rust and dirt

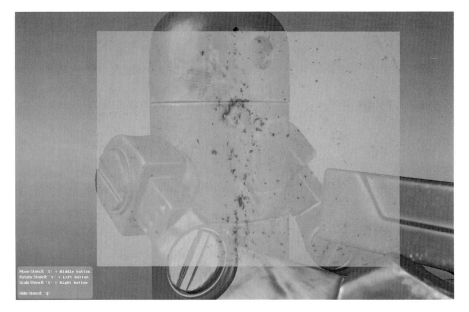

4. Find some surface areas where water would pool or areas where leaks would have made the surface scratches and dents rust over time. Paint some rust on those areas (Figure 4.18). Based on the Rust Stages.jpg image in the Chapter 4\reference folder, notice that rust has a more orange and light red color in deeper, fresher areas and gets more of a dull, dark, red sheen on the outer edges.

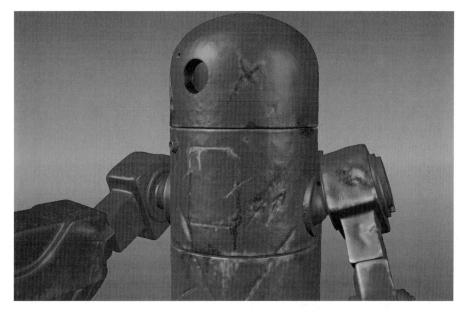

Figure 4.18

Rusty areas

5. Using the Dry Brush tool and a dark brown color, paint some dirt on areas that that have raised, sculpted surface patterns. This is a perfect brush to add a patina to your model.

6. Use the Pencil tool to draw fine lines to fill in scratches and areas where you want to add some fine detail.

7. Save your scene. Right-click the paint layer in the list of Paint Layers and click Export Selected from the drop-down menu. Save it as **weathering.tga**.

The Decal Layer

For the decal layer, you will use 512 × 512 bitmaps as stencils and paint insignia on Bertie:

1. Click the Layers window drop down menu and select New Layer from the drop-down menu. Create a new 2K TGA paint layer and call it **Decal**.

2. In the Image Browser, navigate to the Stencils\Decals folder on the DVD. I have created 11 decals you can use on Bertie. These are simple .tif image files with an alpha layer. You can load them in Photoshop to modify them. I have also included an empty template called decal_template.tif you can use to paint on to create your own decals. You can also use this template to make a 512 × 512 stamp too.

3. Pick a decal and set it as a stencil. Use the S key + left, middle, or right button combinations to scale, position, and rotate the decal.

4. Using the Projection tool, and the `bw_bristol2.tif` stamp, gently draw out the stencil on the surface of the model. If you set your tool Strength to 3, you can apply the stencil in an additive way, which gives it a more realistic look.

5. Save your scene, and then right-click the decal layer in the list of Paint Layers and click Export Selected from the drop-down menu. Save it as **decal.tga**.

The Specular Layer

The specular layer is a grayscale image that specifies what degree of specularity our surface has. We can indicate which parts are shiny and which parts are not. As you can see in Figure 4.19, the image on the left has a specular layer, and the image on the right does not. The image on the left looks far more realistic.

1. Click the Layers window drop-down menu and select New Layer from the drop-down menu. Create a new 2KB TGA specular layer and call it **specular**. You need to specify Specular as the channel in the Create New Paint Layer dialog box.

2. Note that the specular channel is not in the same grouping as the diffuse layers.

3. In the interest of time, I imported the `galvanized_steel_tileable.tga` image as the base specular layer, and used the Paint Brush tool to paint on areas that will be shinier by choosing light gray or white, and areas that will not be shiny with black.

Figure 4.19

Difference between a model that has a specular layer and one that does not

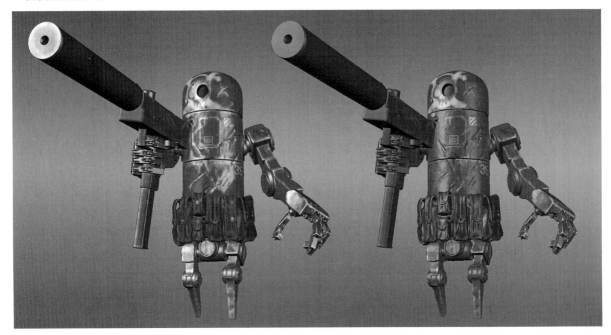

4. Because the robot and gun are of different metals, you can apply a different specular value to the gun than the rest of Bertie.

5. Notice that if we do a good job with the specularity, we will have a very realistic model, even if we turn the rest of the layers off (Figure 4.20).

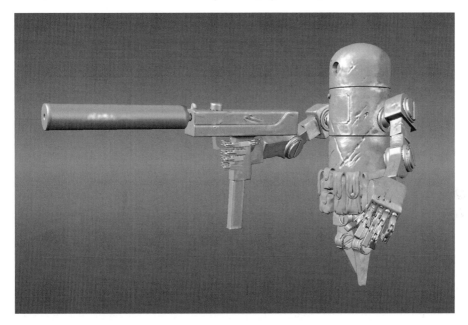

Figure 4.20

The model with only the specularity paint layer

6. Rusty areas are not specular, so make sure not to apply specularity to them. Some of the decals could be less or more reflective, so apply some specularity to them as needed.

7. Save your scene. Then right-click the specular layer in the list of Paint Layers and click Export Selected from the drop-down menu. Save it as `specular.tga`.

Mudbox allows us to paint a specular map in real time so we can see the final results as we are working on the model.

Compositing the Layers in Photoshop

Now that you are finished texture-painting the model, you can take the textures into Photoshop for further manipulation. Load the `Bertie_map_composite.psd` file (Figure 4.21) into Photoshop and notice the various layers and their opacity. This would be a good place to paint details that you were not able to do in Mudbox, because Photoshop has numerous brushes and layer-compositing tools that you can manipulate to get the exact look you are going for.

Figure 4.21

**Texture layers
manipulated in
Photoshop**

Summary

In this chapter, you have gone through texture-painting an imported model of Bertie the robot. You have seen how critical a good UV layout and efficient UV shell distribution in UV space are to the texture-painting process. You have learned the difference between materials and textures and how you need to reverse-engineer the look of objects around you to determine their material properties and their texture layers.

You also have learned about paint and texture layers and their functions in Mudbox. You have seen how in Mudbox you can use opacity levels and layer order to control how layers are composited on top of one another. You have learned the importance of gathering and compiling reference material to aid in the modeling and texture-painting process. And finally, you texture-painted Bertie with various layers to get the final result.

CHAPTER 5

Digital Sculpting, Part I

Digital sculpting is one of the two most significant applications of Mudbox, 3D painting being the second. In this chapter and the next, you will focus on the sculpting tools and the workflow to create a digital sculpture. In the next chapter, you will go through a fictional scenario of sculpting a lead female character in pose for a video game.

For this project, you will be in the early stages of development, during which you will need to determine a look for the character. Imagine that the producers and director have asked you to develop the look and come up with some 2D renders and turntables of the character to include in promotional material for the game. You are given little direction except that the character is a synthetic human, 20 to 30 years in age, athletic, nimble, and graceful. In this chapter, we will go over some of the basics leading up to the start of the project in the next chapter. We will cover the following topics:

- Understanding digital sculpting

- Planning the sculpture

- Sculpting in stages

- Determining the best base mesh for sculpting

- Understanding the Mudbox sculpt tools and their properties

Understanding Digital Sculpting

Digital sculpting software is relatively new, and there are significant advances almost annually that enable us to take advantage of the faster processors and graphics card technologies to create amazing art.

There are two areas of expertise required to become a good digital sculptor. First and foremost, you need a strong background in some aspects of fine art that are pertinent to digital sculpting. A solid background in artistic observation, gesture, composition, human and animal anatomy, and three-dimensional sculpting in a traditional physical medium, such as clay, will make a huge difference in the quality of your work. If you don't have this background, there are plenty of excellent schools, extension classes, books, DVDs, and online tutorials that can help. This is an area that all artists continuously develop and cultivate throughout life. The second area of expertise, of course, is understanding the workings of the Mudbox sculpting tools. Knowing which tools to use and developing a quick and smooth workflow will help bring your ideas and visions to fruition.

Planning the Sculpture

Planning is best done with a clear vision of the outcome. In production, requirements are handed to you by a producer or art director, and they vary in depth and granularity, ranging from minute detail to very broad-stroke concepts.

The easiest way to start is with concept art, a rough sketch, descriptive words, or reference pictures rather than a blank cube or sphere. As we discussed in Chapter 4, "Painting and Texturing an Imported Model," even if you are given strict guidelines about what is needed, it is always a good idea to gather as much of your own reference material as you can so you can draw inspiration and ideas from it. Do your own research on the topic by spending time finding video footage, images on the Internet, movies, or books on the subject matter. After you are familiar with the subject matter, sketch some examples or use some of your reference material to determine what your sculpture will look like.

It is also a good practice in the planning stages to think about some of the framing angles of your final sculpture. Even though sculpture is three-dimensional, some views will make the best features of the sculpture stand out. Although Michelangelo's *David* is a masterpiece viewed at any angle, it is placed, lit, and presented in the Gallerie dell'Accademia in a way that represents its best features for visitors. Also, photographers have photographed it at succinct angles that really bring out its beauty. If you are going to present your final material as a 2D image, it is best to have a good idea of which features of your model you will want to highlight.

The next stage in planning is determining the base mesh. In this case, you will model the base mesh in Maya. Even though the Human Body primitive mesh provided in Mudbox is an excellent base mesh to start with, you are going to start with a simpler base mesh that you can more easily pose. This will also be good practice for you, to understand how to build simple base meshes in case the ones provided in Mudbox will not work for your sculpture or subject.

Another important consideration during planning is the final pose in which you will present your character. You should also research this when you are building your reference sheet. Characters are designed, sculpted, and presented in the generic bind pose, similar to the pose that the Mudbox Human Body primitive mesh is in, but as discussed earlier in this book, it makes for a really boring presentation of the character. Although you will model our sculpture in Maya in the bind pose, you will pose the model with Mudbox 2011's new posing tools.

If the model you will be working on is to be animated, chances are that at some point it will undergo rigging in the pipeline's animation software, whether it is Maya, Autodesk Softimage, or 3ds Max. Rigging involves building a skeleton with joints and effectors (Figure 5.1), and then skinning or binding the parts of the model to corresponding areas of the skeleton. After binding the character, weight-painting determines the effect of the skeleton on the various parts of the skeleton rig. Further rigging actions include creating controls that make your model easy to manipulate and animate, and writing animation scripts to automate movement. A well-rigged model will enable you to easily pose the figure in multiple poses and then animate it. However, rigging the model yourself just to pose it is an involved and time-consuming process.

Figure 5.1

Skeleton rig in Maya

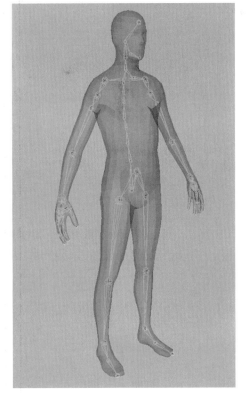

In earlier versions of Mudbox, you or someone else would have had to rig your model, pose it, and bring it in for sculpture. Another option would have been to use the transpose tools in ZBrush or 3D-Coat on your model, which would have required learning another program if you were not already familiar with it. However, the transpose tools in ZBrush are pretty powerful and well worth the investment in time to learn. A couple of excellent books with instruction on the transpose tools are *Introducing ZBrush* by Eric Keller and *ZBrush Character Creation: Advanced Digital Sculpting* by Scott Spencer (both published by Sybex in 2008). That said, the Posing toolset introduced in Mudbox 2011 makes it really easy to address most of your posing needs. I will cover the Posing toolset and posing our model in the next chapter.

Another consideration during the planning stage is the UV layout. If your sculpture is to be painted and presented in color, you have to make sure that your model has UVs. After posing our model, you will use Headus UVLayout to lay out the UVs. If you do not have the Headus tool, you can use Maya's UV tools, or whatever UV layout software you are familiar with. In my workflow, I use the tools that I am familiar with to get the fastest acceptable results.

I have found it extremely useful to spend a good chunk of a project's time on the planning stages, and to get as much personal and organizational approval then because it saves me tremendous amounts of time and frustration in the later stages of the work.

Sculpting in Stages

Even though certain views and lighting make a sculpture's prominent features stand out and its beauty shine, the sculpture still needs to work from all angles. Taking that into consideration is critical, to make sure the proportions and gesture of a sculpted model work from all angles before doing anything else.

In sculpting, the first stage of our sculpture or model is called the *blocking stage*. In this stage, we work on the overall shape, proportions, dimensions, flow, and gesture of the sculpture. Even though the outcome of this particular stage might not be very compelling to look at, it is by far the most important stage, because whatever is done correctly or incorrectly in this stage will only be amplified in the stages ahead.

When sculpting in clay, this stage is done by posing an armature and then putting on chunks of clay to get the general shape. In digital sculpting, this sculpting stage is done by creating a base mesh and posing it. There are many approaches to this. You could model and create your base mesh in a pose, or you could model a generic base mesh and pose it after the fact. You don't need a lot of geometry to get the general pose and gesture of a sculpture. In Figure 5.2, you can see that the general pose gesture and flow of the model are visible even though we have used a very low-polygon base mesh of about 600 polygons.

The next stage after the blocked-in model is to sculpt the surface shapes and planes that make up the surface of the model. Look at objects around you and imagine them as three-dimensional objects made of planes. A good example of this is the human head. Although you see no flat planes on a face, there are underlying planes that give the surface its shape. I have provided a Mudbox model on the DVD for you to see the planes of the face; it is called `planes_of_the_face.mud` and is in the `Chapter 5` folder of the DVD (Figure 5.3).

Figure 5.2

Blocked-in shape

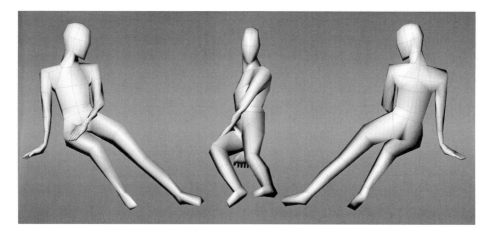

Figure 5.3

Planes of the face

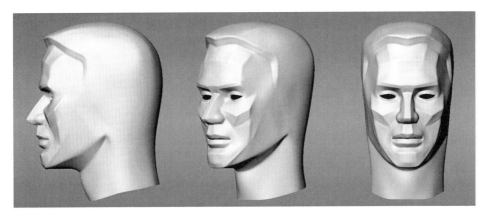

Please note that this model is not a 100 percent accurate representation, and there are some surfaces that look like planes but are not coplanar. However, this model does get the point across of how a human face is composed of different planes, and that these planes vary dramatically in their angles and the lines of intersection that make up the shape of the face.

Load the model from the DVD and tumble around it to get an idea of this concept. A common problem many beginning sculptors run into is not taking planes into consideration while sculpting. This makes their models fall apart the minute they turn it and look at it from a different angle. If you notice this issue with your sculptures, look at objects around you and see if you can determine the planes that make up the shape. It would also be a good idea to pick some of the meshes provided in Mudbox and use the Flatten tool to determine the planes that define the model.

After blocking in and sculpting the surface shapes comes the second sculpting stage that refines, or rounds, the planes to more-organic shapes while your sculpture is still loose and rough. The final stage is sculpting in the fine detail. Because the fine detail is what people see first and find interesting on a subject, beginning artists and sculptors tend to draw or sculpt these before going through the prior stages, and then notice that their sculpture somehow does not work. Perfectly sculpted wrinkles and pores on a face will only amplify mistakes made in the first two stages.

It is critical that you have all your proportions, gestures, and planes correct in the first blocking stage. Then you can focus on refining the shape and finally start adding the surface details.

Determining the Best Base Mesh for Sculpting

As mentioned, after you have your concept art, your digital sculpture has to have a starting point. This could be a premodeled mesh that either you or someone else models in a 3D application, or a 3D scan mesh, or one of the provided primitives in Mudbox if your final sculpture falls within the supplied categories. In fact, some of the most amazing digital sculptures I have seen online have started from a cube or sphere.

Remember that all you need to sculpt are polygons, and you could keep subdividing any primitive or mesh to get the polygons you need for the results you want. The challenge with this method is that you could end up taking your digital sculpture in directions requiring you to add parts with new geometry, because the geometry you have is being stretched. For example, say you need a humanoid character with six fingers, and you start out with the Human Body primitive that is provided in Mudbox. You will have to use the Grab tool and pull out the extra two fingers in an area around or between the existing ones. Well, there just isn't enough geometry there to do that, so you will have to subdivide the model to create more geometry. As you are subdividing your model to get enough geometry for the additional two fingers, the ten fingers you started with and the body are getting denser geometry that you do not need. Furthermore, the added geometry is using up your computing resources and slowing down your workflow. The solution to adding more geometry in areas where you don't have it or to changing the underlying starting mesh is to re-topologize your model.

Re-topologizing a model is changing the base topology of the model while maintaining the high-resolution detail. It can be done in many ways. The most common way is to bring a dense version of your high-resolution mesh into a 3D application, such as Maya, 3ds Max, or Softimage, and use the surface of the high-resolution mesh as a template to build a new underlying base mesh. After you have done that, you reapply your already sculpted detail to this new base mesh while also getting the additional geometry needed for the changes. Note that you need to create or modify the UVs for this new base mesh. Mudbox has some powerful capabilities to re-topologize by using its Sculpt Model Using Displacement Map feature. You will see this in the next chapter when you take a dense 3D scan of a head and apply it to better topology.

Approaches to Using a Base Mesh

There are two differing approaches to using a base mesh for digital sculpting.

The first is to start sculpting and to re-topologize at a later point in time. The benefit of this approach is that you have no barrier to your creativity at the onset of the project. You can start with a primitive or a very simple base mesh, and take your sculpture in any direction you desire without any extensive planning or modeling from the onset. However, you might run into a situation where you need more geometry, in which case you would need to interrupt your creative process to re-topologize and then continue sculpting.

The second approach is to give your final sculpture some thought and planning before you begin, and either model or obtain a base mesh that will accommodate the geometry you need for your final result. The benefit of this approach is that you will not have any interruptions during the creative process of sculpting and you could very well take your model to completion without having to re-topologize.

Neither of these approaches is perfect, because sometimes you might start out by sculpting from a primitive and never need to re-topologize, and sometimes you might plan your base mesh ad nauseam and still end up needing to re-topologize. Thus, it is a good idea to know about both approaches and decide which direction to take based on your project.

I presently favor the second approach in my workflow, and start by planning a good base mesh at the outset. However, I know and greatly admire many amazing digital artists who use the first approach of starting with a primitive.

I find that I have better results and a smoother workflow when I start with a base mesh that fits the guidelines discussed in Chapter 3, "Detail-Sculpting an Imported Model," where the geometry is as follows:

- Evenly distributed, two-Manifold geometry
- Composed of edges with a valency of five or less
- Composed of quads

And with UVs, that have these features:

- No overlap in UV shells
- A spacing of at least 4 to 6 pixels between the UV shells
- A correct UV winding order
- Minimal stretching or compression

Understanding the Mudbox Sculpt Tools and Their Properties

You went through a brief overview of the Sculpt Tools tray and the Sculpt tool properties of the various Mudbox sculpting tools in Chapter 2, "The Mudbox User Interface." In this chapter, you will go deeper into the sculpt tools and their properties to understand how you can use them to bring the intended shapes into your digital sculpture.

The two basic functions we can perform on a surface are either to pull it out or to push it in. With drawing, we balance positive and negative space to represent our intended image. In essence, we do the exact same thing in three dimensions with sculpture: We add or subtract surface depth to get the shapes we want. In Mudbox, we add to or subtract from a surface by pushing or pulling the surface of the model. The various sculpting tools give us the illusion and comfort of using traditional tools to achieve the caking on or scraping off of surfaces, but in essence we are just balancing negative and positive 3D space by pushing in or pulling out geometry. Another important factor in how our eyes recognize the shape of our sculpture is the way light shines off the indentations and protrusions of the surface.

Size and Strength

The two most used and universally common properties of every sculpt tool in Mudbox are its Size and Strength properties. The *Size property* represents how large of an area the tool will impact, and the *Strength property* represents how deep the tool will push in or pull out the surface. You can manipulate these properties in one of two ways: you can type a value in its field or you can use the B and M keys and click (or tap with a tablet) and drag visual cues on the surface of the model. The Size property is represented by a circle, and the Strength property by a line perpendicular to this circle at the center.

Invert Function

The third-most-used property of a sculpt tool is Invert Function. Every sculpt tool except the Grab tool has this property. The Invert Function property is extremely useful because it inverts the effect the tool has on the surface. For example, if Invert Function is selected, the sculpt tool will depress into the surface of the model (instead of pulling out the surface, as it does when Invert Function is not selected). The check box for this property is useful only if the majority of your strokes are in the reverse orientation of the tool. The best way to get the same effect as Invert Function is to hold down the Ctrl key.

SLIDERS IN MUDBOX

Sliders in Mudbox represent a range of values—for example, the Size property slider range is bracketed by values of 0 to 100. However, the numbers that bracket a range do not represent the limits of how small or large the tool size could be. You can have a tool with a size of 200, or 152, or even 10,000 if you type the value in the text box next to the sliders. When you hit Enter after typing a value larger than the existing limit, the typed value becomes the maximum value for the corresponding slider. This is the case with most of the sliders in Mudbox. For example, if you type 200 in the Size text box, your tool will take on that size, and 200 will become the new maximum on the right of the slider, so if you move the slider to the left, the Size will count down from 200. The same process works for the minimum value on the slider, too. If you type in a smaller size than the minimum value, that value will become the new minimum.

You can also set any value within the bracketed range to be the new maximum of the range by moving the slider to the desired number, and then double clicking the slider. This will set the new maximum to the number the slider is on.

Keyboard Shortcut Workflow

Even though each and every sculpting tool has many properties, there are only a few that you will be constantly manipulating in your workflow while sculpting. These are as follows:

- Navigating the 3D view with the Alt key
- Changing the tool Size
- Changing the tool Strength
- Smoothing the model by using the Smooth tool
- Changing the effect of the tool on the surface by using Invert Function via the Ctrl key

While sculpting, you can move your cursor back and forth between the model in the 3D view and the Properties tray on the right, but it is infinitely faster for your workflow if you use hot keys for the preceding functions, so you can keep working on your model without having to move back and forth. The following "Expert Tip" indicates are the settings I use; you can use the same ones or come up with your own based on your workflow.

EXPERT TIP

Because you use the Alt key to move the camera around your sculpture, the Ctrl key to invert the function of the brush, and the Shift key to activate the Smooth tool, your hand is constantly pressing and releasing keys in one of the two bottom corners of the keyboard, depending on whether you are right- or left-handed. It's a good idea to place other commonly used functions in this area as well.

For example, because I am right-handed and use the stylus or mouse with my right hand, I use the bottom-left corner of the keyboard to press Alt and Ctrl, I assign the Size function to the Z key (instead of B), and the Strength function to X (instead of M) because it helps my workflow tremendously. I also assign these five keys to the function buttons on the Wacom tablet so that if I am sitting back, and my hand can't reach the keyboard, I can use just the tablet's function keys to perform these functions. The other benefit to keeping your hand in the vicinity of these keys is that you also have very close and easy access to Undo and Redo, which are Ctrl+Z and Shift+Z.

The way to customize keyboard shortcuts is to click Windows → Hotkeys (Window → Hotkeys on the Mac) and find the function in the list of functions in the dialog box, and then type in your desired value. For example, find Change Brush Size and set the key to Z (case does not matter) and LMB (left mouse button), and then find Change Brush Strength and set the key to X and LMB.

Place other tools or options that you use frequently in the same vicinity by using the A, S, D, C, Q, and W keys.

Also note that the tools in the Sculpt Tools tray are mapped to the number keys in the same order as they appear in the initial default setting of the application. So the number 1 on your keyboard corresponds to the Sculpt tool, 2 to the Smooth tool, 3 to the Grab tool, and so forth.

Falloff Curve

The next important sculpting property is Falloff. The Falloff property is available for all the sculpting tools. Falloff represents a curve that indicates the strength of the tool from its center to its outer edge (Figure 5.4). The leftmost corner of the falloff curve represents the center of the tool, and the rightmost corner represents the edge, so the falloff curve itself represents only half of the tool and is mirrored to the left to encompass the entire brush. The top-to-bottom portion of the falloff curve represents the Strength of the tool.

Figure 5.4

The falloff curve

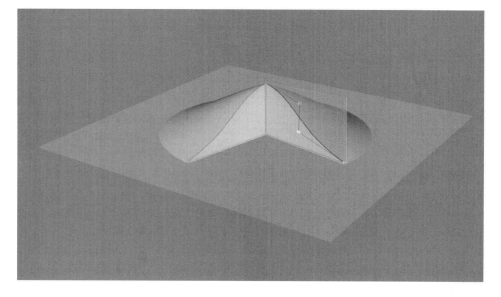

The shape of the falloff curve can be adjusted by moving the four curve points. The two curve points on each end can be moved only up and down because they represent the center and the edge of the tool. The two center curve points can be moved anywhere in the falloff curve graph area.

You can make the falloff curve into a straight line for a planar drop-off by aligning the curve points accordingly. Figure 5.5 shows you an example of the default falloff curves in the Falloff tray and their results on a plane. Incidentally, a plane is a great primitive to try out the various sculpting tools with their settings to get a good idea of their function.

As you make your own falloff curves, you can save them to the tray for future use by clicking the Store To button underneath the falloff curve in the tool Properties tray. The Snap check box allows you to snap the curve points on the grid. Figure 5.6 shows some user-created falloff curves and their result on a plane.

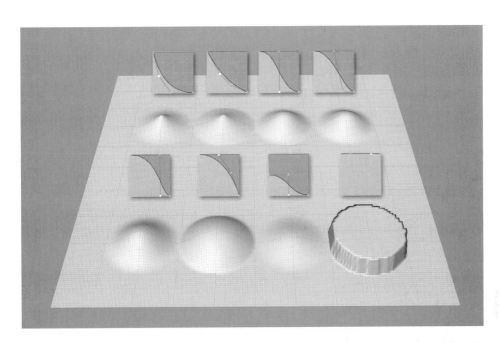

Figure 5.5

The default falloff curves on a plane

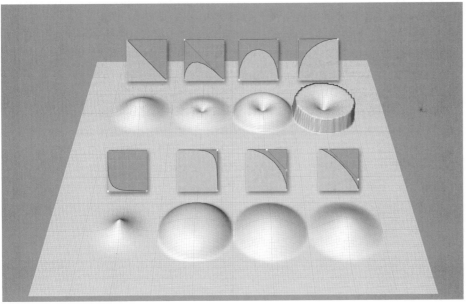

Figure 5.6

User-created falloff curves

A falloff curve that I use a lot, but that is not part of the default set, is a falloff curve with both middle curve points snapped to the leftmost corner, or center of the brush (Figure 5.7). I use this falloff in addition to the Sculpt tool to create sharp edges instead of using the Pinch tool.

Figure 5.7

Sharp-edge falloff brush]

To create this falloff curve, do the following:

1. In the Sculpt Tools tray, select the Sculpt tool.

2. In the properties of the Sculpt tool, expand the Falloff section if it is not already expanded.

3. Select the rightmost curve point and move it to the bottom-right corner.

4. Select the leftmost curve point and move it to the top-left corner.

5. Select the two middle curve points, one at a time, and move them to the bottom-left corner.

6. To add this falloff to your Falloff tray, click the Store To button and select Falloff from the drop-down menu.

Your curve should look like Figure 5.7.

Mirroring Geometry

Besides the Undo function, the other big advantage to digital sculpting is mirroring, or symmetrical sculpting. Using mirroring while sculpting enables you to sculpt one side of your sculpture and have the exact same strokes and shapes mirrored on the other side. Mudbox has some very powerful mirroring capabilities in its sculpting tools.

There are two ways to sculpt when using mirroring, or symmetry. The first is to turn mirroring on and sculpt, in which case the strokes you do on one side are duplicated on the other. The other way is to sculpt one side and then mirror your sculpture after the fact.

The Mirror property, another property that all sculpting tools have, is a drop-down menu that lists the various mirroring options. The first three mirroring options will mirror your work along the world axes. The next three options enable you to mirror along the model's local axes, treating the pivot point, or center of the object, as the center of mirroring.

The last and most unconventionally powerful mirroring option is the Tangent option. This enables you to mirror a topologically symmetrical object along a topological axis that you set up. Topologically symmetrical models have an equal number of faces on each half of the model, even though those faces are in different locations. There is usually a dividing edge loop that divides the model in half.

To work with the mirroring capabilities in Mudbox go through the following steps:

1. From the Chapter 5 folder on the DVD, load the pinup_pose.mud file (Figure 5.8).

2. If the wireframe is not on, press the W key to turn it on. Also, make sure the grid is on by choosing Display → Grid.

3. From the Object List tray, select cube 2.

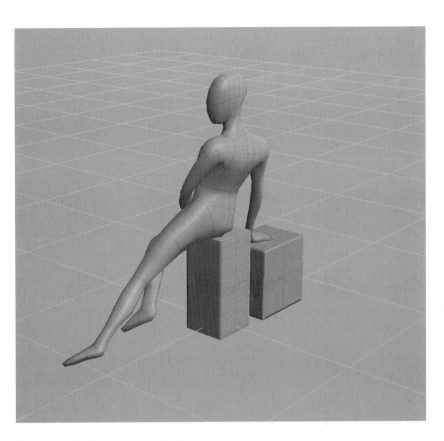

Figure 5.8

A model in an asymmetrical pose

4. From the Sculpt Tools tray, select the Grab tool.

5. In the Properties tray for the Grab tool, click the Mirror drop-down menu to show the mirror options (Figure 5.9).

6. Without clicking, move your cursor over the options while looking at the selected cube in the 3D view. Notice how a visual grid pops up in the display to show you the plane of symmetry. As you go through the first six options, you see the plane of symmetry grid; however, when you get to the last option, Tangent, nothing happens.

7. Experiment while using the Grab tool on the cube by enabling some of the first six mirror options to see the results. After you are finished, select the pinup_pose model object from the Object List tray.

   The pinup_pose model is a topologically symmetrical model, even though it is not in a symmetrical pose. The line that divides the model in half that starts at the top of the head and goes all the way to the crotch area is twisted, but there are an equal number of faces on each side of the model divided by that line.

Figure 5.9

Mirror drop-down menu

8. Hover the mouse cursor on the model and press Pg Dn to drop the model down one subdivision level, to level 0. We are moving down to the lowest subdivision level because we need to select at least two faces that are adjacent to, and on opposite sides of, the edge loop dividing the model in half. Doing this at the lowest subdivision level is the easiest way because the polygons are large and easy to select, and we can be sure that we are selecting the same number of polygons on each side.

9. From the Select/Move Tools tray, select the Faces tool.

10. On the model, select the four left and right faces that make up the face. Click on both sides of the center line of symmetry to select the two faces (Figure 5.10). They become highlighted in yellow. Make sure not to select any other faces besides the four on opposite sides of the center line of symmetry of the face. Alternately, you can select the two faces on the model's back or chest that straddle the center line of symmetry if that is easier for you. If you accidentally select a face you didn't intend to, you can easily deselect it by clicking it again.

11. Choose Mesh → Set Topological Axis. This picks the line between the selected faces as the axis of symmetry. If this does not turn on Tangent mirroring for you, click the Mirror drop-down menu and select Tangent.

Figure 5.10

Select both left and right faces straddling the symmetry line.

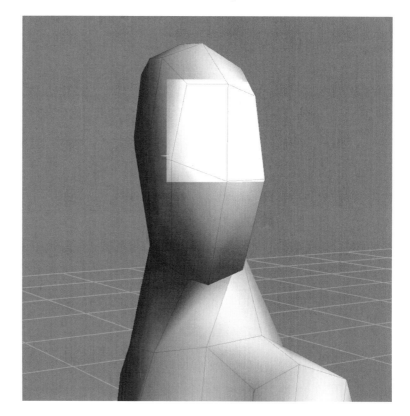

12. In the Sculpt Tools tray, select the Grab tool and click once on the model.

13. Hover the mouse cursor on the model and press Pg Up to go up one subdivision level.

14. Move your cursor on the body of the model and notice how the mirrored cursor moves along the other side. Even though the model is in an asymmetrical pose, we can still sculpt symmetrically.

15. Press Shift+D until you subdivide your model to level 6. Press W to hide the wireframe.

16. Pick a sculpting tool such as the Wax tool; sculpt on the model to see how it mirrors on the other side. Experiment with different tools, Sizes, Strengths, and Falloffs to sculpt on the face and body to get an idea of how the Tangent Mirror works. Figure 5.11 is an example of what I came up with during 15 minutes of sculpting.

After tangent symmetry is set up, it gets saved with the model so you can use it at a future time.

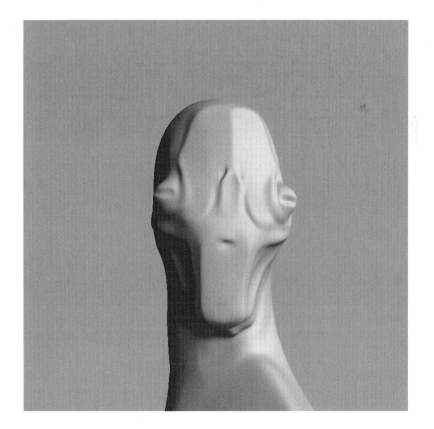

Figure 5.11

Tangent mirror sculpt

TOPOLOGICAL SYMMETRY AND SUBDIVISION LEVELS

Tangent mirroring set on one subdivision level carries over to all the other subdivision levels only if your model is composed entirely of quads. If not, then it is set for only the subdivision level you are on, and if you want to use topological symmetry on different levels, you have to set the topological axis again on that level.

Symmetry is a huge time-saver and makes our lives a lot easier while sculpting symmetrical subjects. However, at times when you are sculpting, you might forget to turn on symmetry, which could be very frustrating. There are a couple of ways to overcome this.

One solution is to generate a 32-bit displacement map and use a 2D image-manipulation tool that can handle 32-bit images to copy, flip, and paste the sculpture from one side to another.

However, there is a way to do this in Mudbox that is a lot easier. For example, say we sculpted the ear on one side of the head and inadvertently turned off tangent symmetry in our model before we started sculpting the ear. There is a way to mirror the ear to the other side after the fact. This works with all mirroring, and luckily also with topological tangent symmetry as well. We will go through this example with the model we have been working on, where we sculpted the ear on one side and need to transfer it over to the other side (Figure 5.12).

1. From the DVD, load the ear_symmetry.mud file from the Chapter 5 folder of the DVD. Tumble the camera around the model to see that there is an ear on the left side, but not on the right.

Figure 5.12

Ear not mirrored

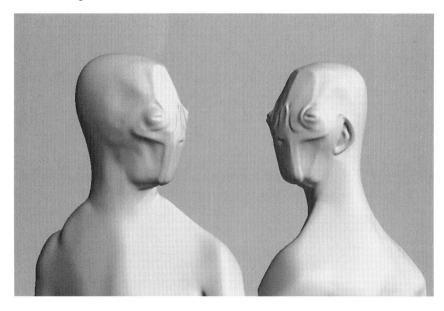

2. Notice that there is a sculpting layer called `ear_1f` in the Layers tray. Mirroring by using this technique works only if you are sculpting on a layer, so make sure that you create at least one sculpting layer, even if you don't need one. Click the view circle next to the layer to hide the ear, then again to show it.

3. Choose the Freeze tool from the Sculpt Tools tray.

4. In the Freeze tool properties, select Tangent from the Mirror drop-down list. Make sure Strength is set to 100.

5. Paint the entire ear (Figure 5.13). Note that because we have tangent mirroring on, there is a blue frozen area where we want the new ear to go.

Figure 5.13

Freeze tool painted on left ear

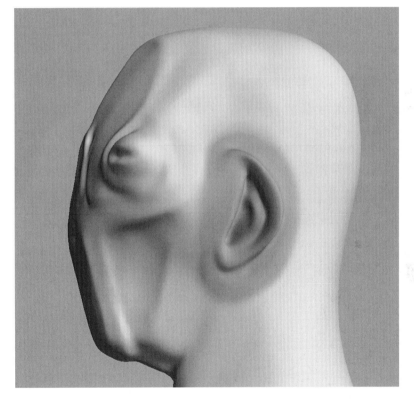

6. Choose Edit → Invert Freeze to freeze all the geometry except the two ear areas. The entire model is now blue except the two ear areas.

7. Click the Faces tool in the Select/Move Tools tray and select Off in the Mirror drop-down list, because we want to select only the side we want to mirror to the other side. Click anywhere on the ear to select the side to mirror from. The area you click turns yellow.

8. Make sure the `ear_1f` layer is selected and click the Layers tray drop-down menu → Mirror → Tangent to mirror the ear to the other side (Figure 5.14).

9. Choose Edit → Unfreeze All to unfreeze the entire model.

10. Notice the mirrored ear on the other side. Do some smoothing and cleanup and you are done (Figure 5.15)!

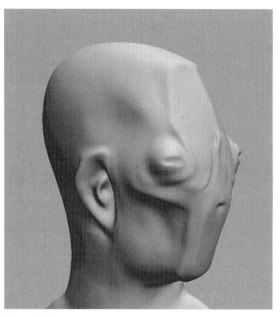

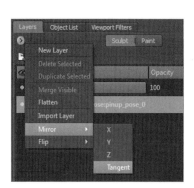

Figure 5.14

Tangent mirror in Layers window menu

Figure 5.15

Mirrored ear

Use Stamp Image and Stamp Spacing Properties

The Use Stamp Image property enables you to use stamp images in combination with the sculpting and paint tools to sculpt or paint with the stamp image as the tip of your tool. This is mostly useful to create interesting repeating detail on the surface of your model. For stamps to be effective, you need to make sure that your model is subdivided appropriately to show the granularity level of the stamp on the surface of the geometry.

While sculpting, the stamp image's opacity values are used to mask which parts of the image get modified versus which parts do not. Black values on the stamp image produce absolutely no modification, while white values produce the most; the values in between have changes applied to the geometry based on their value.

To use stamps to sculpt, select the Use Stamp Image check box in the tool's Properties tray. Stamps can be applied with certain levels of uniformity, or randomness, based on the settings of the Use Stamp Image properties.

The stamp image can be flipped and rotated by using the Flip and Rotate buttons on top of the stamp image in the Use Stamp Image properties.

An important capability of using stamps to sculpt is using the Orient to Stroke function. This can be toggled on or off by clicking the Orient to Stroke button above the stamp thumbnail in the Use Stamp Image properties. This will allow the orientation of the stamp to follow the orientation of your stroke (Figure 5.16), like tire tracks orient themselves to the direction of a car.

The Randomize option lets you apply randomization based on the sliders to add rotational, horizontal, vertical, scale, and opacity jitter to your stroke with the stamp applied. In Figure 5.17, notice how we get a completely random-looking corroded effect by just using the Sculpt tool with one stamp, and turning on the randomize effects of the Use Stamp Image properties.

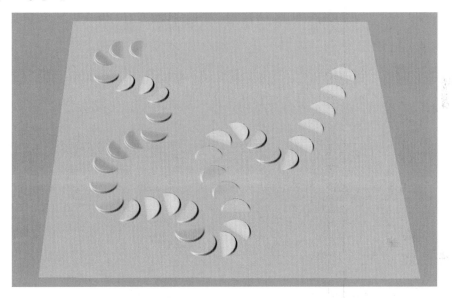

Figure 5.16

Orient to Stroke

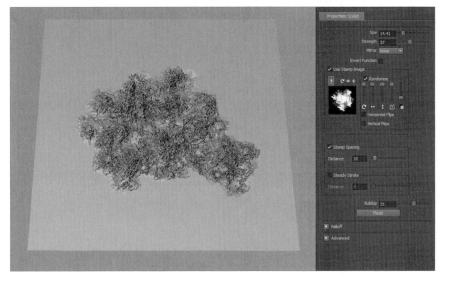

Figure 5.17

Randomize application of the stamp

The Stamp Spacing property sets the rate at which the stamp image repeats on a stroke. It works whether or not the Use Stamp Image check box is selected. You should manipulate this property only if you want more gaps in your stroke or, more realistically, if you want none or fewer.

Steady Stroke

Steady Stroke is available for all sculpting tools except Imprint. It enables you to sculpt a more even or straighter stroke. This is done by displaying a vector when you begin your stroke. When your stroke has moved the distance specified in the Distance text box of the Steady Stroke property, the stroke is then applied to the model.

Steady Stroke is extremely useful when you want to sculpt lines or patterns that portray a smooth continuity in direction. If you want to sculpt in an actual straight line, or a shape that is more controlled and rigid, you can use the Curves option.

Using Curves in Mudbox

If you work with 2D illustration applications such as Adobe Illustrator, or NURBs in Maya, you are familiar with how useful curves are. In Mudbox, you can use built-in curves and modify them, or you can draw your own curves as guides to sculpt.

The curve tools are found in two places. To create a curve, choose Create → Curves and choose from a Circle, French Curve, Straight Line, or Square. Even though you might not think of straight lines or squares as curves, the reason they are called such is because they are constructed as curves. You can also create a curve by choosing Curves → New Curve and clicking to draw the curve points in the 3D view; use Undo (Ctrl Z) to undo the last point, and press Enter to end the curve creation process. If you want to close your curve, choose Curves → Close Curve.

You can edit the curve by selecting it in the Object List and moving the curve points.

To manipulate a curve, press C on the keyboard and use the left, middle, and right mouse or stylus buttons to rotate, translate, and scale the curve, respectively.

To duplicate a curve, choose Curves → Duplicate Curve.

To snap your tool to the curve to sculpt along it, select the curve in the Object List and press Enter, and then move the cursor to the curve. As it gets close to it, the cursor will snap to the curve.

SNAP TO CURVE AND STAMP SPACING

Sculpt or paint tools will snap to an active curve only when their Stamp Spacing property is turned off. Deselect the Stamp Spacing check box in the tool's properties to enable a tool to snap to the curve.

You can sculpt repeating stamp patterns along the curve by choosing Curves → Stroke on Curve and filling in the dialog box with the number of stamps you want on the curve (Figure 5.18). This is very useful if you are going to have a repeating pattern along a curve or line, such as rivets, nails, sewing stitches, staples, and so forth.

Figure 5.18

Stroke on Curve dialog box

STROKE ON CURVE WITH MULTIPLE OBJECTS

Stroke on Curve works only if the starting point of your curve is on the object you want the stroke to be on. If you have multiple objects, the one that the starting point of the curve is on will get the stroke.

Buildup and Flood

Buildup, which is available for the Sculpt, Smooth, Pinch, Flatten, Foamy, Spray, Repeat, Wax, Scrape, Fill, Knife, Smear, Bulge, Amplify, Freeze, and Mask tools, indicates the rate at which the tool will reach the Strength value.

For example, if you have a Strength of 100 and a Buildup of 50, you will get to the full Strength value with a very short stroke, whereas if your Buildup value is 10, it will take you longer.

Experiment with strokes on a plane that is subdivided five or six times with the Sculpt tool Strength set at 100 and Buildup at 10, 20, 40, 60, 80, and 100 to see the effects. The default Buildup for the Sculpt tool is 40, just in case you need to set it back to its default value. It's always a good idea to note the default value of a property because it is the value that the developers have deemed as a default average.

Flood, which is available to only the Sculpt, Smooth, Pinch, Flatten, Freeze, Foamy, Spray, Repeat, Wax, Scrape, Fill, Knife, Smear, Bulge, Amplify Mask, and Erase tools, applies the function of these tools uniformly on the entire surface of your model in one click of the Flood button. It's a great way to add uniform thickness and smoothness to the entire model. Note that Flood does not apply the function of the tools to surface areas that are hidden, frozen, or affected by a stencil.

Update Plane and Whole Stroke

Update Plane is a property of the Flatten, Wax, Scrape, Fill, and Amplify tools, located in the Advanced section of the tool Properties tray. When Update Plane is not selected at the onset of a stroke, a plane is determined based on the stamp's tangency to the contact point, and all the points on the surface are pulled in the direction of that plane for the duration of the stroke. For example, if you start the stroke on a sphere and move to its edge, you will create a plane tangent to the sphere from the point you clicked on it (Figure 5.19).

Figure 5.19

**Wax tool with
Update Plane off**

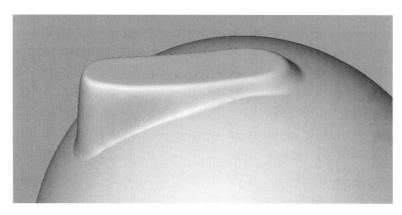

However, with the setting selected, the plane toward which the surface is pulled gets redetermined and updated for each stamp update in a tool stroke (Figure 5.20). Having Update Plane selected is the desired setting while sculpting with the preceding tools, because the brush adheres to the curvature of the sculpted surface instead of the plane of the stroke's initial contact.

Figure 5.20

**Wax tool with
Update Plane on**

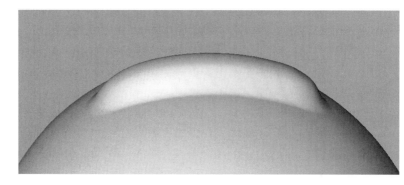

Whole Stroke is also a property of the Flatten, Wax, Scrape, Fill, and Amplify tools and is located in the Advanced section. It causes the plane toward which the surface is pulled to be recalculated and updated for each vertex affected by the current tool stroke, as opposed to each stamp update with the Update Plane function. The result is a slight variation of the Update Plane property, where a more planar effect continues throughout the stroke.

Sculpting Tools Recap and Prioritization

Before we get deeper into the tools, I want to mention that using and developing a large number of sculpting tools is not critical, just as it is not critical when you are doing traditional sculpting. Based on what you are trying to sculpt, you will determine a few tools that work best for you and continue to use those to get the shapes you want. You can customize the settings of a tool and save your custom variant if you discover you are repeating tool customization tasks. Save your custom tool by clicking on the tray's window drop-down menu and then clicking Add Tool.

The Sculpt and Wax tools are the workhorses of Mudbox, especially with the enhancements introduced in Mudbox 2010. In this version, the Update Plane option has been added to the Wax tool, giving it properties similar to adding clay to a traditional sculpture. The Wax tool is best used with the square stamp, to give the illusion of adding strips of clay to your sculpture.

The Flatten tool is another one of the most useful tools in Mudbox. You can use it to define planes while sculpting and to create flat surfaces.

The Foamy tool is a variation of the Sculpt tool with a softer result.

With all the properties and stamps you can apply to these tools, many new implementations remain to be discovered. I will cover a few that I use when we sculpt the model in the next chapter.

The Pinch tool is useful for creating creased corners. However, use it with caution because as it compresses and stretches geometry to create the effect, it creates undesirable topological effects.

Notice the nice crease created on the edge of a car by using the Pinch tool with Steady Stroke on (Figure 5.21). Although this looks like a nice hard edge, upon further examination, we notice that polygons are crammed in together to produce this crease, while adjacent polygons to those pinched to form the crease are stretched out(Figure 5.22).

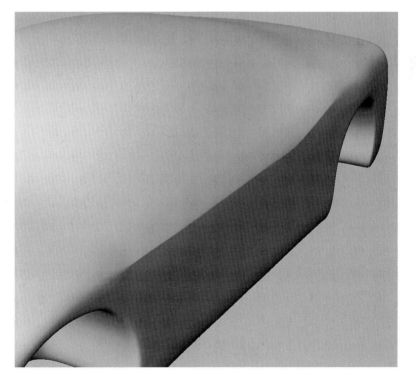

Figure 5.21

Pinch tool with Steady Stroke on to create nice pinch on the edge of a car

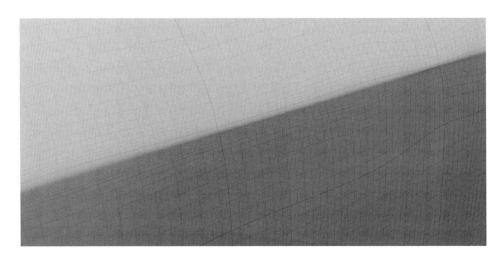

The Smear tool has a similar property of moving vertices on the model's surface. The Smear tool could also cause undesirable effects when texturing or sculpting.

The Spray, Repeat, and Imprint tools enable you to place stamps on the surface of your model. You should be familiar with the Spray and Imprint tool because you have used them in previous chapters. The Repeat tool enables you to repeat a stamp along your stroke. This tool is extremely useful for creating repeated patterns such as stitching, rivets, screws, or nails on a path.

Freeze Tool

Even though you can lock sculpting on an object in the Object List, the Freeze tool enables you to freeze, or lock, certain vertices of the geometry so you cannot modify or sculpt them. The frozen faces get painted blue at varying opacities to indicate the amount of freezing. A fully opaque blue locks completely, while partially opaque blue allows the vertices to move slightly when a sculpting tool is applied.

To paint areas you want frozen, click and paint on the model. The painting takes into consideration all your tool settings such as Size, Strength, Falloff, Buildup, and Steady Stroke. In addition, you can erase the frozen area while holding down Ctrl, and smooth the edges of your frozen area by holding down Shift. Note that to smooth the areas of the edges of a frozen area, you need to have the Smooth & Paint Values check box selected in the Advanced section of the Freeze tool properties tray.

You can freeze your entire selected model by choosing Edit → Freeze Selected. You can invert the frozen areas by choosing Edit → Invert Freeze. To clear all frozen items, choose Edit → Unfreeze All.

If you are familiar with ZBrush, Freeze is analogous to Mask in ZBrush. If you are a user of both applications, note that what is referred to as the Mask function does something completely different in each application.

Erase and Mask Tools

Both the Erase and Mask tools are used to erase or remove sculpting from layers. Neither one of the two tools works on the base mesh of a model; you have to have at least one sculpting layer to use them.

The Erase tool erases the sculpting on the layer to reveal the original base mesh, or other layers beneath it. Once something is erased, the only way to bring it back is through Undo. If the model is saved and loaded, there is no way to bring back what was erased.

The Erase tool erases sculpting on the current selected layer only. Nothing changes on the other layers or the original base mesh.

The Mask tool does the same thing as the Erase tool, but with a couple of big differences:

- It is nondestructive, meaning when you mask out an area, you can restore it by erasing the mask, or inverting the function of the Mask tool by holding down the Ctrl key while applying a stroke to the masked areas of the model. This is stored with the model so you can restore what was masked in later sculpting sessions after the model has been saved and reloaded.

- You can mask out with opacity values, which gives you more options and control over what the Erase tool does. This means that when you mask out an area, the Strength setting lets you determine how much depth you are erasing.

To clear the mask completely, turn on Invert Function in the Mask tool properties window, and click Flood.

To understand the function of these tools better, you will go through an exercise of using the Mask, Erase, and Freeze tools to add a wetsuit to the Human Body starter mesh. Follow these steps:

1. Choose File → New Scene to start a new Mudbox session and load the Human Body primitive mesh.

2. Press Shift+D three times to subdivide your model to level 4.

3. Create two sculpting layers and name them **wetsuit** and **Hood**.

4. Choose the Gesso material from the Material Presets tray.

5. Click the **wetsuit** layer to select it and click the Sculpt tool to bring up its properties in the Properties tray.

6. Type **0.4** in the Strength text box to set the strength of the tool.

7. Click the Flood button in the Sculpt tool properties to flood the wetsuit layer with the Sculpt tool. This makes the model look a little thicker.

8. Click the Mask tool and make sure you have a Strength of 100 and change the Size to 7 or 8. You will be adjusting the size as you go through the next steps to accommodate for sculpting on the different areas of the model.

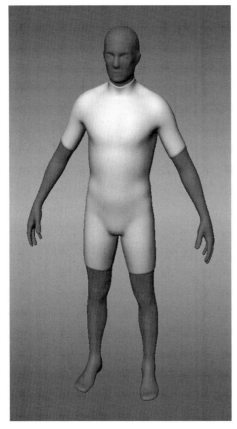

9. Click the Show/Hide Mask button in the Layers tray. This highlights the masked areas in a reddish color. This is just a cosmetic effect, to show you the masked areas with a color.

10. Turn on mirroring by selecting Local X from the Mirror drop-down menu in the Mask tool properties.

11. Use the Mask tool to mask the head, hands, and legs of the model (Figure 5.23).

12. To create dive booties, we need to re-add them. Hold down the Ctrl key and erase the masked area on and above the feet to redraw the booties (Figure 5.24). Remember that you can continually add and subtract the material as needed.

Figure 5.23
Masked head, arms, and legs

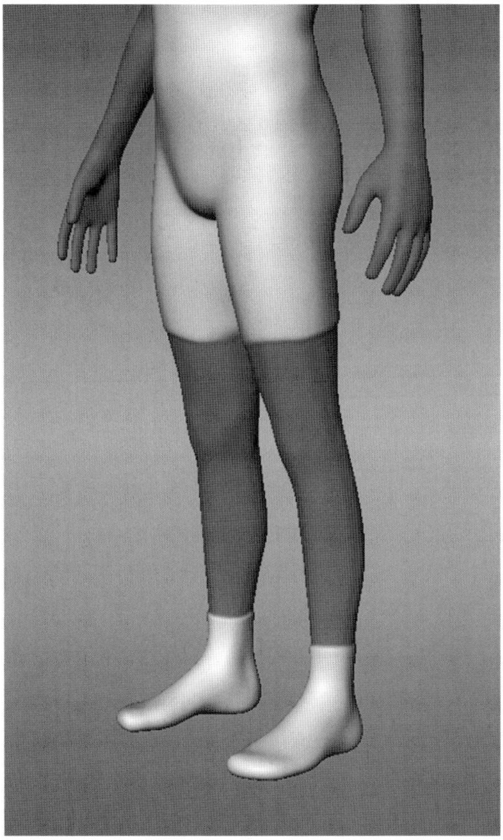

Figure 5.24
Add wetsuit booties by holding down the Ctrl key.

13. Click the Show/Hide Mask option to hide the reddish hue of the mask. Note that you can toggle the View Layer circle next to the layer name `wetsuit` to hide and show the wetsuit layer and reveal your starting figure. Make sure you have the `wetsuit` layer visible for the next step.

14. Click the Freeze tool and make sure you have a Strength setting of 100.

15. Mask out a hood area on the model (Figure 5.25).

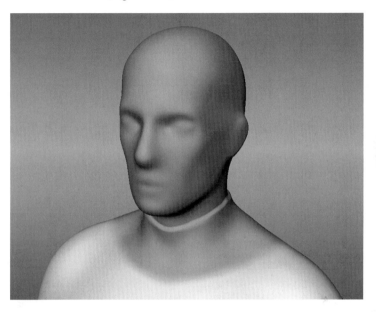

Figure 5.25

Masked hood

16. Click Edit → Invert Freeze or press Shift+I to invert the frozen area to everything but where we will be adding the hood.

17. Select the hood layer in the Layers tray.

18. Click the Sculpt tool and click Flood again in its properties.

19. Choose Edit → Unfreeze All to unfreeze the body. Notice that the hood now covers the head with a little bit of overhang on the shoulders.

20. Click the Erase tool and make sure you have a Strength setting of 100.

21. Erase an area on the hood to reveal the face (Figure 5.26). Do this with care, because you cannot add the erased areas back as you were able to with the Mask tool.

22. Use the Smooth tool to smooth out the lip between the neck of the wetsuit and the hood (Figure 5.26).

As you can see masking, freezing, erasing, and sculpting layers are extremely useful for creating models that can be modified on a layer-by-layer basis.

Figure 5.26

Erase the face area on the hood.

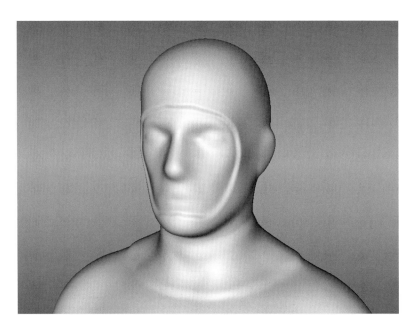

Summary

In this first of our two digital sculpting chapters, you have learned the importance of planning your sculpture, the different stages that a sculpture will go through to get to the final result, and how to determine and plan the base mesh for your sculpture. You also looked deeper into some of the important sculpting tools, their functions, and properties. In the next chapter, you will use these concepts and tools to create a digital sculpture.

CHAPTER 6

Digital Sculpting, Part II

Continuing from the preceding chapter, you will now move on to modeling a very simple human base mesh in Maya and making slight modifications for it to be a female. Then you will create UVs for the model by using Headus UVLayout. After this point, you will have a simple human-form base mesh that you can easily pose. You will then pose the base mesh with the new posing toolset in Mudbox 2011. Finally, you will subdivide the model and sculpt it.

This chapter includes the following topics:

- Modeling the base mesh in Maya

- Laying out the UVs in UVLayout

- Posing the base mesh

- Sculpting the model

- Sculpt using a vector displacement map

Modeling the Base Mesh in Maya

In this section, you will build a very simple human base mesh in Maya. You will start with a Cube primitive, extrude it, and use the Split Polygon, Insert Edge Loop, and Cut Faces tools to create the base mesh (Figure 6.1).

Figure 6.1

Base mesh models

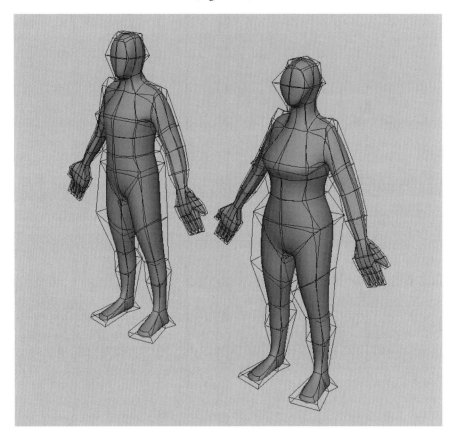

The reason you are not using the humanoid base mesh that comes in Mudbox is that, even though it is a good humanoid model for sculpting, it has a high polygon count that could prove more difficult to pose than the simpler mesh you will be modeling.

Maya is not the only application in which you can create a base mesh; any 3D application that enables you to do polygonal modeling and export your results as an .obj or .fbx file will also work. I have included a video, Chapter6-part1-Modeling_the_base_mesh_in_Maya .mov of me modeling the human base mesh on the DVD in the Chapter 6\Videos folder. I have also provided a female and male version of the result of the work in this section as human_basemesh_male.obj and human_basemesh_female.obj files in the Chapter 6\1 - base_ mesh folder on the DVD.

You will use the eight-head scale (Figure 6.2) to make this human base mesh. Note the eight-head scale intersection lines on the parts of the body. If you are familiar with drawing human anatomy, you should already be familiar with this; if not, there are plenty of great drawing and anatomy books that will give you measurement and scale guidelines to the human body. You could use image planes for the front and left view-ports to model, but in this case, because you have a perfectly acceptable human mesh in Mudbox, you will use it as the guide to create the simple base mesh.

Follow these steps to create the base mesh:

1. Start Mudbox and load the Human Body primitive from the Welcome screen or click Create → Mesh → Human Body.

2. From the Select/Move Tools tray, select the Objects tool and then select the model.

3. Click File → Export Selection and export the model as **Mudbox_HumanBody.obj**.

   Next you will set the grids in Maya to accommodate for the English measurement system, to show a grid line at every foot for a 6-foot-tall person. One foot is 30.48 centimeters, so if you are using Maya's default working units of centimeters, you will now have a grid line every foot that is divided by 12 subdivisions to indicate inches.

4. Start Maya and go to the options for the Grid by clicking on the options box to the right of Display → Grid menu selection. This brings up the Maya Grid Options dialog box.

5. In the Size setting for the grid, type **16** in the Length and Width text box and type **30.48** in the Grid Lines Every text box. Finally, type **12** in the Subdivisions text box (Figure 6.3). Click Close to close the Grid Options dialog box.

   You will now load the Mudbox Human body.obj file into Maya and set it as a template.

6. In Maya, click File → Import and select the Mudbox_HumanBody.obj file that you exported from Mudbox.

7. Click on the model to select it. Click the Show or Hide the Channel Box/Layer Editor icon to bring up the Layer Editor.

8. Click the Create a New Layer and Assign Selected Objects icon to create a display layer and add the Human Body model to it.

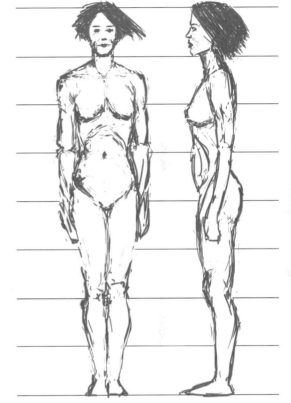

Figure 6.2

Sketch of a human figure composed of eight head lengths

Figure 6.3

Grid options

Click the middle square in the Layer Editor so it displays the letter *T*. This will set the objects in this layer, in this case, the human body, to be a template. Setting an object as a template makes it possible for you to see the objects, but you cannot select them. We are doing this because we are using this model as a reference. You might also want to click on the name of the layer and name the layer as something more useful (Figure 6.4).

Note that the model is about 6 feet tall. It is also eight heads tall (Figure 6.5).

Next, you will create a polygon cube and extrude some faces. Because the body is symmetrical along the y-axis, you will delete a symmetric half of the mesh, model half of the mesh, and then mirror it to the other side to get your final result.

9. Click options box to the right of the Create → Polygon Primitives → Cube menu selection, and type **30.48** in the Width, Height, and Depth text boxes in the Polygon Cube options dialog box. Click the Create button for a 1-foot cube centered on the origin (Figure 6.6).

10. Move your mouse to the front viewport and press the spacebar to expand the viewport. Make sure your cube is selected and click the Move Tool icon on the top left of your Maya interface or press the W key on your keyboard.

Figure 6.4

Mudbox Human Body model and Layer Editor

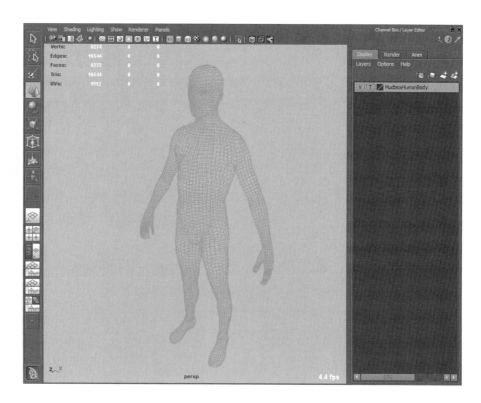

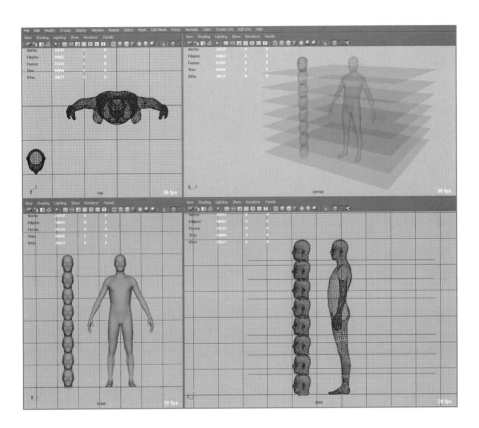

Figure 6.5

Mudbox Human Body model, eight heads tall and six feet tall

11. Use the green up arrow to drag your cube upward so that the top corners of the cube are aligned with the armpits of the model (Figure 6.7).

12. Press the spacebar and in the perspective viewport, right-click on the box and select Face from the marking menu (Figure 6.8). This enables you to select faces.

13. Rotate the model by pressing Alt and clicking and dragging the mouse in the perspective viewport so you see the top face of the cube. Then select the top face of the cube by clicking it with the left mouse button (Figure 6.9).

14. Make sure that the polygon menu set is active and that the drop-down menu in the top-left corner of the Maya toolbar reads *Polygons*. Press the spacebar, move your mouse cursor to the front viewport, and click the spacebar again. Click Edit Mesh → Extrude. Use the up arrow to extrude the cube upward, and the red square on the right to scale the extruded face in so it is approximately the width of a head (Figure 6.10).

Figure 6.6

Cube options

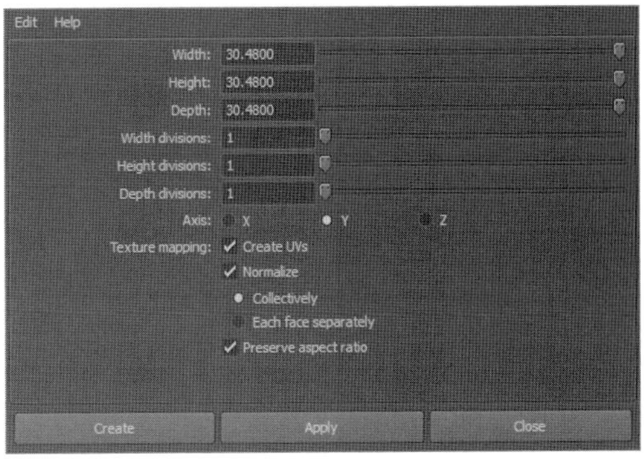

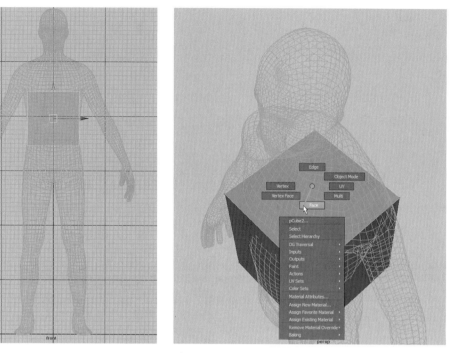

Figure 6.7

Move the cube up.

Figure 6.8

Select Face from the marking menu.

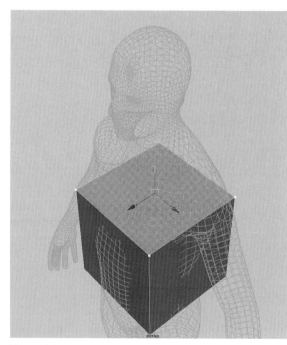

Figure 6.9

Select the top face of the cube.

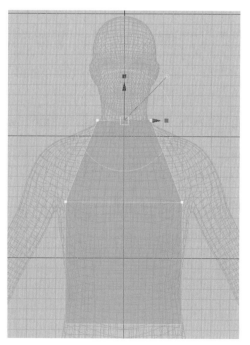

Figure 6.10

Extruded and scaled face

15. Click Edit Mesh → Extrude to extrude another face to the top of the head (Figure 6.11).

16. Press the spacebar and in the perspective viewport, rotate the model by pressing Alt and clicking and dragging the mouse until you see the bottom face of the cube you started with. Then right-click on it with the left mouse button to select it.

17. Press the spacebar, move your mouse cursor to the front viewport, and click the spacebar again. Click Edit Mesh → Extrude. Use the blue arrow to extrude the face downward, and the green square on the right to scale the extruded face in so that it is the length of the gap between the legs (Figure 6.12).

18. Click Edit Mesh → Insert Edge Loop Tool, and then click anywhere in the middle area of the model to create a vertical edge loop.

19. In the Channel Box, click PolySplitRing1 and type in a weight of **0.5** (Figure 6.13). This makes the edge loop you created move to the middle of the model.

20. Press the spacebar and in the perspective viewport, right-click on the model and choose Face from the marking menu. Select the left face on the initial cube you created, and then hold down the Shift key and double-click in the face above the one you have selected. This selects an edge ring (Figure 6.14).

21. Press the Delete key to delete the selected faces.

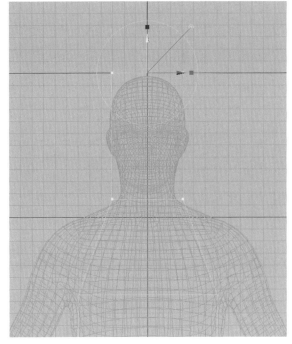

Figure 6.11

Extruded head

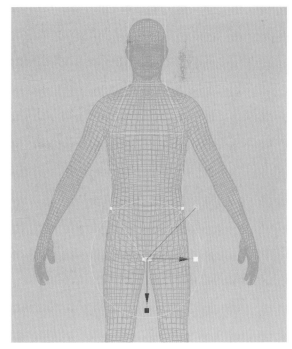

Figure 6.12

Extruded hip

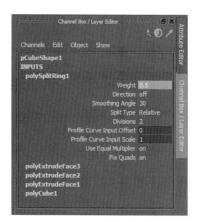

Figure 6.13

Splitting the polygon in the middle

22. Double-click on the remaining faces and press the Delete key again (Figure 6.15).

23. Press the Delete key to remove the selected edges. You now have half the model, which will be easier to work on, and when you are finished, you can mirror your work. Another reason that this is a good way to model is that it ensures that the model is topologically symmetrical, which as you saw in the previous chapter, is how you can still mirror-sculpt on a model that is not posed symmetrically.

24. Rotate your model, select the face for the leg, and click Edit Mesh → Extrude to extrude out the leg. Click the circle handle attached to the extrude manipulator to switch from local to world axes. Switch back to the front viewport, click the green arrow, and pull down the leg. Use the red arrow, the red square, and the rotate manipulators to move, scale, and rotate your extruded face so that your newly created leg overlaps with the leg of the reference human (Figure 6.16).

25. Select the shoulder face and click Edit Mesh → Extrude to extrude out. Use the Move, Scale, Rotate controls to extrude out the shoulder (Figure 6.17).

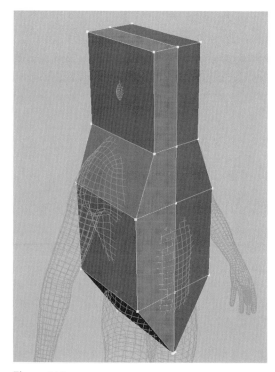

Figure 6.14

Selected edge ring

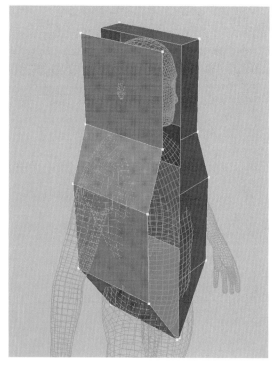

Figure 6.15

Remaining faces

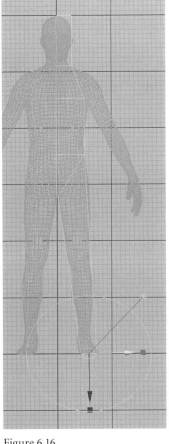

Figure 6.16

Extruded leg

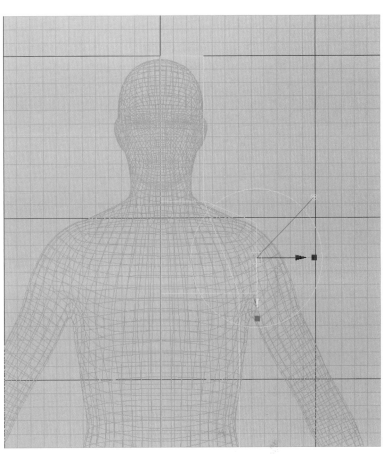

Figure 6.17

Extruded shoulder

26. With the shoulder face still selected from the preceding step, click Edit Mesh → Extrude to extrude out the arm. Use the Move, Scale, and Rotate controls to extrude out the arm to about where the wrist would be on the reference figure (Figure 6.18).

    Now you will use the Cut Faces tool to add more geometry to the model. The Cut Faces tool draws a line in the view window to define the cutting plane, which will draw edges on the selected face where the cutting plane intersects. You will start with the arm and use the Cut Faces tool to create an edge loop that will be the elbow.

27. In the front viewport, click and drag a rectangle on the arm to highlight the entire face of the arm. Click Edit Mesh → Cut Faces Tool. Notice that your cursor changes shape and you see the message Click-Drag to Cut. Click the location where the elbow would be and drag your mouse until you get an angle that best represents the pivoting of the elbow. Do the same to create two more cuts on the arm to divide the upper and lower arm (Figure 6.19).

Figure 6.18

Extruded arm

Figure 6.18

Extruded arm

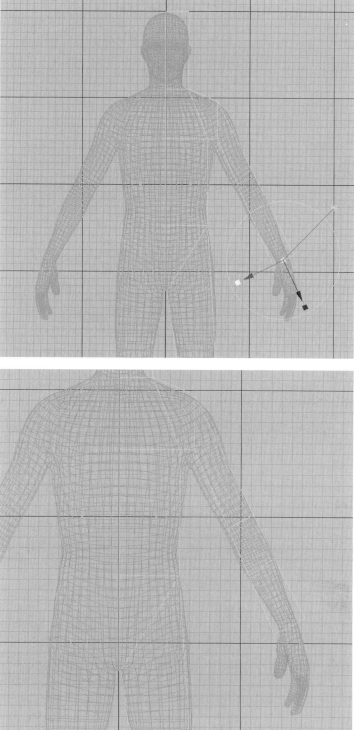

Figure 6.19

**Edge loops
on the arm**

28. Press the Q key, select the entire face of the leg, and use the Cut Faces tool to do the same thing for the leg that you did in the previous step. In addition to the two cuts to separate out the upper leg and the lower leg, add a third cut to mark a line where the top of the foot would be (Figure 6.20).

29. Finally, add two edge loops on the head—one at eye level, and another at the top of the neck. Then add another edge loop on the torso to divide it in half (Figure 6.21). Remember to press the Q key to select the faces before using the Cut Faces tool. You can hold the Shift key down before you let go of the mouse button to restrict your cutting line to 45-degree increments. This comes in handy to draw perfectly horizontal cutting planes.

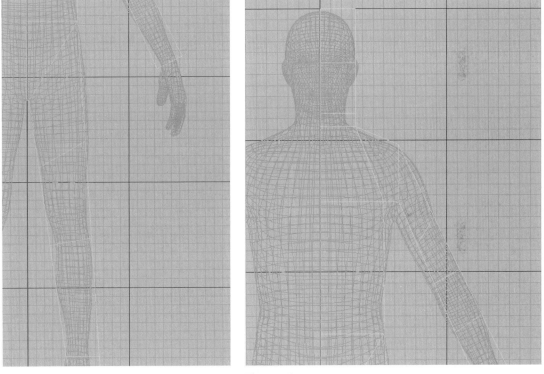

Figure 6.20
Edge loops added to the leg

Figure 6.21
Edge loops added to the torso and head

30. Go to the side viewport. Right-click on the model to bring up the markup menu, and then select Vertex to get into vertex selection mode. Select and move the vertices by using the drag rectangle mode to make sure that the inner vertices are also selected. Align all the vertices to a loose outline of the reference figure. If you have trouble determining which vertex belongs to the arm, you can either toggle between different

viewports or work in the four-viewport mode, going back and forth between viewports. Note that you are just aligning the side outline at this time; you will do the rest later. Your end result should look like Figure 6.22. Note that the face and the foot are not outlined because you are going to extrude them.

31. Under the Edit Mesh menu, make sure that there is a checkmark next to Keep Faces Together. In the side viewport, right-click on the model to bring up the markup menu, and select Face to get into face selection manipulation mode. Select the two front-facing faces of the head and click Edit Mesh → Extrude to extrude out the faces to the front (Figure 6.23). Use the same method of vertex manipulation as you did in the preceding step to align the newly created vertices. Note that the extruded faces also create a couple of faces on the inside of the model, which you need to select and delete.

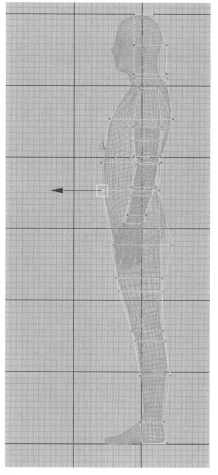

Figure 6.22

Align vertices to the reference character.

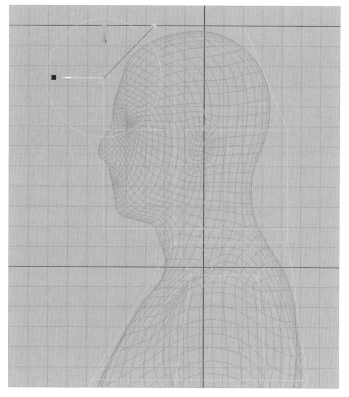

Figure 6.23

Extruded face

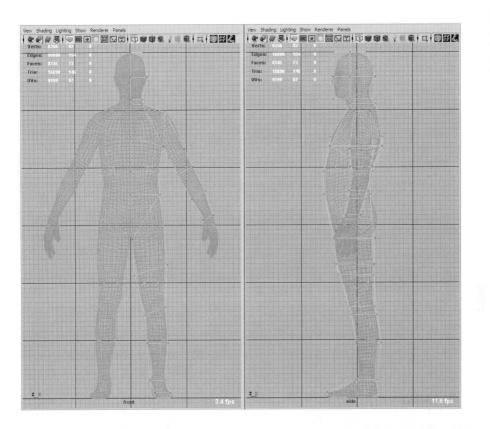

Figure 6.24

Align vertices to the reference character in the front viewport.

32. Use the same method of vertex manipulation as you did in step 27 to align the vertices in the front viewport (Figure 6.24). Make sure you don't select any of the vertices on the y-axis because that is the axis you are going to use to mirror the model.

33. At this point you will add an edge loop to the arms to create some geometry to model the hands. Click Edit Mesh → Insert Edge Loop Tool. Click on the shoulder line and drag your mouse so it evenly divides the shoulder line (Figure 6.25). The progress so far is available for you on the DVD as human_base_mesh - step 30.ma in the Chapter6\1- base_mesh folder.

34. With the new edge loop, you need to slightly modify the topology to add some more geometry to the head and to accommodate the flow of the arm. Click Edit Mesh → Split Polygon Tool and draw the edge connecting the upper-mid arm to the shoulder (Figure 6.26).

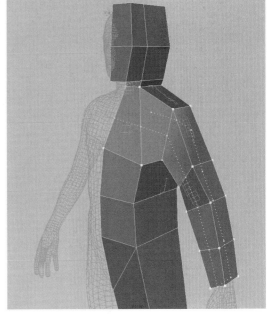

Figure 6.25

Edge loop added to the arm

Figure 6.26
Edge loop added to the edge of the arm by using the Split Polygon tool

Figure 6.27
Edge in the middle of the chest

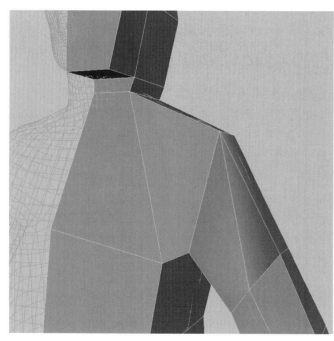

Figure 6.28
Edge loop deleted

Figure 6.29
Connect edges by using the Split Polygon tool.

35. Select the edge indicated in Figure 6.27. Ctrl+click it and use the marking menu to select Edge Loop Utilities in the right corner. From the marking menu that comes up, select To Edge Loop and Delete (Figure 6.28).

36. Click Edit Mesh → Split Polygon Tool to connect edges as displayed in Figure 6.29.

37. Select the edge in Figure 6.30 and press Delete on your keyboard to delete it.

38. Finally, you will use Edit Mesh → Extrude to add the hands. Note that you will not model the hands to match those of the reference model. You will make the hands with the palms facing forward, and then you can modify the pose to easily accommodate the twist in the forearm with the posing tools later. In the perspective view, select the two faces of the bottom of the arm, extrude them out to about where the thumb begins, and then extrude again until you get to the knuckles (Figure 6.31).

39. Select the two outer faces and extrude out twice so that your second extrusion is at about the base of the thumb of the reference model (Figure 6.32). Do the same on the other side, but just extrude out once.

Figure 6.30

Selecting the edge to delete

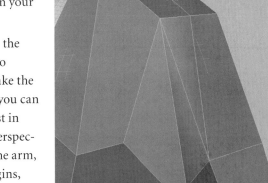

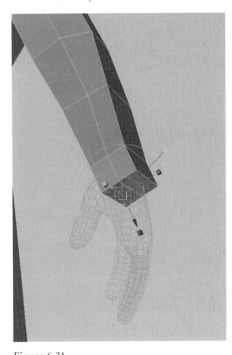

Figure 6.31

Extruded base of the arm

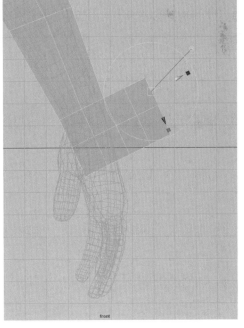

Figure 6.32

Extruded hand and base of thumb

40. In the front viewport, adjust the vertices of the base of the hand the same way as in Figure 6.33.

41. Extrude the four inner fingers out to about where the knuckles of the reference model are. Use the yellow cubes to scale them in a bit and then use the green arrow to translate them back (Figure 6.34).

42. Extrude the thumb out once, scale and translate the extruded face, and extrude it a second time to match the shape of a thumb (Figure 6.35).

43. Click Edit Mesh and deselect Keep Faces Together. In the perspective viewport, select the faces that would make the four fingers and extrude them out, use the red and green cubes to scale them in a bit, and extrude them again a second time (Figure 6.36). At this juncture, you could extrude them out one more time to create the three joints of a finger, but you have enough geometry for the pose you need.

44. Select your model, and then right-click to select Object Mode from the marking menu. Click Mesh → Mirror Geometry to bring up the Mirror Options dialog box. You will want to mirror our model in the negative X direction, and you want to make sure that Merge with the Original and Merge Vertices are selected. Click the Mirror button in the Mirror Options dialog box to create a mirror of your model (Figure 6.37). The progress thus far is available for you on the DVD as `human_base_mesh - step 41.ma` in the `Chapter6\1 - base_mesh` folder.

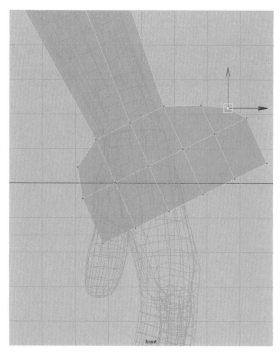

Figure 6.33
Arrange the vertices of the base of the hand.

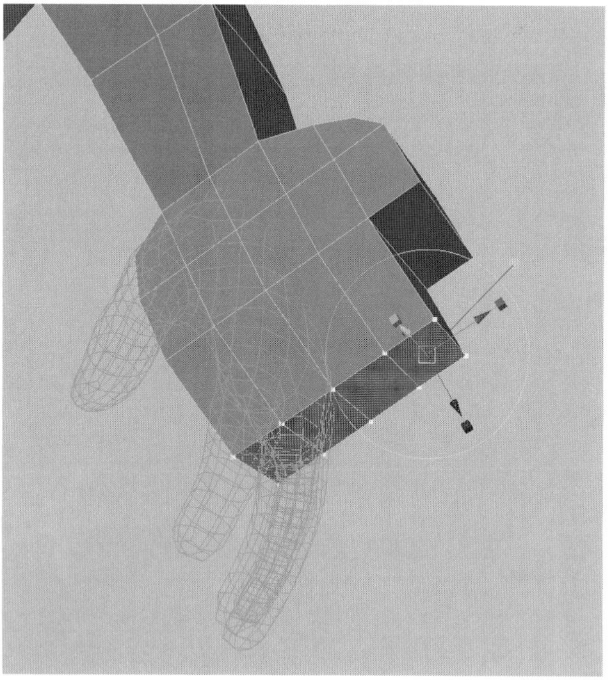

Figure 6.34
Extrude out the four inner fingers.

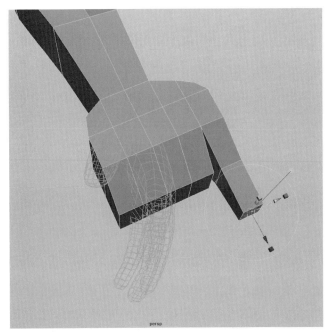

Figure 6.35

Extruding out the thumb

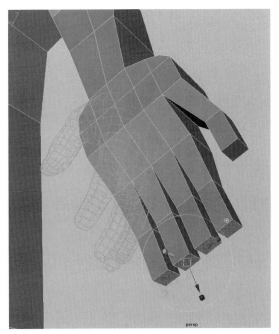

Figure 6.36

Extrude out the four fingers.

45. You are almost finished with the model; you just need to make a few adjustments to make the base mesh look more like the reference model after it is subdivided. Before you do that, you need to turn on a couple of options to help you with final adjustments. Double-click the Move tool and make sure that Reflection is selected under the Reflection section. Also make sure that X is the selected reflection axis.

46. In the perspective viewport, press 3 to turn on smooth mesh preview and click Shading → X-Ray to make the base mesh you just created transparent (Figure 6.38).

47. Right-click on the model and choose Vertex from the marking menu. Start moving the vertices to get a shape that is as close as possible to the reference model. Remember, the hands do not need to change in pose; you just need to make sure the proportions look correct (Figure 6.39). Note that as you modify the vertices, the modification is reflected to the other side because Reflection is turned on in the Move Tool options.

48. Press 1 and notice that as you get back to the unsmoothed version of the polygon, it looks very odd, but this base mesh will produce a base mesh similar to the reference model when you subdivide it in Mudbox. The progress thus far is available for you on the DVD as human_base_mesh - step 44.ma in the Chapter6\1 - base_mesh folder.

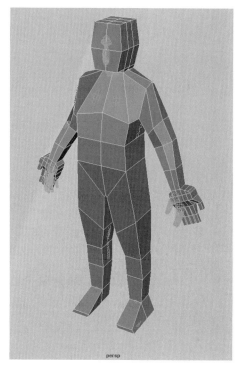

Figure 6.37

Mirrored model

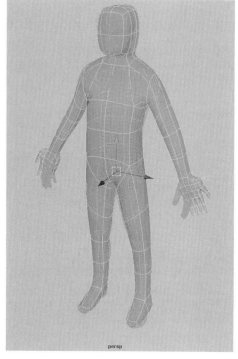

Figure 6.38

Perspective viewport with a smoothed, transparent model

Figure 6.39

Adjusted model

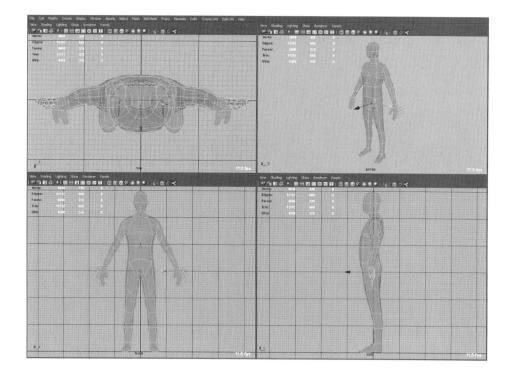

49. Make sure you have the `objExport.mll` (or bundle on the Mac) plug-in loaded by clicking Window → Settings/Preferences → Plug-in Manager and checking to make sure the Loaded check box is selected for `objExport.mll` (or bundle on the Mac). Right-click on your model in the perspective view, choose Object Mode, and select your model. Select the options for File → Export Selection, choose OBJexport from the File Type drop-down list, and scroll to the end and make sure that all the File Type Specific Options are turned off (Figure 6.40). Click Export Selection and save your base mesh as **human_base_mesh_male.obj**.

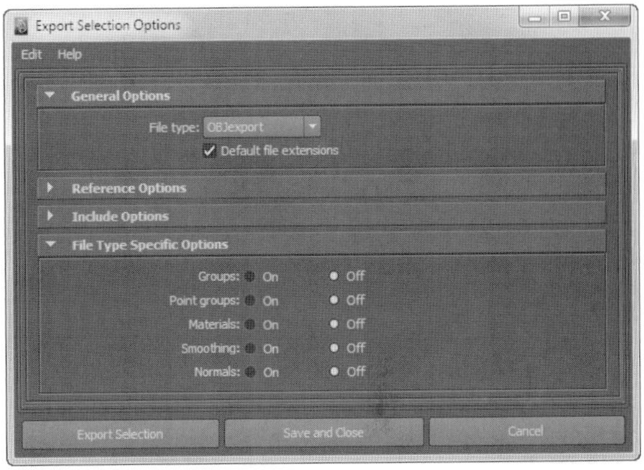

Figure 6.40

Export Selection options

One last thing to do, because our intended sculpt is that of a female, is to make a female version of this base mesh. This is very easy and requires making only minor adjustments. First, you need to note that the general anatomical differences in the two sexes at the detail level of the body we have are as follows:

- Lower and larger pelvis as the center of gravity of the female body
- Narrower shoulders
- Longer neck
- Smaller hands and feet
- Smaller, rounder head

Women generally also have larger cheekbones, a softer jaw line, a less-pronounced chin, and a larger space between the eyebrow and upper eyelid, but don't worry about that at this juncture.

50. Adjust the pixels on your model to account for the five differences listed. Notice that even at this low level of detail, you can tell the difference between the two sexes from the simple silhouettes (Figure 6.41).

51. Export the female version of your base mesh and call it **human_base_mesh_female.obj**.

The progress thus far is available for you on the DVD as `human_base_mesh - step 46.ma` in the `Chapter6\1 - base_mesh` folder.

You are finished with creating our very simple yet effective human base meshes that you can use to sculpt on. However, you still need to lay out the UVs of this model, which is what you will do in the next section.

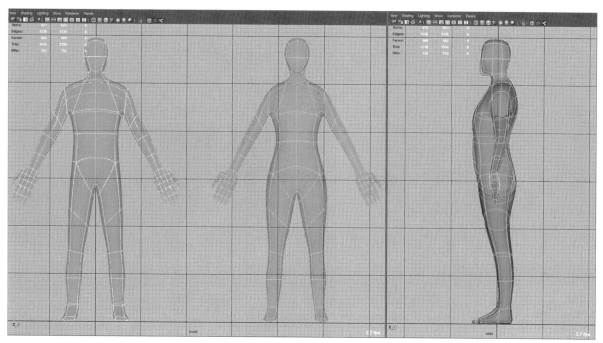

Figure 6.41

Differences in the male and female base meshes

Laying Out the UVs in UVLayout

I have found Headus UVLayout to be the easiest and fastest way to create UVs for our model. You can use it as a stand-alone application or interact with it through plug-ins or scripts that are available for the most popular 3D applications. You can download a trial version of the software from www.uvlayout.com, and it is available for sale in different configurations for different customer needs. I have found the pro version to be well worth its asking price because of the amount of time and aggravation it saves you. The website also has plenty of great videos to teach you how to use the software in addition to showing off the amazing feats this software can perform. The camera navigation in UVLayout is the same as it is in Maya and Mudbox. I have included a video, Chapter6-part2-UVLayout.mov on the DVD in the Chapter 6\Videos folder, of my laying out the UVs of the base mesh in UVLayout.

The steps you will go through to create UVs are the following:

1. Load the human_base_mesh_female.obj file.

2. Find good places for seams to cut to separate the mesh.

3. Flatten the pieces into UV shells and pack them in 0 to 1 UV space.

4. Export out the .obj file with the new UVs.

One thing to note is that I will not discuss UVLayout in depth, but will go through only what you need to do to create the UVs for this base mesh so you know where to start to create UVs for the base meshes you make for various projects. If you are comfortable laying out UVs in Maya or your preferred 3D application, please do so and skip this section. I have also provided finished versions of the model with UVs laid out for you on the DVD so you can just read this portion and then load the .obj file with the UVs into Mudbox for the next stage.

1. Start UVLayout, click Load, and navigate to where you saved your human_base_mesh_female.obj file and open it, or load the one from the Chapter6\1 - base_mesh folder. Make sure that New is selected, which tells Headus to disregard any UVs that the model has because you will be creating new ones (Figure 6.42).

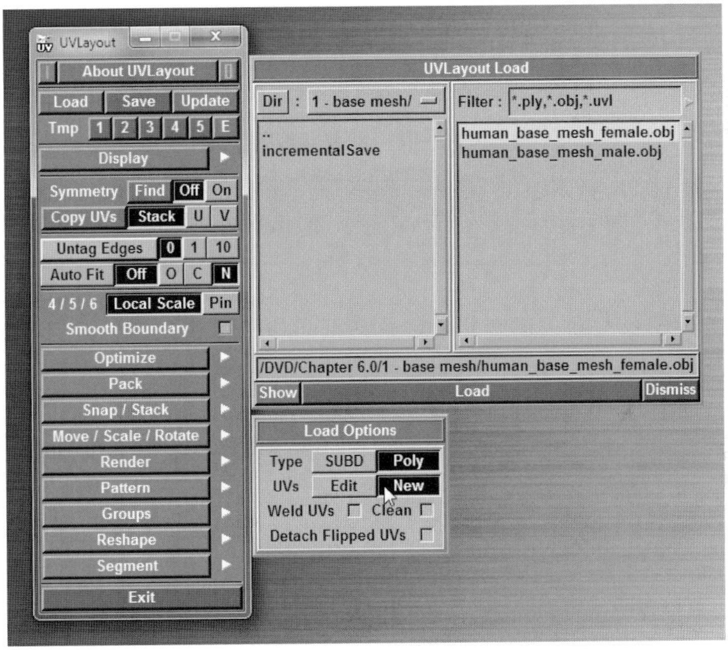

Figure 6.42

Headus open dialog box and settings

Headus will load this model into its Ed view or UV view. You can cycle between the three views (UV view, Ed view, and 3D view) by pressing the 1, 2, and 3 keys, respectively, on your keyboard. You will use the Ed view when you cut the seams and separate out the various shells.

2. Again you can use symmetry and do half the work. Press 2 to be in Ed view. Click the blue Find button next to the word Symmetry, click on an edge that is in the middle of the model, and press the spacebar. This colors half your model a darker shade of gray to indicate that symmetry is on (Figure 6.43).

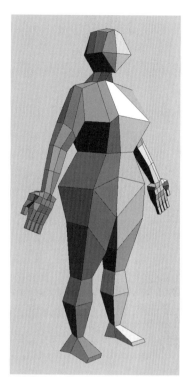

Figure 6.43

Symmetry activated in UVLayout

3. The head is always a good place to start. Move your cursor to any edge on the neckline and press the C key. This will mark that edge for cutting and it will also select its edge loop in yellow. Press Enter to perform the cut and separate the head (Figure 6.44).

4. Cut a seam from the tip of the forehead to the base of the back of the neck. Cut another horizontal seam across the back of the head. If you cut seams that you didn't mean to, move your cursor onto the edge you intend to weld and press the W key. Press Shift+S to separate the cut seams (Figure 6.45). Place your pointer on the head and press the D key to drop it into UV view. Press 1 to see the dropped head in UV view.

5. Cut seams around the wrists, legs, and arms, as in Figure 6.46. While pressing the spacebar, you can click and drag the pieces to move them.

6. Cut a seam in the back of the arm and press Shift+S to open up the seam (Figure 6.47). Move the cursor onto any one of the two arms and press the D key to drop both arms into UV view. Press 1 to see both arms and the head in UV view, and then press 2 again to return to Ed view.

7. Cut a seam along the inside back edges of the leg, and press Shift+S to open up the seam. Move the cursor onto any one of the two legs and press the D key to drop both of the legs into UV view.

Figure 6.44

"Off with her head!"

Figure 6.45

Seams on the head

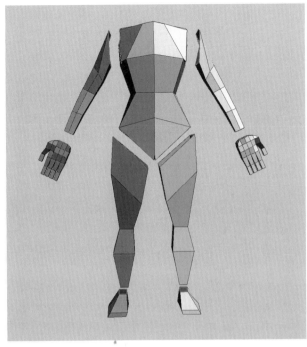

Figure 6.46

Cut seams and separate out feet, legs, and arms.

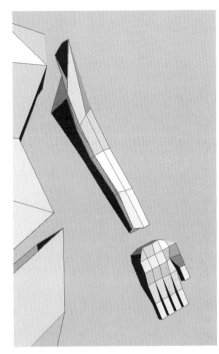

Figure 6.47

Seam along the arm

8. Cut a seam in the torso in the back (Figure 6.48). This might prove a little difficult because there are intersecting planes in the model. Take your time and rotate around the model to find the seams and then press the C key to cut them. You can also go to the Display menu and move the X-Ray slider to the left to make the model a little more transparent so you can see the intersection lines better. If you make accidental cuts, move your cursor to the edges you accidentally marked for cutting, and press the W key. Move your mouse cursor on top of the cut piece and press Enter to separate that piece out. Note that there are three areas that need to be separated. The first seam is from the neckline to the top of the shoulders, the second area is the sides, and the third is the bottom rear. When you are finished cutting and the pieces separate, move your cursor onto the cut pieces and press the D key to drop them into UV view.

9. Cut a seam around the soles of the feet and press Enter. Then cut a seam on the inside of the ankle and press Shift+S to open up the seam (Figure 6.49). Move your cursor onto the cut pieces and press the D key to drop them into UV view. At any point, if you want to frame whatever pieces are left in Ed view, press the Home key and it will show all the components that have not been dropped into Ed view.

Figure 6.48

Cutting seams to separate out the front and back torso

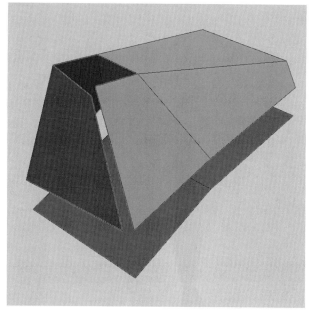

Figure 6.49

Cutting seams on the foot

10. The only two items left are the hands, and you need to cut seams in only one hand because the mirroring actions will repeat on the opposite side. Cut seams on the top and bottom of the hands (Figure 6.50), dividing each hand into three shells. Move your cursor onto each of the pieces and press the D key to drop them into UV view.

Figure 6.50

Seams on the hand

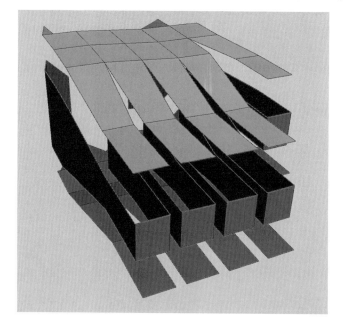

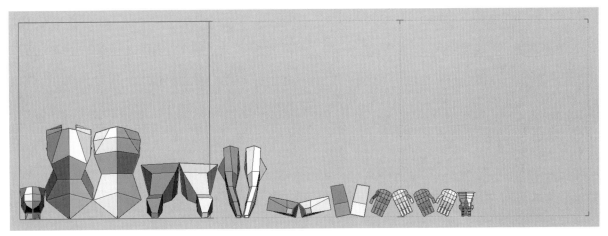

Figure 6.51

**UV shells in
the UV view**

You are finished cutting the seams and have all the shells ready to be flattened. Because of symmetry, you need to flatten only one side of the model and copy the work over to the other.

11 Press 1 to go to UV view; notice that all your shells are arranged at the bottom of the view (Figure 6.51) and they look as though they are still in the shape they were when you dropped them into UV view.

12. You can work on the shells anywhere on the screen. Don't worry about the arrangement just yet; you will arrange them when you are finished flattening all the shells. Click on the shell for the head to select it, press the spacebar, and click and drag with your middle mouse button to move it to an empty space in UV view.

13. With your mouse cursor on the head, press the F key to flatten it a little. You can also press the spacebar and the F key to continuously flatten until you press the spacebar again to stop. Or, you can just press Shift+F to activate the Bloat Then Reflatten function and watch as the head first gets stretched out and then flattened to completely unfold. This process alone is why using software such as UVLayout will cut hours of drudgery out of UVing.

The Bloat Then Reflatten function does a decent job of flattening the head. Headus UVLayout uses a color code to identify ideal, stretched, and compressed faces. Yellow indicates an ideal face, red is stretched, and blue is compressed. The shades of the aforementioned colors indicate how stretched or compressed the faces are. Solid blue or red is undesired. Solid yellow and the lightest possible shades of red and blue are what you strive for. As you see on the flattened head UV, there is a hint of a darker red in the bottom half of the face. Because this is an important area that will be painted and sculpted, you want to make sure you get them to be green.

14. Press Ctrl and middle-mouse click and drag on the vertices of the face to move them in a direction causing the face color to turn yellower. Remember, you need to do this only on the lighter side of the face. Move the vertices slightly until you have a shade close to the lightest shade of yellow, and when you are finished, move your mouse cursor on top of the half of the face that you worked on and press the S key. Notice that the S key mirrors the contents of the lighter mirrored area to the darker one (Figure 6.52).

15. Press 3 to go the 3D view. Press the T key to place a checkered pattern on the face. Press the T key again to get a more granular display with a grid and numbers. Tumble your model around the head and observe the effects of wrapping a texture on your model with all the stretching and compressing visible. You can also see the underlying shades of green, red, and blue, especially if you have solid blue or red areas. Going back and forth pressing 1 and 3, repeat step 14 until you are satisfied with the results (Figure 6.53). The pattern might look a bit skewed. but that is due to the very little geometry you are working with. As this model subdivides, you can reload it into UVLayout and do further refining.

16. Repeat the process performed in step 15 on all the other pieces of the model until you have the model completely flattened out. Remember to press the S key to mirror your work to the other side. Most of the pieces will flatten out pretty easily. The chest might need some extra work, but because you have very little geometry, the task is fairly simple and quick. When you are finished, you will have all the shells flattened all over the UV screen and you can press 3 to see the pattern all over your model (Figure 6.54).

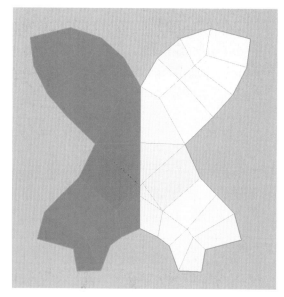

Figure 6.52

Flattened face

Figure 6.53

Texture-check the UVs

Figure 6.54

**Fully UVed model
with textures**

17. The next step is to pack all the pieces together. You can click on the individual pieces and use spacebar+left-click and drag to rotate them. Pressing the S key while clicking on the pieces mirrors them and also has the added benefit of placing them next to your piece. You can either manually arrange the pieces in the first UV tile or let the software do it for you. To manually move the shells, click on the shells to select them and then hold down the spacebar and middle-click and drag on the shells; they will turn pink, and you will be able to position them anywhere on the screen. You can also resize the shells by using the spacebar+right-click and drag combination, but this is not something you need at this juncture. To have UVLayout arrange the shells for you, click the Pack button, which will expand the packing options for you. Select Best, because you have only a few shells and the time taken will be nominal. You might want to revisit this with Fast or Mid in the future for models that have more polygons if UVLayout is taking too long to arrange your shells. Type **6** in the

Bleed text box to make room for 6 pixels between the UV shells and the borders of the 0 to 1 UV tile. Click Pack All and watch UVLayout arrange your pieces for you (Figure 6.55).

I find that I need to do a bit of arranging myself to get a little more space efficiency and proximity of shells to patterns (Figure 6.56).

I have included the files `pre_drop.uvl` and `final.uvl` on the DVD in the `Chapter 6\2 - UV` folder. You can load these into UVLayout to catch up to the progress or see my work.

18. Finally, you will save the model as **`human_base_mesh_female_UV.obj`**. I have included my version of this model as well, on the DVD in the `Chapter 6\2 - UV` folder.

I hope you have seen how UVLayout can simplify the process with its amazing capabilities of Symmetry, Bloat and Reflatten, and the automatic packing of the UVs. There are plenty of other extremely useful capabilities that I did not have the time to get into, so make sure to look at the videos on the website.

You now have a model with UVs ready to import into Mudbox for posing and sculpting.

Figure 6.55

UVs packed by UVLayout

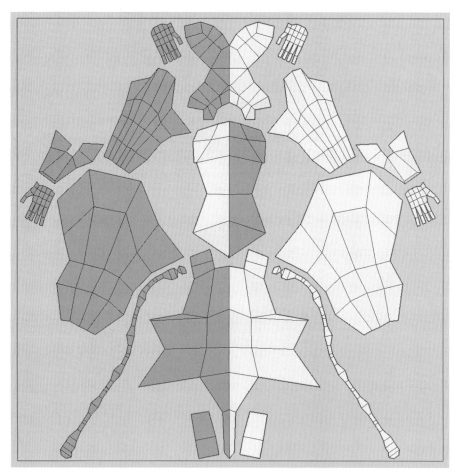

Figure 6.56

**Minor adjustments
to the UV
arrangement**

Posing the Base Mesh

A good pose makes or breaks your model's presentation. It's always ideal to have a live model in front of you as a reference to sculpt the pose. If that's not available to you, 2D reference images work, but you need a good understanding of anatomy to figure out the weight distribution and balance of the angles beyond what is on your image. Having images from different angles helps but if you do not, you might want to consider either doing the pose yourself or coercing a friend.

You should pay attention to balance so the pose looks plausible. Make sure you know where the plumb line and the center of gravity are on the posed figure. Do the pose yourself to get an idea of balance and weight distribution because that will help you with the balancing of your model. Think of the weight of the various masses of the body and how they influence the strain on the muscles. Ask yourself, If your model was printed as a solid, would it stand or fall over?

When posing a model, I always start with the three defining shapes of the body: the head, ribcage, and pelvis. Posing these three correctly makes the rest of the work easier, and if these shapes are not posed correctly, your entire pose will look unrealistic. The order in which these shapes are posed is up to you. Some people like to start with the pelvis, others with the head, and yet others with the biggest shape, the ribcage. So take your time in posing these three shapes, and the extremities will fall into place.

Finally, make sure to focus on the model's gesture. Make sure you have rhythm lines in the pose for your audience's eyes to follow. Study some of the classics; try to emulate some of the same poses yourself with your models. You might get a whole new level of appreciation for them.

Using the Posing Toolset

With the introduction of the posing toolset in Mudbox 2011, you can now pose, position, transform, and scale your models into various stances without exporting your model to other applications. This capability removes yet another noncreative step from your workflow. Although the posing toolset is primarily aimed at posing characters, this capability can also be used to deform, move, bend, and twist noncharacter models. The four tools of the posing toolset are Create Joint, Pose, Weights, and Move Pivot. These are found in the Pose Tools tray.

You can pose your model by using the Create Joint tool to place pivot points called *joints* on your model. These joints act as origins for translating, rotating, and scaling sets of vertices. After you place your joint on the model, you indicate which vertices it manipulates by drawing out a weight vector in the direction of the parts of the model you wish to manipulate (Figure 6.57).

Figure 6.57

Joint, weight vector, and joint boundary ring

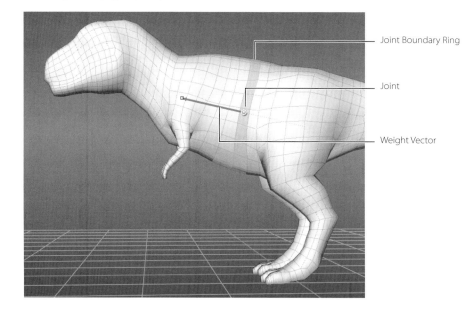

Joint Boundary Ring

Joint

Weight Vector

The color of the weights, which is green by default, can be customized by clicking Windows → Preferences → Color (Mudbox → Preferences → Color on the Mac) and adjusting the Joint Weight color.

The region of influence is indicated in saturation levels of green; solid green areas will be influenced the most during posing (Figure 6.58), and the rest of the green areas will be influenced by their degree of saturation.

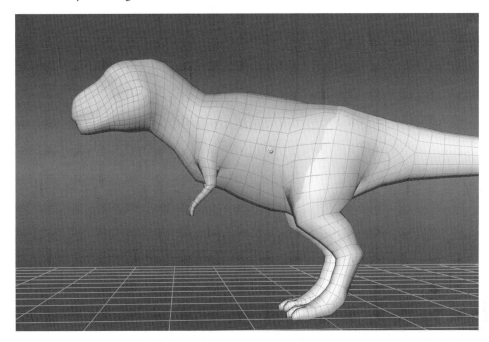

Figure 6.58

Region of influence here as the upper body of the dinosaur

The region of influence surrounding the joint fades based on the Falloff curve property, which is the only property for the Create Joint tool. This falloff curve can be adjusted the same way as adjusting it for sculpting or painting tools. The falloff determines how the weight changes between the area that is fully weighted (green) and the area that is completely not weighted (not green). Between those two extremes, the weighting can change linearly, exponentially, or however you specify based on the curvature of the falloff curve before creating the joint. You will see the results of this as the green coloration feathers off gently or with a sharper edge.

You can subsequently move the joint to a more suitable position by using the Move Joint Pivot, and also by adjusting the degree of influence, referred to as the *weight*, by painting it on in green or erasing it with the Weights tool. The Weights tool is identical to a paint tool in its usage.

Then you are ready to use the Pose tool to rotate, translate, and scale the weighted areas associated with the joint. The transformations of your pose use the camera view as a plane of reference. Clicking and dragging left and then right by using the left mouse/stylus button rotates the component about a vertical axis through the joint and planar to the current camera view (Figure 6.59). You do not need to click on the model; clicking anywhere on the screen works.

Figure 6.59

Rotating the area of influence

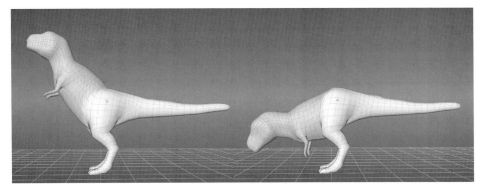

If you click and drag on the joint itself while pressing the left mouse/stylus button, a forward or backward motion rotates the component about a horizontal axis through the joint and on the same plane as the current camera view (Figure 6.60).

Figure 6.60

Rotating the area of influence by clicking and dragging on the pivot and moving the mouse forward or backward

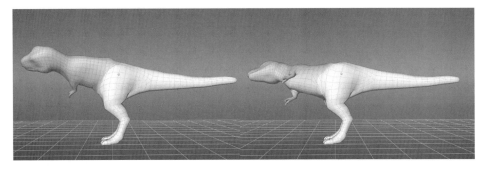

If you click and drag on the pivot itself while pressing the left mouse/stylus button, a left or right motion rotates the component about a vertical axis through the joint and on the same plane as the current camera view (Figure 6.61).

Figure 6.61

Rotating the area of influence by clicking and dragging on the pivot and moving the mouse left or right

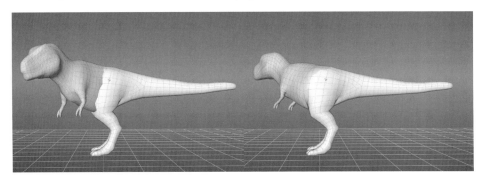

To move the area of influence, click and drag on the region of influence with the middle mouse button (Figure 6.62). Notice that the geometry is stretched when you do this. You need to use the Smooth tool afterward to evenly distribute or relax the polygons. You might also want to export out the model and add a few more edge loops to the stretched-out area.

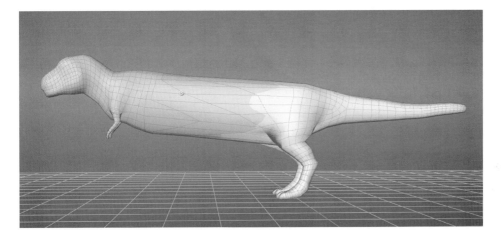

Figure 6.62

Moving the area of influence by middle-clicking and dragging

To scale the area of influence, click and drag on it while pressing both the left and middle buttons on your mouse or stylus (Figure 6.63). Notice also that the geometry is stretched in or out and is not in the same scale as the rest of the model.

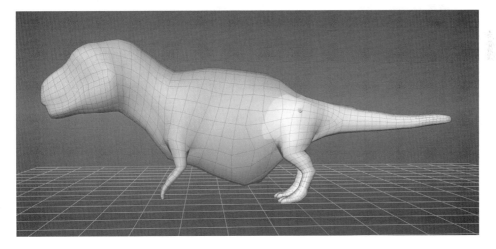

Figure 6.63

Scaling the area of influence by left+middle-clicking and dragging

You can invert the parts of the model that are to be posed by the region of influence when using the Pose tool by pressing the Ctrl key before clicking and dragging with any button to perform the rotate, move, or scale operation on an inverse selection of the area of influence (Figure 6.64).

Figure 6.64

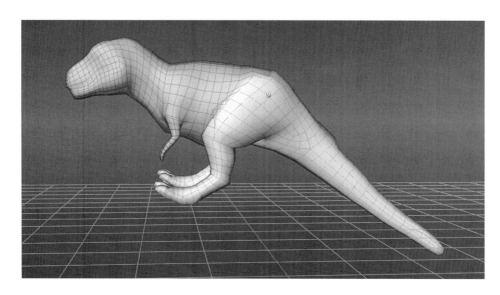

One of the most powerful capabilities of the posing toolset is posing multiple objects
at the same time. This capability is extremely useful when you are posing a head with
eyeballs as two separate objects, or a human figure with multiple clothing or accessory
objects that need to be posed along with the body. The method for doing this is simple:
You paint weights on the separate objects you need to move as well as on the part of the
object that you are posing. For example, suppose we have the dinosaur in Figure 6.65 and
a scenario where his tail has skewered three balls. If we pose the tail, we would need to
move and position each of the three balls to accommodate for the pose, and if subsequent
poses needed to be done to the tail again, we would have to repeat moving and positioning the three balls every time. With the posing toolset in Mudbox 2011, this process is
made much easier.

Figure 6.65

**Three balls on a
T. rex tail**

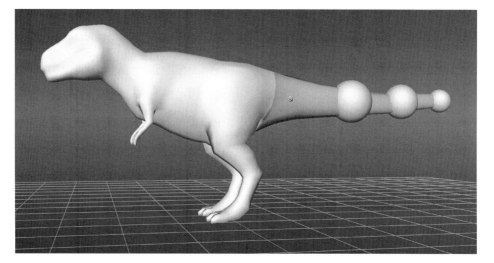

After you draw the weight vector on the tail, which highlights the areas you will be able to pose in green, you can use the Weights tool to paint the three balls so they are within the influence of the tail pose. Choose a larger Size for the Weights tool than the size of the balls to paint the weights on faster.

Follow these steps to pose multiple objects:

1. Start Mudbox and load the `multi object pose.mud` file from the `Chapter 6` folder of the DVD. In the Object List, notice that there are four independent meshes in the scene: the T. rex and the three spheres.

2. From the Pose Tools tray, select the Create Joint tool and draw a weight vector on the tail (see Figure 6.65 earlier).

3. From the Pose Tools tray, click the Pose tool and pose the tail; notice that the three spheres do not move with the tail (Figure 6.66).

Figure 6.66

Posing the tail without the three spheres

4. Press Ctrl+Z to undo the pose so the tail is in its original position, or reload the file and add the joint by repeating steps 1 and 2.

5. Click the Weights tool and choose a brush size larger than the spheres. Then paint weights on the spheres so they are completely covered in green (Figure 6.67).

6. Use the Pose tool to pose the tail; note that the three spheres now move with the tail (Figure 6.68).

Figure 6.67

Weight-painted spheres

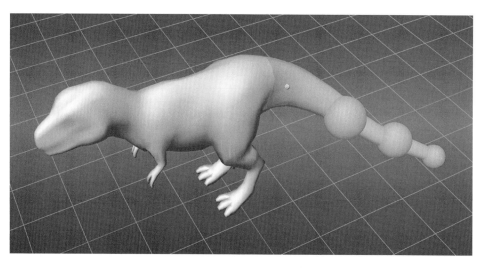

Figure 6.68

Combined pose

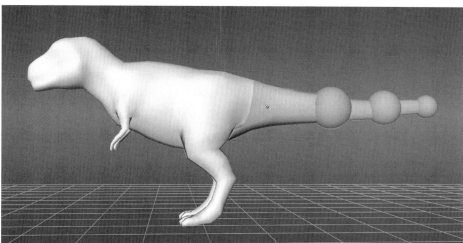

Mesh objects get weight-painted individually, so if you click on a mesh, such as one of the spheres, you can continue to paint weights on the object, and only that object until you release the click, even if you move your brush onto other objects. This is also true when 3D painting. When you start a stroke on a mesh, you will paint only on that mesh, whether using the paint tools or the Weights painting tool, until you release the stroke. This makes it inconvenient to paint across multiple meshes, but extremely convenient if you intend to limit your work to one mesh.

An important thing to remember when posing is that Mudbox is primarily a sculpting program, so even though you have the new powerful and versatile posing toolset, your main posing tools are still the sculpting tools, primarily the Grab tool to move geometry around, and the Smooth tool to evenly redistribute the polygons after you move them around. Your workflow will be faster if you mostly use the Grab tool on the pose until you run into a limitation, such as rotation, that it can't address, or until you determine that your workflow would be faster if you were to use the pose tools for the specific scenario. The reason for this is that you can continuously use the Grab tool and adjust your model versus creating a joint, moving the joint, painting weights on the joint, and then posing it. That said, the Grab tool cannot do the work of the posing toolset, because some poses would be impossible to do with the Grab tool. It will take some practice working with the posing toolset and the sculpting tools for you to determine your best workflow for getting the perfect pose.

It is also best to pose your model at the lowest subdivision level possible because you then manipulate fewer vertices and polygons with the Grab tool or the posing toolset, allowing your workflow to progress much faster. This is the reason you modeled a human base mesh with the minimal geometry in Maya previously in this chapter. The model is easier to pose at this lowest subdivision level than at higher subdivision levels, and you can always drop down to the lower subdivision level and make the adjustments further on in the progress. You should be able to get your pose with the blocky view of the low-res mesh. In Figure 6.69, you can see the pose with the minimal geography. After the base pose is set, you can then move up in subdivision levels to do more fine-tuning of the pose and sculpt details.

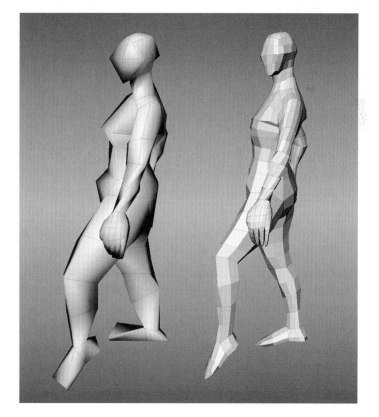

Figure 6.69

Blocked-out pose at lower subdivision levels

Posing the Model

In this section, you will pose the human base mesh you modeled earlier in Maya; you will start with the head, then the chest/ribcage and pelvis, and finally the arms and legs. I will be using references that I have collected over the years to create a collage of poses from various images. You can do the same, or try to do a pose of a classic sculpture such as Michelangelo's or Donatello's *David*, or any sculpture by Rodin or Degas.

I will go through posing the head, pelvis, legs, and an arm, and the methods used to pose them are the same for the rest of the model. Go through and pose the model yourself. You can load the fully posed model `Pose_4_body.mud` from the `Chapter 6\3-pose` folder of the DVD and examine the pose of the model I worked on. A couple of things before you get started:

- Pose your model subtly and incrementally instead of making huge pose gestures. This will help you adjust the topology and polygon distribution as you go along versus major changes in a pose that might need much more work to adjust.

- Place each pose on a separate sculpt layer so that you can easily undo it by deleting the layer or adjusting the opacity of the layer to fine-tune your pose.

Even though you have a very low-polygon-count model with the base mesh, you can define the gesture of the model here with the pose:

1. Either load the model you created the UVs for in the previous section, or load the `human_base_mesh_female_UV.obj` model from the `Chapter 6\2 - UV` folder of the DVD.

2. Create seven sculpt layers called **head**, **ribcage**, **arm_lf**, **arm_rt**, **pelvis**, **leg_lf**, **leg_rt**. Save your model as **pose_1.mud** so you have a ground-zero file to work from.

3. Place a joint on your model by clicking the Create Joint tool on the Pose Tools tray and clicking and holding down the click on the neck of your model to set the pivot or origin of your pose (Figure 6.70). When you create a joint, it is automatically positioned at the center of the ring of faces of the joint boundary ring; in this case, that would be the middle of the neck. Do not release the click yet, because you will be dragging out the weight vector in the next step.

4. Drag out a weight vector to set the region of influence, which is determined by how far you drag the weight vector from the joint location. The farther out you drag the weight vector, the less weight you will get closer to the origin. Therefore, drag your weight vector to about the top of the head (Figure 6.71) because you want the posing operation on the head to manipulate the whole head with little to no falloff. You want the head to have a solid green color after you let go of the mouse or stylus.

   This same operation of dragging out of the weight vector also lets you set a joint boundary ring, which is a solid green ring perpendicular to the weight vector that outlines where the region of influence begins in relation to the joint. This operation results in a region highlighted in green that you subsequently can pose with the Pose tool.

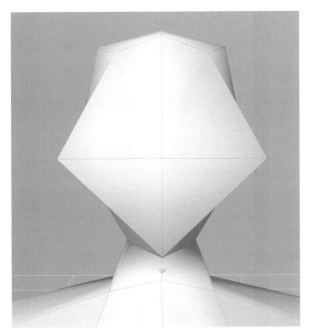

Figure 6.70

Click on the neck to set your joint.

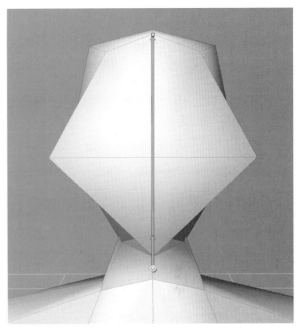

Figure 6.71

Drag out the weight vector to the tip of the head.

5. Now that you have created a joint and set the region you want to manipulate based on the weight vector, you need to look at our model to determine whether the origin of rotation is what you need. It is not—because you want to rotate the head at the base of the skull versus the middle of the neck—so you need to move the joint up to that area. Using the Move Pivot tool, click and drag the joint up into the head so it is aligned at the base of the skull, halfway between the bottom of the neck and the top of the head (Figure 6.72). You might need to navigate the camera to a few different angles to make sure your joint is centralized in your model. After you move a joint, it is no longer placed at the center of the joint boundary ring, or your volume, so you will need to adjust it from at least three angles to make sure it is placed where you need it to be.

Figure 6.72

Move the pivot to the base of the skull.

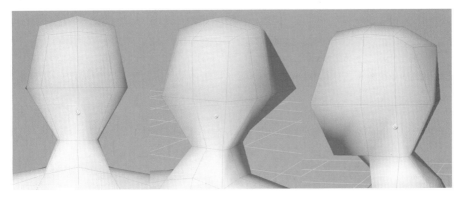

6. Click on the head sculpt layer in the Sculpt Layers window. You have created a joint and set the area you need to pose, so now you will click the Pose tool to perform the pose. Notice that as you move your cursor onto the model, the cursor changes as you move it onto the pivot versus the rest of the model (Figure 6.73).

Figure 6.73

Cursor change on the joint and on the model

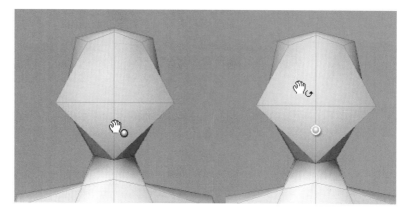

7. With the cursor on the pivot, click and drag in a left or right motion while pressing the left mouse/stylus button to rotate the head until it is turned slightly left (Figure 6.74).

Figure 6.74

Rotate the head to the left.

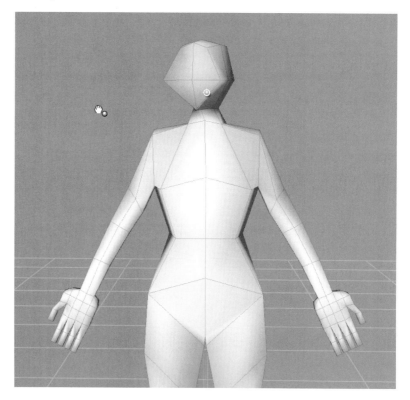

8. With the cursor on the pivot, click and drag in an up or down motion while pressing the left mouse/stylus button to rotate the head until it is turned slightly up (Figure 6.75).

9. While looking at your model head-on, click and drag left or right using the left mouse/stylus button while your cursor is not on the pivot, to tilt the head slightly to the left (Figure 6.76).

10. With the cursor on the pivot, click and drag while pressing the middle mouse/stylus button to move the head slightly to the left so the neck doesn't look broken (Figure 6.77).

11. In the Sculpt Tools tray, click the Grab tool. In the Sculpt Layers window, click on the head sculpt layer and adjust its opacity. Notice that the pose will now go from the neutral position you had it in to the posed position. If you are happy with your final pose, leave the opacity at 100. If somewhere in between works better for you, leave the opacity at that level.

    That's all there is to the mechanics of posing. The art of posing is something you will work on for a long time.

12. To pose the ribcage, first select the ribcage sculpt layer in the Sculpt Layers window, and then place a joint around where the belly button would be. Using the Pose tool, pose the ribcage so your model is leaning to the left a little and bending back. Add a little twist of the torso (Figure 6.78).

13. With the Pose tool still selected, click on the ribcage sculpt layer. Using the same methods as before, hold down the Ctrl key and click and drag the model to pose the bottom half of the body. Adjust the legs so they angle back (Figure 6.79). This messes up the plumb line, and makes the model look like it is floating, but you will fix this in the next stage. You have just posed the pelvis.

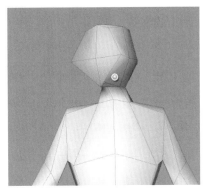

Figure 6.75
Rotate the head up.

Figure 6.76
Cursor on the pivot point

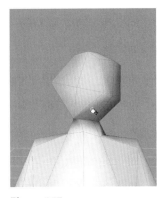

Figure 6.77
Tilt the head.

Figure 6.78

Rotate the torso back and twist to the right.

Figure 6.79

Pose and rotate the pelvis back.

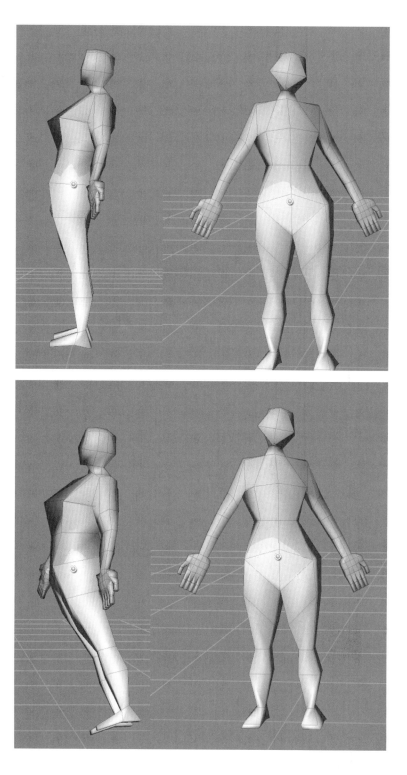

14. Next you will pose the legs. Select the `leg_rt` layer in the Sculpt Layers window. Place a joint on the leg (Figure 6.80).

15. Move the pivot to where the ball joint of the femur would be (Figure 6.81).

16. Use the Weights tool and paint on the pelvis area of the model to remove the weights on that area. Remember that you would need to hold down the Ctrl key to erase. You might want to increase the Strength to 100 to make sure you erase all the weight on the pelvis. Remember that the value of green determines how much an area will move when you pose it.

17. Use the Pose tool to rotate the leg forward and to the right (Figure 6.82).

18. Create a new joint at the knee and bend the shin back and out by using the Pose tool (Figure 6.83).

19. Click on the `leg_lf` sculpt layer. Pose the left leg, moving it straight down and in, using the same routine (Figure 6.84).

20. Finally, we will pose the right arm. Click on the `arm_rt` sculpt layer to select it. Then place a joint starting on the base of the arm and drag out (Figure 6.85).

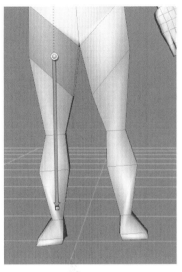

Figure 6.80

Creating a joint on the right leg

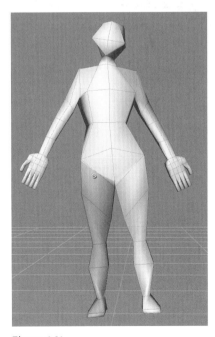

Figure 6.81

Move the joint to ball joint of the femur.

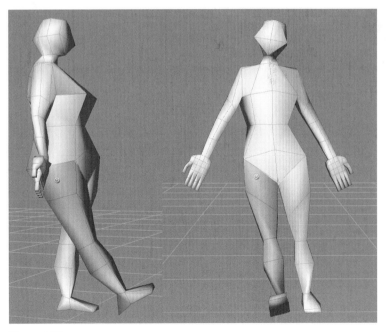

Figure 6.82

Rotate the leg forward.

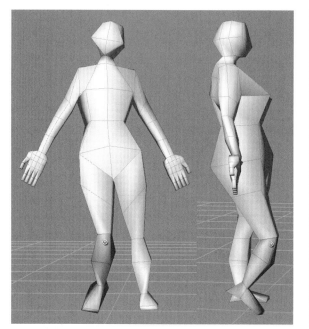

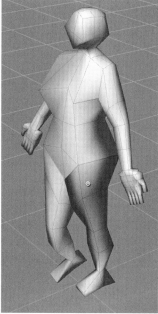

Figure 6.83

Rotate the shin back.

Figure 6.84

Pose the left leg.

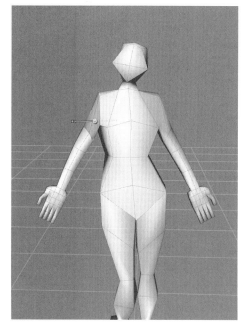

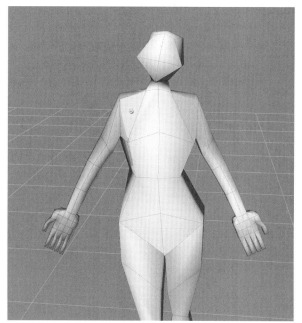

Figure 6.86

Move the pivot to the shoulder.

Figure 6.85

Create the joint on the right arm.

21. Move the pivot to where the scapula, or the shoulder blade, would be (Figure 6.86). Remember to move the camera around to make sure that the pivot is where you want it to be inside the model. You might need to use the Weights tool to remove any green shading on the shoulders.

22. Rotate the arm a little. If the shoulder or the armpit swings out with the arm, use the Weights tool to paint off the weights in that area. Rotate the arm so it is up (Figure 6.87).

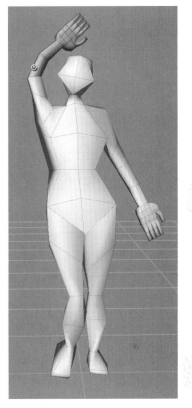

Figure 6.87

Rotate the arm up.

23. Place a pivot on the elbow and bend the forearm (Figure 6.88).

24. Place a joint in the middle of the forearm. Click and drag on the pivot to rotate the forearm (Figure 6.88). This rotation can get radical because the of the way the radius and ulna of the forearm twist to accommodate the hand rotating a full 180 degrees. To accommodate for a more radical rotation, you can move the pivot a few times down the forearm and rotate in increments. Pose the other arm the same way.

25. From this point on, we will make adjustments by using the Grab tool. Although a lot of these edits can be made with the posing toolset, it is a lot faster and easier to make the changes by using the Grab tool. Press Shift+D to subdivide the model to level 1. Notice the blocky shapes have become smoother and curvier (Figure 6.89).

26. Use the Grab tool, and start moving the polygons at this low subdivision level to flesh out the gesture and bring out the major anatomical shapes and dimensions. The pose of the model I am going with is a collage of some reference pictures I have from various fashion pictures I have collected over the years. Go down in subdivision levels to make major adjustments if necessary.

Try the posing tools at subdivision level 1 to see how the tools work at higher resolutions. After working with the model for about 15 to 20 minutes by using the Grab and Smooth tools, I came up with the result in Figure 6.91 that we will take into the next section to further sculpt it.

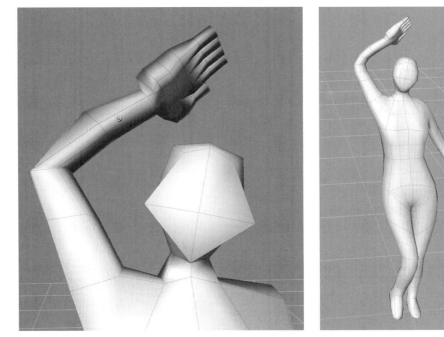

Figure 6.88
Bend the forearm.

Figure 6.89
First level of subdivision

Figure 6.90
Fully posed model

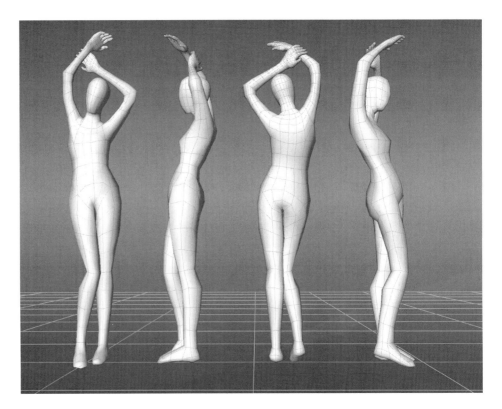

Sculpting the Model

Now that you have posed the model, it is time to start subdividing and sculpting. However, you are not quite finished with the posing. After subdividing your model, either before or after you start sculpting, you will notice that there are some parts that look out of place with the pose as it pertains to balance, gesture, proportion, or anatomy. Some of these can be fixed with the Grab tool, but certain types of motions, specifically rotation of extremities on a pivot, cannot be accommodated with the Grab tool in Mudbox. You might need to revisit some of the posing toolset and Rotate, Scale, and Translate sections of the model.

Figure 6.91

Posed divided model

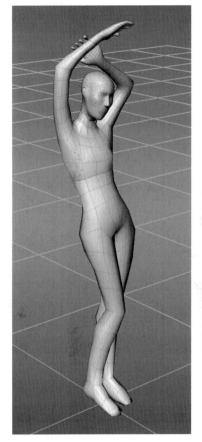

1. Open the file `01_sculptstart.mud` from the `Chapter 6\04 - sculpt` folder on the DVD (Figure 6.91).

    Notice that it is the same model we posed earlier. The only difference is that the level 1 subdivided model we worked on in the preceding section has been exported as an `.obj` file into Maya and separated into five pieces: the head, body top, body bottom, left hand, and right hand. This has been done by selecting the faces representing the five parts and using the Mesh → Extract function of Maya. The reason for this is that separate pieces can now be individually subdivided to the needed level of detail instead of subdividing the whole model. For example, we will need more geometry to get the details of the face versus the other parts of the body, and instead of having a very dense model to accommodate for that, we can now subdivide the different parts to the lowest detail level that will give us the polygon resolution we need. The other change is that the head we started out with has been replaced with the `basic_head` mesh that is provided in Mudbox. The reason for this is that the head mesh provided in Mudbox has better topology than the one we had in our base mesh and it can very easily be translated, scaled, and rotated to fit the same area.

SCALING CAN BE AN ISSUE WITH THE SCULPTING TOOLS IN MUDBOX

You will notice that if you scale down a mesh in Mudbox, the sculpting tools will act on it the same way they would when it was on the larger scale. You will get unpredictable and uncharacteristic results as you try to sculpt, because the sculpt tools will react to the model as if it were in its original scale. For example, if we just added the basic head mesh to the model and scaled it down, it would manifest this problem. The solution is to scale the head down, export it as an `.obj` file, and then import it back in.

You will also notice that the material used is the Gesso material. I find the Gesso material instead of the default glossier brown to be my favorite while sculpting because it does a good job of contrasting light and shadows for the shapes. As I am getting closer to the finished model, I change over to the default material and change the color to white because that adds a little more glossiness and specular highlights to the model. I am sure you either have or will develop your own preferred material to sculpt in.

2. Subdivide the body_top, body_bottom, hand_lf, and hand_rt parts to level 1 but make sure that you have Smooth Positions deselected in the Subdivision Options dialog box Figure 6.92). This will maintain the form you sculpted in while you posed the model, and works well only if you are going from level 0 to level 1.

Figure 6.92

Deselect Smooth Positions only for subdivision level 1

Make sure you select the Smooth Positions check box for subsequent subdivisions. At higher subdivisions, if this option is not selected, you get a faceted subdivision, and unless you are going for that look, you will have to do a lot of work smoothing out the creased facets (Figure 6.93). With experience, you will learn how a model subdivides and how shapes shift, shrink, and get smoothed by the operation.

Figure 6.93

The difference between subdividing with Smooth Positions off and on

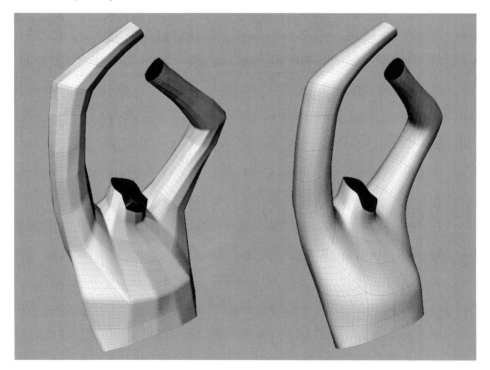

SCULPTING ON DIFFERENT SUBDIVISION LEVELS

One of the most critical skills you will need to develop when sculpting in Mudbox, or any digital sculpting application that has multiple subdivision levels, is to know how and when to sculpt your model at the different levels. Always start with the lowest levels to get the general shape you want, and work your way up in subdivision levels. Go back down in subdivision levels again if you need to make adjustments that would be faster and easier with less geometry.

In my experience, new digital sculptors often go immediately to the higher subdivision levels and start working there, mostly on minor details, even low-frequency detail, without fleshing out the main form at the lower subdivision levels. You could have an immaculately detailed model with the most beautiful facial pore representation or intricate reptilian scales, but the whole package falls apart if the basic shapes, proportions, balance, and anatomy are not sound at the lower subdivision levels. Note that we paid a lot of attention to this even with our initial base mesh model.

3. At subdivision level 1, use the Grab tool with a large Size to make major adjustments and a small Size to move vertices or proximity of vertices. Remember that the tool will move the polygons on the surface based on your falloff curve.

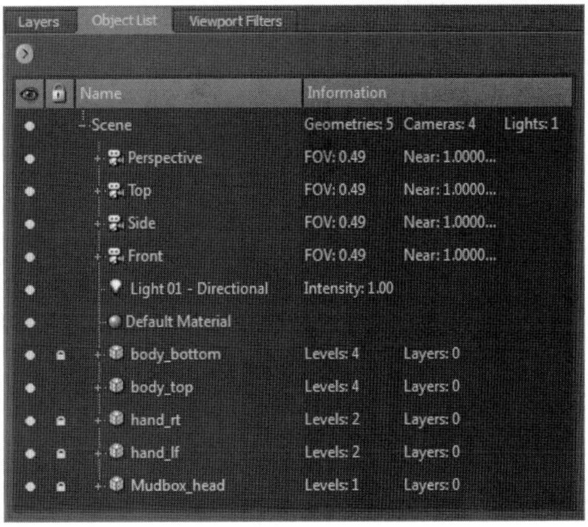

Figure 6.94

Locking all the meshes except body_lowermesh

4. Use the lock capability in the Object List to lock all the meshes of the model you don't want to accidentally manipulate by clicking in the padlock column next to the name of the object (Figure 6.94). You can also use the visibility option to turn visibility of objects on or off if they are getting in the way.

5. Use the Flatten tool to define planes. Even though you are at this very low level of subdivision, many of the major planes on the body can be defined here—for example, the underarm area, the face, and so forth. Think of these planes as scaffolding on top of which you will build up or down the desired shape on the next subdivision level.

6. Even at this low subdivision level, you can use the Wax tool to bulge out or push in details where the geometry allows.

Remember to use the Size and Strength keyboard shortcuts to continuously adjust the effect of the tool on the surface. Also remember to constantly keep tumbling around your model to examine your changes from different vantage points to see whether they are working. You might have spent a long time on a feature such as the bulk of the ribcage from one angle and then notice that it completely throws off the physical shape of the ribcage from other angles. Sculpture is created on a three-dimensional canvas and needs to work from any vantage point.

I personally like to sculpt on lower levels with the wireframe on, because topology matters at the lower levels. The last thing you want to do is scrunch up vertices to obtain a shape that would unevenly subdivide certain areas so they do not contain enough geometry, while others have plenty of geometry that is not needed. Much of your sculpting at this level is working on a base-level mesh, so the rules of having a good base mesh carry over, specifically, keeping an even distribution of quads.

7. Use the Smooth tool to constantly adjust the polygon distribution and smoothness of the surface. Make sure you work with lower strengths so you don't completely smooth out features on the surface. It's better to run over a surface multiple times than to completely erode and smooth out a shape you spent a lot of time developing. While you are tumbling around, also use different shading to see some features that you were not able to see in the default smooth shading.

8. Right-click in the 3D view and deselect Smooth Shade; this gives you the best depiction of the topology with a faceted version of the model. Right-click in the 3D view again and select Flat Lighting; this will give your model a silhouette look. You might want to tumble around your model with the wireframe on to see whether the silhouette is working, and then for the ultimate test, turn the wireframe off and look at your model. Zoom in and out while you are looking at your model in this silhouette mode (Figure 6.95). If your silhouette works at this level, it will work at every level, because this is the first shape your eyes will interpret. I have found squinting and looking at the model at this stage helps tremendously.

9. Press l and click-drag your mouse or stylus around to change the lighting on your model. This is also a good way to find areas of the shape of the model that need adjusting (Figure 6.96).

10. Use the Grab, Smooth, Flatten, and Wax tools to sculpt as much as you can until you start running into the limitations of this subdivision level. You will notice the limitations when you are trying to refine a shape, but you just don't have enough geometry.

11. Subdivide all the parts of your model to level 2 and continue to refine the shapes by using the preceding methods. Save your model at every subdivision level and at every point that you are satisfied with the result of your work. Remember to also use layers to easily get to a starting point in case things don't go well.

12. Isolate areas to work on them, or see their cross sections by using the Faces tool from the Select/Move Tools tray to select the faces you want to work on (Figure 6.97). They get highlighted in yellow. Then click Display → Hide Unselected to hide the rest of your model and work only on the desired section. To bring everything on your model back, click Display → Show All, or press the U key.

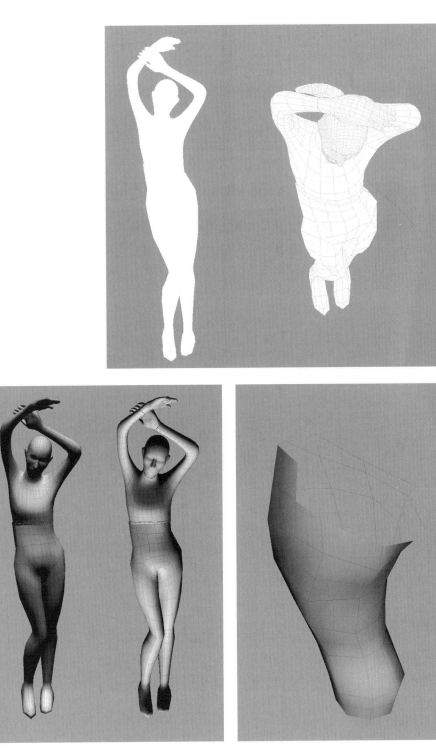

Figure 6.95

**Silhouette of model
at level 2**

Figure 6.96

Different lighting on the same model

Figure 6.97

Cross section of a leg

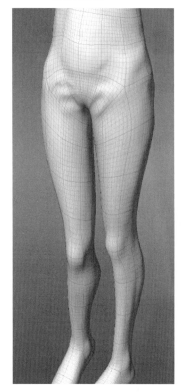

13. When you run into the limitations of a subdivision level, subdivide the model and continue using the Grab, Wax, Smooth, Flatten, and Bulge tools to start refining the sculpture. Remember, you can always activate the Smooth tool by pressing the Shift key so you do not have to keep going back and forth between the Smooth tool and the others.

14. At level 3 you will be able to sculpt some more-defining shapes and details such as folds, indentations, and line definition (Figure 6.98). In my model, I have created the knees and ankles, added some line definition to the shins, and introduced some folds on the pants.

From this point on, the sculpting actions are the same. You subdivide the model and sculpt on it until you run into limitations of the level and need more geometry. Save your work before you subdivide you model, because you might want to go back and modify the model at that lower subdivision state. You could also add your new subdivision level on a new layer, and keep saving the same file. Either way is a good way to go back to the last known good state that your model was in just in case things go awry at the higher subdivision level, which incidentally also affects the lower subdivision levels.

As you get to higher subdivision levels, remember that your file size is growing significantly. That's another reason to exhaust the capacity of a subdivision level before adding another one—so you won't get to higher subdivision levels that add no shape value, and create large files that hinder your productivity by slowing your machine down with the extra geometry.

Using the Mudbox Sculpting Tools

While working with three-dimensional sculptures, you are constantly dealing with form, volume, and surface. The Mudbox sculpting tools are used to give your sculpture form, to add or subtract volume, and finally to define surface shapes and patterns.

Even though Autodesk has the Sculpt tool as the first tool on the left in the Sculpt Tools tray, I have found the Grab tool to be the tool I use most frequently while sculpting. In fact, I reorder my tools in the frequency I use them, specifically the first four (Figure 6.99).

I use the Grab tool frequently to establish form, pushing and pulling volume, and adjusting and moving surface details. You can use the Grab tool to move large volume around, such as adjusting the hip size of our model (Figure 6.100).

WORKFLOW OPTIMIZATION BY REORGANIZING THE SCULPT TOOL TRAY

Remember when we set the tool size to the Z key and the tool strength to X to improve workflow? Well, there is another workflow tip that will speed up your workflow, and that is the order of the tools on the Sculpt Tools tray. You should order the tools according to how frequently you use them. In my workflow, I use the Grab tool most frequently, so I want it to be the first tool on the list. Then I use the Wax tool, the Flatten tool, and then the Bulge tool. Of course, the Smooth tool is probably used as frequently as the Grab tool, but I can always quickly switch to it by pressing the Shift key. The reason why the order of the tools is important is not for the visual cue, but because the tools are mapped to the numbers on your keyboard in the order in which they appear. In my case, I can get to the Grab tool by pressing 1, the Wax tool by pressing 2, and so forth. This makes my workflow faster because I can keep my brush on the sculpture while I change tools. To move the tools, click them with the middle mouse button, and with the button pressed down, drag the tools to the desired location.

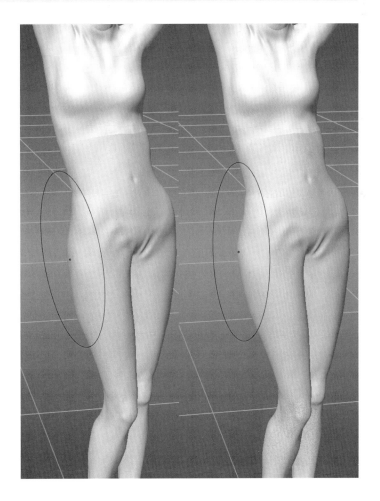

Figure 6.100

Using the Grab tool to pull out the hip

The size and falloff of the Grab tool determine how destructive it is to sculpted detail. Therefore, make sure to use an appropriate falloff with enough feathering on the edges (that is, a curve closer to the bottom) to make sure you don't disturb too much detail if you are working at higher subdivision levels. Better still, drop down in subdivision level to do the same action if you don't need to adjust things based on any high-frequency detail.

You can also use the Grab tool with a smaller size and strength to push or pull smaller areas of the surface if the volume you are trying to affect is not uniform—for example, pushing in the inside or pulling out the edges of an ear.

You can also use the Grab tool to adjust the surface by shifting parts along the surface—for example, if you misplace the belly button to the left when you create it, you can use the Grab tool to move it to the right.

Remember to use additive strokes instead of bigger ones until you are fully comfortable with the effect the tool has on the surface. You can of course always use Undo, and sculpt on a layer too.

The next tool I use frequently is the Wax tool, paired with a square stamp. I find this tool to be indispensible for adding shaped volume to a model, similar to pressing on clay to a practical sculpture. The inverse effect is also tremendously helpful for subtracting shaped volume (Figure 6.101). You can then use the Smooth tool to smooth out the rough outline. There are many Mudbox digital sculptors who use the Sculpt tool interchangeably with the Wax tool for this purpose; you can experiment with both to determine what works best for your workflow.

Figure 6.101

Using the Wax tool with the square stamp to define the shape of the scapula

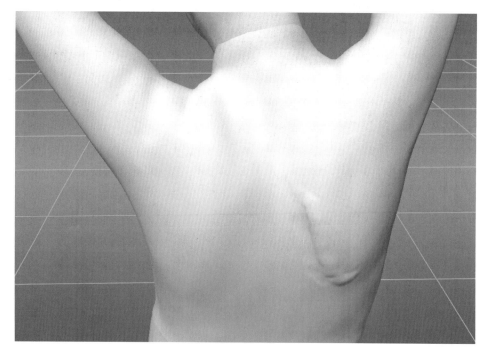

This Wax tool, with minor rotate and strength randomization, and no falloff (Figure 6.102), makes for a good effect of a chiseled surface (Figure 6.103). I use this to sculpt out the rough form, sometimes to smooth out later, and sometimes to give the model the effect of looking like a Giacometti sculpture surface.

To define crisper edges, the tendency of many artists is to use the Pinch tool. However, I get the same results without the cost of scrunched-up geometry by using the Sculpt or Wax tools with a very sharp falloff (Figure 6.104). This will punch in or pull out a sharp line, and you can use the Flatten tool on both sides of the line to get the shape of a sharp edge. You will also want to use Steady Stroke to get straighter edges.

Another extremely useful effect with the Wax tool is to use a sharp falloff and a small brush size to sculpt lines on the surface—for example, the border of the lips as additive (Figure 6.105), or the nasolabial fold as a negative.

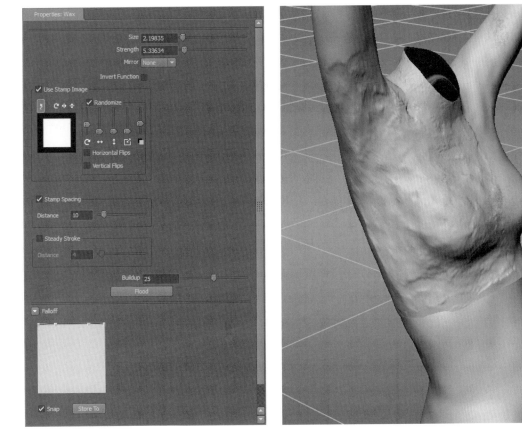

Figure 6.102
Wax tool settings

Figure 6.103
Using the Wax tool to get a chiseled surface look

Figure 6.104
Wax tool settings

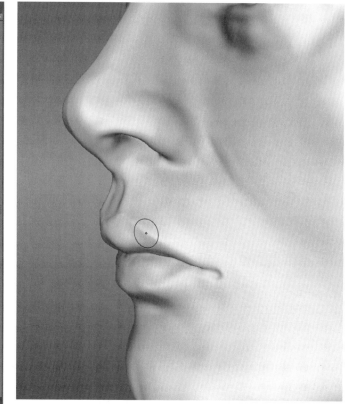

Figure 6.105

Using the Wax tool with a small size and sharp falloff to sculpt sharp features

The Flatten tool is useful for establishing planes on the surface and smoothing out features in places where the Smooth tool would just soften the details. I find it extremely useful with low strength levels to polish surfaces.

The Bulge tool is also extremely useful for inflating areas. Think of it as an air compressor to inflate areas like a balloon. An example of where the Bulge tool would be useful is on really thin arms that you want to bulk up. The Bulge tool works a lot faster than using the Grab tool on the perimeter.

To readjust the spacing of the quads at the lower subdivision levels, the Smear tool, used sparingly at these levels, redistributes the quad spacing if the Grab or Smooth tools are not doing the job. When you get to the higher subdivision levels, topology does not matter as much if you have done the needed work along the way to make sure you maintain as good a quad distribution as possible. An even subdivision of polygons will give you even geometry to work on in the higher subdivision levels.

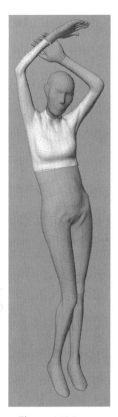

EFFECTIVE USE OF THE WIREFRAME ON YOUR MODEL

As you get to the higher subdivision levels, displaying the wireframe on the model gives you a very dense wireframe, which slows down your work and does not really provide any help. I usually set the Limit Wireframe option to level 0 or 3 in the Windows → Preferences → Render (Window → Preferences on the Mac) dialog box so that I get the wireframe of the lower subdivision level on the higher-resolution model. I find this useful to see the topology, and it also makes for a good visual.

Completing the Final Sculpting Stages

I have included my sculpting of the model at various stages on the DVD for you to examine how much work I did before subdividing. I will from this point forward post pictures of the progress at each level and give you any additional guides as to any tools or processes I used that we have not talked about already.

At subdivision level 3 (Figure 6.106), I bulked out the muscle structure and fixed as much of the anatomy as possible, added some clothing wrinkles. On this level, I used mostly the Grab, Wax, Smooth, Flatten, and Bulge tools. I used the Grab tool for pushing and pulling the surface to sculpt the shape. I used Flatten with small strength values to establish the planes. I used Smooth to smooth out areas that get too pixilated or stretch in undesirable directions.

At subdivision level 4, I did some further refining as I did on subdivision level 3 (Figure 6.107).

At subdivision level 5, I started to work on some of the features of the face (Figure 6.108).

This would be a good time to turn on the Ambient Occlusion viewport filter. It will give you a better idea of the finer details introduced at this subdivision level by darkening the occluded areas on the surface.

At this point, I added a couple of Mudbox Sphere primitives to create eyes. I then used the Translate and Scale tools to position them. I then exported and reimported them to overcome the scaling issue.

Your progress on the model from this point on is dependent on your artistic and aesthetic abilities as well as the time you are willing to spend. You can either use my progress to date, modify it, or start a new project of your own with what you have learned. The work is mostly based on repetition of the previous sculpting steps and your knowledge of anatomy, balance, gesture, and aesthetic.

I have included a video, `Chapter6-sculpting_Athena.mov`, of my following the preceding steps, sculpting various parts of the model, and narrating what I am doing on the `Chapter 6\Videos` folder of the DVD.

Figure 6.106

Level 3 subdivision progress

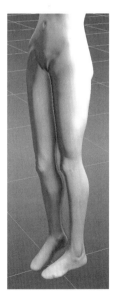

Figure 6.107

Level 4 subdivision progress

Figure 6.108

Sculpting the face with Ambient Occlusion turned on

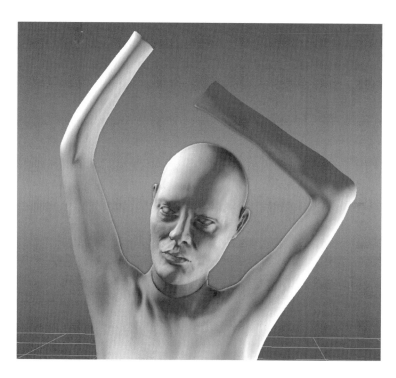

Sculp Using a Vector Displacement Map (VDM)

A *displacement map* is a grayscale 2D image that records the height of points on a surface. Even though displacement maps are extremely useful, they record only height information, which means that when we have surfaces that are orthogonal to the displacement, such as undercuts or overhangs, the displacement information represents only the highest surface. Vector displacement maps (VDMs) overcome this issue because a VDM is a 32-bit floating-point color 2D image that records height as well as directional information for points on the model.

We cannot use VDMs to assign topology from an original model or 3D scan to a destination model unless the VDMs have identical vertex topology, or the destination model has an identical subdivision level of the original. If your two models have identical vertex topology or have identical subdivision levels, using a VDM produces no artifacts when you apply the extracted VDM to the target model.

Where VDMs are extremely useful is for creating VDM stencils and stamps that can be used with the 3D sculpting tools to re-create features on the surface of the model.

Remember that your model needs to have UVs in order for you to be able to extract maps. Extracting a VDM is similar to extracting a displacement or normal map with the Maps → Extract Texture Maps command. In the Maps to Generate section of the Extract Texture Maps dialog box, select Vector Displacement Map. Most of the contents of the dialog box should be familiar to you except the Vector Space attribute.

Mudbox in Color

In this color section, you will find some images created by artists using Mudbox as well as some images from the book that better portray their intent in color.

Thanks to artists Maik Donath, Marcia K. Moore, Kenichi Nishida, Andreja Vuckovic, Rudy Wijaya, and Pete Zoppi. (All images are used with permission.)

The final mental ray renders of the egg model from Chapter 1. On the left is a render of the egg with the displacement map applied to the low-resolution model, and on the right a render with the normal map applied to the low-resolution model.

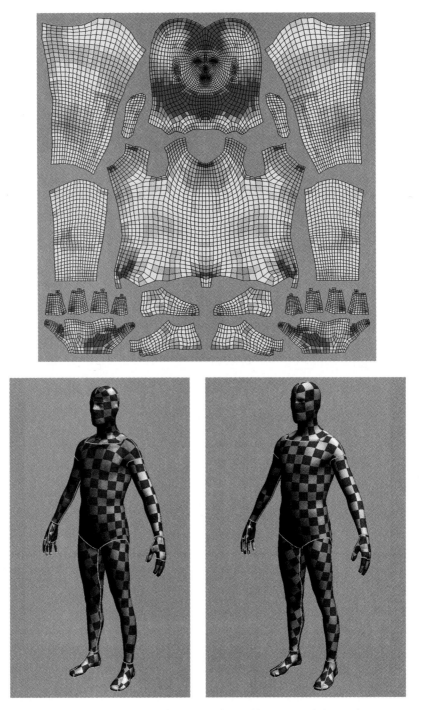

Figures 3.10 (top), 3.11 (bottom left), and 3.12 (bottom right) in color to indicate the colors in UVLayout where there would be stretching (indicated in red) and compression (indicated in blue) of textures on the UVs. ■ Figure 3.11 indicates the effects of the compression and stretching on a checkered pattern. ■ Figure 3.12 indicates the corrected UVs with minimal stretching and compression of textures.

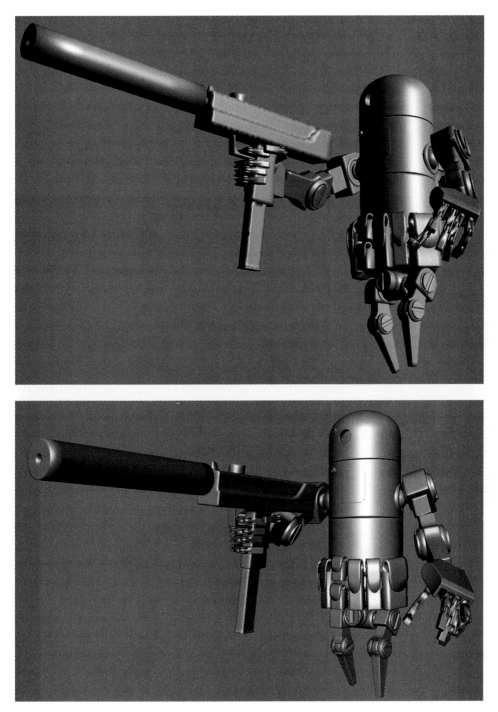

Figures 3.30 (top) and 3.31 (bottom) indicate the objects, highlighted in yellow, that need to be selected for the exercise steps.

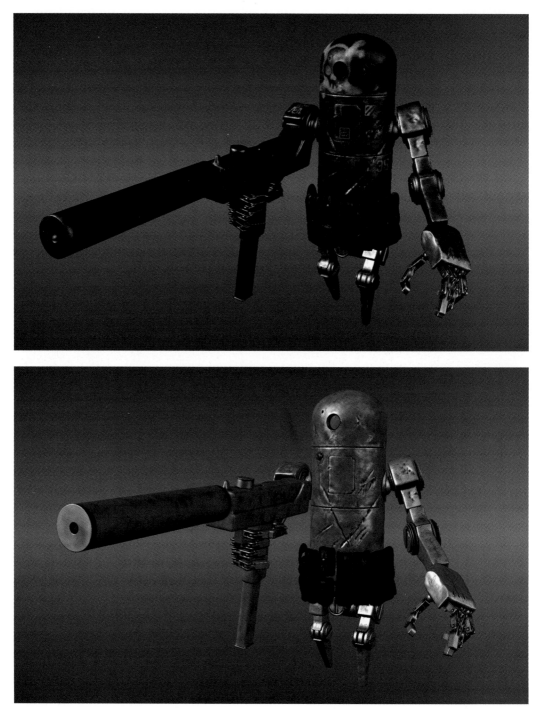

Figure 4.3 (top) is the final result of my work for 3D texture painting Bertie in Chapter 4.
■ Figure 4.5 (bottom) shows Bertie with just the base coat paint layer and specular layer rendered with the Ambient Occlusion viewport filter.

Figure 4.19 (top) indicates the difference in the model with (left) and without (right) specular layers. ■ Figure 4.20 (bottom) shows the model with just the specular paint layer.

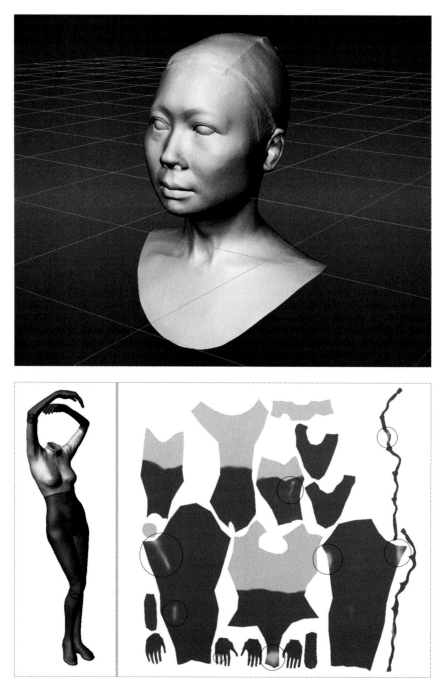

Figure 7.26 (top) shows the final result of the 3D scan data cleanup. ▪ The circles in Figure 8.3 (bottom) indicate the areas that were not painted in the 3D view, but can easily be painted in the flattened UV view.

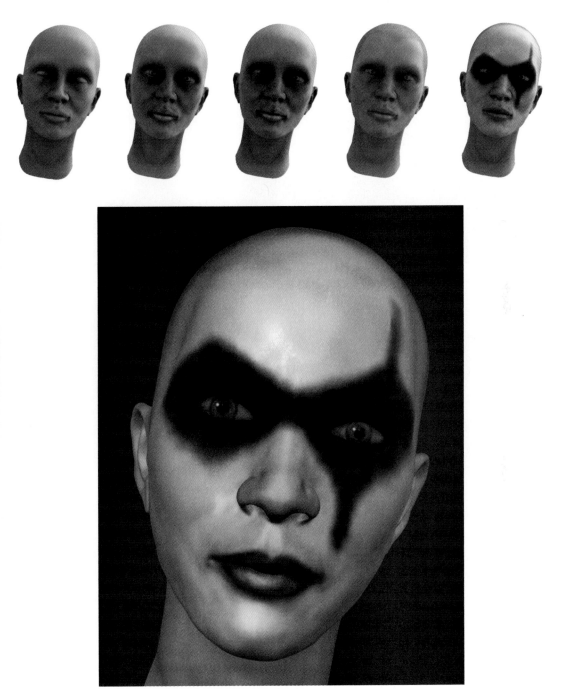

The paint layers of the face from the head model in Chapter 8 (top). ■ The composited paint layer result (bottom).

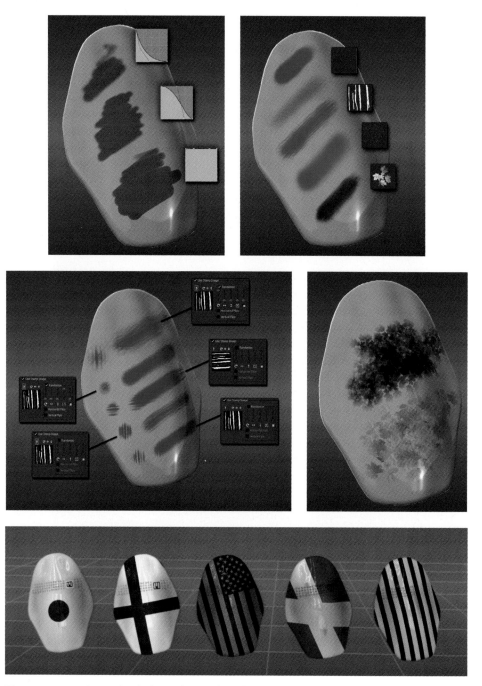

Figures 8.28 and 8.35 (top) show the results of various falloff settings and stamps as brush tips. ■ Figures 8.36 and 8.37 (middle) indicate the results of brush settings and projection painting results. ■ Figure 8.43 (bottom) represents the results of various 3D paint tests.

Figure 9.39 (left) shows Athena rendered in Mudbox. ■ Another render of Athena (right) rendered in KeyShot similar to Figure 9.50 but at a different angle and with an added base.

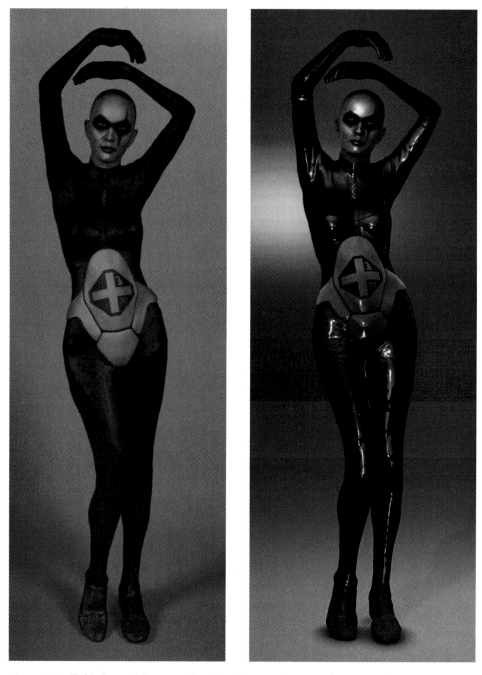

Figure 9.67 (left) shows Athena rendered in Maya using mental ray. ■ The image on the right shows Athena composited in Photoshop.

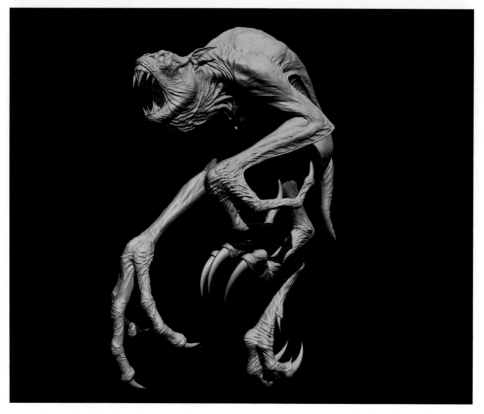

The First Assailment by Peter Zoppi (top), www.zopfx.com. Software used: Maya, Mudbox, Photoshop, mental ray. ■ *Flying Creature* by Kenichi Nishida (bottom). Software used: Mudbox, Maya.

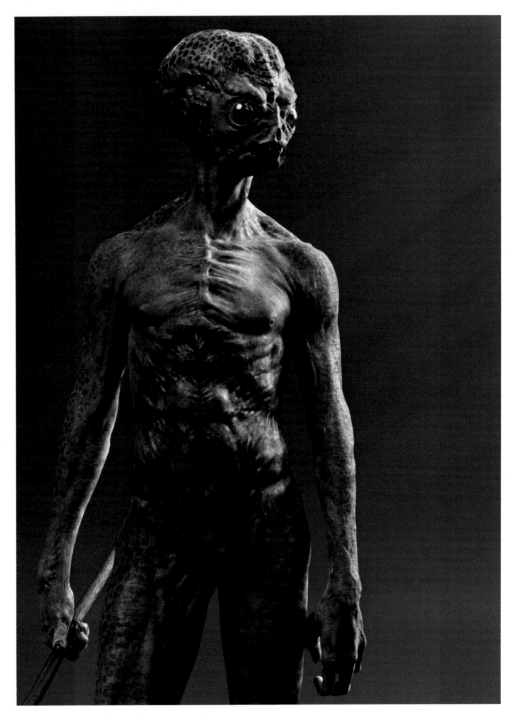

Alien Lifeform by Peter Zoppi, www.zopfx.com. Software used: Maya, Mudbox, Photoshop, mental ray.

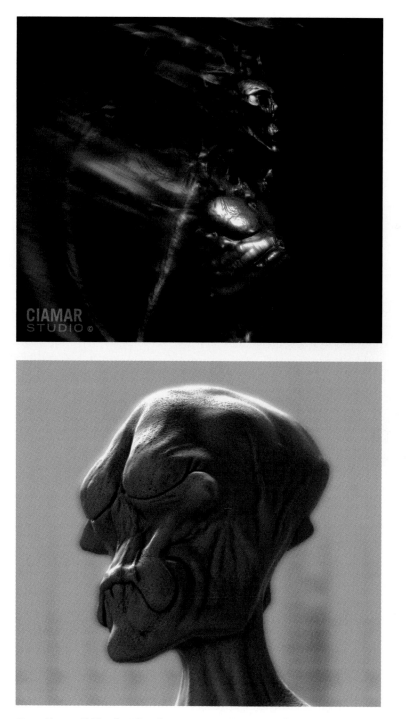

Boar Shape-Shifter by Marcia K Moore, Ciamar Studio and MkM Designs (top). Software used: Mudbox, Photoshop. ■ *The Blind Seer* by Ara Kermanikian (bottom). Software used: Mudbox.

Creature by Kenichi Nishida. Software used: Mudbox, Maya, Photoshop.

Scorpion by Kenichi Nishida (top). Software used: Mudbox, Maya, Photoshop. ■ *Bertie* (design copyright Ashley Wood) by Ara Kermanikian (bottom). Software used: Mudbox.

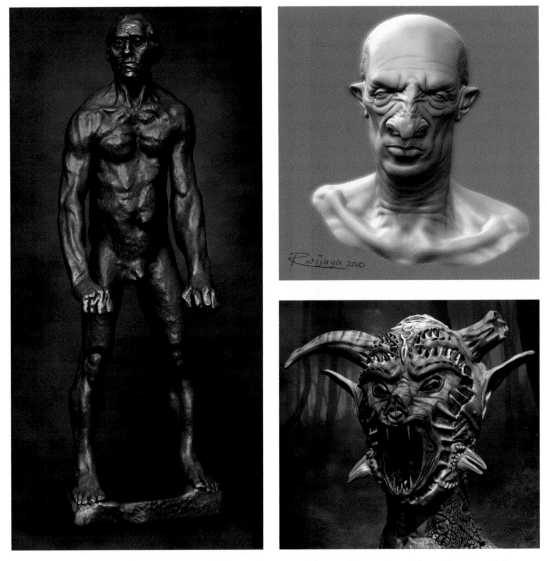

Jean d'Aires-Nu by Andreja Vuckovic (left). Software used: Mudbox, Maya, Photoshop. ■ *Alien Captainbust* by Rudy Wijaya (top right). Software used: Mudbox, Photoshop. ■ *Baphomet* by Maik Donath (bottom right). Software used: Mudbox.

The Vector Space attribute can have one of three values:

Tangent: This default setting indicates a vector space defined by the normal, tangent, and the binormal. You would use this setting if the model deforms during animation.

Object: This indicates the local coordinate space for the model. You would use this method if the model will not need to deform during animation.

World: This indicates the coordinate space of the 3D scene. You would use this if the model is not to be animated or deformed.

Note that the image size will determine the captured detail of the VDM. For extremely detailed models, use higher resolutions. You can extract VDMs from models with UVs outside the 0 to 1 range, in which case, each UV tile is extracted as a separate image file and saved to the extracted files directory. The files will use the naming convention of `<filename>_u1_v1_vdm.tiff`, where the number value next to the U and V would be the coordinates of the tile.

Follow these steps for an example of how to extract a displacement map and then use it to transfer your sculpture to another surface:

1. Start Mudbox and load the `ear.mud` file from the `Chapter 6` folder of the DVD (Figure 6.109). This is a model of an ear that I sculpted on a plane when I was practicing sculpting ears. It has seven subdivisions. Click on the ear to select it.

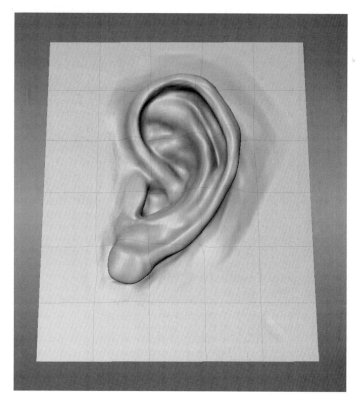

Figure 6.109

Ear sculpt with seven subdivision levels

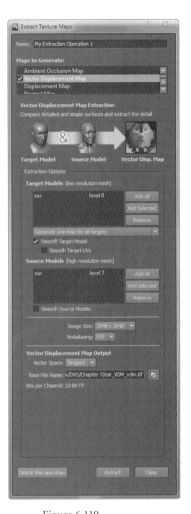

Figure 6.110

VDM extraction dialog box settings

2. Click Maps → Extract Texture Maps → New Operation, and select the Vector Displacement Map check box. The dialog box expands for you to input the VDM extraction parameters. Note that the ear model is loaded at levels 0 and 7, respectively, in the Target Models and Source Models list boxes (Figure 6.110).

3. Set the image size to 2048 × 2048 and click the folder button to the left of the Base File Name text box. Choose a name and location to save your file. Note that you can choose either the 32-bit `.tif` or `.exr` file formats.

4. Tangent is the default Vector Space option, and it is fine for what we need.

5. Click the extract button to create the VDM 2D, 32-bit color image file. When the extraction is finished, you will get a confirmation dialog box. Click OK to close it (Figure 6.111).

6. You are now finished with the ear model. Click File → New Scene and create a Basic Head mesh. Select the Flatten sculpting tool and set its Mirror property to X. Press the W key to turn on the wireframe. Flatten the ear protrusions on the model so they are flush with the head (Figure 6.112). You might be tempted to use Smooth, but that contracts the polygons, and you want the topology to stay put. This is a time where the wireframe is indispensible.

7. In the Image Browser, navigate to the VDM file you just created and select it as a Stencil. While holding down the S key, align the VDM ear to the head. Based on Edouard Lanteri's location parameters for the top-to-bottom distance of the ears, scale the ear to span the distance from the bottom of the nose to the top of the eyebrow (Figure 6.113). You can adjust the scale of the ear to match that distance on this model and then move the ear to its location (Figure 6.114).

8. Select the Sculpt tool with the default properties, making sure that the Mirror property is still set to X. Click on the model and drag. This will sculpt the ear with all of its cut-ins and shapes onto the head, and mirror the results to the other side (Figure 6.115).

With some minor sculpting, you can easily fix some of the alignment anomalies and match the ear to the head (Figure 6.116). The mirror option comes in very handy here. You can use this same method for all sorts of details and find it a huge time-saver to create a reference set library of parts to use. You can see a video, `Chapter6-VDM.mov`, of my going through the exercise steps in the `Chapter 6/Videos` folder of the DVD.

Figure 6.111

Map extraction confirmation

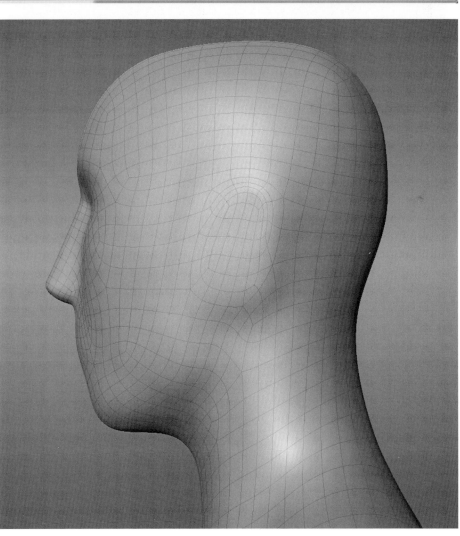

Figure 6.112

Flatten the ears on the Basic Head mesh.

Figure 6.113

Scale the ear to span the distance between the bottom of the nose to the top of the eyebrow.

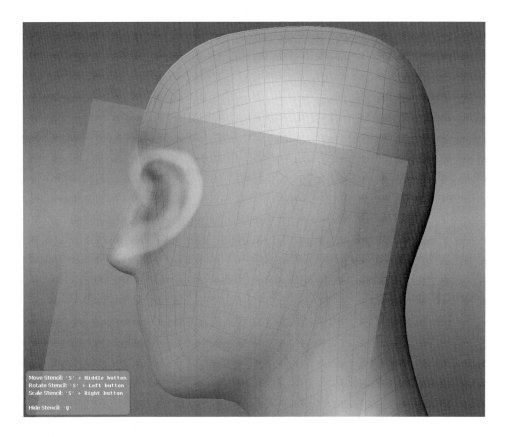

Figure 6.114

Move the ear into position.

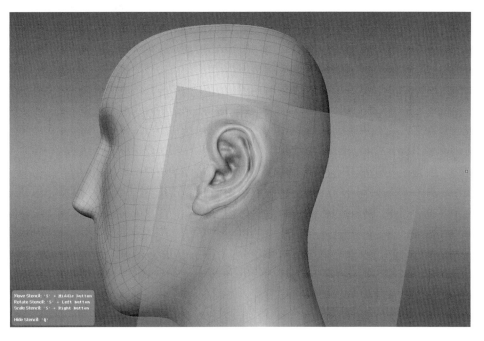

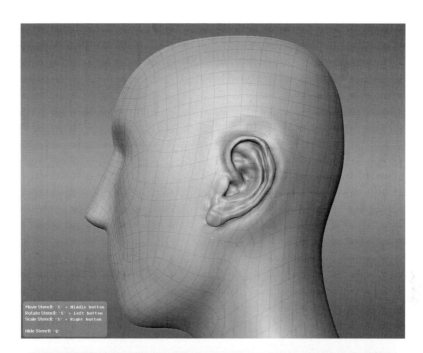

Figure 6.115

Sculpt the ear shape by using the VDM as a stencil.

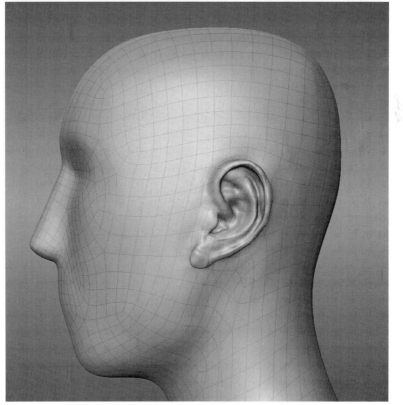

Figure 6.116

Sculpted ear on the Base Head mesh

Summary

We have now covered the sculpting capability in Mudbox. In Chapters 1, 3, 5, and 6, you have gone through the process of making a simple shape of an egg and giving it surface details. You have sculpted surface details on a prebuilt model to give it a more realistic look. Finally, you have created a base mesh, made the UVs for it, and then posed it and sculpted on it in Mudbox.

You have gone through the process of planning your sculpture, going through the stages of sculpting, base mesh modeling, creating UVs, and posing the model. You have covered all the sculpting tools and sculpting layer functions. You have also gone through an example showing shortcuts, techniques, and workflow to sculpt a model.

Here is a summary of the points to remember when posing a model:

- Pose with the Grab tool first.
- Pose your model at the lowest subdivision level possible.
- Pose the head, ribcage, and pelvis before the arms and legs.
- Pay attention to the balance and weight distribution.
- Focus on the gesture and flow of the connecting shapes.
- Pose your model on a new sculpt layer.

Here are some summary points on sculpting:

Sculpt around your model Don't stay on one angle or specific feature too long; keep moving around the sculpture as you would when you are working on a three-dimensional object. Camera controls should be second nature to you, and you should be able to move around your model to get to a specific angle without even thinking about it while you work. Sculpt the overall model instead of being stuck working on one specific area. Continuously tumble around your model and work on different areas, and keep thinking of your sculpture as a holistic piece that needs to come together.

Topology Remember to turn Wireframe and Smooth Shading on and off to see how the polygons are deforming under your sculpture. You don't want a large concentration of polygons in a place where you don't need them, and a scarcity of them in an area where you need to sculpt details.

Silhouette Turn on Flat Lighting to see the silhouette of your model, because the silhouette is one of the key ways we recognize and distinguish shapes. Finally, remember to zoom in and out on your model because there are good or bad features that will show up when it is very small. If gesture, shapes, and proportions look good small, it is very likely that they will also look good when you zoom in on the model.

Subdivision levels You need to sculpt at every subdivision level and not just the highest subdivision levels. The lower subdivision levels give you the blocked-in shape. Gesture, balance, and proportion should look good at the lower subdivision levels. Critical landmarks on your model should be sculpted and visible at the lower subdivision levels such as 2 or 3. For example, if you are sculpting a human body, critical anatomical bony landmarks such as the top of the sternum (front center of the ribcage), the olecranon of the ulna (elbow protrusion), the crest of the ilium (the hipbone), the great trochanter of the femur (top of leg bone), and the patella (knee protrusion) should be apparent at the lower subdivision levels. Exhaust what you can sculpt in the lower subdivision level before you move on to the higher one. Also remember that you can go back down to lower subdivision levels when it makes sense to make changes that are more related to the form of your sculpture, without affecting the details on the higher levels.

Sculpt layers Layers are an extremely powerful capability in Mudbox. You can use them for a variety of reasons, such as a save point for when you are sculpting, a variation of the pose of your sculpture, a blend shape, areas that you want to mask from others, or a location to bring in modified versions of your sculpture where you changed the pose or modified the UVs.

Use shortcut keys to make your workflow fast. When you notice that you are pausing to find and click a tool or a feature, make a hot key for it and move it to a location in close proximity of your hand that is on the keyboard. Also remember that your tablet has sensitivity levels, so use that to your advantage to give your strokes a light or heavy touch.

The Grab and Wax tools are the primary workhorse sculpting tools. Use the Grab tool to adjust the overall shape, and the Wax tool to add gesture to the shape. The Flatten and Bulge tools would be the next most frequently used tools. Use the Flatten tool to establish the planes on your model and the Bulge tool to inflate surfaces that are in close proximity where the other tools are not as effective.

Light Make sure to press l and click and drag your stylus or mouse to see your model lit at different angles. The way the surface of your sculpture looks is a product of light and shadow on the surface, and moving the light will reveal your model in a … well, a whole new light.

In the next chapter, you will see how to bring scan data into Mudbox as yet another way to create models that have a greater resemblance to real people and objects.

CHAPTER 7

Working with 3D Scan Data

Every Mudbox sculpture starts out as a polygon mesh. You could start with one of the 10 provided with Mudbox—for example, the sphere that you sculpted into the egg in Chapter 1, "Getting Your Feet in the Mud: The Basics of the Mudbox Production Pipeline." The sculpture could also start out as a full mesh modeled in a 3D application such as Maya, 3ds Max, Softimage, or Modo. An example of this is the model of Bertie that you worked on in Chapter 3, "Detail-Sculpting an Imported Model," and Chapter 4, "Painting and Texturing an Imported Model." Bertie was modeled, rigged, and posed in Maya and brought into Mudbox for detail sculpting and painting. You could start with a downloaded base mesh from the Mudbox Community on the AREA or from many online websites, for free or for a nominal price. Finally, a model can be brought in as a 3D scan from a 3D scanner, which is a device that generates a polygon mesh from a physical 3D object. Just as 2D scanners, which are now very inexpensive and common, are used to scan pictures and text, 3D scanners are used to scan 3D objects.

In this chapter, you will go through the benefits and limitations of 3D scan data. You will learn how you can use Mudbox's sculpting tools to overcome these limitations and clean up the 3D scans. You can then generate displacement maps from the scan data and map them to usable topology.

This chapter includes the following topics:

- Understanding the benefits and challenges of 3D scan data

- Using 3D scanners

- Reviewing scan data import considerations

- Importing 3D scan data and re-topologizing in Mudbox

Understanding the Benefits and Challenges of 3D Scan Data

Three-dimensional scanning is a quick, simple, and fairly inexpensive process used to generate near-perfect likenesses of people and props. When CG models are required as stunt doubles for real actors in movies, advertisements, and characters in video games, it is critical to have a believable likeness. The data generated by a 3D scan is indispensible for creating models that represent that required likeness.

Although the scan process is quick, simple, and fairly inexpensive, in almost all cases, the generated 3D scan data does not replace the needed 3D model. For example, the basketball player or film/TV actor model generated by the 3D scan is not the model animators will use to animate the basketball player for a video game or the actor for an impossible stunt.

There are several reasons for this. One is that 3D scanners sample points on a body's surface to create a likeness of the shape without giving any consideration to topology or polygon count. The data from 3D scans is usually in the order of millions of triangles arranged in a completely random pattern to represent the surface of the scanned subject (Figure 7.1). Even though the representation is perfect, the makeup of that representation is not.

Figure 7.1

Triangle soup

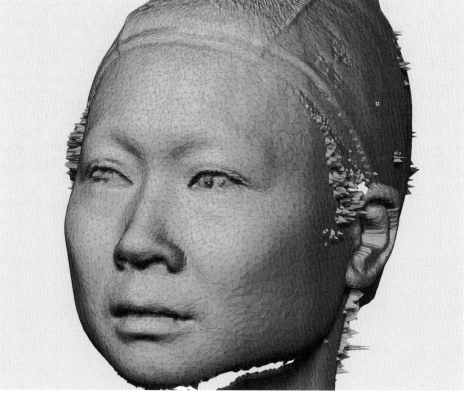

IMAGE COURTESY OF ICON IMAGING ©

Yet another challenge is that even if the most skillful scan artists use the best scanners to scan a model that poses for the scan, they would still get a resulting 3D mesh that had anomalies. Just the slightest movement of a human subject—even ones who are able to stand relatively still during the scan process (which entails having multiple scanners moving around the person and scanning bands of points on the surface of the body)—always generates undesirable surface anomalies, such as ripples or stretching (Figure 7.2).

Three-dimensional scanners also have difficulty working around occluded areas on the surface that fold over or have holes; we see this with 3D scan data of ears and areas under the chin. This is because blind spots exist that the 3D scanner cannot scan. It is also difficult to scan details such as hair or surfaces that are transparent or reflective. These result in anomalies and holes on the resulting 3D scan (Figure 7.3).

Data from a 3D scan can be used with minimal processing only when the object is to be rendered in a stationary position. Even in these cases, the model still needs to be cleaned up of 3D scan anomalies and optimized to reduce the polygon count so that rendering engines can process the data and render the scene in a reasonable time frame.

On the flip side, it would take an extremely talented modeler and sculptor to create a model from scratch to match the precision and likeness of a well-recognized person that our discerning eyes will accept. This talent is a limited and expensive resource. In addition, the sheer volume of models needed for production cycles of games, movies, and advertisements is getting greater while the time frame within which they are needed is getting shorter. By today's standards, it would just not be feasible, for example, to model and sculpt the likeness of an entire sports team or a movie cast in the time allowed for a seasonal game or the production schedule of a movie or TV show.

Figure 7.2

Ripples and stretching of a 3D scan

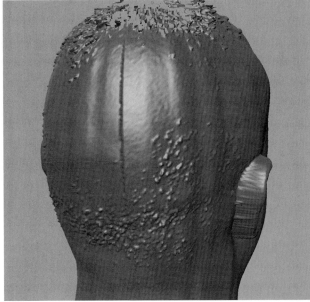

IMAGE COURTESY OF ICON IMAGING ©

Figure 7.3

Scans showing a blind-area hole under the chin, anomalies on the ear, and reflective eye and hair

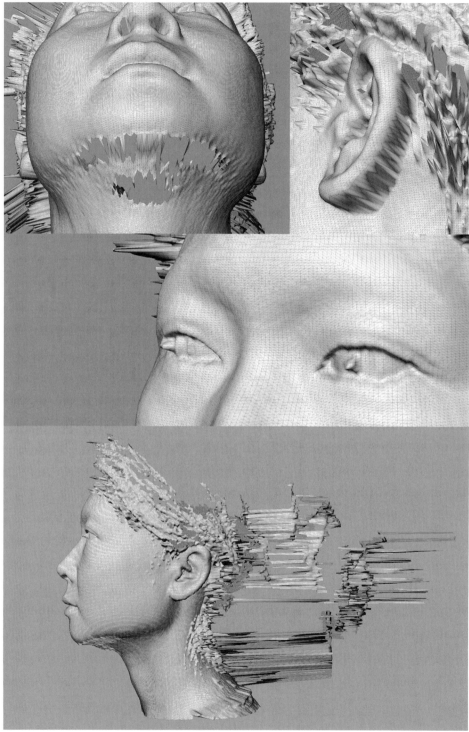

The solution to all these challenges is to start with a 3D scan of the subject, remove the anomalies from that scan, and transfer the likeness onto a polygonal topology that can be animated. This process is called *3D scan cleanup and re-topology*. The 3D scan data is an excellent starting point to get the perfect likeness of a model. If you have modeled using image planes, think of the 3D scan data as a 3D image plane you can use as a reference to build the perfect model with the ideal topology. Starting with 3D scan data saves many hours of modeling work as it generates convincing likeness, accurate proportions, and comprehensive surface details (Figure 7.4).

Modelers and digital sculptors use the 3D scan data as a starting point and utilize the complex 3D scan mesh as a template to snap on their own points and polygons with the needed topology. This used to be a time-consuming process, but it is getting a lot less so, and much easier because of re-topology tools and plug-ins for major 3D modeling software.

Recently, with the introduction of digital sculpting tools such as Mudbox and ZBrush, this process has gotten even easier. Because digital sculpting software such as Mudbox enables the manipulation of multimillion-polygon models, modelers and digital sculptors can now easily use the sculpting tools to clean up the scan data, and then use a library of generic base mesh models onto which they wrap or project the 3D scan detail with relative ease and speedy results.

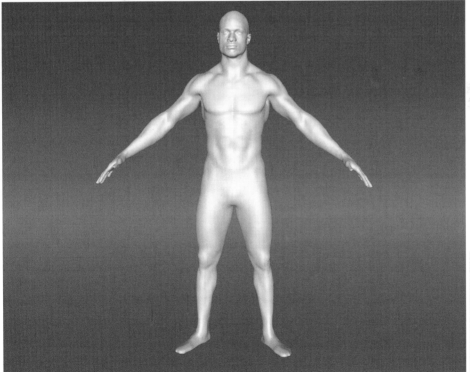

Figure 7.4

An image of a perfectly scanned subject ; image provided by ICON Studio

IMAGE COURTESY OF ICON IMAGING ©

Using 3D Scanners

Three-dimensional scanners are machines that sample points on the surface of objects and create a set of 3D coordinates that represent these points. The density of these sampled points depends on the resolution of the scanners, and, of course, the denser the points, the more accurate the scan. Also, depending on your needs, some scanners also enable you to scan the same subject at different scan densities (Figure 7.5).

The information gathered by the 3D scanner is fed into 3D scan software that outputs the 3D scan mesh model. Because you can represent a plane by using three points in 3D space, the 3D scan software then algorithmically determines the optimal way to attach the scanned 3D coordinates into planes represented by triangles. The resulting mesh is a set of 3D coordinates and a list of which points are attached in triangles and then output in an exportable format such as an `.obj` file.

Figure 7.5

Images of two objects scanned with varying scan densities

IMAGE COURTESY OF ICON IMAGING ©

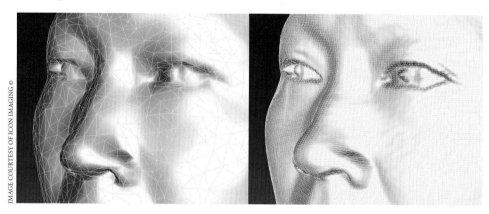

Types of 3D Scanners

There are many types of 3D scanners, such as laser, structured-light, light detection and ranging (LIDAR), photometric, surface-transmitter, and touch-probe scanners. All of these scanners produce information that can be processed and refined in Mudbox. However, the two that are most commonly used are laser and structured-light 3D scanners.

Laser scanners employ an array of lasers and cameras to record the coordinates of points on the surface of the scan subject (Figure 7.6). They are the most commonly used 3D scanners and are produced by companies such as Cyberware, Konica Minolta, and NextEngine.

Structured-light scanners project patterns of parallel stripes that are observed by cameras at different viewpoints. These patterns on the surface of the scanned object appear geometrically distorted because of the surface shape of the object, and the cameras can triangulate the distortions into their locations in space. Structured-light scanners are produced by companies such as GOM International (ATOS scanners) and Steinbichler Optotechnik (Figure 7.7).

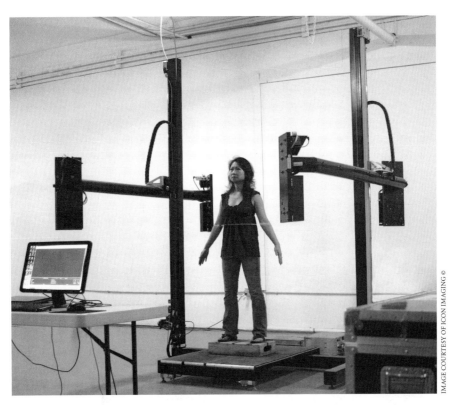

Figure 7.6

A full-body laser 3D scanner

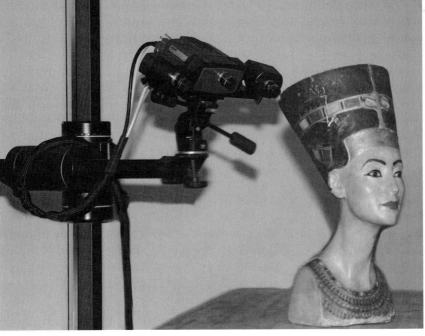

Figure 7.7

A structured-light scanner

LIDAR measures the range of distant objects determined by calculating the time delay between the transmission of a laser pulse and a reading of the reflected signal. LIDAR is used mostly to scan points on distant large objects such as buildings.

Photometric scanners use silhouette, or photometric image data to generate the coordinates of the points on the surface.

Surface-transmitter scanners employ small transmitter objects that are placed on the surface of the object to transmit coordinates. These are used mostly for capturing motion, but they can also be used to get key defining coordinates of large objects.

Touch-probe scanners generate the 3D coordinates based on a sensor on a swiveling or robotic arm touching or colliding with the subject. Examples of these are 3D scanners produced by companies such as FARO Technologies and MicroScribe.

Three-dimensional scanning is still very much a developing technology with implementations in many scientific and commercial fields. Even though we have scanners that can capture perfect renditions of people and objects, advancements in research and development (R&D) labs are pushing the limits of precision, scale, speed of scanning, and ways of generating and manipulating the information.

Scanned Object Size

Figure 7.8

A 3D scanner used to scan a head

IMAGE COURTESY OF ICON IMAGING ©

Theoretically, we are able to scan objects of any size, either by a single scan or by stitching together multiple scans. The most commonly scanned subjects are people's faces (Figure 7.8) or bodies (Figure 7.9), because they have unique identifying characteristics that are instantly recognizable, and yet are difficult and time-consuming to model, sculpt, and re-create.

To accommodate for that, most commonly used 3D scanners are made to scan a face or a body. However, some scanners are made to scan larger objects, such as cars or statues (Figure 7.10), or smaller objects, such as a maquette (Figure 7.11) or action figure. Scanners can also scan multiple parts of an object and combine the scan pieces into one complete model.

Most professional-grade 3D scanners are industrial-size devices used by professional 3D scanning companies. There are, however, smaller, less-expensive 3D scanners available that are the size of a cereal box, such as the NextEngine 3D scanner (Figure 7.12).

When you need scans of objects of varying sizes, you need to consider scan accuracy. Three-dimensional scan accuracy can range from meters for larger objects to millimeters and microns for smaller ones. Some scanners are able to sample points at the accuracy levels they publish, and others use algorithms to make approximations that fill in points between physical sample ranges. Of course, the data quality of the scanners that produce results based on sample points versus algorithmic approximation is more accurate, and less prone to softness in detail.

The data generated from 3D scans of heads or bodies are in the range of 500,000 to 1 million polygons (triangles). A maquette can be in the range of 1 to 10 million polygons. Some detailed car interior scans can go above the 50 million polygon range. There are detailed scans, such as the one done on Michelangelo's *David*, that exceed 1 billion polygons.

Figure 7.9

A 3D scanner used to scan a body

IMAGE COURTESY OF ICON IMAGING ©

Figure 7.10

A 3D scanner used
to scan a large
statue

Figure 7.11

A 3D scanner used
to scan a maquette

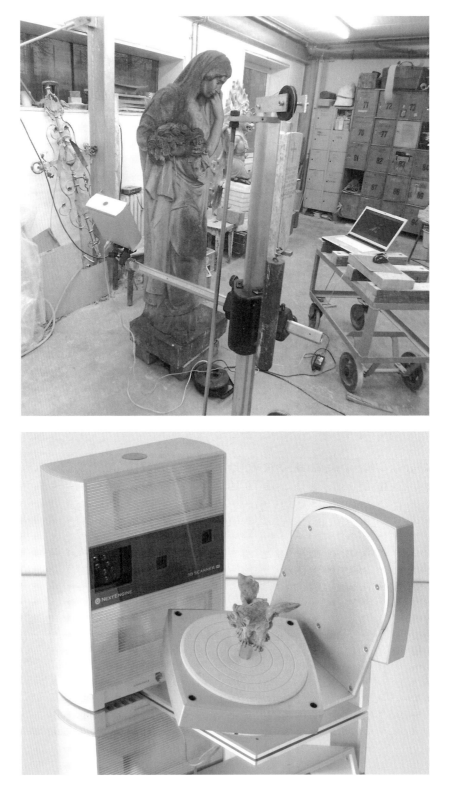

Figure 7.12
**A NextEngine
scanner**

Most 3D scan data is collected and interpolated by scanning software that exports the results in formats readable by 3D and computer-aided design (CAD) applications. Most commonly, the file formats produced by 3D scanners are .obj, .ply (Polygon File Format), or .stl (Stereolithography). In Mudbox we will use the .obj format because it is the only one that's supported.

Reviewing Scan Data Import Considerations

After you have the 3D scan data in .obj format, you load it into Mudbox to look at the results. As mentioned before, the polygon count you will be working with is in the 500,000 to 1,000,000 polygon range for a head or body, so Mudbox can easily handle that number of polygons. This would be a good way to visualize our model, and use the Rotate and Scale tools to arrange the model and orient it to the center of the screen.

Direction of the Normals

One thing to make sure of is the direction of the normals. You need to make sure that the scan application exports the .obj file with normals facing outward. You get a visual cue of this in Mudbox as you load the model. If you get scan data with normals facing inward (Figure 7.13), you can either re-request the data with the normals facing outward or load the data into a 3D application and reverse the normals.

After you have the model loaded and positioned, you should visually check it for scan anomalies and take notes as to where they are, because you will have to fix them later.

Figure 7.13

A 3D scan of a head with normals facing inward

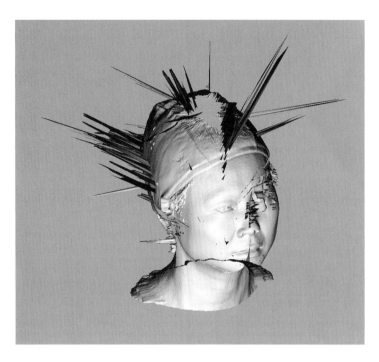

Common Anomalies

Generally, 3D scanners have problems with the following surfaces:

- Occluded areas that are blind spots for the scanner
- Perfectly horizontal surfaces
- Random spikes from floating particles in the air that may get caught in the scan
- Reflective surfaces
- Extremely dark or black surfaces that absorb light
- Shiny surfaces that reflect light irregularly
- Small multidirectional fibers such as hair
- Surfaces with uniform textures or materials
- Surfaces that have transparent or refractive properties

Some of these anomalies can be fixed before the scan. For example, to get a surface scan of a transparent, glass soda bottle, we would have to paint it with some opaque paint or add a layer of opaque powder. To get rid of anomalies caused by hair, we would have the model wear a skull cap. To get rid of anomalies caused by reflective surfaces, we would coat the surface with a nonreflective substance. Other anomalies can be fixed after the scan by sculpting the corrections.

Importing 3D Scan Data and Re-topologizing in Mudbox

In the rest of this chapter, you will go through the process of bringing 3D scan data into Mudbox and mapping the detail onto a more manageable topology. If you will not use 3D scan data, this process is also critical to the Mudbox workflow because you would use this exact same process to re-topologize a sculpture you created from scratch that needs to be mapped onto a more manageable topology. Let's say, for example, you sculpted a creature's head by using the Sphere primitive. It started out as a sketch, but you got some amazing results and wanted to get better topology to continue to add more detail or to send the model off to be animated. The process used to apply your sculpt onto a more accommodating topology mesh would be the same method we will be going through to re-topologize a 3D scan.

In the rest of this chapter, you will load a 3D head scan and go through the following steps to apply a new topology to it:

1. Load the 3D scan data into Mudbox.

2. Edit some of the anomalies in an external 3D application.

3. Add the Mudbox Basic Head primitive to the scene and align it to the 3D scan.

4. Extract a displacement map.

5. Apply the displacement map back on the model by using the Sculpt Model Using Displacement Map function.

6. Sculpt out the anomalies and add sculptural details.

   Let's get started.

Loading 3D Scan Data into Mudbox

The 3D scan data you will work with in this chapter is provided by Icon Imaging, one of the leading studios that specializes in very realistic and complex 3D scanning, modeling, and imaging (I have included information about Icon Imaging in the acknowledgments section at the beginning of this book). The scan artists at the company used a Cyberware 3D head scanner, which orbits 360 degrees around a subject's head, to produce the scan data. Typically, 3D scan houses offer various levels of data cleanup services, but I asked for this data in its rawest form to give you an idea of the anomalies that happen during a typical scan. The resulting scan (Figure 7.14) has some excellent examples of anomalies.

1. Start Mudbox. Choose File → Import and import the Chapter 7\raw_head_scan.obj file from the DVD. Click OK to close the warning dialog box. This warning dialog box will always come up if you are importing a high-resolution mesh with no subdivision levels. It will take from a few seconds to a few minutes, based on your system, to load the 3D scan mesh. Choose the white Chalk or Gesso material from the Material Presets tray. In the Object List, note that the 3D scan has 374,408 polygons.

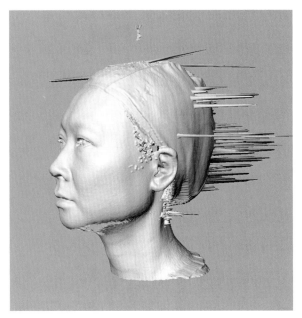

Figure 7.14

A 3D scan of a head with anomalies

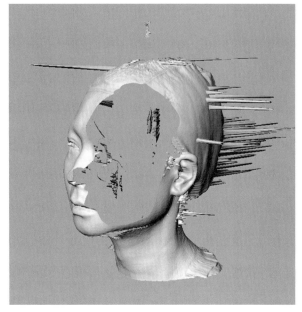

Figure 7.15

The model intersecting the near clipping plane

2. Zoom in on the scanned head. Notice that as you get "closer" to the head, and it starts getting bigger, a big hole appears in the model (Figure 7.15).

This happens because the model is intersecting your near plane. The *near plane* is also referred to as the *near clipping plane*, and it defines how close the camera sees. The reason that the model is cutting out is because the default near plane value of 1 does not give you enough room to see the entire image. You can remedy this situation by selecting the Perspective camera in the Object List tray, and setting the Near Plane attribute to 0.1 (Figure 7.16). If you are not able to see the model, remember to press the A key on your keyboard to center the model in the viewport.

Figure 7.16

The Near Plane attribute for the Perspective camera

3. Tumble around the model and look at the captured detail of the face in addition to all the anomalies. The most obvious ones are the porcupinelike spikes and the holes at the top and the bottom of the chin and the cap. You will also see some little spikes from the hair, between the top of the hair and the cap, and the reflective eyeballs. There is a little anomaly on the top of the head from the calibration pendulum of the scanner. Notice the subtle ripples on the face from the scan. This is most noticeable below the right eye and the neck area. Notice that there is a sharp drop-off behind the ear, where there is an occluded area. Finally, even though this scan was completed in under a minute, note the ridge line in the back, indicating where the scan

started and ended (Figure 7.17). This is considered a good scan of someone who is very experienced at being scanned, and as you can see, there still are some unavoidable anomalies.

4. Choose Create → Mesh → Basic Head to add the Mudbox Basic Head primitive to the scene. You might be surprised, because you will not see anything happen. That's because the Basic Head scale is significantly bigger than the scanned head image. Press the A key, and you will see the Basic Head primitive but not the scanned head. As you tumble around in your scene, you will notice that the 3D scanned head is tiny compared to the Basic Head primitive. This is another big anomaly to take into consideration: the scale of the 3D scan.

Editing Anomalies in an External 3D Application

Even though it is possible to clean up all of the anomalies in Mudbox, I find it easier to do some of the cleanup in another 3D application that gives me more control over deleting polygons. In either Maya 2010 or Softimage 2010, you can easily import the 3D scan data and delete the polygons that make up the spikes. It is a process that takes very little time because you can bulk-select the spike pivot points and the polygons they contain, and then delete them. I also deleted the pendulum geometry above the head because it was not needed.

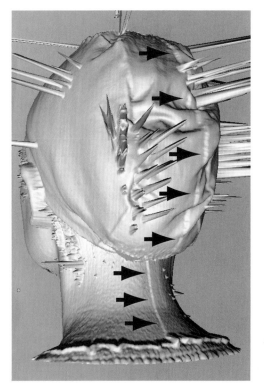

Figure 7.17

The ridge line representing the start and end of the 3D scan

The next thing I did was export the Basic Head primitive from Mudbox as an .obj file and import it into Softimage 2010. I translated, rotated, and scaled the 3D head scan to approximately match the same size, orientation, and centered position as the Basic Head Mudbox primitive. I exported the edited 3D head scan from Softimage 2010 as head_scan_Softimage_edit.obj for you to use for this chapter.

The 3D scanning companies that you get your 3D scan from will, in most cases, do this cleanup for you, but it's also good to know how to do the edits yourself just in case you need to. Here are the steps:

1. Choose File → New Scene without saving your prior work. Then choose File → Import and import the Chapter 7\head_scan_Softimage_edit.obj file from the DVD. Again, click OK to close the warning dialog box that comes up. Choose the white Chalk or Gesso material from the Material Presets tray. Notice that the bigger spikes are gone, but all the other anomalies are still there.

2. Press the W key on your keyboard to bring up the wireframe on the face (Figure 7.18).

Figure 7.18

The wireframe from the raw 3D scan

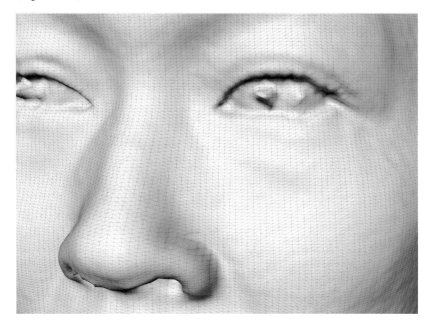

3. You can now see why this model, while instantly recognizable as the scanned person, is completely not feasible to sculpt, patch up, or animate. Select the face by clicking the Objects tool in the Select/Move Tools tray. Click the UV View tab in the main viewport. Notice that the 3D scan does not have any UVs, nor would you want to UV a model this messy. Click back on the 3D view and press the W key to turn off the wireframe.

Adding and Aligning the Basic Head Primitive

What you need to do is take the best of what the 3D scan has to offer and apply it to a more manageable mesh. In this case, you will use the Basic Head primitive from Mudbox. You could use one of the many human head base meshes that are available on the Internet for free or, of course, one of your own. As you already know, the Basic Head base mesh in Mudbox has UVs and has a topology you can subdivide and sculpt.

1. Choose Create → Mesh → Basic Head. This adds the Basic Head primitive to your scene. Notice that there is a little overlap of both the meshes. Select the Basic Head and subdivide it one level by pressing Shift+D.

2. In the Object List, click the padlock icon next to the `head_scan_Softimage_edit_0` object to lock it. You need to do this because you want to make sure you don't move any of the points on the scanned 3D head.

3. Select the Grab tool from the Sculpt Tools tray. Using appropriate Size and Strength, align key landmarks (Figure 7.19) of the Basic Head primitive to those of the 3D scanned head. Press the W key to turn on the wireframe and make sure that your quads are well spaced and not overlapping or squashed together. Your alignment does not have to be precise, but the landmarks should roughly overlap those on the 3D scan.

4. By the time you are finished, your head should look more or less like Figure 7.20. You can import `Mudbox_basic head_edit.obj` from the DVD to check your work.

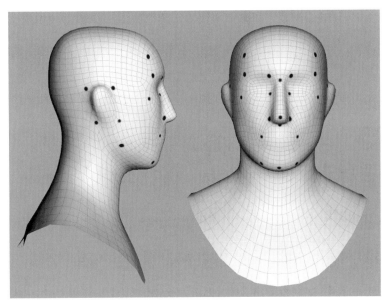

Figure 7.19
Key alignment landmarks on the face

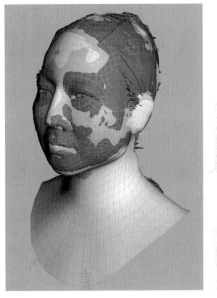

Figure 7.20
The aligned Basic Head primitive mesh and 3D scan mesh

Extracting a Displacement Map

In this section, you will be extracting the displacement map of the 3D scanned head—but with a twist. You will use the 3D scanned head as the source model and the Basic Head primitive as the target model during your extraction. This will extract the displacement, or surface depth information, of the high-resolution mesh and map it onto the UVs of the Basic Head.

1. Choose Maps → Extract Texture Maps → New Operation.

2. Select the Displacement Map check box to expand the dialog box and bring up the options for extracting a displacement map. All the settings that we will discuss can be seen in Figure 7.21.

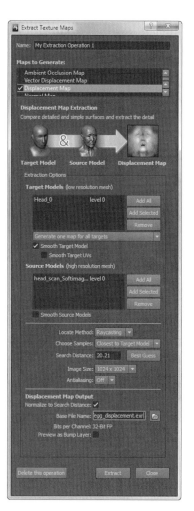

Figure 7.21

**Extract the Texture
Maps dialog box**

3. Next to the Target Models (Low Resolution Mesh) list box, click the Add All button. This adds both the 3D head scan and the edited Basic Head primitive to the list. Click the 3D scan data head (head_scan_Softimage_edit_0) and click the Remove button.

4. Do the same for the Source Models (High Resolution Mesh) list box but remove the Basic Head primitive (Head_0) from the list.

5. Make sure Locate Method is set to Raycasting, and for the Search Distance option, click the Best Guess button. This sets the total distance that samples can be taken from the target model to the source model based on the distances between the bounding boxes of the two.

6. In the Choose Samples list, make sure Closest to Target Model is selected. This creates the displacement map with samples closest to the target model.

7. Select an Image Size of 4096 × 4096, because you want to use the maximum map size to get the most detail from the 3D scanned model.

8. Click the folder icon next to the Base File Name text box and type **3Dscan_displacement** or a name of your choice for your displacement map. Select OpenEXR [32 Bit Floating Point, RGBA] as the file format and click Save. Again, this does not generate or save the displacement map; it just sets the name.

9. Make sure the Preview as Bump Layer option is not selected.

10. Click the Extract button to extract the displacement map. This opens the Map Extraction Results dialog box, which shows you the progress of the extraction.

11. The dialog box tells you that your map extraction finished without errors and the operation completed successfully. Click OK, and click Close to close the Map Extraction Results dialog box.

12. Click the Image Browser tab in the main viewport and navigate to the folder in which you extracted the displacement map. Examine the displacement map (Figure 7.22). You can use the + or – keys to increase or decrease the stop value, respectively, to see the level of detail the image has at different exposures. Also note that the displacement map has been extracted to match the UV map of the Mudbox Basic Head primitive.

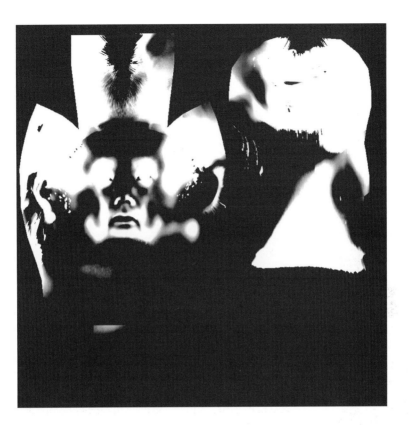

Figure 7.22
The extracted displacement map at an Exposure Stop value of 0

Applying the Displacement Map to Sculpt on Desired Topology

At this juncture, you no longer need the 3D scan model. You will delete it and wrap the displacement map you generated to add the details of the 3D scan to a subdivided version of the Mudbox Basic Head primitive.

1. Select the 3D head scan (`head_scan_Softimage_edit_0`) in the Object List tray, right-click on it, and select Delete Object. This leaves the Mudbox Basic Head primitive you edited earlier. Select the head (`Head_0`) in the Object List and press Shift+D four times to get about 512,000 polygon subdivisions. We can further subdivide our model, but a good guideline is to get as close to the same number of polygons as the 3D scan model, which is 374,408.

2. Choose Maps → Sculpt Model Using Displacement Map → New Operation.

3. From the Target Mesh list box, select the only mesh in the scene: `Head_0`.

Figure 7.23

**A good topology
of quads with
details from the
3D scan data**

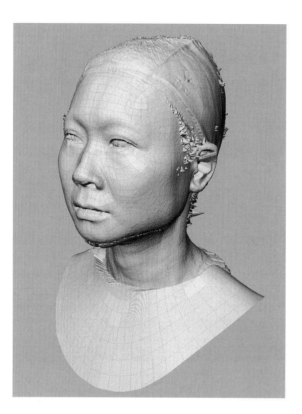

4. Click the three dots next to the Displacement Map text box, select the displacement map you generated in the previous section (`3Dscan_displacement.exr`), and click Open.

5. Click Go. This displaces your Basic Head primitive.

6. Note that you now have the exact same model of the 3D scan, but if you press the W key, you will see that it is no longer composed of triangles and n-gons but of quads that the Basic Head primitive was composed of (Figure 7.23). You have solved one of the big problems you had.

7. Tumble around the head and notice that the holes have been filled, and that's another problem solved. But the model has a lot of little spikes, surface inconsistencies where the holes used to be, anomalies behind the ears, and so forth, that still need to be fixed.

Sculpting Anomalies and Adding Details

You can no longer solve any of the remaining anomalies automatically. You will need to use good old digital sculpting to get the model to look like the scanned subject. Fortunately, this is not too difficult and is perfectly suited for Mudbox. To sculpt out the anomalies, it is easier to start at the lower subdivision levels and work your way up.

You will initially use three sculpt tools—the Smooth, Grab, and Flatten tools—and then use the Sculpt and Wax tools to sculpt some details. Always remember, it is a good idea to use sculpt layers and to save often. It is also a good idea to use lower Size and Strength settings and work your way up.

1. Press Pg Dn until you are at level 1. Use the Grab and Smooth tools to move the polygons in the neckline area so they align. Use the Smooth tool to straighten some of the artifacts that can be seen at this level. Remember to use an additive approach to smoothing by using a lower Strength setting, testing it out, and then gradually working your way up to a greater Strength or applying the Smooth tool with the weaker Strength a few times to get the desired effect. Use the Grab tool to gradually lift up the top of the head where the hole used to be. By the end of your work, your sculpture should look like Figure 7.24.

2. Step up one level to level 2 by pressing Pg Up. Repeat the process in step 1 to sculpt out the anomalies that show up. Note that there are still anomalies in the areas you fixed on level 1, but they are less severe than they would have been had you not done the work on level 1.

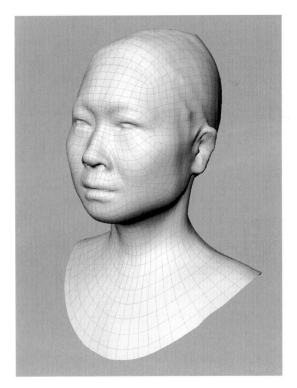

Figure 7.24

The cleaned-up subdivision level 1 head

3. Step up to level 3 by pressing Pg Up. Now you can see some of the anomalies in more-granular detail. At this level, as you are getting rid of anomalies, you could just as easily also soften up needed surface details. So, from this point on, it is a good idea to use a lighter hand on the tablet and really work with smaller tool sizes and a lower Strength setting. Start out with the Smooth tool and move the tool in a circular motion over the anomalies to reduce their size. If the spikes persist, try using the Flatten tool, or drop back down a subdivision level and work on the same area.

> You might be tempted to press Shift to switch to the Smooth tool. However, this might prove problematic if you have the Smooth tool's Remember Size property selected. Pressing the Shift key will then revert to your last set Smooth tool and Size. I recommend that you do not have this option selected so that your smoothing size and strength match those of the tool you are using before you press the Shift key.

4. Step up to level 4 by pressing Pg Up. You can now see the anomalies in even more granular detail. Repeat the same work to smooth the anomalies. If you get into severe areas that need repair—for example, the neckline (Figure 7.25)—you can use the Flatten tool in combination with the Smooth tool to straighten up that area.

Figure 7.25

Spikes that need to be cleaned up by using the Smooth and Flatten tools

5. Press Shift+D to add another subdivision level, level 5.

6. Work with even more detail and fix the rest of the anomalies. Don't worry about losing some high-frequency detail such as skin pores or wrinkles, because those can easily be added at a later point. You might also lose some detail in areas critical to the sculpture, for example, some wrinkles on the cap or inside or around the ear, but those are easy enough to sculpt after you are finished with the cleanup.

At this point, the cleanup is done. Now is the time to sculpt the missing details, such as the inside of the ears, the indentation behind the ears, the nostrils, and all the other areas that you feel need detail.

I have included the version I worked on, named `3DScan_cleanup_final.mud`, on the DVD in the `Chapter 7` folder (Figure 7.26). I also included a couple of Sphere primitives, `eye_lf.obj` and `eye_rt.obj`, that you can use for the eyeballs. To add the eyeballs, import the two `.obj` files and use the Translate tool from the Select/Move Tools tray to position them. After they are positioned, you might want to sculpt the slight bulge of the cornea. I did not do any high-frequency detail on my version. In fact, I removed all the high-frequency detail because I was shooting for a more statuesque result, but you might want to add detail to your heart's desire. I have also included a video, `Chapter7-working_with_3D_scan_data.mov`, of my going through the entire process in the `Chapter 7\Videos` folder.

When you are finished, you have a model with a believable likeness of the 3D scan subject, with UVs and usable topology that you can 3D-paint, further sculpt, or move into the next stages of the pipeline to get animated or 3D printed.

Figure 7.26

The cleaned 3D scan with quad topology, UV map, and 3D scan data detail

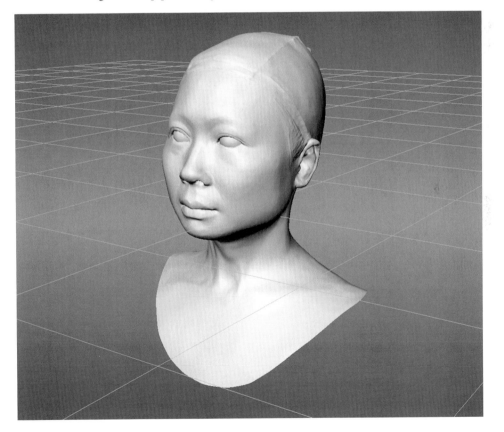

Summary

Three-dimensional scanning is an efficient method for getting near-perfect likenesses in little time, with very little specialized effort, and for nominal cost by using tools such as Mudbox.

The displacement map generation and the Sculpt Model Using Displacement Map technology in Mudbox, paired with the digital sculpting tools, have proven a great asset to many production pipelines.

CHAPTER 8

3D Painting

Mudbox 2011 painting tools, paired with an image-editing application such as Photoshop, give you limitless possibilities to paint your digital sculptures. Some of the basics of 3D painting and texturing were covered in Chapter 4, "Painting and Texturing an Imported Model."

This chapter includes the following topics:

- **Painting your sculpture**
- **Generating UVs on subdivision levels and painting directly on UVs**
- **Painting on layers and using blend modes**
- **Using color, stamps, and stencils**
- **Workflow to Adobe Photoshop and back**
- **Loading textures into Maya**

Painting Your Sculpture

At a recent exhibit at the Getty Villa in Malibu, California called The Color of Life: Polychromy in Sculpture from Antiquity to the Present, featuring polychrome (multi-colored) statues and the uses of color in figural sculpture, it was interesting to see examples of historical sculpture that we are used to seeing in their innate rock or stone finish, represented in the original vivid colors in which they were painted.

One particular statue caught my attention because at first sight I thought it was a live person lying on the ground. It was a human-sized statue of a naked male figure called the *Dying Gaul* by John De Andrea. This contemporary work is based on an older Roman statue, which in turn was based on a lost Hellenistic statue to commemorate Attalus of Pergamon's victory over the Celtic Galatians. The form of the sculpture, which was made of casts of molds of human body parts, was perfect, but what made the statue stand out for me was how realistic it looked in the way it was painstakingly painted with acrylic to complement the form.

Painting a three-dimensional object has many similarities to two-dimensional painting and some significant differences, too. The overall color theory, balance, and application might be the same as two-dimensional painting, but you do not have to concern yourself with painting light and shadows because that is taken care of by lighting and rendering your model. What you need to be mostly concerned with is representing the material properties, and the appropriate hue, saturation, and value of the applied paint and textures. Your 3D paint and texture should complement the form and shadows of your sculpture, add the intended realistic or stylistic look, and bring out its beauty. Painted 3D sculpture is all around us in the form of cars, toys, scale models, movie props, and many other objects. Look around to find out what works and what doesn't in painted sculpture.

Generating UVs on Subdivision Levels and Painting Directly on UVs

As you have already seen in Chapter 4, in Mudbox models need to have UVs before they can be painted. This applies to any subdivision level you intend to paint, and Mudbox, by default, does not generate UVs for every subdivision level you create. Mudbox can, however, generate UVs based on the UVs you have on the root subdivision level at any point in time, or generate them as you are creating the subdivision level.

Ideally, you should paint your models at the highest subdivision level, because unlike sculpting, there are no visual benefits to painting your model at lower subdivision levels, and there is a huge benefit to painting your model in its most detailed subdivision level. However, if you notice that painting your model at the highest subdivision level is sluggish and slow because of the complexity of your model or if you need to reduce graphics processing unit (GPU) memory usage, then you would need to paint it at a lower subdivision level. In that case, you need to make sure that UVs exist at the particular subdivision level you are intending to paint.

Even if your base mesh or model starts out with UVs, by default, Mudbox does not create the UVs for every subdivision level because they increase the overall RAM and GPU memory requirements and might limit your ability to work on your model because of memory constraints. To find out if the subdivision level you are in has UVs, select the model and click the UV View. If no UVs appear, there are no UVs for that particular subdivision level, even if they exist at the base level or other subdivision levels of the model. If that's the case, you need to create UVs for the current subdivision level in one of three ways:

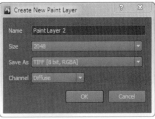

Figure 8.1

Create New Paint Layer dialog box

- If the model has UVs on the base or lower levels and you paint on a subdivision level that has no UVs, upon your first stroke Mudbox will automatically create subdivided UVs of the mesh and come up with the Create New Paint Layer dialog box (Figure 8.1).

- Select the mesh at that specific subdivision level by selecting your model, pressing the Pg Up or Pg Dn keys, and then clicking Mesh → Recreate Level UVs. Note that if you need to step up and down in subdivision level after the initial selection, you can either reselect the mesh and press the Pg Up or Pg Dn keys, or hover your cursor on the mesh and press Pg Up or Pg Dn.

- You can also generate UVs at the same time you subdivide the model by selecting the Subdivide UVs option in the Mesh → Add New Subdivision Level dialog box on Windows (Figure 8.2), or the Mesh → Add New Subdivision Level Options on the Mac.

Figure 8.2

Add New Subdivision Level dialog box

Note that turning this option on will automatically subdivide UVs every subsequent time the model is subdivided, so it is best to leave it deselected to save memory and to check it only when you intend to create UVs for that particular subdivision level. Keep this option selected as a default only if you know you need UVs at every subdivision level of your model.

High-resolution textures spread out over multiple UV tiles will quickly use up limited graphics memory if all textures are set to display simultaneously. If you have a model with multiple UV tiles with at least one paint layer, only one texture tile will show in 3D View, the default being the first quadrant tile. You can selectively and manually load the remaining texture tiles to display them. Before you do that, the tiles are assigned a random color to indicate their unloaded state in 3D View. This enables you to see the location of each of the tiles, and know which texture tiles are currently loaded or unloaded on the model.

To toggle the display of a texture tile and all its paint channels on a model, place the cursor over the texture tile region and click the up arrow key. To show all texture tiles on a model, press Ctrl+up arrow key, and to hide them, press Ctrl+down arrow key.

When you subdivide your model, UVs are not smoothed by default; however, when you do need the UVs smoothed, you can select the Smooth UVs check box in the Mesh → Add New Subdivision Level dialog box (Figure 8.2). You would want UVs smoothed if your model is eventually to be rendered as a subdivision surface in a target application that supports UV smoothing, similar to Mudbox.

As of Mudbox 2011, you can use Mesh → Flatten to UV Space, or press Alt+T to have the flattened UVs appear in 3D view, so if needed, you can paint on them in a flattened view. This creates a copy of the model with vertex positions that are identical to the UVs on the model, and the original model is made temporarily invisible to let you paint on the 2D UVs. After you are finished painting on the flattened UV view, click Mesh → Unflatten from UV Space, or press Alt+T to display the model in 3D.

Painting on flat UVs was something you had to do external to Mudbox in an image-editing program, but now you can do it right in Mudbox and use all the sculpting and painting tools on a flattened version of the UVs. This is extremely useful for making minor topology adjustments to resolve stretching issues by using the Grab tool. One of the most useful implementations for this capability is to paint areas that are not visible or are in an occluded area on the 3D sculpture. An example of this is Figure 8.3, in which the model's pants and gloves were painted with the Paint Brush tool in the 3D view. Even though the parts we want painted look like they are covered completely by paint, when we go into flattened UV view, we see that all the areas I have circled do not have paint on them. This would be an issue if the model were to be animated and those parts appeared unpainted in a different pose of the model. You will go through an example of this in the following steps, in which you will color the bottom half of the body and the gloves in one color, and the rest in a different color.

The following steps go through the process of painting a model in flattened UV space:

1. Start Mudbox, and from the `Chapter 8` folder of the DVD load the `body.mud` file. If it is not at subdivision level 5, move your cursor on the mesh and press Pg Up until it is.

2. From the Paint Tools tray, choose the Paint Brush and click on the model. Click OK to create a new paint layer, and then click OK to accept the defaults for the Create New Paint Layer dialog box.

3. In the properties of the Paint Brush tool, click Color and choose a bluish-gray color, or any other color of your choice (Figure 8.4). Make sure the strength of the tool is at 100, and adjust the size on the model to get a large and comfortable setting to paint the model with the least number of strokes.

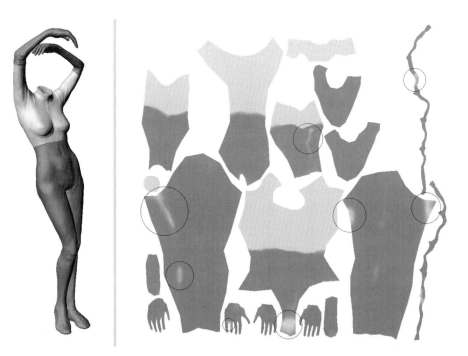

Figure 8.3

The circled area on the flattened UVs shows areas that were not painted in the 3D view (see color insert).

4. Paint the pants in the blue color by spinning the model around, making sure you apply paint to all the parts of the pants that are visible. Adjust the brush to a smaller size to paint the edges. Do the same with the gloves. When you are finished, your result should look like the image on the left of Figure 8.3. Use the Paint Erase tool to remove paint from areas that you crossed over but did not wish to paint on.

Figure 8.4

Color Chooser

5. Either click Mesh → Flatten to UV Space, or press Alt+T to view your model in flattened UV mode. Notice the unpainted areas within the boundary of what you painted, as you can see in the left side of Figure 8.3.

6. Press the W key to show the wireframe on the flattened UVs, and using the Paint Brush tool, fill in those areas to ensure that you have complete coverage of paint for the areas you need to have painted (Figure 8.5).

7. What you want to do next is color the remaining parts of the model orange. Still in flattened UV mode, choose orange as your color and paint on the unpainted parts of your model. After you are finished, click Mesh → Unflatten from UV Space, or click Alt+T again to view your model in 3D view. Notice that you might need to do some painting on the seams of the UVs on the 3D model and make some minor corrections

between the edges where the two colors meet. However, for the most part, flattening to UV space is a nice quick way to paint your model and make sure the color covers all the areas within the boundaries of the areas you are painting.

You can also manipulate the vertices on the flattened 2D view of the model's UVs by using sculpting tools such as the Grab tool to adjust the UV positions and have your adjustments affect your model.

Figure 8.5

Paint the gaps in color on the flattened UVs.

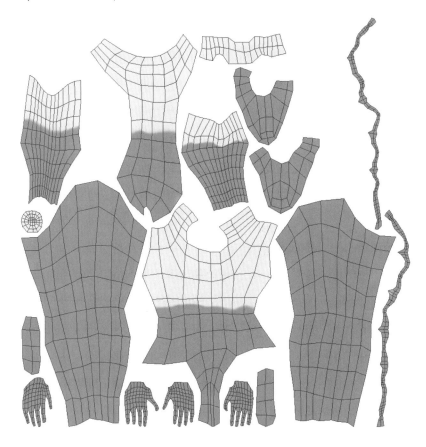

Painting on Layers and Using Blend Modes

Being able to paint your model by using layers is one of the most useful capabilities in Mudbox. It gives you the capability to combine and composite your layers to get your intended final image. You can use paint layers for separating disparate features of your texture, as we did with Bertie in Chapter 4, where we separated the base coat, the weathering, and the decals on separate layers. You can also use them for separating channels such as Diffuse, Specular, Gloss, Bump Map, Normal Map, or Reflection Mask.

Each layer acts like a painted acetate transparency, and the layers stack up to form the final image. You can adjust the order of the layers, which determines what part of each map carries through to the next. You can also specify the opacity of each layer, and a blend mode that works similar to blend modes in Photoshop.

As already mentioned, paint layers need to belong to one of seven paint channels that get composited into the final look of the texture on the model. When you create a new paint layer, you are asked to specify which channel type it is. The default is Diffuse, and the rest are Specular, Gloss, Incandescence, Bump Map, Normal Map, and Reflection Mask. Note that the Channel menu will list which channels are available, depending on the material type currently assigned to your model. You can choose from the following types of channels:

Diffuse: The flat color of the layer.

Specular: The areas on the layer that indicate the color and intensity of specular highlights.

Gloss: The areas of the layer that indicate the size of the gloss reflection highlights on the specular map.

Incandescence: The areas on the layer that simulate the emission of color from a material independent of lighting in the scene.

Bump Map: Bump values on the model.

Normal Map: RGB values that indicate the normals on the model.

Reflection Mask: A layer for painting a mask to allow or restrict the application of the reflection map.

Note that the Mudbox Material used in the 2009 and 2010 versions of Mudbox had some additional channels such as Specular 2 and Gloss 2, and did not have others such as Incandescence and Normal Map. It also had some naming differences such as Bump Value instead of Bump Map. The channels in the older Mudbox Material are still supported with later versions of Mudbox to maintain compatibility; however, they are not available to you when you are creating materials.

Order of Paint Layers

Paint layers are grouped in their respective channels, and each channel can have several layers. Even though that's the case, chances are you will have multiple paint layers in only the Diffuse channel because most of what you need in the other channels will likely be satisfied with a single layer. One reason that you would need different layers for the other channels is to have different variations of the channel that you can turn on and off—for example, if you were to test two specularity maps that add shine to different areas on the model.

The order of visibility of layers in a channel is top to bottom. The topmost layer is the outermost layer, and the rest stack inward like layers in an onion. If you have a fully opaque layer and it is the topmost layer, you will not be able to see the inner layers. The only way to see the inner layers is either to have an alpha channel in the image that controls its areas of transparency, or to change the opacity of a layer by adjusting the opacity slider.

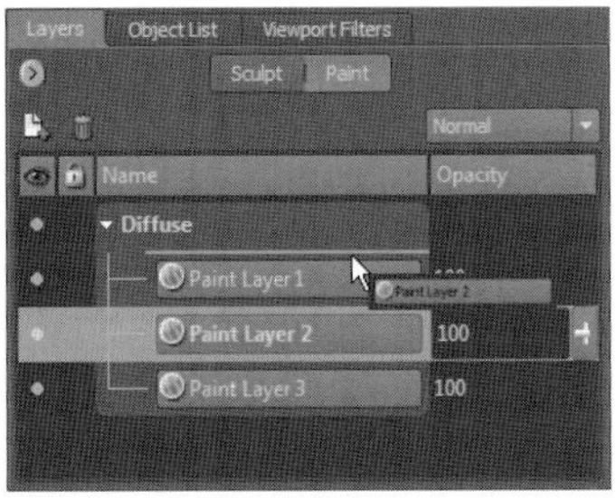

Figure 8.6

Reordering paint
layer 2 to precede
paint layer 1

Paint layers can be rearranged, merged, duplicated, or deleted as needed. To rearrange a layer, simply click on the layer you intend to move, and drag and drop it in its new slot in the Layers window (Figure 8.6).

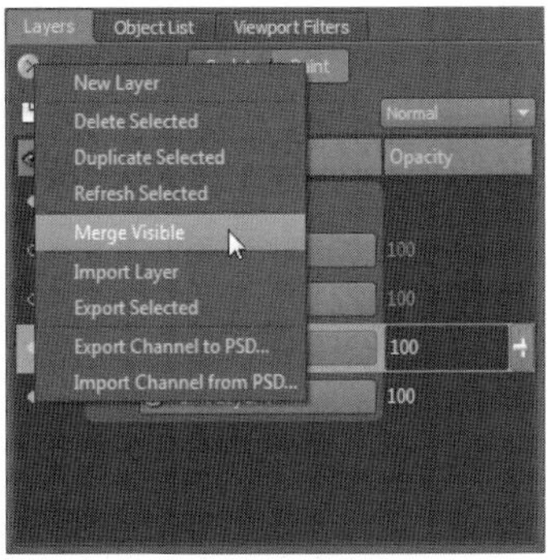

To merge layers, first turn off the visibility to all the paint layers that you do not wish to merge by clicking the circle in front of the name of the paint layer so it is an empty circle. Then click Merge Visible from the Layers window drop-down menu to merge all the paint layers that are visible and have a filled circle in front of the paint layer name (Figure 8.7).

Figure 8.7

Merging visible
layers 3 and 4

To delete or duplicate a paint layer, first select it by clicking on it, and then right-click and select Delete Selected or Duplicate Selected, respectively, to perform the desired operation (Figure 8.8).

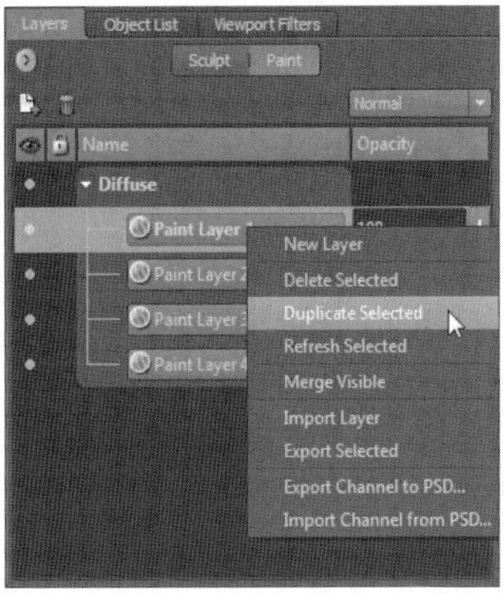

Individual paint layers can be exported in a variety of file formats for processing in external applications, such as 3D applications, game engines, and image-processing software. This can be done by clicking to select the paint layer you want to export and then right-clicking and choosing Export Selected.

Figure 8.8

Duplicating
paint layer 1

You can also individually import an image to be a new paint layer from a variety of file formats. To do this, select the paint layer on top of which you want to create a new paint layer, right-click, and choose Import Layer from the drop-down menu. After you navigate to and select the file you intend to import as a paint layer, you will be asked to choose which channel it goes into by the Select Channel dialog box (Figure 8.9).

Figure 8.9

Select the paint
layer into which you
wish to import your
image.

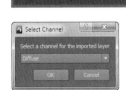

You can also import or export multiple paint layers grouped as a channel in and out of Photoshop as a `.psd` file. The layers, their order, and blend mode will be preserved as you do the import and export operation.

Follow these steps to walk through an example of working with multiple paint layers within Mudbox and Adobe Photoshop.

1. Start Mudbox, and from the Chapter 8 folder of the DVD load the head.mud file. Select the Layers menu and click Paint to view the paint layers. If you see none, click once on the head in the 3D viewport, which will then bring up six Diffuse layers, a single Specular, and a single Gloss layer (Figure 8.10).

2. Click layer visibility circles to the left of the paint layer names to hide all the paint layers. Note that you can show or hide an entire channel by clicking its layer visibility circle. As you hide each layer, you can see the layers beneath. Figure out how each layer affects the others and the overall view by showing and hiding the layers. You can also adjust the opacity of each layer to see its effect. Note that setting the opacity of a layer to 0 is the same as hiding it. Spend as much time as needed to see the effects of the layers and their interaction with each other and the material of the head. Click on the eyes and notice that each eye has its own diffuse and specular layer.

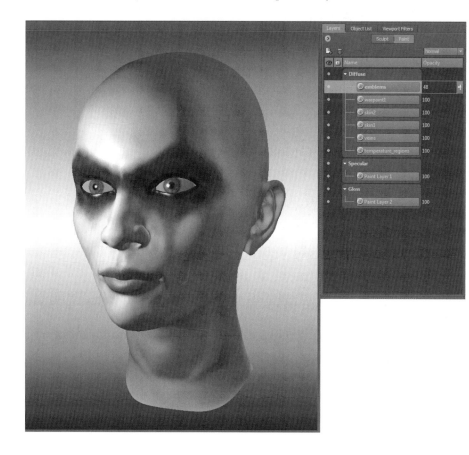

Figure 8.10

Multiple paint layers on the model

Figure 8.11

Multiple paint layers on the model

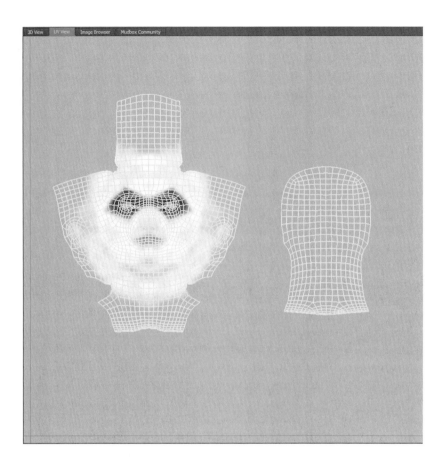

3. Turn all the paint layers back on, and change their opacity to **100**, or reload the file from the DVD. Click on the head and press Pg Dn five times to get to subdivision level 0. Press the W key to show the wireframe on the head. Click the UV View tab to take your image into UV view. Click on each of the paint layers to view it in UV view (Figure 8.11). Note that the layer visibility circles for the channel and the layer have to be full for this to work. The UV view will show only individual paint layers.

4. Click the 3D View tab, press Pg Up five times to get the head to subdivision level 5, and press the W key to hide the wireframe. Press Alt+T or click Mesh → Flatten to UV Space; this displays the UVs. Note that even though the face flattened out to its UVs, the eyeballs are not flattened to UV space. In the Object List, click the visibility circles of Eye_1f and Eye_rt meshes to hide them. Note that the visibility of the Head mesh is also turned off. Right-click on the Front camera and select Look Through from the drop-down menu. Zoom and pan your model until the two UV shells of the face fill the 3D view. Now click the Layers tab and notice that you can view and hide the individual layers (Figure 8.12).

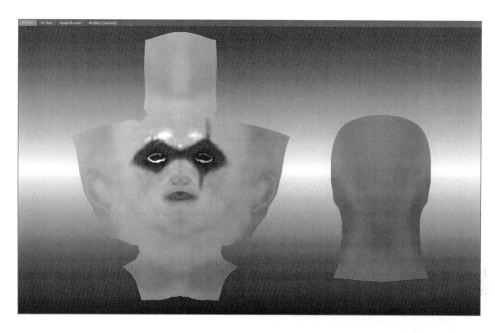

Figure 8.12

Model flattened to UV space seen in the Front camera

Figure 8.13

Set the wireframe limit to 0

5. Click Windows → Preferences (or Mudbox → Preferences on the Mac) and expand the Render section. Type **0** in the Limit Wireframe to Level text box (Figure 8.13). This limits the wireframe displayed on the model to level 0 and closes the preferences dialog box.

6. Press the W key to display the wireframe (Figure 8.14). In this view, in essence, you are able to paint on a flattened UV view of the model by using all the painting tools of Mudbox exactly as you would if you were working on the UVs in an image-editing program. The advantage here is that you can show and hide the different layers to see how they composite, and also flip out of flattened UV space by the simple toggle of pressing Alt+T. Experiment typing in **1**, **2**, and **3** in the Limit Wireframe to Level text box in the preferences to see the wireframe detail on both the flattened-to-UV-space and 3D-space version of the model.

Figure 8.14

Wireframe on the flattened-to-UV-space model

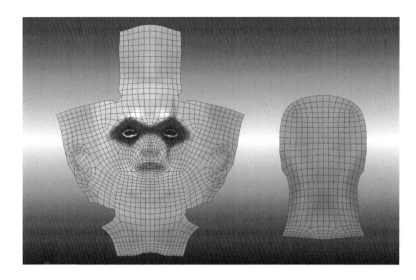

7. Experiment using the Mudbox painting tools on the flattened-to-UV-space model. Note that you can use stencils to projection-paint on the surface as well as use stamps and all of the various tools available to you in Mudbox.

8. Go back to the perspective view by right-clicking on the Perspective camera in the Object List and choosing Look Through Selected from the drop-down menu.

9. Click on the head, and turn off all the paint layers by clicking their layer visibility circles to view the base material (Figure 8.15).

Figure 8.15

Model with all textures turned off on the head

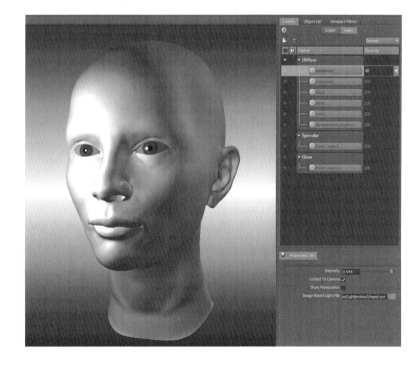

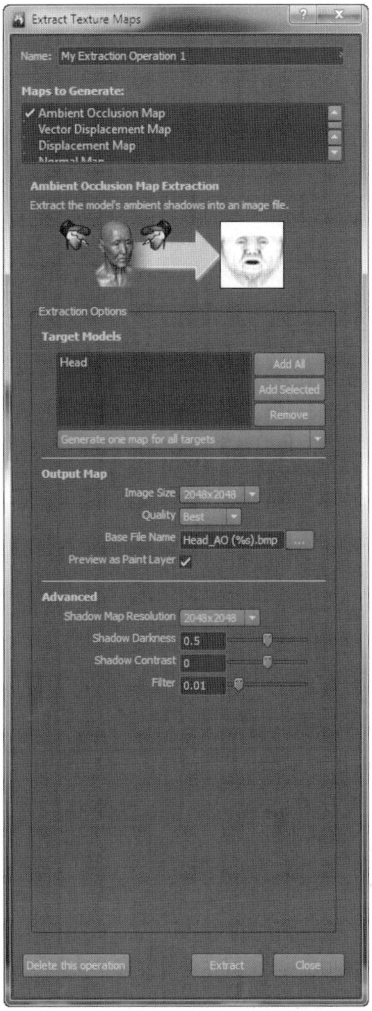

10. Click Maps → Extract Texture Maps → New Operation, and select the Ambient Occlusion Map check box. For the Target Models, click the Add All button, and then individually select all the added meshes except Head and click the Remove button. You can select multiple objects by holding down the Ctrl key and clicking on them. For the Output Map, select an Image Size of 2048 × 2048. Select Best for the Quality. Type **Head_AO** in the Base File Name text box. Make sure the Preview as Paint Layer option is selected because you want to have the generated Ambient Occlusion map added to your list of layers. It will be added in the Diffuse channel. Choose a shadow map resolution of 2048 × 2048, and click Extract to generate the Ambient Occlusion map (Figure 8.16).

11. After the map is extracted, rename it **Head_AO**. Notice that as you turn the visibility on, the Ambient Occlusion paint layer will obstruct all layers beneath it to show only the Ambient Occlusion map, in which the occluded areas are darker than the ones that are not. You will apply the darkening of the occluded areas to your original composition but not completely cover it with the white areas of the Ambient Occlusion map. To do this, use a blend mode for your layer composition. The blend operation that shows the darkened areas through while hiding the light areas is called Multiply and is available from the blend mode menu in the Layers window (Figure 8.17). Choose the Multiply blend mode for the Ambient Occlusion paint layer. Notice that the occluded areas get darkened and the rest of the model shows through.

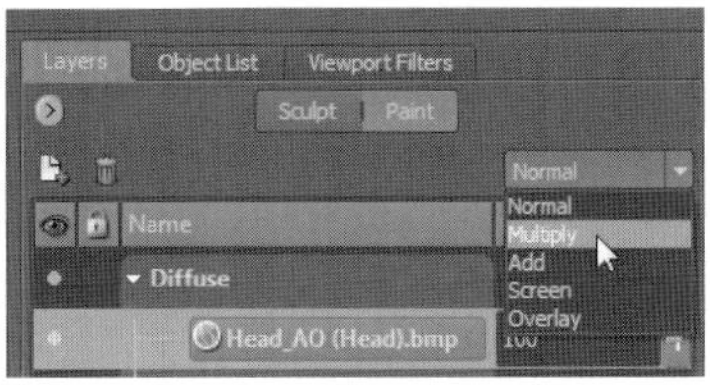

12. As powerful as the painting and compositing features are in Mudbox, they are by no means as extensive as those of Adobe Photoshop, and all its image processing features and ecosystem of third-party plug-ins, filters, brushes, actions, and other extensions. However, you can export channels with all their layers

Figure 8.16

Extract Texture Maps dialog box to extract the Ambient Occlusion map

Figure 8.17

Blend mode menu

Figure 8.18

Export Channel to PSD

and blend modes into Photoshop if you need to use those capabilities. To do that, click Export Channel to PSD in the Layers window drop-down menu (Figure 8.18).

13. After you specify where to save the PSD file and name it, Mudbox will export all the layers with their opacity and blend modes into a PSD file. If you have Photoshop installed on your machine, this command will even open up Photoshop for you and load the PSD. After the export is done and Photoshop is loaded with your composited layers, if you minimize Photoshop or switch back to Mudbox, you will notice a dialog box (Figure 8.19) that is waiting for you to update the PSD so Mudbox can re-import the PSD and place your Photoshop edits back into your paint layer structure.

14. If you look at your image in Photoshop (Figure 8.20), you will notice that all the layers are available to you to paint on except the top and bottom layers, which are locked. The top layer has the wireframe guide, and the bottom layer has the diffuse color of the material. You can now individually work on all the layers and then re-import them into Mudbox by clicking the Re-Import Diffuse_Channel.psd button in the dialog box. If you dismissed the dialog box by clicking Close, you can use the Import Channel from PSD menu item in the Layers window drop-down menu (shown previously in Figure 8.18). Also note that each of the layers has an RGB and alpha channel in the Photoshop channels list.

Figure 8.19

Dialog box to re-import the PSD file into Mudbox

15. Experiment adding some elements and processing the various layers, and then save your PSD file. Re-import your changes into Mudbox to see the results of your edits.

Figure 8.20

The Diffuse channel of our Mudbox model loaded into Photoshop CS4

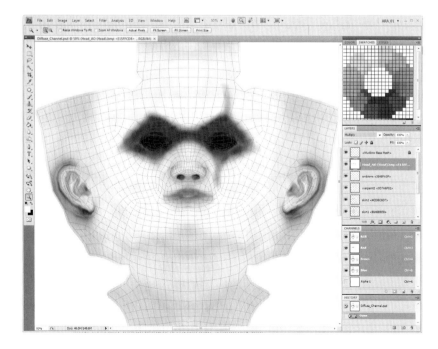

As you briefly saw in the preceding exercise, blend modes are extremely useful for compositing layers of 3D textures. Note that the Ambient Occlusion, or AO, layer needs to be the topmost layer, and you need to use the Multiply blend mode to get the needed result. Including Multiply, Mudbox 2011 has five blend modes:

Normal This is the default blend mode for a paint layer. With this blend mode, the composite of all the layers will result in only the top paint layer in the layer stack unless you change the opacity setting to a number less than 100, or it has some transparent regions due to the image having an alpha channel that indicates what parts of it are transparent.

Multiply The value of each pixel in the layer is darkened by a value greater than or equal to the value of pixels occupying the same location on layers on top of it in the layer stack. This blend mode is useful for darkening an image, especially with an Ambient Occlusion map. Multiplying with white does nothing, while screening with black produces black.

Add The value of each pixel in the layer is brightened by a value less than or equal to the value of pixels occupying the same location on layers on top of it in the layer stack. Although Screen seems to do the same thing as the Add blend mode, the lightening effect produces no change in contrast because the mode is applied in a linear fashion, producing a more extreme lightening result than Screening.

Screen The value of each pixel in the layer is brightened by a value less than or equal to the value of pixels occupying the same location on layers on top of it in the layer stack. The resulting effect is the opposite of the Multiply blend mode. Screening with black does nothing, while screening with white produces white.

Overlay This is a combination of Multiply and Screen: The value of each pixel is multiplied if the layer on which the mode is set is in the bottom 50 percent of the overall brightness of the image, and uses the Screen blend mode if the layer on which the mode is applied to is in the top 50 percent of the overall brightness. The base color on the layer is not replaced but is mixed with the blend color to reflect the lightness or darkness of the original color. This mode is useful for replacing patterns and colors while preserving the highlights and shadows of the base color.

Using Color, Stamps, and Stencils

The way we see anything we are working on is by the arrangement of color elements on a plane. Many factors go into that arrangement, be it atmosphere, light, scale, proportion, gesture, balance, weight, reflections, refractions, material, surface, or of course, color. In most cases, the colors in your image can range from generated/synthesized to inherited or somewhere in between.

Choosing a Color in Mudbox

To generate or synthesize a color in Mudbox, use the Color Chooser (Figure 8.21).

Figure 8.21

The expanded Color Chooser

The color of your model in Mudbox is determined by the properties of your material and its relationship with the lighting in your scene. The color is affected by the reflectivity, specularity, gloss, and incandescence properties of the material and how they interact with the color, intensity, and direction of the light. The incandescence property of a material is independent of the lighting in the scene; it is determined by the light emitted by the object itself. Note that the incandescent light emitted by an object does not affect the lighting of the scene or light other areas. The lighting in the scene could be user-created, such as point or directional lights, or image-based lighting (IBL), which emulates the lighting in a high dynamic range (HDR) image.

There are extremely flexible methods of choosing colors in Mudbox. You can select and specify colors for a property or material by using either the color wheel or color palette.

You can choose colors in Mudbox by any of the following methods:

- Visually dialing in the color by using Hue Saturation and Value (HSV) or Red Green Blue (RGB) sliders (see Figure 8.22). You can select colors from any location within

Figure 8.22

Choosing a color by using HSV and RGB values

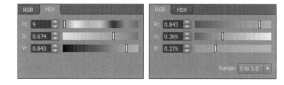

the 3D view. You can also numerically enter color by typing in values for HSV and RGB if you have specific colors that are passed to you numerically.

- Sampling the color off of an image (Figure 8.23). While using this method, you should be aware that if your image is a photo, the color you are selecting is not pure but is

Figure 8.23

Choosing a color from an image or digital photo

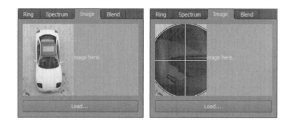

affected by its environment in the image setting. You should look for areas in the image where the color you are looking for has its purest form, with the least distortion from light, reflections, and atmosphere.

- Mixing colors by selecting four base colors and picking your desired color (Figure 8.24) from values blended from the four of them. To do this, drag a color from the color palettes to a corner to have it affect the blend of the other three. Click on

Figure 8.24

Choosing a color from a blend of four colors

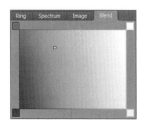

any of the colors in the blended color region to choose your color.

You can also create, load, save, and import color palettes. To create a color palette, drag and drop colors from the Current/Previous color box at the location on the color palette you want it to be. Mudbox will import Adobe Photoshop .aco color sets called *swatches*.

Having a color palette is indispensible when you are painting a subject that has to conform to a color scheme that your art director has set as the mood for your work. These
palettes can come from photographs or other forms of visual inspiration.

To sample colors from an image and place them into a color palette, follow these steps:

1. Start Mudbox and choose the car mesh. Set the Material to Reflective White. From
   the Lighting Presets, choose Late Afternoon. Click on the Paint Tools tray and
   choose the Paint Brush tool. In the properties window for the Paint Brush tool,
   click the Color button to open the Color Chooser (see Figure 8.21 earlier).

2. In the Color Chooser, click the Image tab in the Color Wheel section. Click the Load
   button and load the `Color Palette.jpg` file from the `Stencils` folder of the DVD. It is
   an image I took to capture the
   interaction of colors of a melon
   and plums (Figure 8.25).

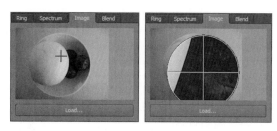

Figure 8.25

**Sampling image
colors in the Color
Chooser**

3. Click and drag on the image
   and notice how your click mag-
   nifies the image to enable you to
   pick specific colors. When you
   find the one you are looking for, let go of the button, and that color will become your
   current selected one.

4. In the Color Palettes section of the Color Chooser, click on the color palette name,
   which is set to Default, and from the drop-down menu select New. Type in a name
   for your new palette and specify a location to save it. This empties your color palette
   so you can fill it with colors from the image.

5. Drag and drop the color from the selected color box to any location on your palette
   to capture that color in the palette.

6. Repeat steps 3 and 5 until you feel you have grabbed a satisfactory number of colors
   from the image. After you are finished, click the Save button to save your changes.
   You have now created a color palette that you can use at future sessions.

You can use an alternate method to step 3. This second method can also come in
handy when you do not care to save the palette but just use colors from an image for a
single session.

1. In the Image Browser, navigate to the `Stencils` folder on the DVD and set the color
   palette file as your image plane. For detailed instructions on how to do this, see
   Chapter 1, "Getting Your Feet in the Mud: The Basics of the Mudbox Production
   Pipeline."

2. Click the + sign in front of the Perspective camera to expand its stencil and image
   plane. Click in the image plane and in the Advanced section of the Image Plane
   properties, set the depth to **1000**, and make sure the Visibility is at **1**.

3. Click the Paint Brush tool if it is not selected. Then click the Color property of the Paint Brush tool, which brings up the Color Chooser. Move the Color Chooser out of the way of your image plane and car model; if you have a second monitor, this would be an excellent use for it.

4. Click the Eyedropper tool either in the Color Chooser palette or the Paint Tools tray, and then click on a location of the picture to sample the color from it. Both the Eyedropper in the Color Chooser and the one in the Paint Tools tray do the exact same thing.

5. And for your prize, click on the car, next, create a new paint layer (the default is fine), and start painting the colors of the photo onto your car, using the shiny material, in a setting lit by an image-based light. In essence, you are sampling colors in real time on a set material and in a specific lighting scenario. This is an extremely powerful capability for doing *what if* analysis of colors of objects in specific settings to see how the generated color becomes an inherited color as a result of its base color, the effects of the material, and the lighting.

The Eyedropper tool is also indispensible for sampling colors off of a model. It enables you to sample a color from your model from the current paint layer. The color chosen does not take into account the lighting and shading on the model; just the true color of the pixel is sampled. It is the same as sampling a color from the model if it were in flat lighting mode in the 3D view.

Paint Using Color, Stamps, and Stencils

You have painted the egg in Chapter 1, and Bertie in Chapter 4, and you are fairly familiar with the painting tools of Mudbox. In this next section, we will cover some of the tools in further detail and introduce some more-advanced capabilities.

The Paint Brush, Airbrush, Pencil, and Paint Erase Tools

The Paint Brush, the Airbrush, the Pencil, and the Paint Erase tools all share the same properties and have functions that are pretty straightforward. One very powerful aspect of the paint tools is that they support symmetry. You can use the Mirror option to paint just as you were able to use it to sculpt, mirroring your paint strokes across all the symmetrical axes as well as the tangent symmetry on objects that are symmetrical but not aligned on an axis.

Follow these steps to use the Paint Brush, Airbrush, Pencil, and Paint Erase Tools:

1. Start Mudbox and load the `plate_dry_brush.mud` file from the `Chapter 8` folder of the DVD. Press the W key to turn on the wireframe. These are armor plates that you will place on the model you sculpted in Chapter 6.

2. On the front top plate, select two symmetrical faces by using the Faces tool from the Select/Move Tools tray (Figure 8.26). Click Mesh → Set Topological Axis to set the topological axis. Click outside the model in 3D view to deselect the faces you had selected. You can now use the topological symmetry of the model to mirror-paint a pattern on the shield.

3. From the paint tools, select the Paint Brush and click on the model. Accept the default options in the Create New Paint Layer dialog box to create a paint layer. Choose a color, paint on your model, and notice how your work is mirrored (Figure 8.27).

The falloff is common with paint tools, and you can use falloffs to feather the edges of the paint you are applying. Notice the effects of different falloffs on the paint on a surface in Figure 8.28. In the falloff used at the bottom of the figure, there is no feathering or smoothness to the edge of the paint. This creates hard edges and the paint appears as though it has been applied with a marker. The other falloffs have a more feathered edge, like that of an airbrush or spray paint.

Using a tablet with pressure sensitivity while working with these tools is also extremely useful because you can use pressure in your paint stroke to apply or erase paint from the model. Drawing or painting while using less pressure gives you more-subtle buildup or teardown of patterns and color.

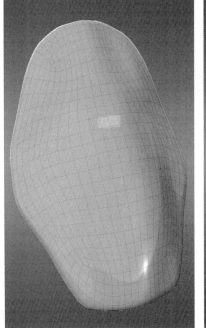
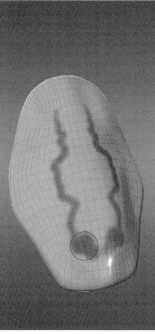
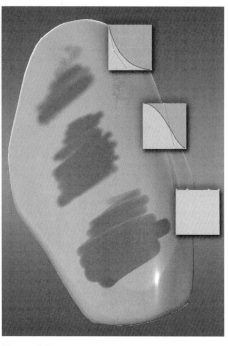

Figure 8.26
Indicating the topological symmetry axis by choosing a face on either side of it

Figure 8.27
Paint mirrored on the topological axis

Figure 8.28
Paint applied with different falloff values (see color insert)

The Clone Tool

The Clone tool works exactly like the Clone Brush in Photoshop: You can set a sampling point by holding down the Ctrl key and clicking on the area from which to sample the color, and then clicking on another location where you want to replicate the colors or patterns of the sampling point. The size of your brush determines the radius of the area you will clone. This is extremely useful to copy a texture or transfer color tone from one

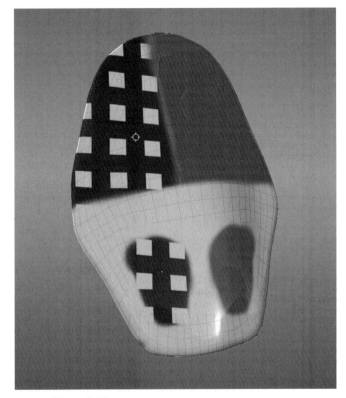

area to another. You can also sample texture from one object to another. Note that the Clone tool works with mirroring, so you can use it on symmetrical objects; however, note that the mirrored brush has its own target. That is, it will clone from a mirror of the sampling area on the mirrored side (Figure 8.29).

The Dry Brush

The Dry Brush tool is useful for conditionally painting on the surface of an object based on the elevation of that surface. You can paint just the protruded areas of a surface with it, and recessed areas while holding down the Ctrl key. It is perfect for painting only protruded or only recessed areas on a surface pattern. It is also extremely useful to add weathering to surfaces.

The Dry Brush tool applies paint depending on whether a face is above an invisible plane that is dynamically calculated as the brush moves on the surface. This invisible plane is calculated by the average positions of vertices on the sur-

Figure 8.29

Using Mirror symmetry with the Clone tool

face that are within the brush ring. The Size property of the Dry Brush affects the height or depth to which paint is applied to the surface, so a smaller brush size provides better control when applying paint on smaller sculpted patterns and shapes.

Mirror symmetry works with the Dry Brush. However, unlike other tools, it applies the effect of the Dry Brush to the mirrored area instead of reflecting an exact copy. The mirrored Dry Brush will act independently on the two surfaces of the mirror. To go through an example of using the Dry Brush, follow these steps:

1. Start Mudbox and load the `plate_dry_brush.mud` file from the `Chapter 8` folder of the DVD (Figure 8.30). Note that this armor plate has a strip of indented dots, and you need to paint the indented parts a dark gray and add some weathering and smears on the edges.

2. From the paint tools, select the Dry Brush and click on the model. Accept the default options in the Create New Paint Layer dialog box, to create a paint layer. Choose a dark gray color and a Strength of 100, hold down the Ctrl key, and paint on the strip of dots on the plate. Experiment with larger brush sizes to see the effects. From the Mirror drop-down list, select Tangent. Note the effect of mirrored use of the Dry Brush in the area where there is a break in the dot pattern (Figure 8.31).

3. Select Off in the Mirror drop-down menu and pick a brownish color by using the Color Chooser. Select the first stamp called bw_acidMetal from the Stamp tray and make sure the Use Stamp Image option is selected in the Dry Brush properties. Release the Ctrl key and paint some streaks around the holes (Figure 8.32).

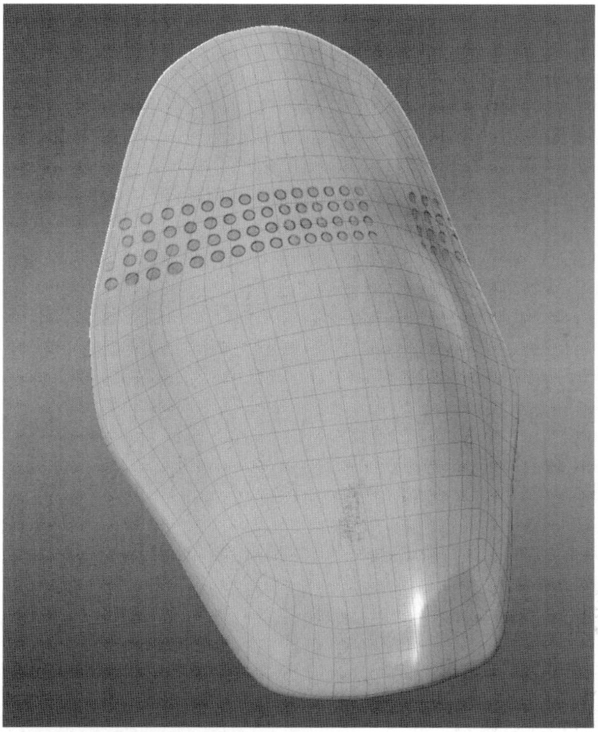

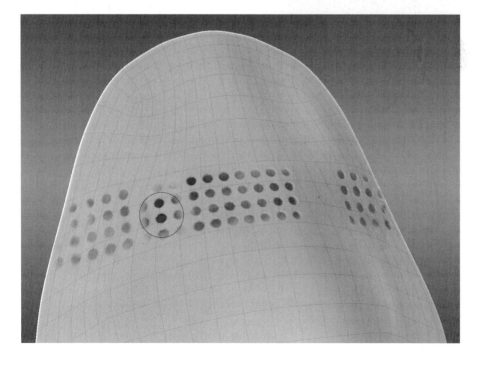

Figure 8.30

Dry Brush on a surface pattern

Figure 8.31

Effects of mirroring while using the Dry Brush on a surface pattern

Figure 8.32

Using the Dry Brush to paint outside the indented holes

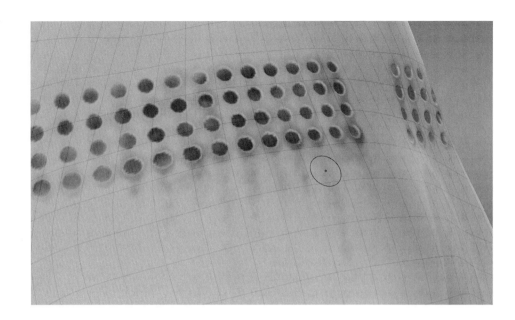

The Blur Tool

The Blur tool blurs the painted area to which the brush ring is applied. The blur effect is applied only to the paint layer you are working on. The difference between the Blur brush in Mudbox and the one in Photoshop is that the one in Mudbox uses the 3D view to calculate the blur. Any operation that changes the screen image, including tumbling and zooming around your model, and turning paint layers on or off, affects the result of the blur, even if you do not change any of the Blur tool properties. Adjusting the Blur Strength property will change the amount the image is blurred; it will also cause the reference image to be recalculated and updated, and that is why you may notice a pause whenever you change it. The size affects the area that is blurred.

Continuing from the example of the armored plate started in the previous section, follow these steps:

1. Use the Blur tool to blur out some of the streaks you make with the Dry Brush.

2. Change the Blur Strength to adjust the amount of blurring and get a feel for how the tool affects the paint on the surface of your model.

The Dodge and Burn Tools

The Dodge and Burn tools enable you to lighten and darken areas on your model. You can chose to affect highlights, mid-tones or shadow areas, or all tonal regions in the areas within the brush ring. I find it a great alternative to the Paint Erase tool to highlight or tone down areas.

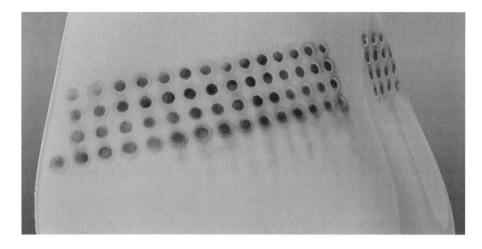

Note that only the color value is affected, while hue and saturation are not. Repeated stroking on the same area will have an additive effect. Change the Strength property to affect the buildup of each successive stroke.

The Exposure property controls the amount of lightening or darkening that occurs. The default setting is 1, which you may want to change only to lessen the effect of the lightening and darkening.

Continuing from the example of the armored plate started in the previous section:

1. Use the Dodge and Burn tools to lighten and darken some of the weathering you applied to the armor plate (Figure 8.33).

2. Change the Affect property of the Dodge and Burn tools to All, and lighten and darken areas of the weathering on the surface.

The Contrast Tool

The Contrast tool increases or decreases the difference between light and dark pixels on the active paint layer to which it is applied. The Contrast property, which ranges from −10 to 10, controls the difference between light and dark pixels. A positive value in the Contrast property increases the contrast, while a negative value reduces it.

Continuing from the example started in the previous section:

1. Try the Contrast tool with varying contrast property values on the model to see the effects on bringing out or muting the edges of your weathering.

2. Try values of −10, −5, 1, 5, and 10.

The Sponge Tool

The Sponge tool makes subtle adjustments to the color saturation of pixels on a texture that is on the active paint layer. The Amount property ranges from −1 to 1; a positive number decreases the color saturation, while a negative number increases it. At the default value of 1, the Sponge tool can be thought of as a tool to sponge off the color of a painted surface.

The Hue Tool

The Hue tool enables you to replace the hue of pixels on a texture that is on the active paint layer with a user-specified color hue. Your stroke will affect the hue only, and not the color value or the color saturation. Unlike other paint tools, the Hue tool does not have a buildup, and its effect is applied on the first stroke. Make sure you cover the entire area you intend to change the hue of in one stroke; otherwise, you will get borders where you stop and restart your stroke.

Continuing from the example started in the previous section:

1. From the Paint Layers window drop-down menu, select Import Layer. From the Chapter 8 folder of the DVD, import the red.tif file. In the Layers window, drag and drop the Red layer so it is below the layer you were working on, so your weathering shows through (Figure 8.34).

2. Make sure you are on the Red Paint layer by clicking on it in the Layers Window and then click the Hue tool in the Paint Tools tray. In the properties for the Hue tool, click the Color button and choose blue in the Color Chooser.

3. With one stroke, paint the image so the red pattern turns blue. Note that the white parts of the texture are not affected. The Hue tool does not affect black or white areas.

Figure 8.34

Reorder the paint layer to apply the Hue tool.

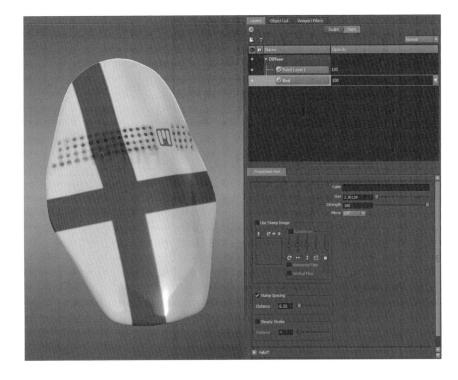

The Hue Shift Tool

The Hue Shift tool shifts the hue by an amount specified in degrees around the color wheel, relative from the current value in a counterclockwise direction. You can enter either a positive or a negative value in the Hue Shift property. The range you can enter is either between 1 and 180 degrees or –1 and –180 degrees.

Continuing from the example started in the previous section:

1. Make sure you are on the Red Paint layer and then click the Hue Shift tool in the Paint Tools tray. In the properties for the Hue Shift tool, type **180** in the Hue Shift text box.

2. With one stroke, paint the image so the blue pattern turns green. Try to do the entire hue shift in one stroke, because if you don't, you will continuously shift the hue. Note that the white parts of the texture are not affected. The Hue Shift tool does not affect black or white areas.

The Invert Tool

Finally, the Invert paint tool enables you to invert the color hue under the region of the brush ring in the current layer.

Continuing from the example started in the previous section:

1. Make sure you are on the Red Paint layer and then click the Invert tool in the Paint Tools tray.

2. With one stroke, paint the image. Try to do the entire inverse in one stroke, because if you don't, you will invert the paint with every stroke. Note that the white parts of the texture are inverted to black.

Paint Using Stamps

Like sculpting, stamps can be used with all the paint tools except the Eyedropper tool. Painting the model with a stamp is much like painting with a rubber stamp. As you click on the model, a stamp is applied to the model, and as you continue your stroke, more copies of the stamp are applied based on the stamp spacing and other stamp properties.

Stamps can be used to apply a recognizable shape such as a grayscale decal, or to create a more random effect to break up the circular shape of the default brush tip. Stamps are very similar to brushes in Adobe Photoshop. You can use one of the many stamps provided for you in Mudbox, or you can use any image or capture and use your favorite brush from Photoshop.

The makeup of a stamp is an image in one of many formats. You can use 8-bit, 16-bit, and 32-bit images, although you can achieve better results especially with sculpting while using 16-bit or 32-bit depth images because of the level of depth detail that can be included in the higher bit depth.

To apply a stamp, you can choose one from the Stamp tray; however, I find that choosing a stamp from the Image Browser is better because you get a larger, more detailed view of the stamp instead of the small thumbnail in the Stamp tray. After you are familiar with the stamps, you can then choose them from the Stamp tray because it takes less time to do so.

**CREATING A BOOKMARK TO YOUR STAMPS AND STENCILS IN THE
IMAGE BROWSER**

In the Image Browser, navigate to the user directory where your documents are stored. In my case, that directory is the C:\Users\<username>\Documents\Mudbox\2011-x64\Data folder in Windows 7. The default stamps and stencils are also stored in the following folders:

(Windows) <drive>:\Program Files\Autodesk\Mudbox2011\stamps

(Windows) <drive>:\Program Files\Autodesk\Mudbox2011\stencils

(Mac OS X) /Users/<username>/Library/Application Support/Autodesk/Mudbox2011/Stamps

(Mac OS X) /Users/<username>/Library/Application Support/Autodesk/Mudbox2011/Stencils

Click the Stamps folder, and you will see larger thumbnails in the strip of thumbnails to the left of the screen and a much bigger version of the stamp in the 2D view of the Image Browser. Now you can see your stamps in much greater detail before you paint or sculpt with them. You can also navigate to your Stencils folder to get larger thumbnails of the default stencils in Mudbox. If you find you are picking stamps and stencils this way a lot, you can add bookmarks to these folders so you do not have to navigate to them all the time. To add a bookmark, navigate to the folder for which you want to add a bookmark, and then click the Bookmarks button in the toolbar and select Add Bookmark from the drop-down menu. From that point on, the bookmark to the folder will be in the Bookmarks drop-down menu. Note that you can also add bookmarks to your texture and reference image folders by using this as well to save you time navigating to the folders every time you need to use an image.

Note that most stamps are square, with resolutions of 256×256 or 512×512, or some are even 1024×1024. Some are grayscale, and some are in color. The Paint Brush tool will allow you to paint with only the grayscale version of the stamp, even if the stamp is in color. To paint with a color version of the stamp, you need to use the Projection tool. Adjust the Stamp Spacing property if you don't want to put down a pattern of the stamps but just a single copy. To more precisely place a stamp, use that stamp as a stencil and use projection painting to place it. The next section provides an example of doing this.

As you have seen, stamps and stencils are images, and you can create and edit them in image-editing programs such as Adobe Photoshop. To create a stamp or stencil in Photoshop, follow the steps in the Help file under Saving Images for Stencils and Stamps as it goes through and details the process of creating an image and choosing the correct settings to save your stamp.

Follow these steps to paint using stamps:

1. Start Mudbox and load the `plate.mud` file from the `Chapter 8` folder of the DVD. Press W to turn on the wireframe.

2. From the paint tools, select the Airbrush tool and click on the model. Accept the default options in the Create New Paint Layer dialog box, to create a paint layer. Choose any color and a Strength of 100. Experiment with different stamps in the Stamp tray to see the effects of painting with the stamp (Figure 8.35).

3. Experiment with the various Use Stamp Image properties to get different results. Use the Paint Erase tool to erase and start over if needed. Notice that slight variations in the properties produce different results (Figure 8.36). Try using stamps with different paint tools to see their effects. Remember that you can also use these stamps to subtract color as well as add it—for example, when using them with the Paint Erase tool.

Figure 8.35

The topmost stroke without using a stamp, and other strokes using various stamps (see color insert)

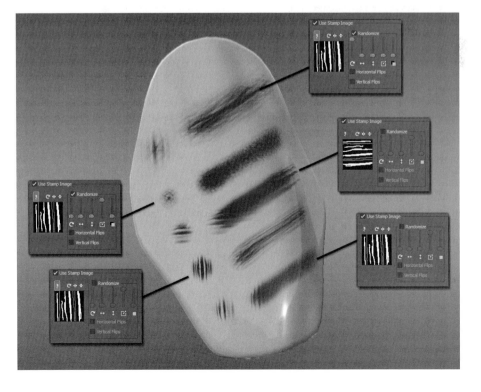

Figure 8.36

Effects of different Use Stamp Image properties (see color insert)

Figure 8.37

Monochrome painted stamps on the top, and color projection stamps on the bottom (see color insert)

To make sure you have the settings you need, remember to select the Use Stamp Image properties every time you select a new stamp. Otherwise, the settings are carried over from your last session.

Projection-Paint Using Stencils

As mentioned in the previous section, stencils and stamps are essentially images. The way we use them determines whether the images are stamps or stencils. In other words, You can use each default stamp image that come with Mudbox as a stencil or any of the Stencil images that come in Mudbox as a stamp.

If your intent is to get a monochromatic pattern of an image, you can use the Paint Brush tool with an image as a stamp, as shown in the monochromatic leaf pattern at the top of Figure 8.37. In this case, it doesn't matter whether the image you are using for a stamp is color or grayscale; the result will still be the painting of the monochrome version of the image.

If your intent is to get a color pattern of the image, use a color image as a stamp and use the Projection tool to paint on the color pattern. To do this, make sure you do not have a stencil selected, because the Projection tool would then prompt you to use it with a stencil. The result is what you see at the bottom of Figure 8.37.

Follow these steps to projection paint using stamps:

1. Start Mudbox and load the `plate.mud` file from the `Chapter 8` folder of the DVD. If the wireframe is on, press the W key to turn it off.

2. Select the Paint Brush tool and pick the color stamp `rbg_leafs.tif`. To find out the name of a stamp, hover on it until a pop-up with the filename comes up. Paint on the top part of the plate to see the effects of using the Paint Brush tool with a stamp. Your results should be similar to the top of Figure 8.37. Experiment with different Use Stamp Image options to see the results.

3. From the paint tools, select the Projection tool and click on the model. Accept the default options in the Create New Paint Layer dialog box to create a paint layer. Make sure the color is white, because that will paint an exact copy of the image. If you used any other color, you would be painting with the hue of that color. Choose a Strength of 100. Ignore the message that tells you to use a stencil.

4. Paint on the model and see the results. If you need a bigger gap in the spacing of the stamps, increase the Stamp Spacing Distance property of the Projection tool. Remember that you can type in values that are more than 100 to get bigger spacing, even though the slider moves to only 100. Try 200 to get results like Figure 8.38.

If your intent is to paint an exact copy of an image onto your model, be it a recognizable emblem or a pattern from an image, you should turn off the Use Stamp Image option and choose the image as a stencil. Then you would use the Projection tools to paint the stencil image onto your model. In this mode, you are manipulating two things to align the image to your model: one is the camera and the other the stencil. You are already very familiar with how to use the camera around your model. However, manipulating the stencil has its own commands. Table 8.1 lists the stencil commands.

You do get a reminder of what these keys are in the bottom-left corner of the 3D View when you have a stencil on.

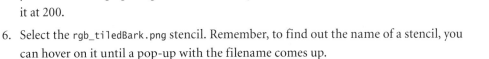

Figure 8.38

Stamp Spacing Distance with the Projection tool

5. Erase the plate by using the Paint Erase tool. Select the Projection tool and make sure that the Use Stamp Image option is turned off in its properties. Also make sure that you set the Stamp Spacing Distance to 10 if you still have it at 200.

6. Select the rgb_tiledBark.png stencil. Remember, to find out the name of a stencil, you can hover on it until a pop-up with the filename comes up.

7. Position the panel so that it points to the front (Figure 8.39). Because the panel is to fit our sculpted model, it is askew from the X, Y, and Z coordinates.

8. Press the S key and click and drag with your left mouse button or press down with the stylus to rotate the stencil so the vertical lines on the pattern align with the angle of the panel (Figure 8.39).

9. Press the S key and click and drag with the middle mouse button or front button on the stylus to move the stencil into position (Figure 8.39).

10. Press the S key and click and drag with the right mouse button or press the back button on your stylus to scale down the stencil so it covers the panel (Figure 8.39). You can use these steps with the stencil shortcuts to interactively to position the stencil.

RESULT	ACTION
Rotate a stencil about its center	S+left button
Translate a stencil	S+middle button
Scale a stencil	S+right button
Hide a stencil	Q (toggle on and off)

Table 8.1

Controls for Translating, Rotating, Scaling, and Hiding Stencils

Figure 8.39

**Painting with
a stencil**

When you projection-paint, you have to account for paint not reaching 3D surfaces that are occluded from your view, or stretching on surfaces that are severely bent from your view, such as the edges of the panel. Think of it as if you were projecting a slide of a picture of a face onto a sculpture of a head. If you are standing to the side of the head, you will see distortions of the image on the nose and side of the head and you will see no image on the back of the head. This can easily be remedied because now you can rotate the model as well to paint in those areas from the existing stencil or images shot of the stencil at different angles.

11. Using the Projection tool at a Strength of 100, paint the panel with the image of the stencil. You will notice that as you press down on the left mouse button or press down on the stylus on the tablet, the stencil disappears and you will start painting the pattern onto the model.

12. After you are finished painting the plate, press the Q key to hide the stencil. Rotate the model to see the stretching on the bent areas of the plate and also on the edges. This can easily be fixed on a nondescript pattern such as the tree bark; you can position the stencil parts and the model to projection-paint a close pattern on the areas that look stretched. You can also use the Clone tool to patch up stretched areas.

If your intent is to paint a monochrome version of an exact copy of an image onto your model, be it a recognizable emblem or a pattern from an image, you should turn off the Use Stamp Image option and choose the image as a stencil. Then you would use the Projection tools to paint the stencil image onto your model while choosing a saturated color.

13. From the Color Chooser, choose green for the properties of the Projection tool. Repaint the stencil and notice that it now has a green tint.

14. Choose black from the Color Chooser for the properties of the Projection tool. Repaint the stencil and notice that none of the detail of the tree bark shows, and you have a completely black image.

15. Press the Q key to view the stencil. Select the Paint Erase tool and then paint the stencil onto the model. Note that this now has a subtractive effect, as paint is erased from the model in the pattern of the stencil.

    Think of the range of color from black to white as the opacity of the stencil. White completely shows the image in its purest form, and as you move to the grays, you are painting darker versions of the image, until at black you are painting with the color black. As you increase the saturation of the color you choose, the more monochromatic you image will get, reflecting only the chosen hue.

16. Press the Q key to hide the stencil. Use the Paint Erase tool to erase the plate, and select the Paint Brush tool. Press the Q key to show the stencil. With the color black still as the color property of the Paint Brush tool, paint the stencil on the plate. Notice that even though we are using a tree bark image, the result looks more like marble.

    Using the Paint Brush tool with a stencil enables you to paint on a desaturated version of the stencil onto the plate.

17. Press the Q key to hide the stencil. Use the Paint Erase tool to erase the plate, and select the Paint Brush tool. In the Image Browser, navigate to the Stencils folder, select the strip.tif file, and set it as the stencil. Notice that the stencil properties appear in the properties section of the East Tray.

18. Switch to the 3D View. The stencil should show up, and the properties for it should still be there. If they are not, you can still get them by clicking on the plus sign to the left of the camera you are using, which in our case is the Perspective camera. This expands the stencil and the image plane associated with this camera. Clicking on the stencil in the Image Browser brings up its properties.

19. Press the Q key to show the stencil if it is not visible. In its properties, make sure that in the Advanced section Use Tiles and Show Tiles are selected. This will tile your image, and if your image is tileable, will create an infinite version of your stencil that you can scale, translate, and rotate to create new patterns. Press the S key to scale, translate, and rotate the pattern of stripes and paint the pattern on the plate (Figure 8.40).

20. Using the Paint Brush tool and an arbitrary color, paint stripes on the plate. Rotate the stencil, and paint again to create a different pattern (Figure 8.41). Note that you can also use stencils as masks to mask off areas on the stencil that are opaque.

Figure 8.40

Repeating the tiled stencil pattern

Figure 8.41

Aggregating patterns

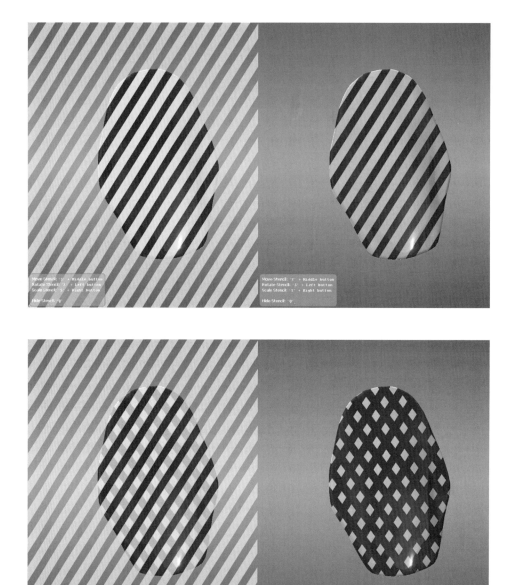

While you have an active stencil, you can still use a stamp to mix the effects—for example, you can use the stamp image to paint a pattern set by the stencil (Figure 8.42).

Note that mirroring and symmetry does not work while you are using stencils. You will find some examples of my experiments with stamps and stencils in Figure 8.43 and in the plate_variations.mud file in the Chapter 8 folder of the DVD.

Figure 8.42

Using stamps and stencils together

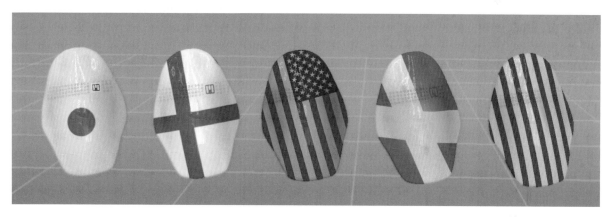

Figure 8.43

Some examples of using stencils (see color insert)

Workflow to Adobe Photoshop and Back

In previous sections, we covered how paint layers in a channel can be exported and imported into Photoshop by using the Export Channel to PSD option in the Paint Layers window drop-down menu. You can also find how to create and import stencils and stamps from Photoshop in the Saving Images for Stencils and Stamps section in the Help file.

However, there are still a few other ways we can interact with the powerful image-editing tools in Photoshop. The next chapter covers a couple of those, but there is one that also pertains to 3D painting.

As mentioned before, you can use many of Photoshop's powerful painting and image-processing capabilities to augment those on Mudbox. One such capability is the ability to paint on text.

Follow these steps to export screenshots into Photoshop CS4:

1. Start Mudbox, and from the Chapter 8 folder of the DVD load the body_logo.mud file. Position the model so the torso is centered in the 3D view (Figure 8.44).

Figure 8.44

Torso centered in the 3D view

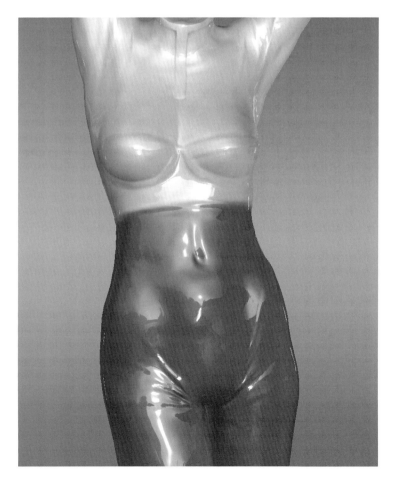

2. Click File →Export Screen to PSD, which brings up the Export Screen Image to PSD dialog box (Figure 8.45). Note that the dialog box has the screen resolution of your current screen along with the option to save the image at double, quadruple, or arbitrary width and height. Click Export to PSD to export the image.

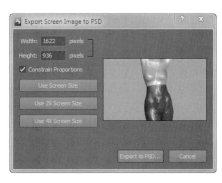

Figure 8.45

Export Screen Image to PSD dialog box

3. Navigate to a location on your hard drive where you wish to save the screen image, and type a name for the PSD file. This saves the file, and if you have Photoshop installed on your machine, opens and loads the file you just saved (Figure 8.46).

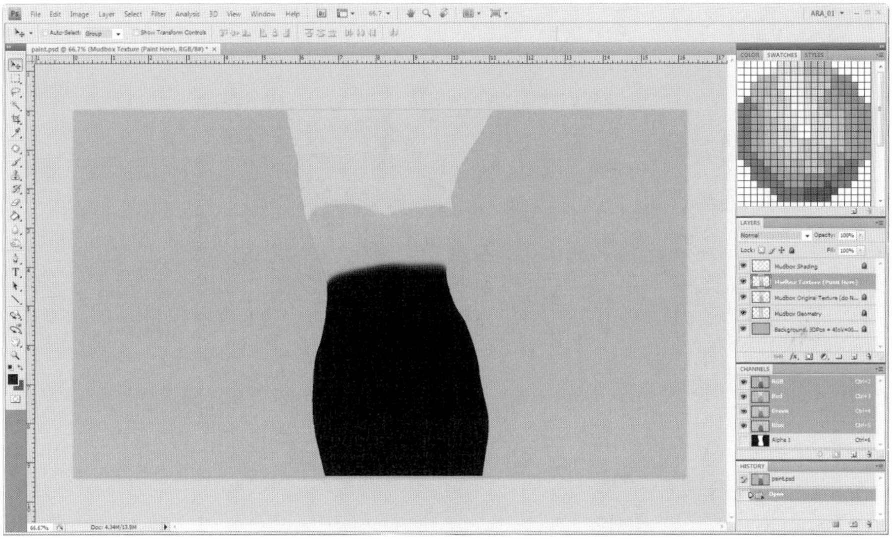

Figure 8.46

Screen image loaded into Photoshop CS4

4. Switch back to Mudbox. Notice that after the file was saved, a Watching File dialog box popped up, giving you two options: to re-import the PSD file or to close the dialog box (Figure 8.47). The Re-Import button is grayed out because Mudbox is watching to see whether a newer version of the PSD file is saved out of Photoshop, in which case the button will be active and you can re-import the modified image and project it onto the model. If you close this dialog box, don't worry, because you can still re-import the PSD file by choosing File → Re-Import From PSD.

Figure 8.47

The Watching File dialog box in Mudbox 2011

Figure 8.48

**Layers of exported
screen image in
Photoshop CS4**

5. Switch back to Photoshop and notice that the PSD file has various layers, all of which are locked except the one that is called Mudbox Texture (Paint here), as you can see

in Figure 8.48. This is the layer onto which you can composite all the work done in Photoshop so it would transfer back into Mudbox. Also note that your image looks different than it did in Mudbox because you are exporting only the flat color of your texture. You can also notice that there is an alpha layer created to mask the background, called Alpha 1.

6. In Photoshop, use the Type tool to type a name on the body of the model, and press the Ctrl key to rotate, scale, and position the text (Figure 8.49). You can also use some of the other tools that you are familiar with in Photoshop to draw or add to the image. Remember that your work will be projected onto the model, so be wary of the edges and changing anything that might alter the uniformity of the texture from the parts that are not visible in the projected image.

Figure 8.49

**Layers of exported
screen image in
Photoshop CS4**

7. In the Photoshop Layers window, right-click on the text layer and select Rasterize Type from the drop-down menu. Right-click on it again and select Merge Down from the drop-down menu. This merges the text with the Mudbox Texture layer. Save your file.

8. Back in Mudbox you will notice that the Re-Import the PSD file button is now active, and upon clicking it you will import the projected text onto the texture of the model (Figure 8.50).

9. Save your scene for use in the next section.

Make sure not to change the layer name for the Mudbox Texture (Paint Here) layer, because the PSD file will no longer re-import into Mudbox. In the next chapter, you will see how you can use the same feature to export the image to composite it in Photoshop with some other layers.

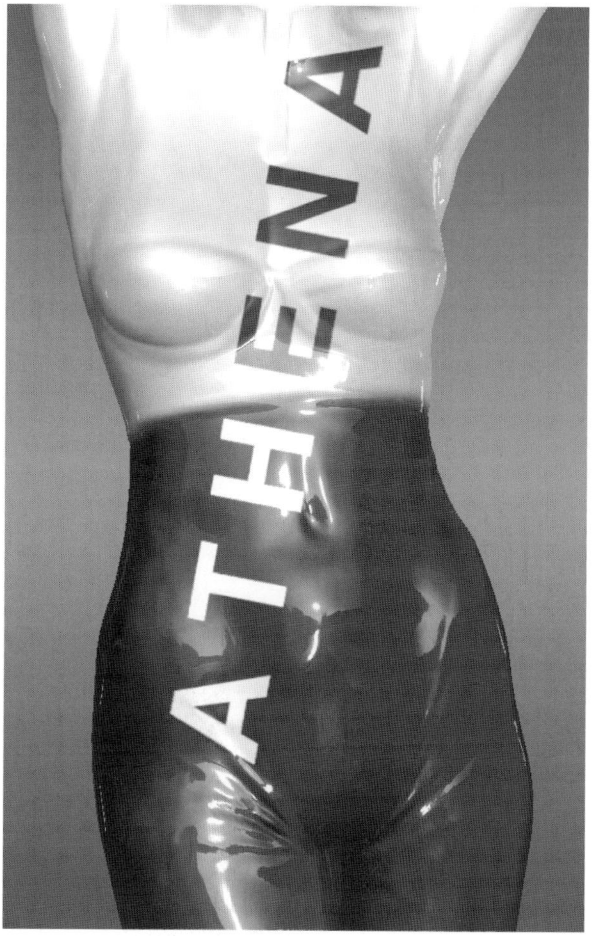

Loading Textures into Maya

After you have painted our model, if your pipeline requires you to send the model to Maya to render, you can export the paint layers in many ways. The most obvious is to use the texture files that are stored when you save the scene, and physically link them to shaders in Hypershade. That's what you did in Chapter 1.

Figure 8.50

Re-imported texture in Mudbox

You can also use the Export to FBX option to export your models to Maya or other applications that support FBX, such as 3ds Max. The FBX export will include the following:

- The mesh, along with top-level transformations and pivot points
- UV texture coordinates
- Cameras, with all their settings
- Image planes, exported with the associated cameras
- Blend shapes
- Joints
- Material textures with Diffuse, Specular, Gloss, Bump Map, Incandescence, Reflection Mask, Reflection Map, and Reflection Strength properties along with the Normal, Multiply, and Add blend modes.

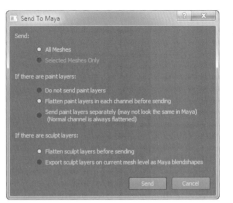

Figure 8.51

The Send to Maya dialog box options

Finally, you can use the easy command to send the model and all the listed FBX properties to Maya 2011, and inversely, use the File → Send to Mudbox command in Maya 2011 to send models to Mudbox.

Upon clicking File → Send to Maya, you will get the Send to Maya dialog box (Figure 8.51). This is where you specify what you want to send.

You can send all the meshes or just the selected ones. You can choose to not send paint layers, send the flattened-by-channel paint layers, or send each layer separately to composite in Maya. Also note that you have the option to flatten all the sculpt layers as well as send them individually as blend shapes.

Follow these steps to export your work to Maya:

1. Start Mudbox and load your scene from the preceding section.

2. Click File → Send to Maya and click OK to accept the defaults.

3. If you have Maya installed, it will launch, and you will have your scene available in Maya. When Maya comes up with a security dialog box, click Allow. You will see the progress of your import in a progress bar at the bottom-left corner of the Maya window.

4. In Maya, open the Hypershade to see your texture already set up (Figure 8.52).

This is a quick and easy way to send your model and textures into Maya.

Figure 8.52

The Shader network in Maya's Hypershade

Summary

Painting your creations in 3D in Mudbox is an easy and natural way to texture and paint your models.

You have seen the versatility of painting a model in 3D as well as in flattened UV space with some powerful painting and image-processing tools. You have worked with compositing multiple paint layers and using blend modes to get the final result.

You have learned how to choose and apply color, and seen the capabilities that stencils and stamps give us in painting patterns and textures onto models. You also have seen how Mudbox can interoperate with Photoshop by sending paint layers as well as projection-painting.

Finally, you have seen how to send textures into Maya. In the next chapter, you will see how to light and render models in Mudbox or export them to render in Maya by using mental ray.

Lighting and Rendering

There are many holy grails in the world of computer-generated imagery, one of which is to get instant rendering results. The rendering stage is still one of the biggest speed bumps to creativity. You have to render each frame to see what it looks like, and as your scene increases in complexity, so does the render time. One of the huge advantages of Mudbox is that all the rendering it does is instantaneous, or real-time. There is no render button. You can interactively sculpt your model, texture-paint it, change material properties, adjust one or multiple lights, and do all of this with viewport filters on while looking at the final result as you are doing the work.

In this chapter, we will go over how to refine and output your render. We will also cover the different lights and their effects on the model.

This chapter includes the following topics:

- **Rendering and using cameras in Mudbox**
- **Lighting your model**
- **Applying visual effects with viewport filters**
- **Creating turntables and recording sessions**
- **Rendering in Mudbox and external programs**

Rendering and Using Cameras in Mudbox

The 3D view is your render window in Mudbox. All the results of your work are rendered there in real time. You can look at the 3D view through any of the default four cameras—Perspective, Top, Side, or Front (Figure 9.1)—which you can select to look through in the Object List.

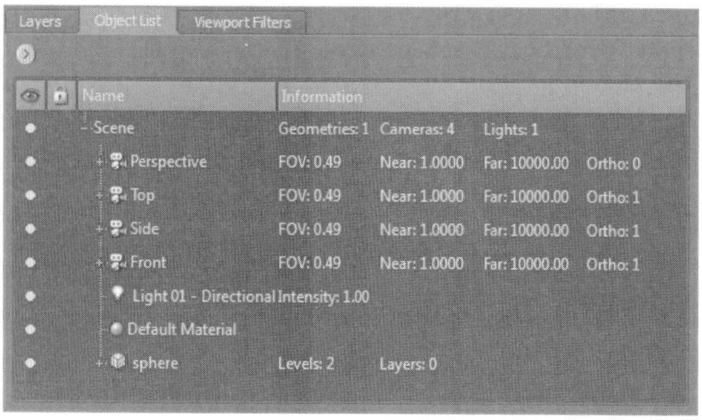

Figure 9.1

Perspective, Top, Side, and Front default cameras in the Object List

If you widen the Object List by dragging the divider on the left, you will see some further information about the cameras to their right, such as the field of vision (FOV), the near and far cutting planes, and whether the display is orthogonal or has perspective.

The camera can be manipulated by its properties (see Figure 9.2). These properties enable you to lock the pan, rotate, and zoom transforms of the camera if you need to do that. The Reset button lets you reset the camera to its original state and to reset all or any of the Roll, Rotate, Track, and Dolly properties.

You can also transform the camera along its 2D view plane. The 2D Transform properties start out unmodified, with default values of a scale of one, zero rotation, and zero shift on either the x- or y-axis. You would need to modify them if you are matching a backplate or real-world camera settings.

If you are working in orthographic diagrams or need to look at your model without perspective of the camera, you would select the Orthographic check box. Note that by default, the Top, Side, and Front cameras have this option turned on, which shows up as a 1 in the Ortho property of the camera in the Object List.

You can set up and use your camera settings in Mudbox or import predetermined camera settings from Maya via FBX. *FBX*, which is short for *Filmbox*, is a proprietary interoperability file format (.fbx) owned and developed by Autodesk. Camera settings are interpolated to yield results that are functionally equivalent; even image planes associated with the camera are also imported.

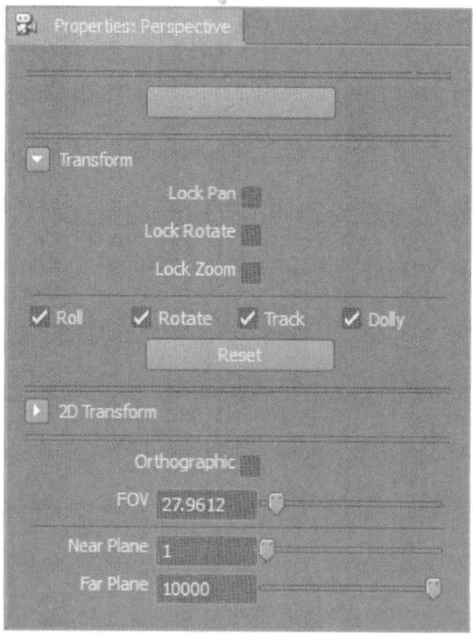

Figure 9.2

Perspective camera properties

Note that you can export only the nondefault cameras from Maya using FBX. The default four cameras are ignored. If you want to export one of the default cameras, you need to make a copy of it by selecting it and choosing Edit → Duplicate. Set the Fit Resolution Gate camera attribute to Vertical in Maya to have a better match of the camera in Mudbox (Figure 9.3).

Each camera has an image plane and stencil associated with it. You can access them and their properties by clicking the plus (+) sign to the left of the camera (Figure 9.4). You can click the stencil or image plane to bring up its properties.

If you have a camera at settings you would like to reuse, you can save it as a bookmark in the Camera Bookmarks tray. You select Add Camera Bookmark from the Camera Bookmarks tray drop-down menu (Figure 9.5) and type a name for your bookmark.

The 3D view also has render modes that you can switch to by right-clicking on the screen and choosing options from the drop-down menu (Figure 9.6). These modes enable you to change the settings of the 3D view and turn on and off settings such as Lighting, Wireframe, and Gradient Background.

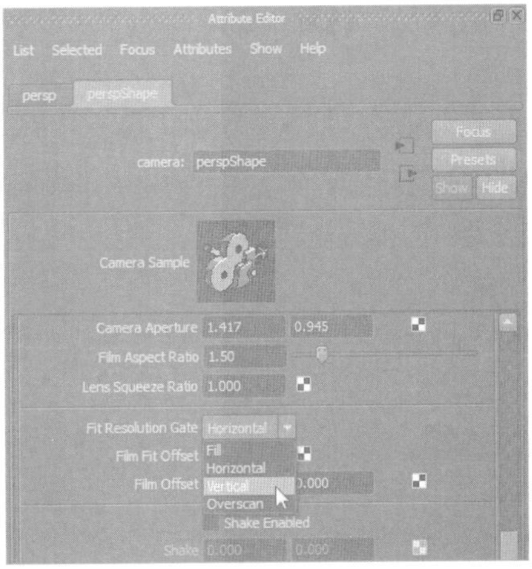

When you have a render you are happy with, you can save it in one of two ways:

- Save your screen as a .psd file by clicking File → Export Screen to PSD. We used this in the previous chapter as a means to projection-paint, but it is also a viable way to export the render of the screen, and you can use the exported layers to composite your image further.
- Save your screen in one of many formats by clicking Render → Save Screen Image. You have to type in a name and the extension of the file format you need to save your image in.

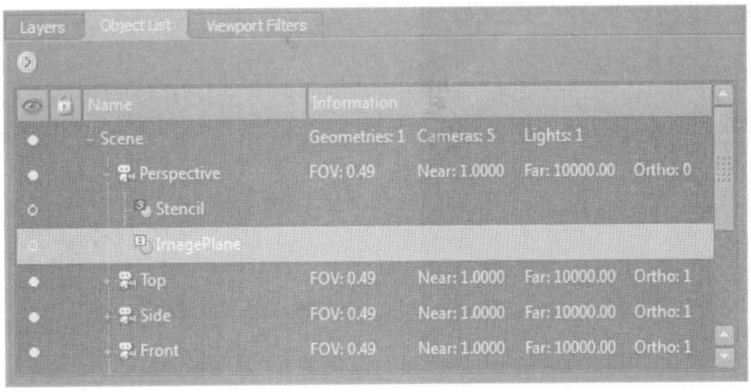

In effect, the contents of both dialog boxes are the same. The only difference is that the outputted .psd file has multiple layers that you can use to composite the image, and the other file formats are flat images.

The reason you have buttons for two or four times the screen resolution is to deal with the aliasing on the edges. If you create an image two or four times the screen resolution, you can then resize the images by half or a quarter in your image-editing application, and get results that give you smoother anti-aliased images.

You can also screen grab, or capture, the image of the 3D view by pressing Alt+P in Windows or Command+Shift+3 in Mac OS X. You will not get any feedback to the 3D view image being captured, but pressing the keyboard combinations will save an image to the following directory on your computer:

Windows: `<drive>:\My Documents\Mudbox\2011`

Mac OS X: `/Users/<user name>/Desktop`

Figure 9.3

Setting the Fit Resolution Gate option to Vertical in Maya creates a better match to the camera in Mudbox.

Figure 9.4

Stencil and image plane that correspond to the Perspective camera

Figure 9.5

Adding a camera bookmark

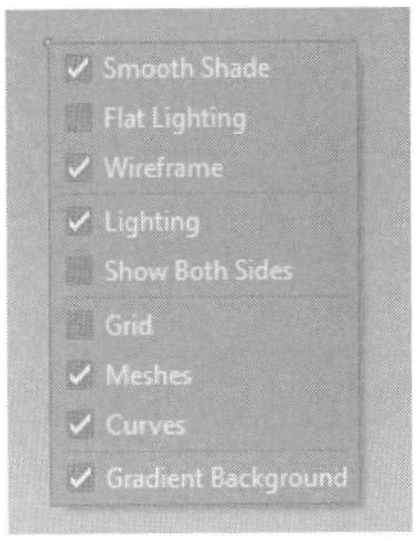

Figure 9.6

3D view right-click menu options

Lighting Your Model

Mudbox allows you to have one of three light types: point, directional, and image-based light (IBL). The default scene loads with a directional light, which you can manipulate by pressing the L key and dragging your mouse or stylus in the 3D view.

Lights can be created by using the Create → Lights menu, from which you can choose one of the three types of lights to add to your scene. You can add multiple point and directional lights, but a scene can have one and only one image-based light.

Each of the lights has its own properties that you can adjust. The light's properties come up in the Properties window when the light is selected in the Object List.

To turn off a light, set its intensity to 0. To delete a light, right-click on it in the Object List and select Delete Light from the drop-down menu.

Point Lights

Point lights emit light in all directions from a point in space. They are best used when you want to add additional light to a specific area, or simulate a light that decays out from a center.

In the light's Properties window, you can choose various settings (Figure 9.7). You can specify the diffuse color of the light and the intensity (you can choose an intensity value greater than 1 if you type that value into the Intensity text box). The Light Decay option enables you to specify how the light diminishes with distance. The Show Manipulator and Show Light check boxes let you translate the light in 3D. The point light is the only light that you can move by using the translation arrows; the other two lights can only be rotated. The Scale property does not affect the application of the light, only the size of the light's representation sphere, which you can turn on by selecting the Show Light check box. You can have multiple point lights in a scene.

The following steps allow you to see the effects of Point Lights:

1. Start Mudbox and load the `Point Lights.mud` file from the `Chapter 9` folder of the DVD. This is a simple scene with three meshes lit by three point lights arranged around the Cube and Sphere objects. The cube and the sphere have the same material, and the backdrop has the default material.

2. In the Object List, click on the key light, and you will see its properties in the Properties tray below. If the Show Manipulator property is selected, and you do not see the light translation manipulators in the 3 view, then unselect and reselect the property to show the translation manipulators of the light in the 3D view. Use the manipulator to move the light around, and notice its effect on the scene (Figure 9.8). Do the same for the other two point lights: bounce and rim. Try to match the lighting of some photographs. When you are finished manipulating the lights, clear all of their Show Manipulator and Show Light check boxes. Note that these lights do not cast a shadow.

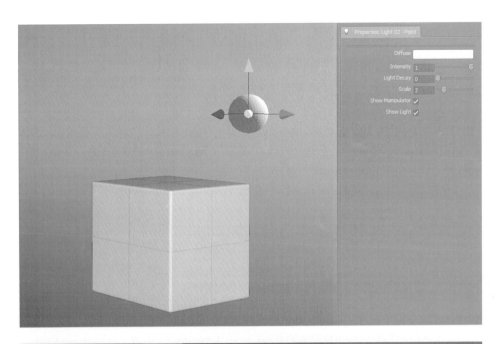

Figure 9.7

Point light attributes

Figure 9.8

Moving a point light

3. Click the cube in the Object List to select it, and click the canvas of the 3D view to remove the yellow highlight. The cube remains selected.

4. Click the Material Presets tab and start selecting the materials in order to see the effect of the lights on each of them. Note that the material for both the sphere and the cube change at the same time because they are both assigned the same material, while the background is not. Repeat step 1 to see the effects of moving the light on the different materials (Figure 9.9).

Figure 9.9

Moving the point
light on different
materials

Directional Lights

Directional lights act as very distant light sources, so that their rays are parallel to each other (Figure 9.10). Directional lights are useful for simulating light from a constant source such as the sun or moon. Directional lights are also the only lights that can cast shadows; you select the Cast Shadows option in the light's preferences. Note that the material in the scene should also have its Receive Shadows property turned on if you want shadows to show up on objects that have the material assigned to them. By default, a newly created Mudbox Material has Receive Shadows and Blur Shadow Edges turned on, with a generic gray color for the shadow. You can change or tint the shadow color by choosing a new one from the Color Chooser.

You can specify a directional light's Intensity, which can be greater than 1 if you type a greater value into the Intensity text box of the directional light's property. As with the point light, you can hide and show the light, which is represented with arrows showing the direction of the light. The manipulator for the light, which you can also show and hide, will bring up the rotate manipulator in the center of the X, Y, and Z coordinates. You can also lock the position of the light to the camera so the effect of the light changes with the rotation or tumbling of the camera.

The following steps allow you to see the effects of directional Lights:

1. Start Mudbox and load the `Directional Lights.mud` file from the `Chapter 9` folder of the DVD. This is a simple scene with three meshes lit by three directional lights that point in three different directions. The cube and the sphere have the same material, while the backdrop has the default material.

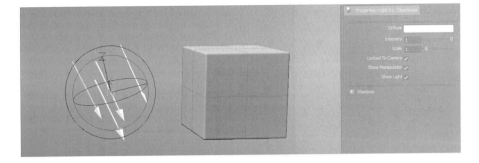

Figure 9.10

Parallel arrows depicting the direction of the Mudbox directional light

2. In the Object List, click the key light, and you will see its properties in the Properties tray below. Select both the Show Light and Show Manipulator check boxes and rotate the light to see its effects on the scene. Note that this light casts shadows because it has Cast Shadows selected in the Shadows section of the properties for the key light. Note that you can change the Depth Map Resolution to a larger size to smooth out the edges of the shadows. Switch it to 2048 × 2048 to see the difference. The other two directional lights can also cast shadows but have Cast Shadows turned off in their properties.

3. Select and rotate the other two bounce and rim directional lights to see their effect on the scene. Try to match the lighting of some photographs.

4. Add three more directional lights by clicking Create → Lights → Directional. Adjust the Intensity properties of the lights you add so that you do not get a blown-out specular effect, as in Figure 9.11.

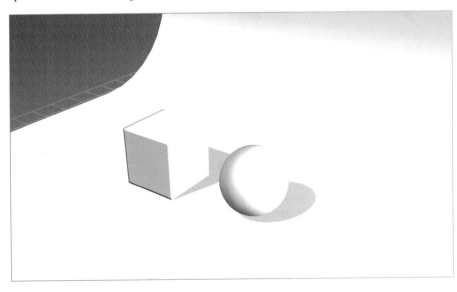

Figure 9.11

Decrease the Intensity property of the lights to reduce the blown-out lighting effect.

5. Rotate the newly added lights so they are at different angles. Note that the lighting gets softer (Figure 9.12). When you are finished manipulating the lights, deselect all of their Show Manipulator and Show Light check boxes.

6. Click the cube in the Object List to select it, and click the canvas of the 3D view to remove the yellow highlight. The cube remains selected.

7. Click the Material Presets tab and start selecting the materials in order to see the effect of the lights on each of them. Note that the material for both the sphere and the cube change at the same time because they are both assigned the same material, while the background is not. Repeat steps 2 and 3 to see the effects of moving the light on the different materials.

8. Add a few point lights and manipulate their Intensity and location to see the effects point lights have on a scene lit by directional lights.

Figure 9.12

Softer lighting results due to the addition of multiple directional lights

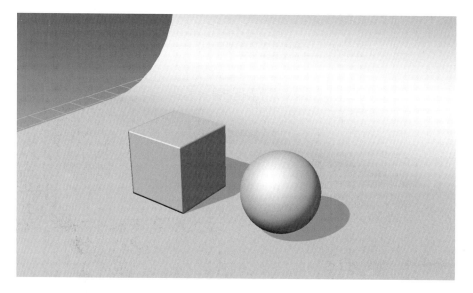

Image-Based Lights

An image-based light (IBL) applies lighting to a model to simulate the lighting in an environment image, which is a digital picture of a naturally or artificially lit scene. Preferably, the image should be a 32-bit high dynamic range (HDR) environment image, which has a greater range of exposure than a standard 8-bit image. Your model is lit with the color and luminance of the environment in the image, in effect simulating the model being in the environment of the image by creating a very realistic distribution of light, even illumination and a more realistic look.

In the Properties window for the light (Figure 9.13), you can modify the Intensity by using the slider. Like the directional light, the image-based light (IBL) can also be rotated only by selecting the Show Manipulator check box. You can also lock it to the camera as you would the directional light. The Image Based Light File property contains the name of the file you intend to use to light your model. You can point to images that you are given, have shot, or have obtained from various resource sites or vendors on the Internet. Mudbox includes a few HDR images that are in the following directories:

- In Windows: `<drive>:\Program Files\Autodesk\Mudbox2011\textures\Lightprobes`
- In Mac OS X: `/Users/<username>/Library/Application Support/Autodesk/Mudbox 2011/textures/Lightprobes`

A scene can have multiple point or directional lights, but only one image-based light. When you create an image-based light, you also replace the reflection map image for all of the materials in the scene with the image in the Image Based Light File property.

The following steps allow you to see the effects of image-based lights:

1. Start Mudbox and load the `Image Based Light.mud` file from the `Chapter 9` folder of the DVD. This is a simple scene with five meshes lit by `Mudbox3PointDefault.tif`, a 32-bit `.tif` HDR image. The two sets of a cube and the sphere have two different materials, while the backdrop has the default material.

2. In the Object List, click the IBL light, and you will see its properties in the Properties tray below. Select the Show Manipulator property and rotate the light to see its effects on the scene. Note that this light does not cast shadows (Figure 9.14). Deselect the Show Manipulator property.

3. Click cube2 in the Object List to select it, and click the canvas of the 3D view to remove the yellow highlight. The cube remains selected.

4. Click the Material Presets tab and start selecting the materials in order to see the effect of the lights on each of them. Materials such as ReflectiveWhite will show a reflection of the image in the image-based light (Figure 9.14).

5. Because the default IBL, `Mudbox3PointDefault.tif`, is made up of an image of three diffused lights, the reflectivity isn't as pronounced. Click IBL Light in the Object List, and from its properties click the button to the right of the Image Based Light File text box to bring up the open dialog box.

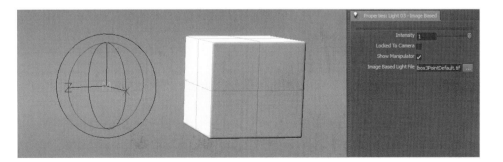

Figure 9.13

Image-based light properties

Figure 9.14

Reflective materials reflect the image-based light.

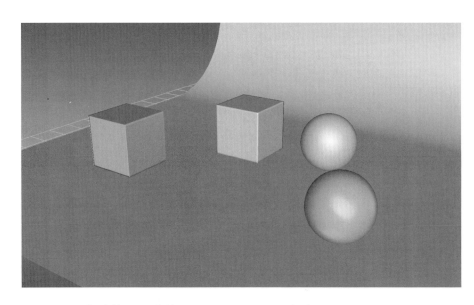

6. Navigate to the following folder in your respective platform:

   In Windows: `<drive>:\Program Files\Autodesk\Mudbox2011\textures\Lightprobes`

   In Mac OS X: `/Users/<username>/Library/Application Support/Autodesk/Mudbox 2011/textures/Lightprobes`

7. Select the `chapel.exr` HDR image file. This sets the image-based light to this image, and also changes the reflection map of all the materials to the same image (Figure 9.15).

8. Repeat step 2 to see the effects of moving the light on the different materials.

Figure 9.15

After you create an image-based light, all the reflection map properties of all the materials in the scene change to the image of the image-based light.

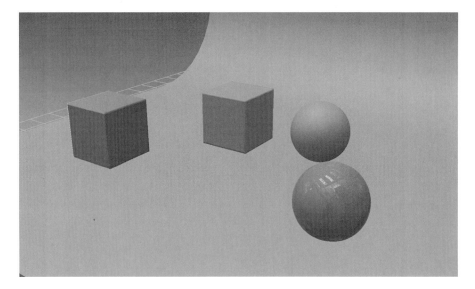

9. Repeat step 10 and choose different HDR images as your IBL.

10. Add a few point lights and a few directional lights. Manipulate their Intensity and location or rotation to see the effects when point and directional lights are added to a scene lit by directional lights. You can have an assortment of point and directional lights, in addition to just one image-based light.

> Note that you have to deselect the Show Manipulator check box before you move off a light to another object, to do anything besides move the light. If things appear stuck after you manipulate lights, go back and make sure you have all the Show Light and Show Manipulator check boxes deselected in all properties of the lights.

Applying Visual Effects with Viewport Filters

Viewport filters are visual effects that you can apply individually or in aggregate to enhance your sculptures and their assigned materials. Provided that your graphics card supports them, visual effects are applied in real time to your 3D view. However, they do consume computing resources and can make working with your model sluggish depending on your hardware configuration, especially if you have more than one viewport filter active at the same time. As a best practice, turn viewport filters off if they don't benefit your workflow, and then back on again to see their effect.

You can add multiple instances of viewport filters by clicking the drop-down menu of the Viewport Filters window (Figure 9.16). The effect of viewport filters is an aggregate of all the filters that are on. You turn the filters on by clicking their name in the list, or adding them from the New Filter menu in the Viewport Filters drop-down menu. The circle to the left of the filter name indicates whether a filter is on or off. You can also click the circle to toggle the filter on and off.

You may notice that there are more filters in the New Filter list than are listed in the Viewport Filters window. There are two extra filters you can add that are specific to features in Nvidia video cards. The nVidiaAOViewPortFilter and the CgViewPortFilter can be added to your list of filters if your video card supports these features. You can go to the Autodesk Mudbox website (http://images.autodesk.com/adsk/files/autodesk_mudbox_2011_system_requirements_us.pdf) to find out the system requirements for Mudbox and the features that are supported for various video cards.

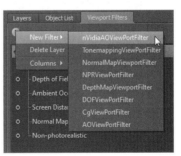

Figure 9.16

Nvidia AO filter

The main reason to use viewport filters is to re-create an environment that mimics some of the attributes of how your sculpture will be rendered in its destination application.

You can also use them to create different versions of your 3D view to composite in a 2D application.

Note that viewport filters and their settings will not save with your scene file. If you want to save the settings, you should make note of them by either writing them down or capturing the screen with the settings by using a screen capture utility.

Ambient Occlusion

The Ambient Occlusion (AO) filter adds realism to your sculpture by approximating the attenuation of light due to occlusion. The result is the darkening of fine detail areas and corners. When you click on the filter, its properties appear in the Properties window below the Viewport Filters window (Figure 9.17).

Figure 9.17

Ambient Occlusion properties

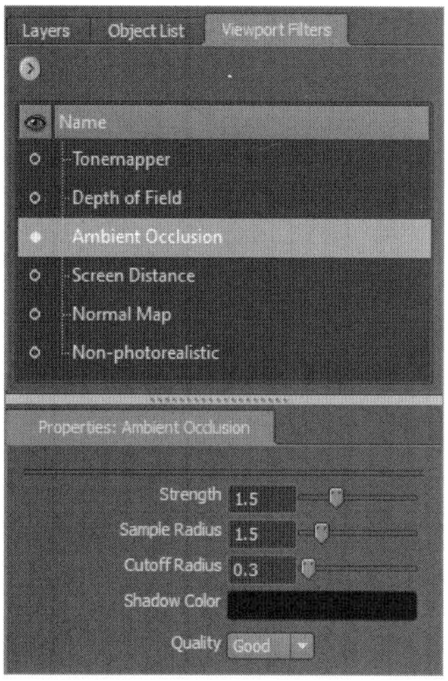

Ambient occlusion is calculated by sampling the results of casting rays in every direction from the surface. Points on the surface that are surrounded by geometry obstructing the cast rays are rendered darker, while others that aren't are rendered lighter. The Strength property controls the intensity of the ambient occlusion. Adjust the Sample Radius based on how detailed your model is. For example, if you have a model in which you see no AO on some details, you need to try a smaller radius. Adjust the Cutoff Radius to specify the distance the rays are cast from the model to calculate occlusion.

You can adjust the number of occlusion samples with the Quality property. Adjust all the other settings before going to a higher-quality setting, because the more occlusion samples you have, the more impact there is on the responsiveness of the model and the refresh rate of a change in the 3D view while manipulating other AO settings.

The second type of Ambient Occlusion filter in Mudbox is the `nVidiaAOViewPortFilter`, which is referred to as the Nvidia AO filter. The properties of the Nvidia AO filter are different from those of the Mudbox AO filter. Some of the properties in both AO filters might stand for the same measurement; however, they are named differently to address the naming convention of the Nvidia video card hardware feature.

One advantage of the Nvidia AO filter is that it enables you to select the Show AO Results check box to see its effects (Figure 9.18). It is extremely useful to individually see the AO results independent of the lighting and texturing of your sculpture, because you can see the effects of the AO unobstructed by textures or lights in the scene, or you can capture an image of it to use as a layer in your final composite.

In the properties of Nvidia AO filter, if the Randomize Dirs setting (which randomizes the direction of the occlusion) is on, the Nb Dirs and Nb Steps settings are ignored. The Randomize Dirs option gives you good results, but you can get results that are better, but more computational, which of course translates to slower interaction with the model. While experimenting, I found that deselecting the Randomize Dirs property and using settings of 100 for both Nb Steps and Nb Dirs, a radius of 1.35, Attenuation of 1, a Contrast of 2, a Blur Radius of 20, and an Ambient Blend of 0.5 produced the results I was going for with this model (Figure 9.19). Try different settings on your own model to see what works best.

Try these two Ambient Occlusion viewport filters together or separately to get the desired look.

The third way to add ambient occlusion to your model is through an ambient occlusion texture map. Extract the map from the Maps → Extract Texture Maps menu command and select the Ambient Occlusion Map option from the Maps to Generate list box (Figure 9.20).

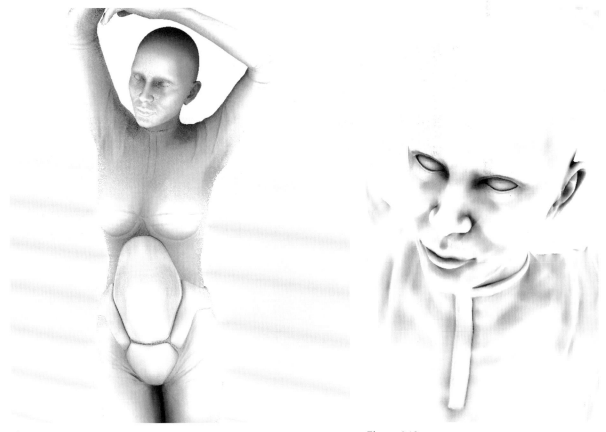

Figure 9.18
Nvidia AO results on the model

Figure 9.19
Smoother AO by changing the Nvidia AO properties

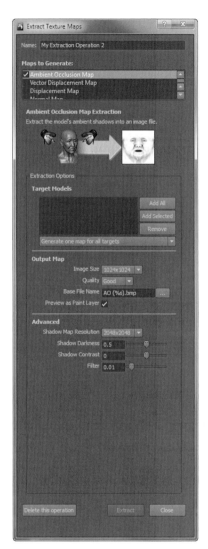

Figure 9.20

Extracting an ambient occlusion map on a model's UVs

This is not a viewport filter, but ambient occlusion results applied to, or commonly referred to as *baked on to*, the UVs of your model and output as a texture map. If you leave the Preview as Paint Layer check box selected before extracting the map, the map is extracted and placed at the top of the Diffuse channel set and multiplied to show only the darkened areas.

Extracting an ambient occlusion map as a texture map has yet another list of settings you need to tweak to get the desired look. As with other texture maps, the image size determines the detail, with the bigger texture maps containing more detail. The Quality setting can range from Fastest to Best and is based on the shadow maps used for the calculation of the map.

The Shadow Map Resolution is the size of the shadow maps that are used in the calculation. Shadow Darkness sets how dark the shadowy areas are on the map, ranging from 0 for no shadows to 1 for very dark shadows. The average default of 0.5 should be fine for most uses. Shadow Contrast determines the contrast between the dark and light colors of the extracted ambient occlusion map. It can range from –1 to 1, where the midpoint and default value of zero is again fine for most uses.

The Filter option sets the sharpness or softness of the shadows. The filter ranges from 0.0001 for sharp and finely detailed shadows to higher values to produce softer and blurry detailed shadows.

To get fast results, set the Quality to Fastest and Image Size to a small resolution. Adjust the other settings and regenerate the ambient occlusion map until you get the results that work for you. After you are happy with the results, bump up the Quality and increase the image size. The map extraction will take longer, but you will have to wait that long only once or a few times instead of having to wait that long while changing the other settings.

The benefit of this method of getting ambient occlusion results is that you can composite the generated map with other texture maps in other 3D programs, such as Maya or 3ds Max. The benefit of the Ambient Occlusion viewport filters is that you can composite them onto 2D images.

Tonemapper

The Tonemapper viewport filter remaps the color values displayed in the 3D view. If you turn on the Tonemapper filter, it will recalculate and readjust itself every time you move the camera and change the contents of the 3D view.

You can adjust the Tonemapper properties to compress, expand, or shift the tonal range of the contents of the 3D view. The Tonemapper is useful for changing the overall brightness of an image to evaluate how the result would look in other environments such as different monitors, films, or games.

Note that if you have the Tonemapper on, it could generate anomalies when you render your scene by using the Render menu.

Screen Distance

Screen Distance, which is also called a *depth map*, generates a grayscale image that is shaded from black to white based on the object's distance from the camera's origin point (Figure 9.21).

Depth maps are useful for image capturing and then using as a layer in a composite 2D image to give it more depth. It is best used with the Multiply layer blend.

It is also useful for creating stencils, stamps, or displacement maps from sculpted objects. You can then use the captured depth map image to sculpt a 2D relief of your object.

Try this by creating a scene with a sphere. In the Front camera view, turn on the Screen Distance viewport filter and save your screen by either clicking Render → Save Screen Image or by pressing the Save 16-Bit Image button in the properties of the Screen Distance viewport filter. Load the image as a stencil or stamp and use it to sculpt. You will notice that it will create hemispheres.

The Properties for the Screen Distance viewport filter enable you to invert and increase the contrast of black and white values of the depth map.

Figure 9.21

Screen Distance viewport filter results

Depth of Field (DOF)

The Depth of Field (DOF) viewport filter simulates the depth-of-field effect of an optical camera lens: a designated area of your subject appears in focus, while objects before and behind it appear blurry and out of focus. You specify the near and far range from the camera (Figure 9.22).

In Mudbox, the DOF filter helps reduce the sharpness and aliased nature of edges and makes your subject look like a real-world photo shot with optical lenses.

Figure 9.22

**Depth of Field
filter results**

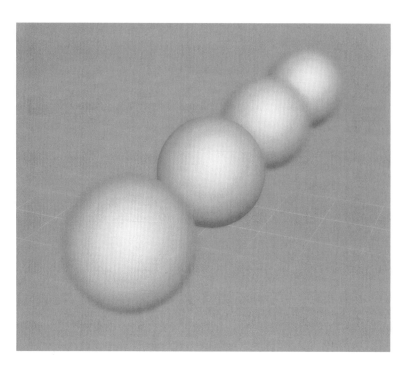

The DOF viewport filter has three properties: Depth of Field, Focus Distance, and Blur Amount. The Depth of Field setting is the distance, in centimeters, that specifies the range of sharp focus; everything within that range will appear sharp and in focus, while anything outside that range will appear blurry and out of focus. The Focus Distance, also in centimeters, is the distance between the camera and the center of the Depth of Field area. The best way to adjust these two settings is to turn the grid on, if it isn't already, and see the effect of the sliders for these two settings on the grid, where the grid line at the Focus Distance is crisp and the blurriness range shows on the gridlines straddling it. When using this filter, I tend to set the Focus Distance first, and the set the Depth of Field setting second. The Blur Amount enables you to set how blurry the area is that is outside the Depth of Field.

Note that your DOF settings are particular to your camera location and will have to be redone if you move the camera.

Normal Map

The Normal Map viewport filter shades objects by using RGB color values to represent the orientation of their surface normals. Like the DOF filter, it is useful as a quick way to create normal maps from your 3D view as a 2D image. You can then use the normal map on surfaces in other 3D software packages.

Non-Photorealistic (NPR)

The Non-Photorealistic viewport filter makes the objects in the 3D view appear as if they were hand-drawn on textured paper (Figure 9.23). It is a great way to represent various angles of your image as a 2D sketch.

You can experiment with the different settings. But most simply, you can turn on this filter and set all the settings to zero and get a convincing-looking sketch of your sculpture. Note that turning textures on for your sculptures influences whether they appear as a subtle tint, and having them off makes your model look more like a drawing.

You can add multiple NPR filters to get a compounded look.

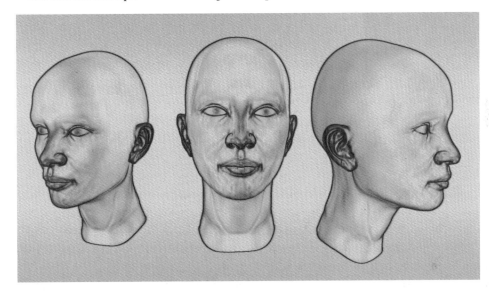

Figure 9.23

Non-Photorealistic viewport filter results

Creating Turntables and Recording Sessions

Besides the Save Screen Image option, the Render menu has two other options that enable you to make movies of your work. The Record Movie option lets you record either the contents of the 3D view or the entire Mudbox window to view or share your work. The Create Turntable Movie option lets you create a turntable animation of your sculpture and save it as a movie file in one of many movie formats.

Record Movie

To record a movie of a work session, click Render → Record Movie.

In the Record Movie dialog box (Figure 9.24), you specify the Width and Height of the movie in pixels. Entering values different from the Actual Size will add either horizontal or vertical padding to fit the aspect ratio of your screen size to the Width and Height you specify. If the Width and Height sizes you specify are larger than the resolution of the user interface, the movie will appear pixelated as the images are sized up.

You specify the timing your movie will record at from the drop-down menu that gives you options at 5, 10, or 15 frames per second (fps), and playback timing of your animation from the drop-down menu that gives you options at 5, 10, 15, and 30 fps.

Figure 9.24

Record Movie
dialog box

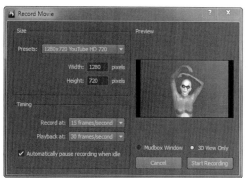

If you set the record and playback rates to identical values, the resulting movie will reflect your actions on screen in real time. However, setting the Record At setting to a lower frame rate and Playback At to a higher rate produces a movie that is more choppy and accelerated and that looks more like a time-lapse video shot at intervals.

You can select the Automatically Pause Recording When Idle check box, which is on by default, to stop the recording whenever the tool cursor is inactive. Recording will continue when the tool cursor is moved again. Make sure to turn this option off if you intend to narrate your work session after the fact in a video-editing program, and are pausing to explain something.

Figure 9.25

Numerical count-
down before
recording

When you click the Start Recording button, a numerical countdown window will appear in the lower-right corner of the application window to indicate that recording is about to begin (Figure 9.25). When it counts down to zero and the recording begins, two new buttons will appear in the lower-right corner of the status line. These buttons will enable you to Pause, Continue, or Stop the recording.

After you press the Stop button, you will get the Screen Recording Complete dialog box (Figure 9.26), which enables you to either abort the session by clicking the Delete Recording button, or save it in one of many movie formats by selecting it in the drop-down menu and clicking the Save As button.

The movie formats that are available are MPEG-4, Adobe Flash, Small Web Format, QuickTime, or File Sequence.

Figure 9.26

Dialog box to input
file path and save
your recording after
you click Stop

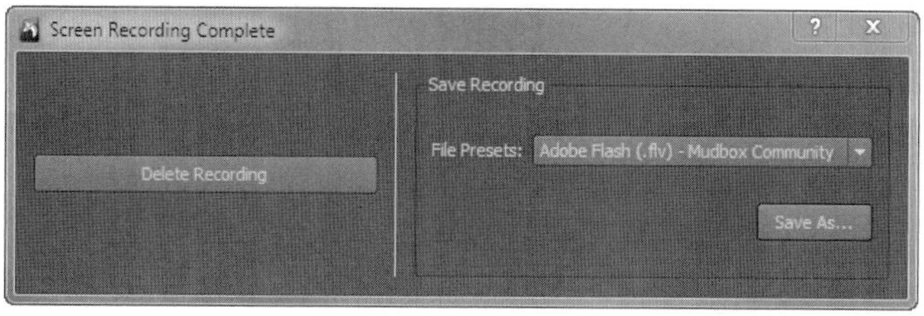

Record a Turntable Movie

Turntables are a great way to show a sculpture from many points of view, because your model rotates 360 degrees. The turntable movie will record a turntable of your model in the state it is in, whether it is at lower or higher subdivision level, or has visible textures or hidden parts. Mudbox renders each movie frame during this process, so it is possible to produce high-quality movies at resolutions greater than the actual image size in the 3D view.

To record a turntable, click Render → Create Turntable Movie. This brings up the Create Turntable Movie dialog box (Figure 9.27).

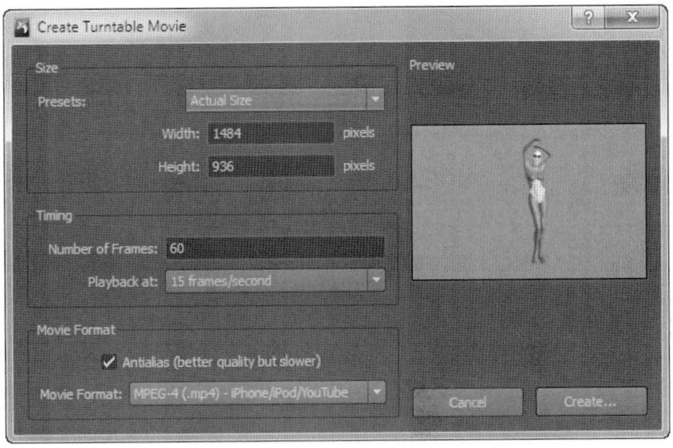

Figure 9.27

Create Turntable Movie dialog box

To create a turntable, your model or scene needs to be centered at the origin so it rotates on its vertical axis uniformly; otherwise, you will get a more elliptical rotation. Note that turntable movies are automatically rendered with a solid color background that you can specify by using the Viewport Flat setting color preference in Windows → Preferences in the Windows version, and Mudbox → Preferences in Mac OS X.

You can specify the Width and Height, Number of Frames, and Playback timing of your animation, as well as the movie format it is rendered in. The combination of these will determine how long your movie takes to render, in addition to the file size of your movie file.

To save time, choose smaller sizes and a small number of frames to see the results of your animation, and then add larger sizes, more frames, and antialiasing if you are satisfied with the results. Antialiasing gives you better-quality movies, but your movie render will take longer.

Rendering in Mudbox and External Programs

To show off your Mudbox work, you need to have your result rendered. Your render could be a single still image, multiple still images showing your subject at different angles or in different environments and lighting, or a sequence of images that make up a movie.

There is a wealth of rendering engines outside of Mudbox that you can use to render your image. Some renderers such as RenderMan by Pixar lend themselves better to animation. Some others simulate the precision of physical cameras by using practical camera settings. Some support different lighting technologies, and some provide a vast array of real-world materials you can apply to your models.

In this section, you will use the render output of Mudbox to create still image renders in Mudbox, and then export them and composite them in Adobe Photoshop. We will also use a software package I have found to be excellent for rendering high-resolution sculptural mesh models called KeyShot by Luxion. KeyShot is a great way to showcase your model as a sculpture without any textures. Finally, as you did with the egg in Chapter 1, "Getting Your Feet in the Mud: The Basics of the Mudbox Production Pipeline," you will export a lower-resolution version of a model with its displacement and texture maps and render it in Maya by using mental ray.

Compositing Mudbox Render Images in Adobe Photoshop

As you have seen, the rendering engine in Mudbox is unlike traditional render engines you are used to, where you compose your scene and then start a render process. Mudbox renders your image in real time, with real-time viewport filters and real-time lighting. You also have the option to use backdrops in your render by adding the camera image plane.

To create high-quality 2D images from Mudbox, you need to use the Render → Save Screen Image, or File → Export Screen to PSD options to output the contents of the screen as 2D images. Although the Export Screen to PSD option is intended for projection painting in Photoshop, you can also use the multiple layers it outputs for compositing purposes. The layers, all of which except one are locked for editing, can be duplicated and used as layers in a composite image. The Save Screen Image outputs only a single layer.

You can also output the depth map and the Show AO results screen for the Nvidia Ambient Occlusion viewport filter as layers to composite as well. In this next exercise, you will create these multiple screens and create a final 2D composite image in Adobe Photoshop:

1. Start Mudbox and load the Athena.mud file from the Chapter 9 folder of the DVD. This is the final results of the work we started in Chapter 5, "Digital Sculpting Part I."

2. Click Create → Camera to add a camera to your scene. In the Object List, the camera is added at the bottom. Right-click on your newly created camera and call it **RenderCam**.

3. Right-click on the RenderCam camera and select Look Through from the drop-down menu. Use camera navigation to position your camera so that you frame the model in the position that you want to capture as your image.

Figure 9.28

Lock the Pan, Rotate, and Zoom camera properties

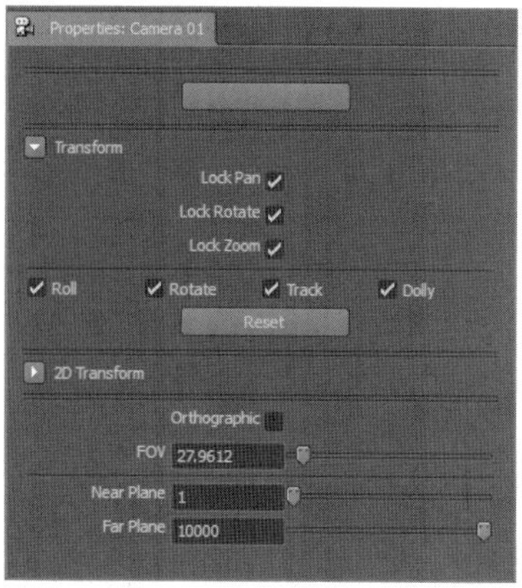

4. When you are happy with the camera positioning, click the Lock Pan, Lock Rotate, and Lock Zoom options to lock your camera (Figure 9.28). Because even a slight motion in the camera can disrupt the composition in the next few steps, locking the camera is an extra step that will save you the frustration of accidentally moving the camera and having to recapture all your screens. Creating locked cameras is also a good way to save views of your model that you can jump to quickly.

5. Click the Camera Bookmarks tab in the South Frame tray, and from its window drop-down menu select Add Camera Bookmark (Figure 9.29). Type **RenderCam** and click OK; this creates an icon image of your screen as a button that you can click in the Camera Bookmarks tray. Now you have a bookmark that you can use to quickly go to the camera view you just created. Note that you have to be looking through the RenderCam for the camera bookmark to get back to your original view.

Figure 9.29

Adding a camera bookmark

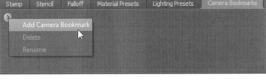

The edges of models in the Mudbox 3D view are jagged (Figure 9.30). These edges could be on the fringes of the model or within the model itself. When you capture your screen to a 2D image, the jagged edges will detract from the polished look of a composited image, and you would need to get rid of them. There are a few methods at your disposal to do that. The most obvious, of course, is to use the Blur brush in Photoshop and soften the edges. Another option is to use the Depth of Field viewport filter and dial in the three sliders in the filter to blur out some of the edges. Another very effective method is to save your image at a higher resolution than what is in the 3D view and then resize the image to its original size in Photoshop. Or you can use a combination of all three of these methods.

Figure 9.30

Jagged edges in the 3D viewport

6. Click the Viewport Filters tab and select the Screen Distance filter. Note that instead of getting a depth map, you get more of a silhouette image. The reason is that the depth map is calculated within the bounding box, or area around all the visible models in your scene. In this case, Mudbox is calculating the distance between the back and front of the backdrop, of which the character takes very little space, and that is why there is no gradation of shading on her body. Even though there is a depth map on the character, the gradation on her covers one or two colors of the range of colors between black and white, and so you see more of a silhouette. To get a more diverse gradation, in the Object List deselect the Visibility circle of the backdrop mesh to hide it. You will now see the difference, as demonstrated in the first two variations in Figure 9.31.

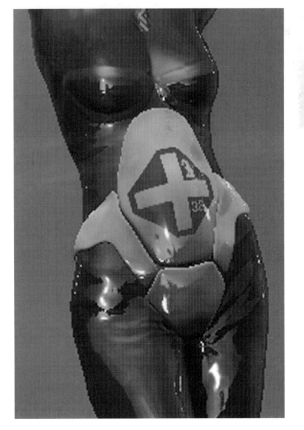

Figure 9.31

**Screen Distance
variations**

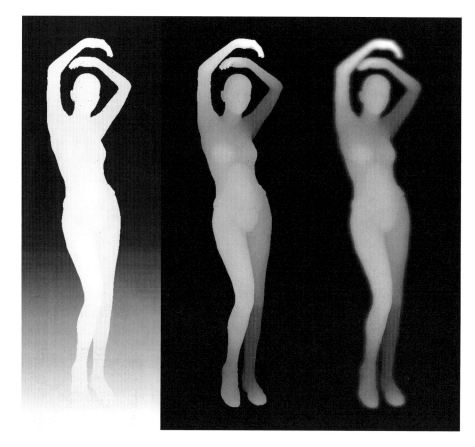

7. Click the Depth of Field viewport filter and adjust the Focus Distance, Depth of Field, and Blur Amount settings to give your depth map an area of focus and to blur out the closest and farthest areas on the character, as seen in the third variation in Figure 9.31.

8. Click Render → Save Screen Image. In the Save Screen Image dialog box (Figure 9.32), click the Use 4× Screen Size button. Save all your screens at 4× resolution to get rid of the jagged edges. You can then change their image sizes to get the resolution you need. Click the Save Image button and save your image as `screen_distance.bmp`.

9. With the Screen Distance and Depth of Field viewport filters still on, click the Ambient Occlusion viewport filter to turn it on. Adjust the Ambient Occlusion settings,

and make sure you choose Best in the Quality property when you are finished making adjustments. On a textured model, I find that adjusting the AO settings is easier with the Screen Distance filter on (Figure 9.33). Click Render → Save Screen Image, and in the Save Screen Image dialog box (Figure 9.32), click the Use 4× Screen Size button and save your image as `mudbox_ao.bmp`.

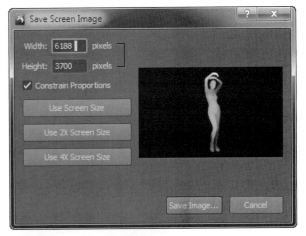

Figure 9.32

Saving the screen image at 4x screen size

10. Turn off the Ambient Occlusion, Screen Distance, and Depth of Field viewport filters, and, if you have a supported Nvidia video card, turn on the Nvidia AO Viewport filter by selecting it from the Viewport Filters window drop-down menu. Click the Show AO results check box to view only the ambient occlusion on the image. Adjust the settings of the Nvidia Ambient Occlusion filter to fine-tune the occluded areas on the character. Turning off Randomize Dirs enables you to bump up the Nb Steps and Nb Dirs and adjust the settings to get a smoother occluded image. When you get an image where the occluded areas are darkest and the transition between the dark and light areas are subtle, click Render → Save Screen Image. In the Save Screen Image dialog box, click the Use 4× Screen Size button, and save your image as `nVidia_ao.bmp`. You can and should save multiple versions of these screen renders with different settings to try them out in your composition.

11. Turn off all the viewport filters and make sure that the Grid and Gradient Background are off by right-clicking on the canvas of the 3D view and deselecting them from the drop-down menu. Click Render → Save Screen Image. In the Save Screen Image dialog box, click the Use 4× Screen Size button, and save your image as `beauty.bmp`. This is the beauty pass. Close Mudbox.

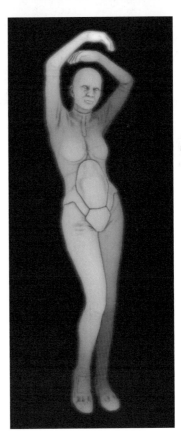

Figure 9.33

Adjusting AO with the Screen Distance viewport filter on

At this juncture, you should have four images to load into Adobe Photoshop to composite into a final image.

12. Open Adobe Photoshop and click File → Scripts → Load Files into Stack, which enables you to load all your files as layers in the same image. In the Load Layers dialog box (Figure 9.34), click the Browse button, navigate to the location on your hard drive where you saved the composition images, and select all four files. Photoshop will load all files as layers, and also align your images so they are on top of each other. However, these layers will not stack up in the correct order.

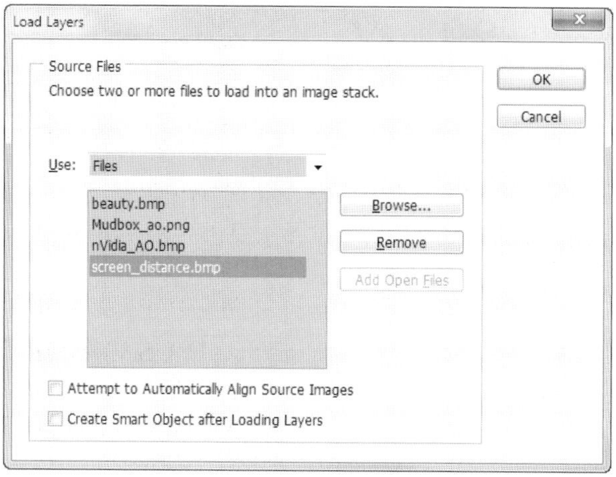

Figure 9.34

Opening all four files in Photoshop

13. Click Layer → New → Layer and call the new layer **background**. Use the Fill tool in Photoshop to fill the background with a bluish-gray color.

14. Drag and drop the layers to order them in the following order:

    nVidia_AO, Mudbox_AO, screen_distance, beauty, background (Figure 9.35).

15. Use the Crop tool and draw a rectangle around the character (Figure 9.36). Click the checkmark on the toolbar to finalize the crop operation.

16. Hide all the layers except the beauty layer by clicking the eye icon in front of them. Select the beauty layer by clicking it in the Layers window. Select the Magic Wand tool and set its Tolerance to 1. Click on the background to select it (Figure 9.37).

17. With the selection on, click the Delete button to delete the background. This should make the background transparent by displaying Photoshop's checkered pattern (Figure 9.38).

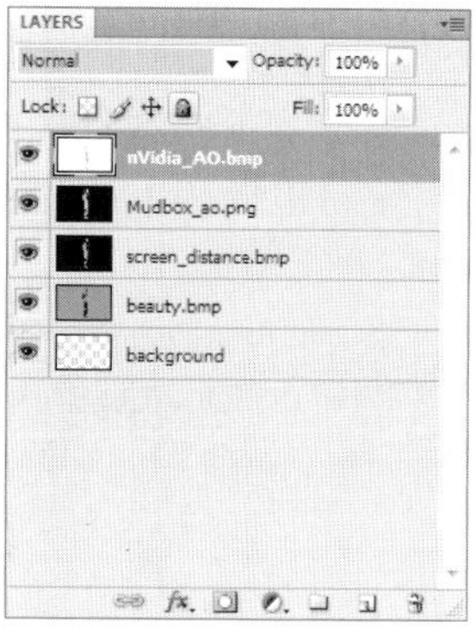

Figure 9.35

Images in Photoshop layers

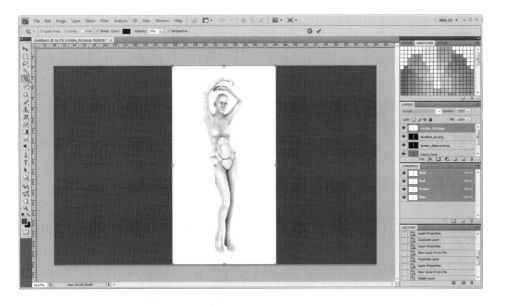

Figure 9.36

Cropping the image around the character

18. With the selection still active, click the eye icon in front of the screen_distance layer in the Layers window, click the layer to select it, and press Delete. This makes the background of the screen_distance layer transparent by displaying Photoshop's checkered pattern and removes the black background around the character. Repeat this step for the Mudbox_AO and nVidia_AO layers. You are now left with just the character in all the layers except the background layer.

19. Click Select → Deselect to deselect the background area.

20. Select the nVidia_AO layer and change its blend mode to Multiply. Do the same for the Mudbox_AO and screen_distance layers.

21. Use the opacity slider for the multiplied layers to get a blend that will show off the character.

22. When you are satisfied with the image (Figure 9.39), save it as a composite image. You can flatten the layers, or leave them for future editing. You can also choose to resize your image into a smaller one if needed.

Figure 9.37

Select the background of the image by using the Magic Wand tool with a Tolerance of 1.

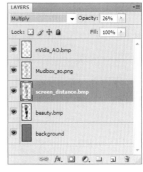

Figure 9.38

Delete the background to make it transparent.

You can now add background images or use the wealth of Photoshop image-processing tools to adjust and refine your image. All the files for this exercise, including the final composite Photoshop `.psd` file can be found on the DVD in the `Chapter 9\composite images` folder for you to examine and compare.

Figure 9.39

Composited image

Rendering Mudbox High-Resolution Models in Luxion KeyShot

I have chosen to include Luxion KeyShot in this chapter because of its ability to load multimillion-polygon high-resolution models such as the models created in Mudbox, and to easily render them with speed and photographic results.

KeyShot is a stand-alone, interactive, raytracing, and global illumination program that works more like a digital camera than a rendering application, and is available for Windows (both 32- and 64-bit) and for Mac OS X.

To go through the steps in this section, you can download a 15-day trial version of KeyShot from www.keyshot.com. If you intend to showcase your sculpture as only a sculpture, using KeyShot is a great way to get quick and beautiful results.

Follow these steps to render a model with KeyShot:

1. Start Mudbox and load the Athena.mud file from the Chapter 9 folder of the DVD. This is the final result of the work you started in Chapter 5.

2. All the meshes should be at their highest subdivision level. From the Select/Move Tools tray, click the Objects selection tool and select the Body, Head, Eye_rt, and Eye_lt meshes in the scene by clicking on them in the 3D view. They should all be highlighted in yellow (Figure 9.40).

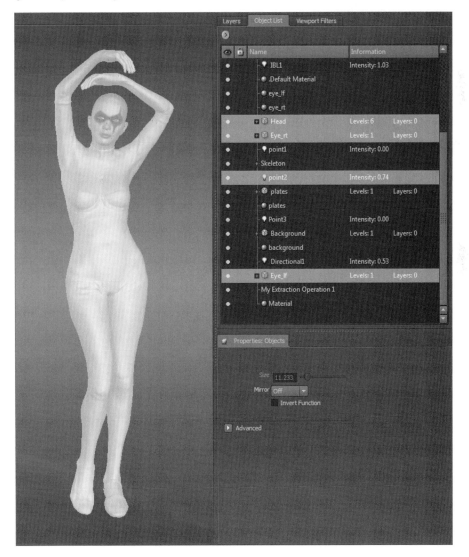

Figure 9.40

All four objects in the scene selected

3. Click File → Export Selection, give it a name, and export the meshes as a combined `.obj` file. Notice the progress bar in the bottom-left corner of the status bar as it completes the export. Note that you have exported a 7,263,232-polygon model, which has resulted in a file of a little more than 800KB. You are not exporting the textures for this section, although you could, and KeyShot is capable of rendering textures. The reason for this is that you are just going to render the model as a sculpture and not a painted sculpture.

4. Close Mudbox and start KeyShot (Figure 9.41).

Figure 9.41

KeyShot interface

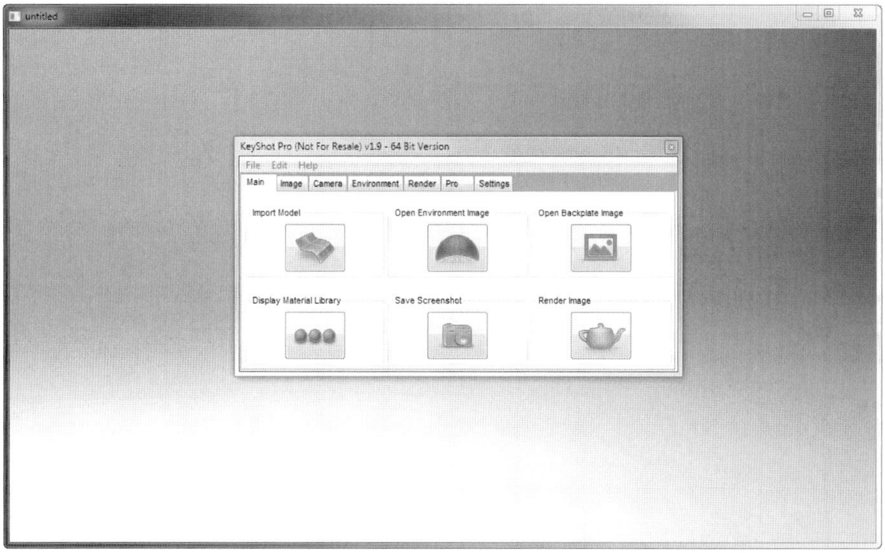

5. Click the Import Model icon and import the `.obj` model from the location you saved in step 3. After you select your model, click Open, and you will get the Import Model dialog box (Figure 9.42). Make sure Calculate Normals is the only option selected and click OK. KeyShot will take a little while to load your model. Because this is a rather large model, it will take a few minutes to load depending on your system configuration.

6. When your model gets imported, it will be lying down on the ground, and you will need to prop it up. First, you need to position the camera; you move the camera in KeyShot exactly the same way as you do in Maya or Mudbox. Position the model in the middle of screen (Figure 9.43).

7. Right-click on the model and select Move Object (Figure 9.44) to bring up the Move Object dialog box.

Figure 9.42

Import Model dialog box settings

8. All you need to do to prop up your model is to rotate it 90 degrees around the x-axis. Type **90** in the X Rotate text box and click Apply (Figure 9.45). Note that shadows are emanating from the model's hips because she is intersecting the ground plane at the location of the shadow. Click the Snap to Ground button in the Move Object dialog

box. This positions the model on the ground, and you will now see the shadow at her feet.

You will notice that the resulting image starts out pixilated, or blocky, and the squares on the screen start getting smaller and smaller until you get a grainy look that after a while becomes a very clear image. Whenever you make a change in the settings of KeyShot, your image will re-render. The render speed is based on the complexity of the scene, including the resolution of the model, the lights, and the materials you choose.

Figure 9.43

Model centered in the interface

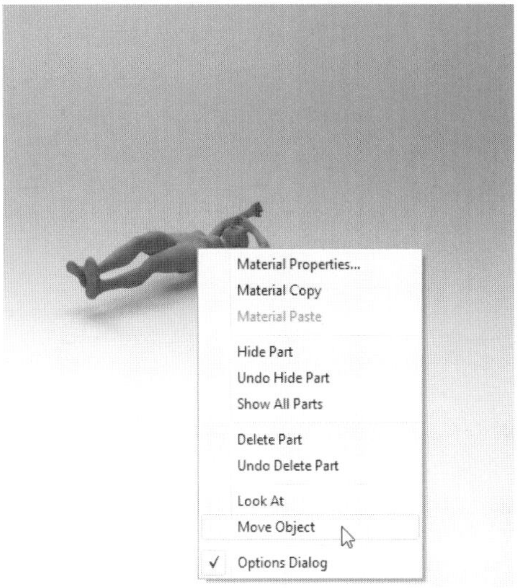

Figure 9.44

Right-click on the model and select Move Object.

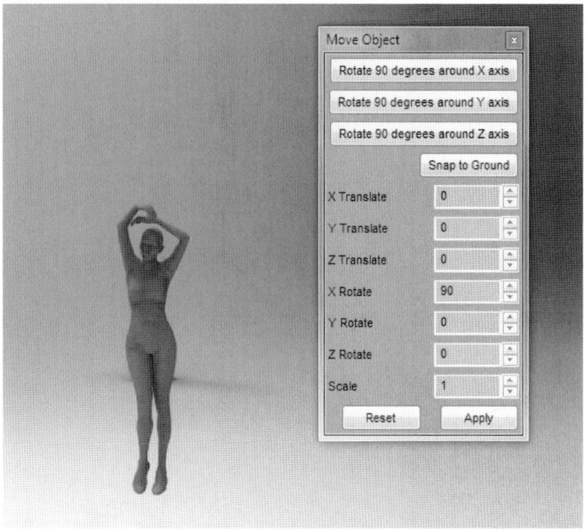

Figure 9.45

Rotate 90 degrees around x-axis.

9. By using the same camera navigation tools as Mudbox and Maya, frame the model. Again KeyShot will re-render the image after you stop. When you are happy with the position, click the Open Environment Image button. This opens up the KeyShot Environments folder, where you can load an image-based light. As in Mudbox, these images will light your model based on the lighting in the image. As in Mudbox, these images are HDR images. Select the HDRLightStudio_car_studio_medium.hdz file. This will light your model.

10. Use the up and down arrows to change the brightness of the light in large increments, and the left and right arrows to change the brightness in smaller increments. Press Ctrl and click and drag your mouse on the model to rotate the environment image, which is similar to pressing the L key in Mudbox. However, the environment lighting image can be rotated around only the z-axis.

11. Press the E key to hide the environment background. The environment light will still light the model, but it will not be visible. You can also still rotate the background image by pressing Ctrl and clicking and dragging on the model even though it is not visible.

12. Click the Open Backplate image button. From the Studio folder in the KeyShot Backplates folder, load the studio_SpotFloor.jpg backplate (Figure 9.46).

13. Click the Display Material Library button to bring up the Material Library (Figure 9.47). Drag and drop some materials onto your model to see what they look like. When you are finished experimenting, click the Other tab and drag and drop the Matte White material onto your model. Use the left and right arrows to change the brightness in small increments until the lighting is not blown out and you can see the fine sculptural detail on the surface of the model.

Figure 9.46

Model with environment image-based light and backplate

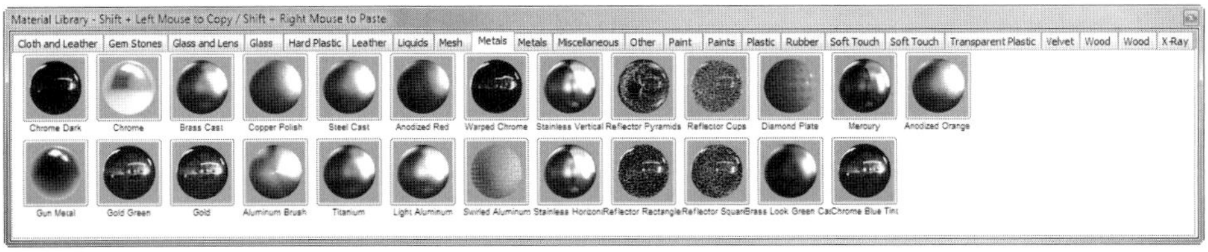

Figure 9.47

The KeyShot Material Library

14. Click the Image tab, and change the Resolution to a larger size depending on your screen size—for example, 1280 × 720. Click the Environment tab and select Ground Shadows and Ground Reflections (Figure 9.48).

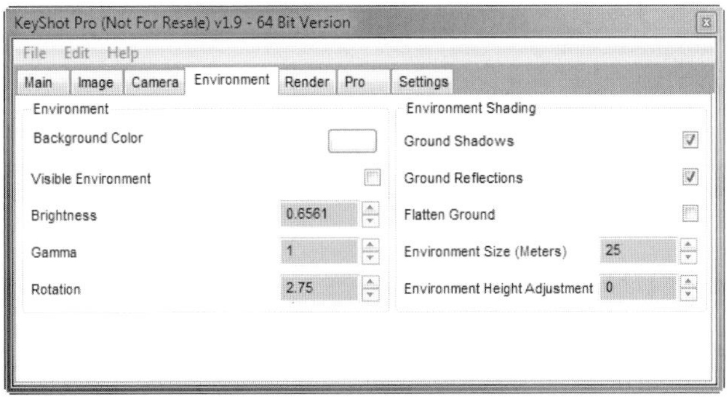

Figure 9.48

Ground Shadows and Reflections options on the Environment tab

15. Make some finer adjustments to the camera and environment light until you are satisfied with the look of the image. Click the Render tab and type the render Width and Height in pixels. Choose an Output Format from the drop-down list. You can choose a .jpg, a .tif, or an .exr file and select the path where you would need to store the image. You can click the Render Image button in the Render tab, or click the Render Image button in the Main tab to render your image. The Rendered image will be placed in the folder you specified in the Save As property in the Render tab (Figure 9.49).

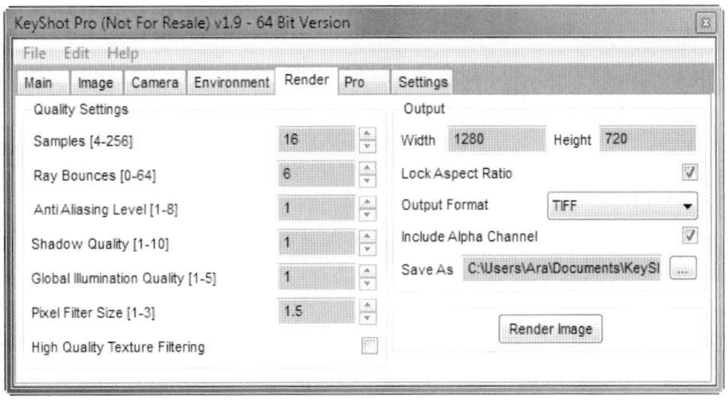

Figure 9.49

Render tab properties

In the Pro version of KeyShot, you are also able to create turntables from rendering a sequence of images, which you can then composite into a video in applications such as Adobe After Effects.

I have found KeyShot to be extremely quick and useful for generating very high-quality renders of multimillion-polygon models in full sculpted fidelity without having to rely on displacement maps and normal maps.

In the Chapter 9\images folder, you will find some examples of high-resolution image renders from KeyShot using models made in Mudbox (Figure 9.50).

In the Chapter 9\Videos folder on the DVD, you can watch the movie Athena_KeyShot .mov. In this turntable render sequence, I have added only a simple stand to the character you have been working with.

Figure 9.50

Rendered image

Rendering in Maya

There are plenty of rendering solutions on the market. Some, like Luxion's KeyShot, are stand-alone. Others are made specifically for one 3D application, such as SplutterFish Brazil for 3ds Max, or for multiple 3D applications, such as Chaos Group's V-Ray for 3ds Max and Maya. Some applications have some powerful and fast renderers, such as the renderer in Luxology's Modo. In addition to all of these renderers, Autodesk Maya, 3ds Max, and Softimage have their built-in renderers, and of course all three also have Nvidia's powerful and versatile mental ray renderer. You have plenty of choices of applications and renderers to take your Mudbox work into for rendering purposes. The methodology and steps of the operation in these applications might be different, but the concepts are the same.

In this section, you will take your character into Maya, and use mental ray to render it. Unlike the preceding section, you will not be taking the high-resolution multimillion-polygon model into Maya, because Maya is aimed at a variety of applications, most notable of which is animation, and animating a multimillion-polygon model is not feasible with today's technology. Just as you did with the egg in the first chapter, you will use a displacement map to depict the detail you sculpted on a lower-resolution version of the model.

You will need to export the following out of Mudbox:

* Low-resolution models of the head and body, exported as `.obj` files, or `.fbx` files. The `.fbx` format has advantages over `.obj` in that you can export the models as well as the textures.

* Displacement maps for the head and body so you can use them to depict the high-resolution detail on the low-resolution mesh models you exported.

* A flattened version of the Diffuse, Specular, and Gloss texture channels.

To export the models individually, you need to select them by using the Objects selection tool, and click File → Export Selection. Note that you need to have your model in the lower subdivision level, because this command will export the model in its current subdivision level. You can select and export multiple objects that will load as a single `.obj` file, but then you would need to separate them in Maya to assign different materials to the individual parts. You can export these models as `.obj` or `.fbx` files by selecting the format from the Save As Type drop-down menu that comes up when you click File → Export Selection.

You have seen the `.obj` file format, and its ability to have both the geometry and the UV data. The `.fbx` format will export both of those in addition to some other features of the model, such as materials, textures, cameras, sculpting layers as blend shapes you can animate in Maya, and more. Some of these features are an exact transfer, and some are modified by the host application.

FBX is a proprietary interoperability file format owned and developed by Autodesk. FBX plug-ins are available for Maya 3ds Max and supported by other Autodesk products such as MotionBuilder and Softimage using Crosswalk.

There are two topics in the help files called Importing Using FBX and Export Using FBX, and both have tables of the features of your scene that transfer in and out of Mudbox using the .fbx file format. You will note that just like the .obj file format, you get perfect compatibility with models and their UVs. However, materials, paint layers, sculpt layers, cameras, image planes, and joints go through conversions that result in functionally equivalent features during the import or export operation. You will also notice that lights do not transfer.

In this scenario, you need to export models, textures, and displacement maps, so you can use .obj, .fbx, or the new and extremely simple Select File → Send to Maya feature, which uses FBX and automates many of the steps and helps speed up your workflow. If you select Preview as Bump Layer when you extracted your displacement map, or imported your displacement map into a bump channel, the Send to Maya option also exports the bump map and adds it as a displacement map in Maya.

1. Start Mudbox and load the Athena.mud file from the Chapter 9 folder of the DVD.

2. You will need to go down in subdivision on both the body and the head to export the lower-subdivision version of them. Use the Objects selection tool to select the body. Press the W key to bring up the wireframe. Move your mouse pointer to anywhere on the body mesh that is highlighted in yellow and press Pg Dn while keeping your pointer on the body until you are at subdivision level 1. Note in the Object List that the model is at 5,088 faces, or polygons.

3. Select the head and move your mouse pointer to anywhere on the head mesh that is highlighted in yellow (Figure 9.51). Press Pg Dn while keeping your pointer on the body until you are at subdivision level 1. Note in the Object List that the model is at 8,008 faces, or polygons.

4. Click Maps → Extract Texture Maps → New Operation to bring up the Extract Texture Maps dialog box. Type **head_disp** as the name for your extraction operation and select the Displacement Map check box.

5. In the Target Models section, click Add Selected, which should add the Head mesh, but the default is to add it at the lowest subdivision level. Click on the words *level 0* to the right of Head, and select level 1 (Figure 9.52). Note that the drop-down list indicates that level 1 is the current level. Select the Smooth Target Model check box.

6. In the Source Models section, click Add Selected, which should add the head mesh. Here the default is to add it at the highest subdivision level, which is what you want. Select Smooth Source Models to get a smoother extraction result with fewer jagged lines and fewer artifacts. If you lose detail due to having Smooth Source Models selected, you can always extract another map with it deselected and compare the results in the Image Browser.

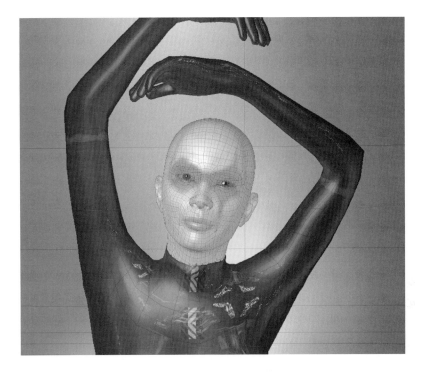

Figure 9.51

Selected head mesh

7. For the Locate Method, you will use Raycasting because it captures the height differences more accurately, particularly when the vertices on the higher subdivision levels have been translated off of the normal compared to the lower subdivision level. Click the Best Guess button and select Test Both Sides.

8. To output a 4K displacement map, choose 4096 × 4096 in the Image Size drop-down menu.

9. Select Normalize to Search Distance. Also select Preview as Bump Layer because we want the generated displacement map to be added to the model as a bump layer, which in turn will be sent into Maya as a displacement map.

10. Click the folder icon to the right of the Base File Name text box. Save the displacement map as **head_disp.exr** and choose the OpenEXR [32 bit Floating Point, RGBA] file format in the Save As Type drop-down menu.

Figure 9.52

Selecting subdivision level 1

11. Click Extract to extract your map. You will see the progress of the operation in the map, and subsequently get a Map Extraction Finished Successfully dialog box. Close this dialog box to return to your scene.

12. Repeat steps 4 through 11, creating another new extraction operation called **body_disp**. Remember to select level 1 in the Target Models section by clicking on the words *level 0* to the

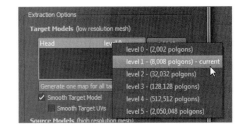

right of Body, and selecting level 1. Save the extracted displacement map as body_disp.exr.

You could at this stage also extrude ambient occlusion maps that you can composite, or bake, onto the texture map. Next you will export the models, the texture maps, and the displacement map, which will be a very simple operation. Before you do that, click Windows → Preferences (Window → Preferences on the Mac), and make sure that you have the link to the Maya executable (maya.exe file) in the Maya text box of the Paths section. In my case, it is C:\Program Files\Autodesk\Maya2011\bin\maya.exe.

13. Click File → Send to Maya. In the Send to Maya dialog box (Figure 9.53), select All Meshes because you need to export them all to Maya. It is important to note that all the meshes will be sent in the subdivision level they are currently in. Also note that you can send individual objects that you should select before clicking File → Send to Maya. This will be useful if you need to isolate a specific object to troubleshoot any anomalies that occur after you get the data in Maya.

14. You want to get the paint layers too, so select the option Flatten Paint Layers in Each Channel before Sending. This will save you time compositing the layers in Photoshop. This will generate a single paint layer for each channel type (such as one for Diffuse, one for Specular, one for Gloss, and so on). Note that this composite texture image will flatten the layers with their applied layer blend modes.

15. Because you are not going to use blend shapes for your sculpting layers, select the Flatten Sculpt Layers before Sending option.

16. Click the Send button, which opens Maya with your exported, textured model. You will get a Maya security warning (Figure 9.54), so click the Allow button to continue the operation. If you have any issues with the transfer, make sure the fbxmaya.mll (or fbxmaya.bundle on the Mac) is loaded in the Plug-in Manager (Window → Settings/ Preferences → Plug-in Manager).

Figure 9.53
Send to Maya Dialog box settings

Figure 9.54
Click the Allow button to pass the Maya security warning.

.*TIF* FILE LZW COMPRESSION NOT SUPPORTED IN MENTAL RAY

It is important to note that the Send to Maya command creates a temporary folder in the Mudbox folder in your user directory, with all the files that are sent to Maya. The textures are all saved by default as LZW compressed .tif files. As they are sent to Maya, where the default renderer is the Maya rendering engine, your textures will render fine. But when you choose mental ray as the renderer, your textures will render out in black, and you will get a sequence of "Failed to open texture file" errors in the Script Editor indicating that the textures were not loaded. The reason for this, again, is that mental ray does not support LZW compressed .tif files. The solution is to add the MUDBOX_NO_COMPRESS_TIFF_LZW environment variable and set its value to 1. Look for instructions on how to add an environment variable for your operating system online.

This will, of course, result in your texture files taking upward of three times the space on your hard drive, but you would be able to see and render them by using mental ray and other software applications that do not support LZW compression in .tif image files. Of course, you could also go to the temp folder on your hard drive where the textures are stored and use an image-editing application such as Adobe Photoshop to convert them to other file formats or non-LZW compressed .tif files.

Figure 9.55

**Character in Maya
in shaded and tex-
tured mode**

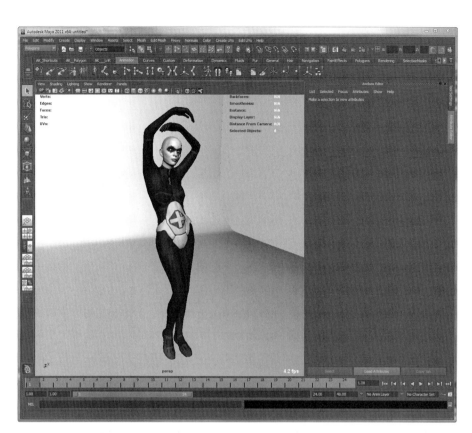

Figure 9.56

**Create a Maya
project.**

17. In Maya, press the F key and navigate the camera to frame the character in the viewport, and then press the 6 key to get a shaded and textured display in the viewport
(Figure 9.55). As you can see, the model, UVs and textures have come across.

18. Click File → New Project. In the New Project dialog box (Figure 9.56), click the Browse button and find a location for your
project. I have saved a version of my project on the DVD in the
Chapter 9 folder. Click the Use Defaults button to populate the
locations, and click Accept to create the Maya project on your
hard drive.

19. Click File → Save Scene and save your scene as **01_athena_start**.
This file will be saved in the Scenes folder of the Maya project
you just set up.

20. Click Window → Rendering Editors → Hypershade to bring up
the Hypershade. Notice that the shaders for the body, head,
the two eyes, and the plates are brought in from Mudbox
(Figure 9.57).

Figure 9.57

Imported shaders in Hypershade

21. Right-click on the head shader and select Graph Network from the marking menu. Examine the shader network that Maya has created with the imported information from Mudbox (Figure 9.58). Notice how all the shaders are directly hooked up to the head shader except the displacement shader, which is connected through a shading engine node. You can see which outputs are connected to which input in the various shaders by hovering your mouse on the line and arrow between them. It is a good idea to see what these connections are so you can troubleshoot them if something does not render correctly. For the most part, the automatic generation of these nodes from the Send to Maya command in Mudbox is perfect and does not need further manipulation. Do the same for the body, eye, and plates shaders.

22. Click Window → Rendering Editors → Render Settings. In the Render Settings dialog box, select mental ray from the Render Using drop-down menu to select mental ray as the rendering engine. If it is not in the drop-down menu, you need to load it from the Window → Settings/Preferences → Plug-in Manager dialog box. It is the Mayatomr.mll plug-in (Figure 9.59). You should also have the OpenEXRLoader.mll plug-in loaded because you chose 32-bit OpenEXR as the format to save your displacement map.

23. In the Quality tab, select Production from the Quality Presets drop-down menu (Figure 9.60).

Figure 9.58

The head shader
network in Maya

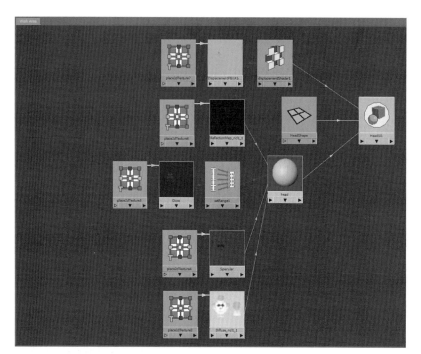

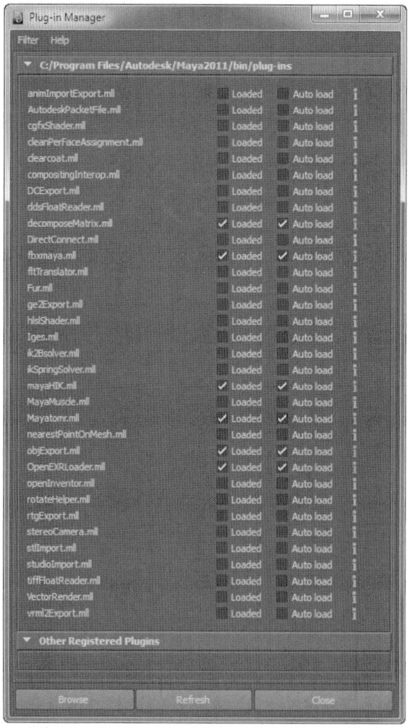

Figure 9.59

The `Mayatomr.mll` plug-in loaded in the
Plug-in Manager

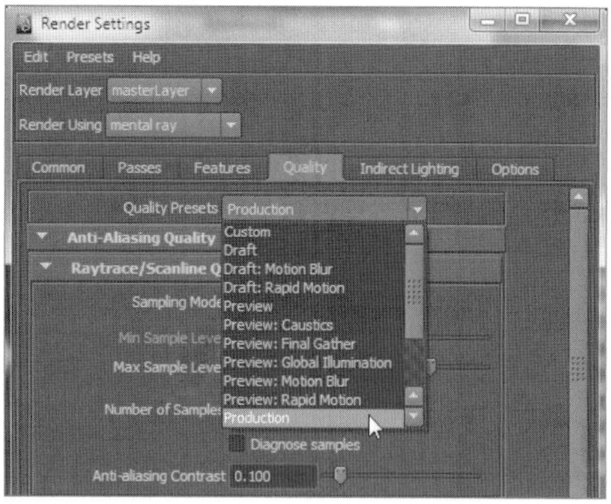

Figure 9.60

Change the quality preset to Production in the
Render Settings dialog box.

24. Frame the head in your viewport and click the Render Current Frame icon on the toolbar.

25. In the Render view, you will notice that the displacement is applied to the head, but the head looks inflated (Figure 9.61). To resolve this, double-click the file node (Figure 9.62) in the Hypershade to bring up its properties. In the Color Balance section of the attributes for the file node, change the Alpha Gain attribute from 1.000 to **0.100**.

26. Render the scene again and notice that the inflated look of the head is gone, and the resulting image looks closer to what you had in Mudbox. The resulting image does, however, have some pixilated areas, especially around the ears and nostrils (Figure 9.63).

27. To remedy the anomalies, you need to apply a mental ray approximation node to set up the displacement tessellation settings for mental ray relative to the detail and subdivisions you had in Mudbox. Choose Window → Rendering Editors → mental ray → Approximation Editor to bring up the mental ray Approximation Editor dialog box (Figure 9.64).

Figure 9.61

Overinflated displacement render

Figure 9.62

**Displacement file
node (center) and
the Alpha Gain attri-
bute changed to 0.1**

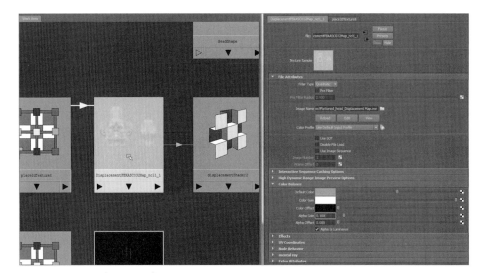

Figure 9.63

**Render anomalies
on ear and nostrils**

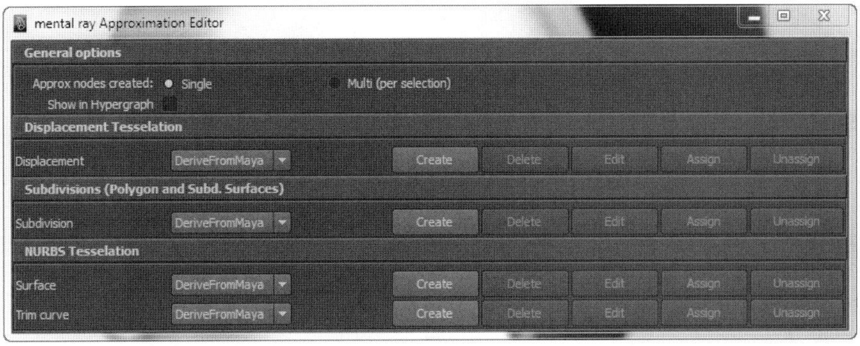

Figure 9.64

mental ray Approximation Editor

28. Click on the head model in the workspace to select it, and click the Create button in the Subdivisions (Polygon and Subd. Surfaces) section of the mental ray Approximation Editor. This creates an approximation node assigned to the head and opens up its attributes (Figure 9.65). The simplest approximation method is specifying Subdivision, and luckily a subdivided model is where you started, so you should correspond the N Subdivisions attribute to the highest subdivision level of the head in Mudbox. The lowest-polygon mesh in Mudbox is referred to as *subdivision level 1*, and it is also the same level at which you exported your low-polygon head. To get to level 5, which is the highest level of subdivision for the head at which we extracted the displacement map, you needed to divide the mesh four times, and that is the value that you need to have assigned to the N Subdivisons attribute.

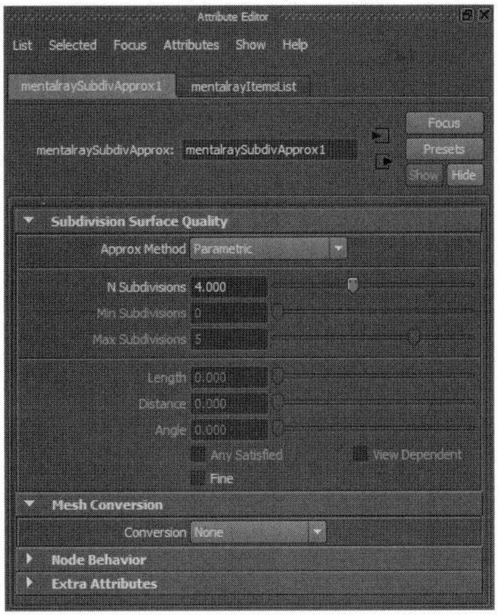

29. Render your image again and notice that the anomalies are gone, and you have a near-perfect representation of your high-definition model (Figure 9.66). Note that this does make your render time longer.

30. Repeat steps 25 through 29 for the body, using 5 as the value for the N Subdivisions attribute.

You now have the representation of your Mudbox work in Maya, and you can add lights and use any of the mental ray features to render our image. I have added lights, a camera, and render settings in the 03_final.ma file in the Chapter 9\Athena\Scenes\ folder of the DVD with renders of the character we created in Mudbox (Figure 9.67).

Figure 9.65

Attributes of the mental ray Approximation Editor

Figure 9.66

**Render results with
the Approximation
Editor**

Figure 9.67

**Model rendered
in Maya using
mental ray**

Summary

The lighting provided with the point, directional, and IBL lights, in addition to the responsive and realistic renderer with viewport filters in Mudbox, will get you well on the way to envisioning your creations. If you need to add to or take your results beyond what Mudbox can produce, Mudbox provides you with ample 2D and 3D export options to load your information into other painting, image-editing, compositing, or 3D applications.

   This brings us to the conclusion of this book. Thank you for reading it. It is my most sincere hope that it has been useful to you, and that you have learned what you need to know about Mudbox to create your art.

About the Companion DVD

In this appendix:

- What you'll find on the DVD

- System requirements

- Using the DVD

- Troubleshooting

What You'll Find on the DVD

The following sections are arranged by category and provide a summary of the content you'll find on the DVD. If you need help with copying the items provided on the DVD, refer to the installation instructions in the "Using the DVD" section of this appendix.

Chapter Folders

The contents of the DVD are organized as chapter folders. In the chapter folders you will find all the files for completing the projects and understanding concepts in this book. For reference, files from the projects are saved at several stages along the process. Some chapter folders also contain a Videos subfolder, which includes .mov files of the stages related to the projects.

Some of the chapter folders include subfolders which contain Maya Projects or other files that need grouping.

> The head scan model on the DVD is provided by Icon Imaging. The Bertie robot model on the DVD is based on paintings and comic books by Ashley Wood. Both models are to be used for education purposes only. Commercial use is not allowed.

3D Primitives

This folder contains some .obj files of 3D primitives you can use as base meshes.

Stamps and Stencils Folders

The Stamps and Stencils folders contain 2D images you will need as stamps and stencils in the lessons in the book, and also add to your library for future use.

System Requirements

You need to be running Mudbox 2011 to fully use all the files on the DVD. Make sure your computer meets the minimum system requirements shown in the following list. If your computer doesn't match up to these requirements, you may have problems using the files on the companion DVD:

> This DVD does not include Mudbox 2011 software. You will need to have Mudbox 2011 installed on your computer to complete the exercises in the book.

- For the 32-bit version of Mudbox 2011:
  - Microsoft Windows 7 Professional
  - Windows Vista (SP1)
  - Windows XP (SP3)
  - Intel® Pentium® 4 or higher, AMD Athlon™ 64, or AMD Opteron™ processor

- For the 64-bit version of Mudbox 2011:

  Windows:

  - Microsoft Windows 7 Professional x64 Edition

  - Windows XP x64 Edition (SP2)

  - Windows Vista x64 Edition (SP1)

  - Intel® EM64T processor, AMD Athlon 64, or AMD Opteron

  Macintosh:

  - Mac OS X 10.6.2

- Intel-based Macintosh computer with a 64-bit processor (Core 2 Duo or later): The minimum system requirements state 2GB of RAM, but 4GB or more is recommended to do the classes in this book especially if you need to have Mudbox and other applications such as Adobe Photoshop or Maya running simultaneously.

- 650MB free hard drive space

- A certified OpenGL, hardware-accelerated graphics card. Refer to the Mudbox 2011 certification chart located at www.autodesk.com/mudbox-hardware.

- Ethernet or wireless network card

- An Internet connection

- A DVD-ROM drive

- Three-button mouse or preferably a Wacom tablet

- Apple QuickTime 7.0 or later (download from www.quicktime.com)

  For the most up-to-date information, check www.autodesk.com/mudbox.

Using the DVD

For best results you'll want to copy the files from your DVD to you computer. To copy the items from the DVD to your hard drive, follow these steps:

1. Insert the DVD into your computer's DVD-ROM drive. The license agreement appears.

> Windows users: The interface won't launch if Autorun is disabled. In that case, click Start → Run (for Windows Vista, Start → All Programs → Accessories → Run). In the dialog box that appears, type **D:\Start.exe**. (Replace **D** with the proper letter if your DVD drive uses a different letter. If you don't know the letter, see how your DVD drive is listed under My Computer.) Click OK.

2. Read through the license agreement, and then click the Accept button if you want to use the DVD.

   The DVD interface appears. The interface allows you to access the content with just one or two clicks.

Alternately, you can access the files at the root directory of your hard drive.

Mac users: The DVD icon will appear on your desktop; double-click the icon to open the DVD and then navigate to the files you want.

All the chapters are individually compressed in their respective .zip files. To use the lesson files for a chapter, copy the .zip file to your hard drive and extract it using the built in zip extraction feature in your operating system or using utilities such as WinZip or 7zip.

Troubleshooting

Wiley has attempted to provide programs that work on most computers with the minimum system requirements. However, your computer may differ, and some programs may not work properly for some reason.

The two likeliest problems are that you don't have enough memory (RAM) for the programs you want to use, or you have other programs running that are affecting installation or running of a program. If you get an error message such as "Not enough memory" or "Setup cannot continue," try one or more of the following suggestions and then try using the software again:

Turn off any antivirus software running on your computer. Installation programs sometimes mimic virus activity and may make your computer incorrectly believe that it's being infected by a virus.

Close all running programs. The more programs you have running, the less memory is available to other programs. Installation programs typically update files and programs; so if you keep other programs running, installation may not work properly.

Have your local computer store add more RAM to your computer. This is, admittedly, a drastic and somewhat expensive step. However, adding more memory can really help the speed of your computer and allow more programs to run at the same time.

Customer Care

If you have trouble with the book's companion CD-ROM, please call the Wiley Product Technical Support phone number at (800) 762-2974. Outside the United States, call +1 (317) 572-3994. You can also contact Wiley Product Technical Support at http://sybex.custhelp.com. John Wiley & Sons will provide technical support only for installation and other general quality-control items. For technical support on the applications themselves, consult the program's vendor or author.

To place additional orders or to request information about other Wiley products, please call (877) 762-2974.

Should the need arise for any errata or replacement files, we will post them at www.sybex.com/go/intromudbox.

Index

Note to the Reader: Throughout this index **boldfaced** page numbers indicate primary discussions of a topic. *Italicized* page numbers indicate illustrations.

Wiley Publishing, Inc. End-User License Agreement

READ THIS. You should carefully read these terms and conditions before opening the software packet(s) included with this book "Book". This is a license agreement "Agreement" between you and Wiley Publishing, Inc. "WPI". By opening the accompanying software packet(s), you acknowledge that you have read and accept the following terms and conditions. If you do not agree and do not want to be bound by such terms and conditions, promptly return the Book and the unopened software packet(s) to the place you obtained them for a full refund.

1. **License Grant.** WPI grants to you (either an individual or entity) a nonexclusive license to use one copy of the enclosed software program(s) (collectively, the "Software") solely for your own personal or business purposes on a single computer (whether a standard computer or a workstation component of a multi-user network). The Software is in use on a computer when it is loaded into temporary memory (RAM) or installed into permanent memory (hard disk, CD-ROM, or other storage device). WPI reserves all rights not expressly granted herein.

2. **Ownership.** WPI is the owner of all right, title, and interest, including copyright, in and to the compilation of the Software recorded on the physical packet included with this Book "Software Media". Copyright to the individual programs recorded on the Software Media is owned by the author or other authorized copyright owner of each program. Ownership of the Software and all proprietary rights relating thereto remain with WPI and its licensers.

3. **Restrictions On Use and Transfer.** (a) You may only (i) make one copy of the Software for backup or archival purposes, or (ii) transfer the Software to a single hard disk, provided that you keep the original for backup or archival purposes. You may not (i) rent or lease the Software, (ii) copy or reproduce the Software through a LAN or other network system or through any computer subscriber system or bulletin-board system, or (iii) modify, adapt, or create derivative works based on the Software. (b) You may not reverse engineer, decompile, or disassemble the Software. You may transfer the Software and user documentation on a permanent basis, provided that the transferee agrees to accept the terms and conditions of this Agreement and you retain no copies. If the Software is an update or has been updated, any transfer must include the most recent update and all prior versions.

4. **Restrictions on Use of Individual Programs.** You must follow the individual requirements and restrictions detailed for each individual program in the "About the CD" appendix of this Book or on the Software Media. These limitations are also contained in the individual license agreements recorded on the Software Media. These limitations may include a requirement that after using the program for a specified period of time, the user must pay a registration fee or discontinue use. By opening the Software packet(s), you agree to abide by the licenses and restrictions for these individual programs that are detailed in the "About the CD" appendix and/or on the Software Media. None of the material on this Software Media or listed in this Book may ever be redistributed, in original or modified form, for commercial purposes.

5. **Limited Warranty.** (a) WPI warrants that the Software and Software Media are free from defects in materials and workmanship under normal use for a period of sixty (60) days from the date of purchase of this Book. If WPI receives notification within the warranty period of defects in materials or workmanship, WPI will replace the defective Software Media. (b) WPI AND THE AUTHOR(S) OF THE BOOK DISCLAIM ALL OTHER WARRANTIES, EXPRESS OR IMPLIED, INCLUDING WITHOUT LIMITATION IMPLIED WARRANTIES OF MERCHANTABILITY AND FITNESS FOR A PARTICULAR PURPOSE, WITH RESPECT TO THE SOFTWARE, THE PROGRAMS, THE SOURCE CODE CONTAINED THEREIN, AND/OR THE TECHNIQUES DESCRIBED IN THIS BOOK. WPI DOES NOT WARRANT THAT THE FUNCTIONS CONTAINED IN THE SOFTWARE WILL MEET YOUR REQUIREMENTS OR THAT THE OPERATION OF THE SOFTWARE WILL BE ERROR FREE. (c) This limited warranty gives you specific legal rights, and you may have other rights that vary from jurisdiction to jurisdiction.

6. **Remedies.** (a) WPI's entire liability and your exclusive remedy for defects in materials and workmanship shall be limited to replacement of the Software Media, which may be returned to WPI with a copy of your receipt at the following address: Software Media Fulfillment Department, Attn.: *Introducing Mudbox*, Wiley Publishing, Inc., 10475 Crosspoint Blvd., Indianapolis, IN 46256, or call 1-800-762-2974. Please allow four to six weeks for delivery. This Limited Warranty is void if failure of the Software Media has resulted from accident, abuse, or misapplication. Any replacement Software Media will be warranted for the remainder of the original warranty period or thirty (30) days, whichever is longer. (b) In no event shall WPI or the author be liable for any damages whatsoever (including without limitation damages for loss of business profits, business interruption, loss of business information, or any other pecuniary loss) arising from the use of or inability to use the Book or the Software, even if WPI has been advised of the possibility of such damages. (c) Because some jurisdictions do not allow the exclusion or limitation of liability for consequential or incidental damages, the above limitation or exclusion may not apply to you.

7. **U.S. Government Restricted Rights.** Use, duplication, or disclosure of the Software for or on behalf of the United States of America, its agencies and/or instrumentalities "U.S. Government" is subject to restrictions as stated in paragraph (c)(1)(ii) of the Rights in Technical Data and Computer Software clause of DFARS 252.227-7013, or subparagraphs (c) (1) and (2) of the Commercial Computer Software - Restricted Rights clause at FAR 52.227-19, and in similar clauses in the NASA FAR supplement, as applicable.

8. **General.** This Agreement constitutes the entire understanding of the parties and revokes and supersedes all prior agreements, oral or written, between them and may not be modified or amended except in a writing signed by both parties hereto that specifically refers to this Agreement. This Agreement shall take precedence over any other documents that may be in conflict herewith. If any one or more provisions contained in this Agreement are held by any court or tribunal to be invalid, illegal, or otherwise unenforceable, each and every other provision shall remain in full force and effect.